4th International Symposium on Affective Science and Engineering and 29th Modern Artificial Intelligence and Cognitive Science Conference (ISASE-MAICS 2018)

Spokane, Washington, USA
31 May - 2 June 2018

ISBN: 978-1-5108-8376-5

Printed from e-media with permission by:

Curran Associates, Inc.
57 Morehouse Lane
Red Hook, NY 12571

proceedings.com

Some format issues inherent in the e-media version may also appear in this print version.

Printed by Curran Associates, Inc. (2019)

Japan Society of Kansei Engineering (JSKE)
Grand Heights 1003
2-55-5 Nihombashi Hamacho
Chuo-ku, Tokyo 103-0007
Japan

jske@jske.org

Additional copies of this publication are available from:

Curran Associates, Inc.
57 Morehouse Lane
Red Hook, NY 12571 USA
Phone: 845-758-0400
Fax: 845-758-2633
Email: curran@proceedings.com
Web: www.proceedings.com

TABLE OF CONTENTS

A1: AFFECTIVE ROBOTICS & EDUCATION

A2: AFFECTIVE INFORMATION & SOFT COMPUTING

A3: AFFECTIVE COMPUTING & INTERFACE DESIGN

A4: ARTIFICIAL INTELLIGENCE

B1: FASHION DESIGN & BUSINESS

B2: COGNITIVE SCIENCE

B3: CONTENT-ORIENTED RESEARCHES

B4: AFFECTIVE DESIGN

A Convergence of Decision-making Criterions in a Human-robot Group

– The Robot Makes a Suitable Decision-making Criterion by Interacting with the Group Members –

Yotaro FUSE*, Hiroshi TAKENOUCHI ** and Masataka TOKUMARU ***

* *Graduate School of Kansai University, 3-3-35 Yamate-cho, Suita-shi, Osaka 564-8680, Japan*
** *Fukuoka Institute of Technology, 3-30-1 Wajiro-higashi, Higashi-ku, Fukuoka 811-0295, Japan*
*** *Kansai University, 3-3-35 Yamate-cho, Suita-shi, Osaka 564-8680, Japan*

Abstract: This paper presents a model to enable robots to create a suitable criterion for decision-making by indirectly interacting with people in a group. Using this model, a robot learns a suitable criterion for the group as a group member through reinforcement learning. When people, who have different personalities form a group, they adjust their criteria to a common criterion for the group. The present study investigates whether the robot can make a suitable decision-making criterion in a group by learning from interactions. Participants and the robot answer easy quizzes that have vague questions without direct conversation. Our experiments reveal that a group consisting of the participants and the robot forms a common criterion in a limited scenario. However, further study is required to reveal a robot's social influence of human.

Keywords: *Social Robotics, Human-Robot Interaction, Group Norm, Reinforcement Learning*

1. INTRODUCTION

In recent years, there has been an increasing effort to develop communication robots. However, currently, communication robots cannot join a multiparty group or conversation. Moreover, to communicate more like human in multiparty situations, they need to learn sociality [1]. Robot models that take sociality into account have previously been proposed [2-4]. These models enable robots to behave cooperatively. However, sociality also means the tendency to form a group and live with the group members. Therefore, in every human society, people cooperate with many unrelated individuals [5].

For robots to behave with sociality in a human society, they need to adapt to rules, namely group norms, which are generated by members of the group without the group members teaching how to behave in the group. People conform to common group behaviors in human groups. Therefore, robots must also learn to behave as a member of a group by observing other members' behaviors. These behaviors are known as group norms [6]. However, all humans have unique personalities, which reflect the dynamic integration of a person's subjective experiences and behavior patterns [7]. Because of unique personalities, people have different criteria for making decisions and can respond differently from one another when faced with the same stimuli [8]. Although people have different personalities and decision-making criteria, the criteria converge into one common criterion when a group is formed.

We therefore propose a model for a robot that creates decision-making criteria by interacting with people in its group. A robot uses the model to learn suitable criteria for the group. When people form a group and face with an unfamiliar situation, they try to adjust their criteria to a common criterion that is suitable for the group. We investigate whether the people and robot's answers converge to a suitable criterion when they answer easy quizzes that have vague questions. Moreover, we use RoBoHoN as a group member of robot in Fig. 1. RoBoHoN is a robot that can speak Japanese and behave in a scenario which we plan [9]. RoBoHoN, that is a height of about 20 centimeters, can be easily put on a desk and can behave and have conversations with human on the basis of a scenario made beforehand. However, it cannot move and behave autonomously.

Figure 1: Laptop and RoBoHoN used in experiments

2. GROUP NORM MODEL

The proposed model enables a robot to create a suitable criterion for decision-making by interacting with people in a group through reinforcement learning. The suitable criterion is a group norm in the group. In this study, we aim a robot system's decision-making on the basis of group norms and investigate whether its decision-makings look like human's. In order for a robot to adjust its behaviors to a group including human, the robot needs to infer a way to behave in the group suitably from the other group members' behaviors while a group norm is forming. Therefore, before a robot behaves in a group on the basis of the robot system, we investigate whether the robot system, taking a group norm into account, makes decisions.

2.1 Decision-making Model

We propose the model that the robot uses to generate a

group norm. The robot's behaviors within the group are determined by this model. The robot recognizes the behaviors of the other group members and compares its own behavior with theirs. Thus, it behaves socially and creates a suitable group criterion by learning from other members' behaviors.

The model uses three stages to learn suitable behavior: decision-making, behavior recognition, and accepting feedback. The inputs pass through these three stages. Inputs in the model consist of others' behavior whereas the output is its own behavior. Moreover, the decision-making module learns the group norm by reinforcement learning.

The decision-making component determines the robot's behavior. The robot then inputs its own behavior into its behavior recognition component. Here, the robot learns a suitable behavior using the hypothesis that people also converge to a suitable behavior in a group. The behavior recognition component also receives the behavior of the other members that the robot observes. These behaviors are then inputted into the feedback acceptance component. On the basis of a combination of the group members' behaviors, the feedback acceptance component sends feedback to the decision-making component. The feedback acceptance component judges whether the robot's behavior suits the group, giving the robot a feedback. The feedback is then inputted to the decision-making component, which uses the feedback to learn how to select suitable behaviors.

The robot continues to adjust the parameters of the different behaviors that it can execute through the repetition of this process. The adjustments are based on whether the participants' behaviors correspond to the robot's own behavior. As the robot's behavior and other participants' behaviors begin to correspond, behaviors within the group become unified.

The decision-making component creates a suitable criterion for group participation by learning the group members' behaviors via reinforcement learning. An agent in the decision-making component is used to make the decisions and has a role in learning suitable behaviors.

2.2 Reinforcement Learning Parameters

Reinforcement learning in this study involves actions, states, a value function, Q values, and rewards. The model has a reinforcement learning environment in the decision-making component in Fig. 3. A robot, using the proposed model, has a set of behaviors that the robot can execute. When such a robot should behave in a real world, an agent in the decision-making component moves on the reinforcement learning environment and decides which behavior the robot should carry out then. Each behavior has a value of each behavior that the robot can carry out in a group.

There are N states and two actions in the environment. The reinforcement learning environment in Fig. 3 consists of these states and actions. The nth state, s_n, indicates a criterion that the robot comes up with at nth time for behaving. The N is a max of the number of states. The actions are a_{dcs} and a_{next}. The a_{dcs} denotes that the

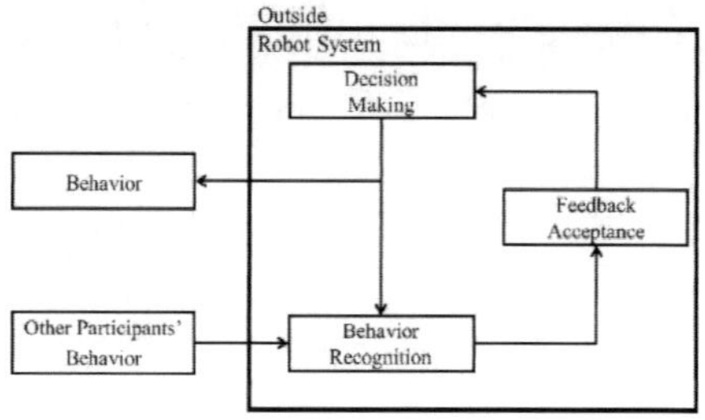

Figure 2: Group Norm Model

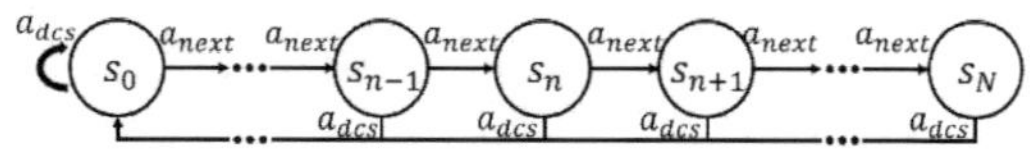

Figure 3: Robot system state transition diagram

agent decides that the robot carries out a behavior based on a present state: a certain criterion, that is may be suitable for a group. The a_{next} indicates that the agent moves from a present state to a next state. When a_{next} is executed, the agent judges the present state is not suitable criterion.

There also are a value function, Q values, and rewards. The mechanism put a high value on robot's adjustment to a group including human. A value function, $V(s_n)$, shows a value of s_n as a criterion in a group. The Q value, $Q(s,a)$, denotes a value of a combination of a certain state and a certain action. When a robot adjusts its behaviors to a group, the robot selects an appropriate way of behaviors for the group while searching the space of states. The values of the ways are derived from value function. In addition, Rewards are used in order to renew the value function. Until the robot using proposed model makes a decision in a group, the robot system executes some a_{next} s and an a_{dcs} while moving from a present state to a next state on the environment in Fig. 3. Every time the agent in the robot system moves to a next state, it has to make a small decision, that is to select either a_{next} or a_{dcs} in a certain state. The value of the small decisions indicates a Q value, derived from a value function. In this case, the equation for renewing the value function at tth step is given in Eq. (1), where γ is a weighting factor, α is the learning rate, and $R^i_{(s_n)}$ is the reward at ith step.

$$V^{t+1}_{(s_n)} \leftarrow V^t_{(s_n)} + \alpha \cdot \sum_{i=1}^{t} \gamma^{(t-i)} \cdot R^i_{(s_n)} \tag{1}$$

The equation of $R^i_{(s_n)}$ at ith step is given in Eq. (2), where M is the number of members in a group that the robot joins (Mth member is regarded as the robot), s_k is a criterion namely behavior at ith step that each group member show in the group, and σ^2 is a sharpness of the $R^i_{(s_n)}$. Additionally, the initial value function of each state are random numbers.

$$R^i_{(s_n)} = R^i_{(s_n;\, s_k,\, \sigma^2)} = \sum_{k=1}^{M-1} exp\left(\frac{(s_n - s_k)^2}{2\sigma^2}\right) \tag{2}$$

Moreover, the Q value, $Q_{(s,a)}$, denotes a value of a combination of a certain state and a certain action. The agent selects an action that has higher value in a state where the agent stays. The equation for deriving Q values is given in Eq. (3) and (4). The conditions of the variables in Eq. (3) and (4) are $m \in \{0,1,2,\cdots,N-1\}, n \in \{0,1,2,\cdots,N\}$, and $l \in \{0,1,2,\cdots,N\}$.

$$Q_{(s_m,a_{next})} = V_{(s_{m+1})} \tag{3}$$

$$Q_{(s_l,a_{dcs})} = \frac{1}{V_{(s_l)} - \max\limits_{n} V_{(s_n)}} \tag{4}$$

The Eq. (4) has two cases in a value of $V_{(s_l)}$. When $V_{(s_l)} = \max\limits_{n} V_{(s_n)}$, the Eq. (5) indicates that the robot feels s_l is appropriate as a group norm.

$$(4) = \begin{cases} Q_{(s_l,a_{dcs})} \to \infty & \left(if\ V_{(s_l)} = \max\limits_{n} V_{(s_n)}\right) \\ Q_{(s_l,a_{dcs})} < 0 & (\quad otherwise \quad) \end{cases} \tag{5}$$

In other words, the agent moves on the environment in order by executing a_{next} or executes a_{dcs} on the basis of the Q value of executing an action in a certain state. However, it's difficult for robots to come up with a certain criterion today. Therefore, a limited scenario of experiments gives a set of the states to the robot in this study.

3. Experiments

3.1 Quiz Environment

In this paper, we prepare quizzes about the descriptive terms of a quantity of dots for participants in an experiment group. Each participant in the group answers the same quiz by clicking a button on a laptop. All the participants recognize each participants' answers after the all participants finish to answer once. This procedure is repeated several times. At first, each participant does not know a right answer, so that they answer the quiz on the basis of their criteria. However, the repetition gets each participant to be affected by the other participants' answers and change their criteria because they do not know a right answer and recognize each answer in the group.

Fig. 4 shows an input screen on the laptop and an example of a participant's answer. Fig. 4(a) shows the initial input screen. Fig. 4(b) shows an input screen after a participant has answered. Fig. 4(c) shows results of the three answers after the three participants have finished the quiz. Fig. 4(a) and (b) have two buttons beneath the white box, labeled "BUTTON" and "FINISH." If the participant clicks on BUTTON once, a black dot appears on the input screen. The number of BUTTON pushes is the number of dots that equals the descriptive term. Every time the participant pushes the BUTTON once, a black dot appears at a random location in the white box. The number of dots indicates the answers of a participant in the quizzes. Additionally, the quiz allows participants to click to a maximum of 100, but participants are unaware that this is the maximum allowable limit. They are, however, able to know the number of dots in their own answer.

Participant answers a quiz whose instructions told them to "continue pushing BUTTON until, in your opinion, you see X." The label X is replaced by a descriptive term that is selected in an experiment. For example, the quiz asks participants to continue clicking BUTTON until, in their own opinion, they see "a considerably large number" of dots. The first participant clicks on BUTTON until they are happy with their answer and then clicks on FINISH. The second and third participants answer in this same way. Finally, the application shows the screen in Fig. 4(c). As a result, the three participants see one another's answers. The participants repeat this procedure five times. At the beginning of each step, they do not know the others' answers. However, at the end of a step, they can see how the other participants have responded.

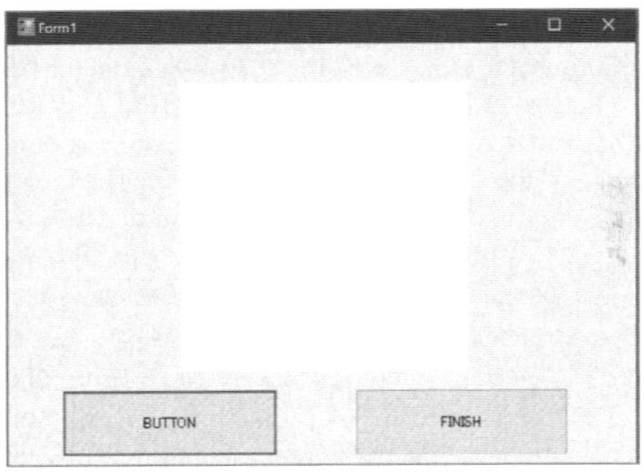

(a) Initial quiz input screen

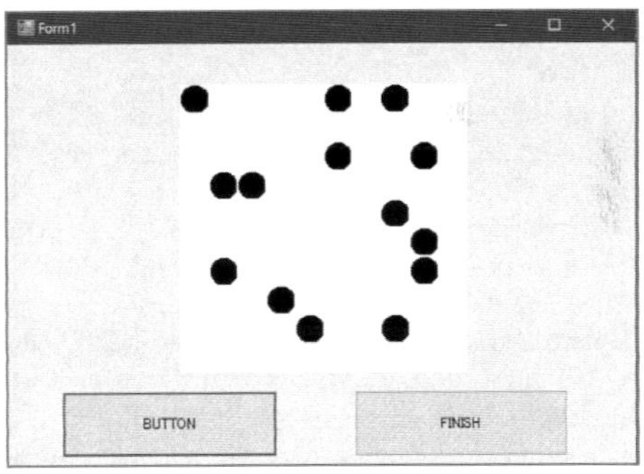

(b) Input screen with the answer

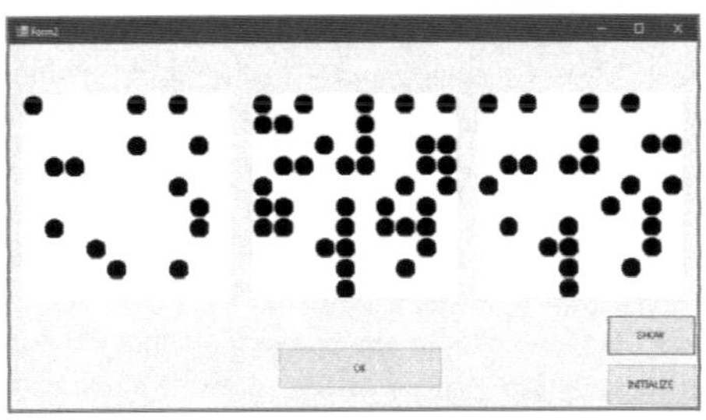

(c) Result at end of a step

Figure 4: Application input screen

3.2 Experiment Flow in a Group Including RoBoHoN

A quiz host controls this experiment. At first, each participant answers the six quizzes about descriptive quizzes without any advice in order to compare answering by his/herself and answering in a group before the experiment. Then, we informed the participants of the existence of the six descriptive terms in the quizzes before the test that they could make their own criteria for each descriptive term. Next, the quiz host introduce the flow of the experiment and RoBoHoN and teaches how to use the laptop before the experiment is carried out. After that, RoBoHoN introduces itself to the other two participants and tells the participants that RoBoHoN intends to join the experiment with the human participants. This is a phase of forming a group, that is, each participant regards the other participants including RoBoHoN as group members. Next, the quiz host decides who answer the quiz at first so that the first and second participant are human group members whereas the third participant is RoBoHoN. When one of the participants have his/her turn to answer a quiz, he/she sits at the chair in front of the laptop. After RoBoHoN finishes to answer, the three participants see one another's answers. As the same time, RoBoHoN checks the one another's answers and learns. When the numbers of dots of human participants' answers are k_1 and k_2, RoBoHoN's robot system recognizes their answers as s_{k_1} and $s_{k_2}$and renews the values by using Eq. (1), (2), (3), and (4). The participants repeat this procedure five times. Table 2 shows parameters of reinforcement learning. M means the number of the participants including RoBoHoN whereas N indicates the maximum number of the states.

3.3 Results and Discussions

Fig. 5 shows the results of three experiments where two participants and the robot in each group answered five questions per experiment. We selected two participants who had large individual differences for certain descriptive terms in each experiment. The horizontal axis shows the step number, whereas the vertical axis shows the standard deviations of the three experiments, which indicate the degree of their individual differences at each step of the three experiments.

Each standard deviation decreases as compared to each fifth step in all the experiments in Fig. 5. This result shows that groups including the robot tend to converge. As a result, we can see that the robot, using the proposed model, adjust its answer to the answers of the group members although the participants recognized that they were interacting with a real robot.

Table 2: Condition of the experiment

M	3
N	100
learning rate	0.1
discount factor	0.1
σ^2	100
initial V values	random number from 1.0 to 1.5

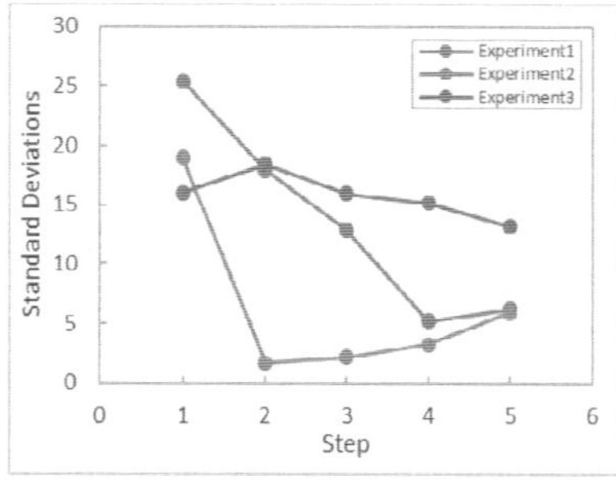

Figure 5: Results of experiments

4. Conclusion

In this study, we proposed a model to enable a robot to create a suitable criterion for decision-making by interacting with humans in a group in a multiparty scenario. In a multiparty quiz scenario, a system uses the model to find a suitable criterion based on observing the other participants in a group. Our results show that the robot adjusts itself to each group and can generate group norms with human participants in limited scenarios when human participants try to form group norms. The experiment results reveal that by using our proposed model the robot adjusts its own behaviors to participants' behaviors. In the future, we will apply robots using the proposed model to elderly care. The robots participant in a group of elderly people and interact with them while considering the social network in the group, so that these interactions are expected to keep and improve their health. Additionally, we plan to investigate how the participants are affected by the robot in detail when the number of group members of the content of the quizzes is changed.

REFFERENCES

1. B. Duffy; Anthropomorphism and the social robot, Robotics and autonomous systems, Vol.42, Issues 3–4, pp. 177-190, 2003-03.
2. H. Salam, O. Celiktutan, I. Hupont, H. Gunes, M. Chetouani; Fully Automatic Analysis of Engagement and Its Relationship to Personality in Human-Robot Interactions, IEEE Access, Vol.5, pp. 705-721, 2016-09.
3. M. Ficocelli, J. Terao, G. Nejat; Promoting Interactions Between Humans and Robots Using Robotic Emotional Behavior, IEEE Transactions on Cybernetics, Vol.46, Issues 12, pp. 2911-2923, 2015-11.
4. S. Iguchi, H. Takenouchi, M. Tokumaru, "Effectiveness of a Sympathy Expression Model for the Bystander Robot", International Journal of Affective Engineering, Vol.15, No.3, pp.223-230, 2016-07.
5. R. Boyd; The Puzzle of Human Sociality, Science, Vol. 314, Issue 5805, pp.1555-1556, 2006-12.
6. D. J. Terry, M. A. Hogg; Group Norms and the Attitude-Behavior Relationship: A Role for Group

Identification, Personality and Social Psychology Bulletin, Vol.22, Issue 8, pp. 776-793, 1996-08.
7. O. F. Kernberg; What Is Personality?, Journal of Personality Disorders, Vol.30, No. 2, pp. 145-156, 2016-04.
8. M. Sherif; A Study of Some Social Factors in Perception, Archives of Psychology, Vol.27, No.187, pp. 5-16, 1934-11.
9. RoBoHoN Official Website; https://robohon.com/global/ (accessed on 2/21/2018).

ISASE-MAICS 2018

Virtual Emotion for Robots

– What, Why, and How –

Yutaka MIYAJI* and Ken TOMIYAMA**

* *The School of Social Informatics, Aoyama Gakuin Univ., 5-10-1 Fuchinobe, Chuoku, Sagamihara, Kanagawa 252-5258 JAPAN*
uta@si.aoyama.ac.jp
** *Future Robotics Technology Center, Chiba Institute of Technology, 2-17-1 Tsudanuma, Narashino, Chiba 275-0016 JAPAN*
drtomiyama@gmail.com

Abstract: We propose a concept of Virtual Kansei for robots and describe our attempts to construct a series of systems for generating virtual emotion, a subset of Virtual Kansei, of a robot. Here, Kansei is a Japanese word that encompasses affection, emotion, and related mental functions. Robots need to have human-like Kansei in order for them to become true partners of humans. The proposed virtual emotion consists of three modules; emotion detector to detect emotional state of the partner, emotion generator to generate robot emotion from partner's emotion, and expression modulator to modify robot motions to express emotion. The emotion detector utilizes facial images, voice sounds, and body motions as inputs and Bayesian networks to integrate the information from three inputs. The emotion generator is a Petri-net that has a feedback structure to represent dynamics of emotion transition. Genetic Algorithm is adopted for adjusting arc weights of the Petri-net. The expression modulator uses an emotion vector to mix basis motions corresponding to the six emotions of Ekman. Experiments and results of three modules are discussed here.
Keywords: *Virtual emotion for robots, Emotion detection, Emotion generation, Emotion expression, Motion modulation*

1. INTRODUCTION

As robots are coming into more personal aspects of every-day human life, they are required to interact more closely with humans. We believe robots need to have a function to have their own Kansei (a Japanese word that encompasses affection, emotion, and related mental function) in order for them to become true partners of humans. Here, we propose and discuss the concept of virtual Kansei for robots and summarize our attempts over 20 years to construct a series of systems for generating virtual emotion of a robot.

2. BACKGROUND

There are many specific fields where the introduction of robots is intensely longed for. Care and welfare field is one such field and we target it as our main application field. Japan is experiencing unprecedented rapid transformation into an aged society where the rate of aging, defined as the ratio of over 65 population versus the entire population, reached 27.3% as of October 2016 and is expected to reach 33.3% in 2036 [1]. This is the reason why the introduction of robotics into care and welfare field is an urgent matter for Japan.

We launched a project on welfare robotics in 1997 and set our objective to develop robot systems that help caretakers. Thus, we arrived at the concept of 'caretaker support robot' that helps caretakers by bearing those workloads which are more fit for robots and creates spare time for caretakers to interact with cared persons in such a way that only humans can do.

One of the more important tasks of the caretaker support robot is to watch the cared person and report not just physical but mental anomalies to caretakers. For this purpose, the robot needs to have a capability to find mental status of the cared person. Furthermore, the robot should be able to keep watching the cared person without irritating him/her. This requires a capability to adjust its reactive behavior to the taste of the cared person. We found out, through extensive observation of actual works of caretakers, that caretakers are matching their mental status with those of the cared person. The caretaker support robot should have this capability of caretakers, namely, the Kansei of the caretakers. Thus, a concept of Virtual Kansei for robots is proposed and studied.

3. VIRTUAL KANSEI AND VIRTUAL EMOTION

The Virtual Kansei, as its name suggests, is a function for a robot to behave like having Kansei. Our approach started from emotion, a major component of Kansei. The emotion is a more accessible component of Kansei because it can be considered in the stimulus versus response framework, which is an input/output relationship in engineering terminology. Therefore, virtual emotion was developed first and this paper reports various attempts and outcomes regarding the virtual emotion.

3.1 Construction of Virtual Emotion

From our series of observations in early studies, we decided to adopt a three-module structure for our virtual emotion: emotion detector, emotion generator, and expression modulator. A conceptual robot control system that includes three modules of virtual emotion is depicted in Fig.1.

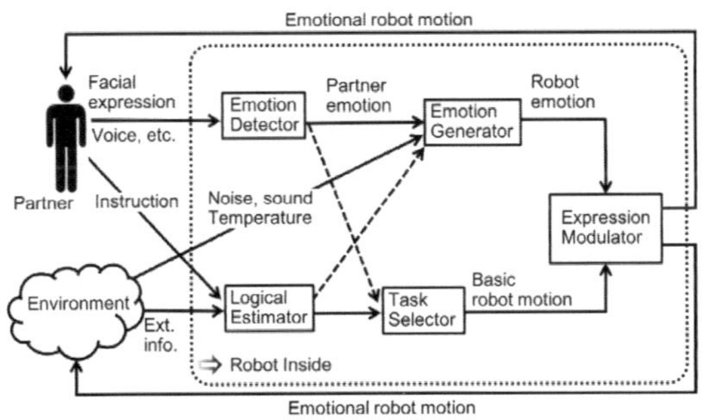

Figure 1: The conceptual robot controller with three virtual emotion modules.

It was found from observations of caretakers that they first identify emotional status of the cared person and then express the emotional state that matches the found emotion of the cared person. Following this observation, we constructed an emotion detector and an emotion generator that takes the partner's emotion as the input.

It is often a case that we do not exhibit our true emotion but express an emotional state that matches the situation. This observation is the reason for the separate module, expression modulator, for expressing emotion. This module is responsible to express robot's emotion by modifying ordinary motions, not by designated gestures.

4. EMOTION DETECTOR

The output of the emotion detector is the partner emotion. Here, the definition of six basic emotions by Ekman is adopted because of its wide applicability [2]. They are; Anger, Disgust, Fear, Happiness, Sadness, and Surprise. We added Neutral to represent non-emotional state to this list. We also decided to treat Surprise separately from other emotions due to its unique characteristics of high speed response time [3].

Emotion detector is structured as a cascade of three parts; the physical feature extraction part, individual emotion detection part, and the emotion state determination part. The input of the module can be facial images, tones of speaking, other bodily motions, or combinations of those. We adopted Bayesian network [4] for emotion detection from each physical input. The adoption of Bayesian network is motivated by the need to integrate the information from multiple sources in identifying the partner's emotion.

4.1 Three Physical Inputs

We first explain physical inputs.

- Facial Images

Ekman and his group proposed Facial Action Coding System (FACS) [2] where facial expressions are clarified by Action Units (AUIDs). The facial image processing part first finds sets of various feature points using Haar patterns from consecutive still face images. The AUID detection part is responsible to identify active AUs using the sets of feature points from the facial image processing part. The developed system extracts 21 AUIDs that are used as inputs to Bayesian network.

- Voice Sound

A standard feature of voice sound is adopted here. Mel-Frequency Cepstrum Coefficients (MFCC [5]) are computed from the obtained voice sound recorded at 16 bit and 16 kHz. We adopted Julius [6], an open source speech recognition engine, for this task. We decided to use 12 coefficients after a set of preliminary analysis.

- Body Motion

We chose physical parameters of the head and both hands as the inputs representing body motion. Kinect for Xbox360 from Microsoft was used to acquire the positions and the accelerations in 3D, that makes a data vector 18-diemnsional. The speed was not adopted because our observation showed speed itself has little influence on the emotion expression.

4.2 Integration of Detected Emotions

As mentioned above, Bayesian networks were used to compute the probabilities of each emotion from the above three physical inputs and the resulted probabilities are combined. This implies that the Bayesian network structure is used to integrate information at decision level rather than the feature level.

The probabilities of six emotions from three Bayesian networks are integrated using mixing ratios as in Kato et al. [4] where the integrated probabilities of emotions are given by the weighted sum of the individual probabilities. The detected emotion is the one with the highest integrated probability.

5. EMOTION GENERATOR

The target is a capability of generating human-like emotion transitions. We have tested several methods for the emotion generator, starting with neural network (NN), then recursive NN (RNN), structured NN (SNN), Petri-net with Genetic Algorithm (PN+GA), Hidden Markov Model (HMM) [7], and a hybrid NN and state space model (NN+SS).

We concentrate on the PN+GA approach here. Petri-net is a modelling tool of discrete distributed systems. It consists of Transitions, Places, Directed Arcs with weights, and Tokens [8]. The main reasons of our adoption of Petri-net are its graphical representation and ease of intentional modification of the network. The former makes it easier to understand how the internal operation pattern changes and that makes the latter possible.

It is noted that the emotion transition is controlled by a dynamics. We experience that we cannot change our emotion suddenly and that we express different emotion even if we are in the same situation. This lead us to adopt models with dynamics and introduced the concept of feedback structure.

5.1 Petri-net + Genetic Algorithm Model

When modelling a system by a Petri-net, we need to determine the network structure and to adjust the weights of the arcs. The emotion generator we developed has four layers: emotion transitions, inner places, inner transitions, and output emotion places (Fig. 2). The first layer is divided into two sets of transitions; one for the input of partner's emotion and the other for the feedback of robot emotion at one step in the past. It is noted that we limited only one each of the input and feedback emotion transitions corresponding to the current emotion (input) and the robot emotion (feedback) is fired.

In this study, the five emotions (Anger, Disgust, Fear, Happiness, and Sadness) are divided into two levels of strong and weak emotions. By adding the Neutral emotion, this makes the total of 11 emotions and accordingly 11 input transitions and 11 output places. The number of the feedback transitions is also 11 and this makes the number of emotion transitions 22. The numbers of middle layer places and transitions are empirically determined as 22 and the corresponding places and transitions are connected by a single arc. The weights of those single arcs are set at prime numbers so that the uniqueness of the network is secured. The weights of arcs from the input transitions to the inner places and from the inner transition to output emotion places are adjusted using Genetic Algorithm so that the input and output emotion transition matches that of a human.

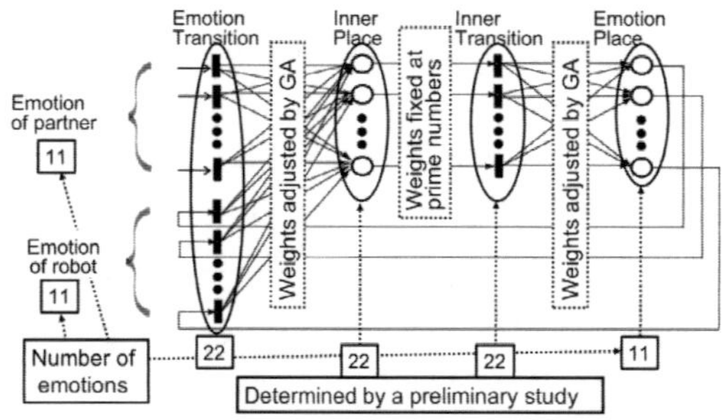

Figure 2: The Petri-net structure of the emotion generator.

6. EXPRESSION MODULATOR

The naming of this module comes from the fact that it is free for a robot to express the generated emotion using many features such as light and sounds and not limited to humanly methods. However, we started our study from modulating motions of robot tasks such as handing an item to the partner. We proposed Motion Modulation System (MMS) for this purpose (Fig. 3).

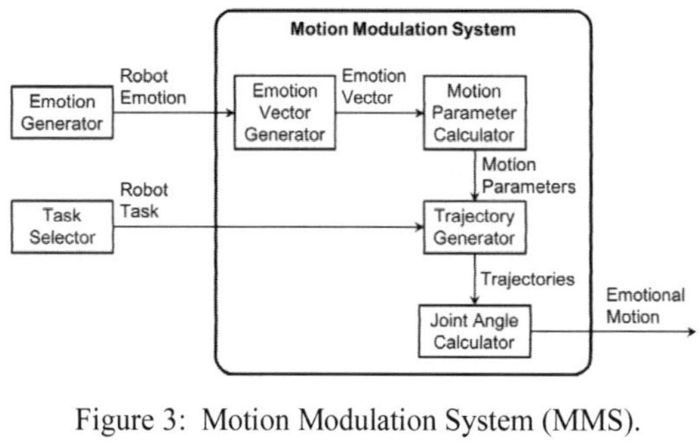

Figure 3: Motion Modulation System (MMS).

The main idea of MMS is to modulate the trajectory of robot motions to achieve a given task without jeopardizing the completion of the task. We first prepared six basic trajectories that can express six basic emotions. At the same time, we devised an emotion vector generator that converts the time-series of single emotion supplied from the emotion generator into a vector of emotions. The emotion vector makes it possible to mix six basic trajectories not only to express mixed emotions but also to give rich variety to robot motion. It is noted that the emotion vector generator can be used as a buffer between the emotion generator and the expression modulator to infuse logical restraints on expressed emotions.

6.1 Generation of Emotion Vector

The emotion vector generator actually generates a time series of five-dimensional emotion vectors excluding the neutral emotion. Each component of the vector will have an integer between 0 and 10. The neutral emotion is expressed by the all zero vector. The adopted algorithm, developed by observing natural human emotion transition, is as follows:

1. At time t, the values of all elements are reduced to half the value at time t-1. If the value is odd, say n, then (n+1)/2 is used.
2. At time t, an emotion is supplied by the emotion generator. Then the element of the vector corresponding to the input emotion will be increased by 5. If the sum exceeds 10, then the value is truncated to 10.
3. If the same emotion is not input for five times, then the corresponding element of the vector is set at 0.

6.2 Motion Parameter MP

It is assumed that the robot motion from the initial point to the final point in 3D space is represented by three cubic spline curves in x-, y- and z-planes with five notes each. The motion parameters MP adjust positions of the internal 3 nodes to modulate the motion between the initial and final points. They are;

- Duration parameter W: Changes the motion duration
- Expansion parameter Ex, Ey, and Ez: Expand trajectories along each axis
- Node position parameter R: Modify the time intervals between nodes

The motion time is prolonged (shortened) from the standard duration when W is positive (negative). The trajectory undulates when there is a mix of signs of expansion parameters. The internal nodes are evenly placed at 1/4 duration of the total time duration when the node position parameter R=0. The nodes are closer to the final (initial) node when R>0 (R<0) and, therefore, the latter (former) part of the trajectory is accelerated. It is noted that there are limits on those parameters due to the hardware limitations.

In a series of preliminary experiments, trajectories corresponding to various combinations of MPs are generated and their emotional impressions are tested for the determination of five basic trajectories for five emotions. The Neutral trajectory is the one with all 0 parameters.

7. EXPERIMENTS AND RESULTS

The experiments and results of individual modules are discussed starting from the emotion detector.

7.1 Emotion Detector

As was explained in Section 4, three physical inputs, facial images, voice sounds, and body motions are used. Separate Bayesian network is developed for each input and the results are combined at the decision level. A set of two samples of six emotions from six experiment participants is used in this experiment. The resulting Bayesian networks and the mixing of three emotion probabilities are shown in Fig. 4. The mixing ratios in Fig. 4 are computed to maximize the matching between the intended emotion and the output emotion. The result of integrating all three inputs is shown here (Table 1). Other results are referred to [9].

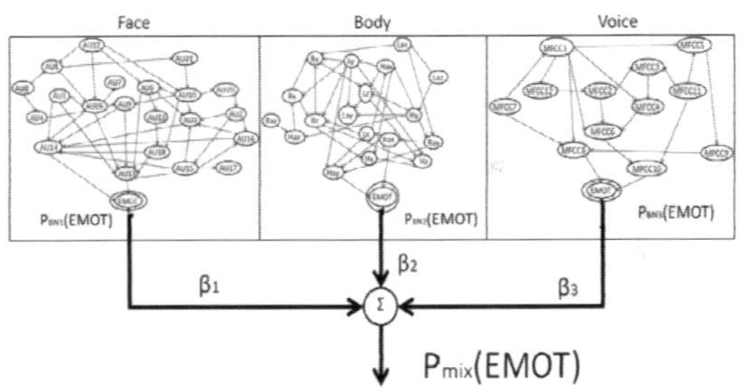

Figure 4: Emotion estimation using Bayesian networks where $P_{mix}(EMOT)$ and β_i are the vector of the integrated emotion and the mixing ratios.

In evaluating this result, we need to consider the nature of human emotion. Through our long history of human emotion estimation studies, we found that human emotion transitions are influenced by many factors such as climate, temperature, noise, physical conditions, and so on. This fact is represented by seemingly multi-valued relationships with any set of inputs. Therefore, the estimation accuracies of over 80%, which are common in deterministic engineering relationships, are only achievable with highly controlled data. It is our experience that those figures are out of reach with natural data and over 70% is a realistic target to achieve. From this point of view, the results shown in this table are satisfactory because the average detection rate exceeds 70%. It is noted that the 'other subject' raw is added to see if an emotion detector developed for a person can be used for other persons. The result shows a possibility. But we decided to develop specialized emotion detector for each partner because humans are obviously adjusting the detection method to each partner.

Table 1: Emotion estimation from all three inputs. $(\beta_1 = 0.48, \beta_2 = 0.20, \beta_3 = 0.32)$

Emotion	Joy	Sadness	Anger	Disgust	Fear	Neutral	Average
Same subject	78.3	67.1	78.5	69.8	66.2	74.8	72.5
Other subjects	74.5	60.9	73.3	65.7	52.4	72.5	66.5

7.2 Emotion Generator

In adjusting the weights of arcs in the Petri-net model, the fitness function is given by the following formula, where the CE, P, S, C_i, and N_i are the numbers of correct answers, pairs in a set, sets, continuous correct answers from the first pair in i-th set, and correct answers, respectively.

$$Fitness = \frac{CE}{C \times S} \quad (2)$$

$$CE = \sum_{i=1}^{S} \sum_{j=1}^{C_i} (N_i - j) \quad (3)$$

Note that this fitness function can place more weight for continuous correct answers. In the evaluation experiment, 40 sets of 6 pairs each were prepared, where a set represents 30 sec time-interval and a pair of emotions is determined for each 5 sec sub-intervals.

Other parameters of GA are set as follows: the chromosome is a collection of all the adjustable weights of the arcs, both roulette and elite selection schemes, two-point crossover, and single locus mutation. The number of individuals and generations are 500 and 10,000, respectively.

The three best individuals are used for evaluation experiment. Here, a two-dimensional emotion model in Fig. 5, which is inspired by the Russel's model [10] is introduced to evaluate differences between emotions quantitatively. There are two locations of Grief, Grifl and Grief2. The distance from Grief is determined by the shorter of the distances computed using Griefl and Grief2.

The error per set given below is evaluated using the same emotion data set yielded in the range of 0.8 to 2.6. Considering the fact that the maximum error of 12, this result is satisfactory.

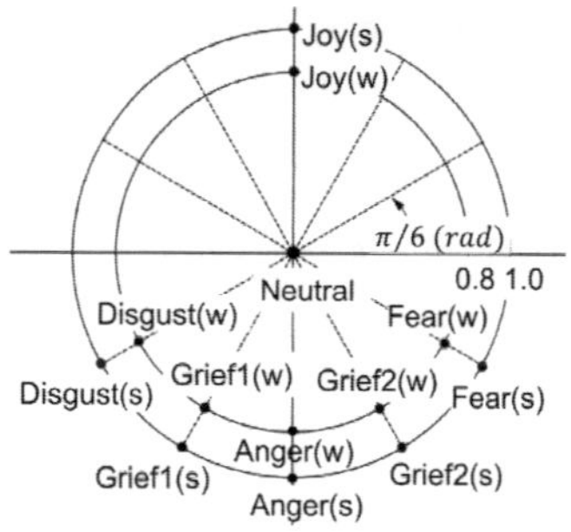

Figure 5: Two-dimensional emotion model inspired by the Russel's model [10]. Here, s and w represent strong and weak emotions.

7.3 Individuation

We found that some inner transitions tend to fire much less than the rest of the inner transitions and that there is a correspondence between the output emotion and the less firing transitions. From this observation, we hypothesized that if we intentionally prohibit the firing of tactically chosen inner transitions then we can control the output emotion. To verify this hypothesis, we deter the firing of the inner transitions [11] and run the test with the same inputs as the evaluation experiment and we obtained the results in Table 2.

Table 2. Comparison of output emotions of Petri-nets between the original and modified ones (m) according to Table 2.

Emotion output	Ori-ginal	Anger (m)	Disgust (m)	Fear (m)	Grief (m)	Joy (m)
Neutral	483	206	341	274	274	194
Anger(w)	1	**2**	1	0	0	0
Anger(s)	29	**343**	19	8	13	23
Disgust(w)	6	7	**160**	0	22	0
Disgust(s)	4	0	**13**	12	6	6
Fear(w)	12	43	28	**66**	10	0
Fear(s)	12	7	33	**224**	7	0
Grief(w)	82	19	32	23	**442**	89
Grief(s)	10	8	28	36	**22**	10
Joy(w)	107	116	84	109	19	**222**
Joy(s)	7	3	6	11	6	**224**

This clearly shows that the planned prohibition of the firing of the inner transitions gave rise to the emphasis of the corresponding emotion in the output emotion (shaded cells). This result shows the possibility of individuation of the emotion generator, namely to tailor-made the emotion generator for each partner.

7.4 Expression Modulator

The motion of handing an object to the partner with the right hand was chosen as the testing task. The right hand grabbing an object simulating a bottle of water is initially resting at the bottom position. Then, the robot moves and extends its hand up to the shoulder height. The neutral motion, serve as the basic motion, is that of the linear motion between the initial and final point over 4 sec duration time. Strictly speaking, the motion of a hand of a robot is determined not only by its positions but also by its posture. Here, the posture is ignored for the sake of simplicity, except the initial and final postures that are fixed.

In preliminary experiments, three values for each PM (W, Ex, Ey, Ez: and R) are chosen and corresponding motions are generated. Then, 16 motions with prevailing features are selected for the main experiment. Those 16 motions were recorded, and their life-size images were shown to participants. 20 participants were asked to evaluate emotional contents of each motion by impression scores of 1 to 3. The resulting scores are analyzed using the canonical correlation analysis to find out the best combination of MPs for each emotion. As the resulting canonical correlations summarized in Table 3 [11], corresponding to the best combinations of MPs show, the motion modulation scheme MMS is promising.

Table 3: Motion Modulation System with best MPs.

Emotion	J	S	A	D	F	(Average)
Canonical correlation	0.77	0.85	0.67	0.82	0.79	(0.78)

8. CONCLUSIONS

Towards the society where robots are integrated to human society as effective supporters, we have been developing Virtual Kansei for robots. Here, we presented the summary of our efforts in developing virtual emotion, an important element of virtual Kansei, for robots. A three-module structure is proposed where each module is responsible for detection of partner's emotional state, generating robot emotion, and expressing robot emotion. The first module, emotion detector, utilizes three physical inputs, facial images, voice sounds, and body motions to compute the probabilities of six emotional states defined by Ekman and Bayesian networks to combine those probabilities to determine the partner's emotional state. The results of experiments show satisfactory detection rates. The second module, emotion generator, takes the partner's emotional state as input and generates robot's virtual emotion using a Petri-net structure with a feedback path for dynamics and GA for adapting arc weights of the Petri-net to reproduce human emotion transition. Motion modulation system (MMS) is proposed as the realization of the third module. Six motions representing six basic emotions are mixed using the emotion vector, which is constructed from the time series of robot emotion generated by the second module.

Three modules need to be integrated together and implemented on a robot to prove the validity of our approach. That is the most important task to be pursued.

ACKNOWLEDGMENTS

There are many care facilities that helped us in understanding the needs of the caretaking field and in proposing the concept of caretaker support robot. We were fortunate to have many enthusiastic students, K. Kamijo, T. Ono, T. Yanadori, J. Kogami to name a few. We acknowledge that this research was launched as a project at the Research Institute of Aoyama Gakuin University, and express our appreciation for financial as well as clerical help.

REFFERENCES

[1] http://www8.cao.go.jp/kourei/english/annualreport/2016/2016pdf_e.html (viewed 3/23/2018)

[2] P. Ekman; An Argument for Basic Emotions, Cognition and Emotion, 6(3/4), pp.169-200, 1992.

[3] M. Zenkyo and K. Tomiyama; Surprise generator for virtual Kansei based on human surprise characteristics, Proceedings of HCI2011, July 2011.

[4] S. Kato, Y. Sugino and H. Itoh; A Bayesian Approach to Emotion Detection in Dialogist's Voice for Human Robot Interaction, Lecture Notes in Artificial Intelligence, Vol. 4252, pp. 961-968, 2006.

[5] http://recognize-speech.com/feature-extraction/mfcc (viewed 3/23/2018)

[6] http://julius.osdn.jp/index.php (in Japanese)

[7] J. Kogami, K. Tomiyama, and Y. Miyaji; Kansei Generator using HMM for Virtual Kansei in Caretaker Support Robot, Kansei Engineering International, 8, 1, pp. 83-90, 2009.

[8] https://en.wikipedia.org/wiki/Petri_net (viewed 3/23/2018)

[9] K. Kamijo and K. Tomiyama; Emotion Estimation Based on Facial Image, Voice Sound, and Body Motion, IASDR2103, KANSEI Robotics Invited Session, Tokyo, 2013.

[10] J.A. Russell; A circumplex model of affect, Journal of Personality and Society Psychology, Vol. 39, pp. 1161-1178, 1980.

[11] Y. Miyaji and K. Tomiyama; Construction of Virtual Kansei by Petri-net with GA and Method of Constructing Personality, Procs. ROMAN2002, 6B4, 2002.

ISASE-MAICS 2018

The Effect of Prices in Red on Mental Simulation

Daiki WAKAYAMA*

** Komazawa University, 1-23-1Komazawa, Setagaya-ku, Tokyo 154-8525, Japan*
dwakayam@komazawa-u.ac.jp

Abstract: The way a product is visually depicted facilitates more/less mental simulation. The imagination difficulty/ease of use of the product impacts on product evaluations such as purchase intentions. Although male consumers perceived greater savings (positive effect) when prices were presented in red, little is known about the impact of price color on mental simulation. This study discusses the effect of prices in red and the effect of visual depiction on mental simulation and product evaluation. This research revealed that there was a discouraging effect of prices in red on mental simulation by right-handed women and their evaluations when the visual stimuli was a mismatch between the product orientation and their dominant hand (e.g., showing a picture of a kettle with the handle on the left).
Keywords: *Price color, Visual depiction effect, Handedness, Mental simulation, Product evaluation*

1. INTRODUCTION

Elder and Krishna (2012) have demonstrated that a match between product orientation and handedness (right/left) facilitates mental simulation more than a mismatch. When product images facilitated more mental simulation, people reported more spontaneous using simulations and higher purchase intentions for the product. Imagination difficulty/ease of product usage impacts on product evaluations (e.g. Zhao, et al., 2012). This phenomenon was called the "visual depiction effect". People seem to process the product images of orientation as a heuristic cue in evaluation.

Puccinelli et al. (2013) have shown that men perceived greater savings when prices were presented in red than when presented in black, whereas women did not. This phenomenon was called the "effect of red price". As discussed by Puccinelli et al. (2013), men seem to process price information less in-depth and use the color of red as a visual heuristic to judge savings. In contrast, when the prices were presented in red, women appear more skeptical of the promotion and perceive fewer savings.

Therefore, it is logical to expect women to perceive difficulty imaging using a visually depicted product with price in red in the mismatch condition in which the product is oriented toward the participant's non-dominant hand. We anticipate right-handed women report less mental simulation lead to lower user-friendliness when visual stimuli containing prices in red orienting the product toward the participant's left hand. The purpose of this study is to provide a demonstration that the influence of price color on mental simulation and product evaluation provided by female participants.

2. METHOD

One hundred sixty-two under graduate students at a private university in Tokyo were recruited to participate in this study. They were assigned to one of four conditions (right black, right red, left black, and left red). Participants were told that they would be evaluating an electric product on several dimensions. They were instructed to view the image and a brief amount of verbal copy before proceeding to answer questions about the product. The stimuli for this study were created by taking an image of an electric kettle with a handle on one side. The picture of the kettle was a black and white photo and which was flipped over a vertical axis to create a mirror image of the kettle without logo marks. Thus, the handle was on either the right or the left side of the kettle. In addition to the image, the stimuli included a price (3,480 yen, price color: red or black; see fig. A1- fig. A4 in the appendix A) presented with the image and a short description of the product (the verbal copy was T-fal Electric Kettle, Justin Plus 1.2l, Body Weight: 970g, Rated Power Consumption: 1250W, Energy saving because keep warm function is not included.). The price and the product information used were based on a price list of Amazon.com at the time of this survey (July 2015).

After viewing the image and reading the product information, participants were asked to evaluate the picture of the kettle on the extent to which they could feel that the product was user-friendly (1 = very user-friendly; 11 = not at all user-friendly). Participants also evaluated the picture of the kettle on the extent to which they agreed with the statement "I had no difficulty imaging using the kettle in my mind" (1 = strongly agree; 11 = strongly disagree) which scale was used as one of three measures of an ease of mental simulation scale (reverse coded) by Elder and Krishna (2012). They were assessed using eleven-point scales. Each scale was used a single-item measure for simplicity. Finally, participants provided basic demographic information by indicating their gender and age, as well as their handedness (right- or left-handed). As suggested in the previous studies, price color and product orientation were key difference variables which can affect processing visual information and evaluating product (user-friendliness). Visual stimuli with prices in red should lead female participants to process it more deeply and more skeptical than visual stimuli with prices in black. A match between product orientation with a price in red and handedness should affect mental simulation more than a mismatch for female participants. That is, if the orientation was directed to the right and the participant was right-handed (coded as a match), participants' perceived user-friendliness of the product will be affected by facilitated mental simulation than a mismatch condition.

3. RESULTS

Of the 162, 67 (41.4%) were men, 94 (58.0%) were female participants, 16 (9.9%) were left-handed.

3.1 Red price effect on imagination difficulty for right-handed female participants

A 2 (orientation: right or left) × 2 (price color: red or black) between-subjects ANOVA with orientation and color as the independent variables and imagination difficulty as the dependent variable revealed a significant two-way interaction between the two factors (F (1,79) = 4.232, p=.043 < .05, *partial* η^2 = 0.051). The analysis revealed that right-handed female participants under the mismatch condition perceived more difficulty of imagination when the price was presented in red than in black ($M_{\text{Right-Black}}$ = 4.61; $M_{\text{Right-Red}}$ = 4.19; $M_{\text{Left-Black}}$ = 3.83; $M_{\text{Left-Red}}$ = 5.35; see Table 1 and Figure 3.1). However, neither the main effect of orientation nor the main effect of price color was significant (M_{Right} = 4.38; M_{Left} = 4.73; F (1,79) = 0.162, p=.689 *n.s.*, M_{Black} = 4.22; M_{Red} = 4.83; F (1,79) = 1.35, p=.249 *n.s.*). The results confirm that there was no red price effect on making evaluations of an imagination difficulty of using the kettle when the orientation matched participant's dominant hand. The results show that the imagination difficulties of using a product was negatively affected by the price color of red in the mismatch condition.

Table 1: Means and standard deviations of right-handed female perceptions of imagination difficulty

					95% CL	
Orientation	Color	*n*	*Mean*	*S.D.*	*LL*	*UL*
Right	Black	18	4.61	2.43	3.40	5.82
	Red	21	4.19	2.23	3.18	5.20
Left	Black	18	3.83	1.65	3.01	4.66
	Red	26	5.35	2.08	4.51	6.19

Note. CL=conficence interval; LL=lower limit; UL=upper limit.

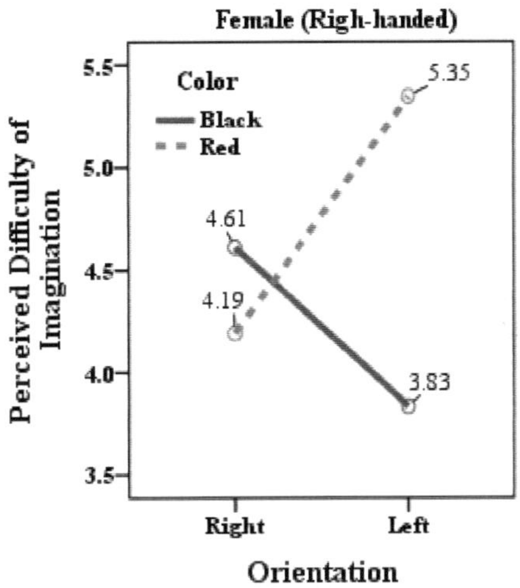

Figure 3.1: Perceived difficulties of imagination

3.2 Red price effect on imagination difficulty for right-handed male participants

A 2 × 2 between-subjects ANOVA with orientation and color as the independent variables and imagination difficulty as the dependent variable revealed neither significant main effects nor a significant two-way interaction effect of orientation and color of price on perceived user-friendliness among men (Table 2).

Table 2: Analysis of variance results for imagination difficulty and user-friendliness among male participants

	Means				F Values		
	Right		Left		Main Effects		Interaction
	Black	Red	Black	Red	Orientation	Color	
Imagination difficulty[a]	4.61	4.21	5.50	4.62	0.655[n.s.]	0.647[n.s.]	0.094[n.s.]
User-friendliness[b]	5.17	4.86	5.67	4.43	0.002[n.s.]	1.117[n.s.]	0.402[n.s.]

NOTE: Male participants
a. Eleven-point scales (1 = "strongly agree"; 11 = "strongly disagree").
b. Eleven-point scales (1 = "very user-friendly"; 11 = "not at all user-friendly").
*Significant at .05. **Significant at .01. ***Significant at .001.
n.s. :Not Significant

3.3 Red price effect on user-friendliness for right-handed female participants

A 2 × 2 between-subjects ANOVA with orientation and color as the independent variables and user-friendliness as the dependent variable revealed a significant two-way interaction between the two factors (F (1,79) = 4.196, p=.044 < .05, *partial* $\eta^2 = 0.050$). Further, examination of the nature of the interaction revealed that right-handed female participants under the mismatch condition (if the orientation was directed to the left) perceived less user-friendliness when the price was presented in red than when it appeared in black ($M_{\text{Right-Black}} = 4.06$; $M_{\text{Right-Red}} = 3.77$; $M_{\text{Left-Black}} = 3.89$; $M_{\text{Left-Red}} = 5.12$, see Table 3). Figure 3.2 graphically presents the means. In contrast, neither the main effect of orientation nor the main effect of price color was significant ($M_{\text{Right}} = 3.90$; $M_{\text{Left}} = 4.61$; F (1,79) = 2.522, p=.116 >.05: *n.s.*, $M_{\text{Black}} = 3.97$; $M_{\text{Red}} = 4.50$; F (1,79) = 1.622, p=.207 >.05: *n.s.*). This result suggests that there was no red prices effect on making evaluations of a user-friendliness when the orientation matched participant's dominant hand. In the mismatch condition, female participants' perceived user-friendliness negatively with the price color was red.

Table 3: Means and standard deviations of right-handed female perceptions of user-friendliness

					95% CL	
Orientation	Color	*n*	*Mean*	*S.D.*	*LL*	*UL*
Right	Black	17	4.06	1.68	3.20	4.92
	Red	22	3.77	1.66	3.04	4.51
Left	Black	18	3.89	1.91	2.94	4.84
	Red	26	5.12	1.45	4.53	5.70

Note. CL=confidence interval; LL=lower limit; UL=upper limit.

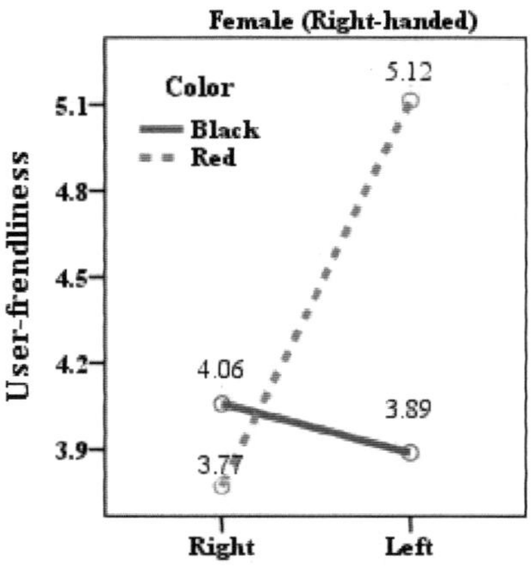

Figure 3.2: User-friendliness

3.4 Red price effect on user-friendliness for right-handed male participants

A 2 × 2 between-subjects ANOVA with orientation and color as the independent variables and user-friendliness as the dependent variable revealed neither significant main effects nor a significant two-way interaction effect of orientation and color of price on perceived user-friendliness among men (Table 2).

4. DISCUSSION

The results demonstrate that female participants reported less mental simulation and lower product evaluations when visual stimuli with a price in red in the mismatch condition (orienting the product toward the participant's left hand) when compared with the price in black, whereas they did not in the match condition. The findings are consistent with our reasoning that when processing the visual stimuli with red color prices within the negatively depicted condition (mismatch), it will lead to a less thorough processing and a negative impact on mental simulation, especially for rating a user-friendly product. Evidence suggests that prices in red play a role for female imaging activities as a discouraging effect. Future research is needed to understand the nature of the effect of red prices on consumers' information processing and judgment.

APPENDIX

STIMULI (a set of picture and price) USED IN THIS STUDY

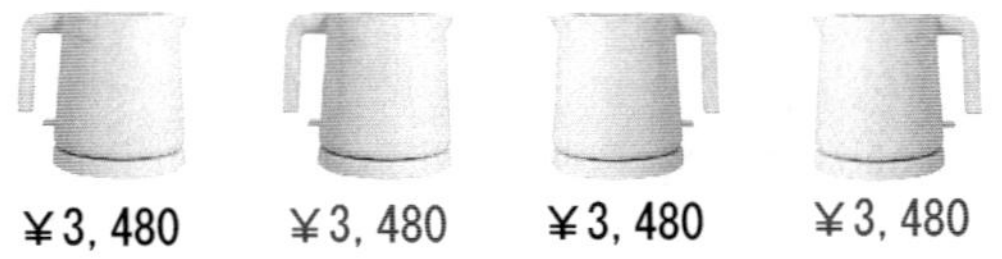

1: **Left Black** 2: **Left Red** 3: **Right Black** 4: **Right Red**

REFFERENCES

[1] Elder Ryan S. and Krishna Aradhna; The "Visual Depiction Effect" in Advertising: Facilitating Embodied Mental Simulation through Product Orientation, *Journal of Consumer Research*, Volume 38, Issue 6, 1 April 2012, Pages 988–1003.

[2] Puccinelli, N. M., Chandrashekaran, R., Grewal, D., & Suri, R. (2013). Are men seduced by red? The effect of red versus black prices on price perceptions. *Journal of Retailing*, *89*(2), 115-125.

[3] Zhao, M., Hoeffler, S., & Dahl, D. W. (2012). Imagination difficulty and new product evaluation. *Journal of Product Innovation Management*, *29*(S1), 76-90.

ISASE-MAICS 2018

Clinical desires to catch signals of human expression

–assisting communication of severely disabled patients with neurodegenerative disorders–

Yugo Narita*, **, Mio Kato ***, Natsumi Nishii ****, Rui Maki *****, Takeo Manabe *****
Takemasa ISHIKAWA ***** and Keiko Fukuroku *

** Course of Nursing Science, Graduate School of Medicine, Mie University, 2-174 Edobashi, Tsu-shi, Mie 514-8507, Japan*
*** Department of Neurology, Mie University Hospital, Mie University, 2-174 Edobashi, Tsu-shi, Mie 514-8507, Japan*
**** Department of Nursing, Daido Hospital, 9 Hakusui, Minami-ku, Nagoya-shi, Aich 457-8511, Japan*
***** Department of Nursing, Komatsu Hospital, 6-45 Maehama-dori, Minami-ku, Nagoya-shi, Aich 457-0058, Japan*
****** Department of Nursing, Mie University Hospital, Mie University, 2-174 Edobashi, Tsu-shi, Mie 514-8507, Japan*

Abstract: The authors present clinical desires to catch signals of human expression, and then ask opinions on communication support for severely disabled patients with neurodegenerative disorders from specialist members of the International Society of Affective Science and Engineering. Two aims were considered. One aim was to detect patients' expressions as a trigger to a switch for an augmentative and alternative communication device and to accumulate facial signals conveying demented patients' good or no-good expressions using a tool that is typically used for providing palliative care for non-cancer patients. The other aim was to determine the examined tool's possibility for evaluation in normal subjects. The knowledge and skills required for communicating with severely disabled patients, especially with amyotrophic lateral sclerosis (ALS), needs to be shared among colleagues in the form of vocational education. In the clinical fields, health-care professionals and undergraduates are too busy to make sufficient time to gain such knowledge and skills. With regard to the proposed tool, we raised the unusual question about whether our desires to catch signals of human expression are too idealistic and infeasible.
Keywords: *human expression, communication, neurodegenerative disorders*

1. INTRODUCTION

The number of patients with neurodegenerative disorders increases steeply in accordance with the aging population [1,2]. These diseases include, among others, Parkinson's disease (PD), dementia with Lewy body (DLB), multiple system atrophy (MSA), amyotrophic lateral sclerosis (ALS) and Alzheimer's disease (AD) [2]. Many clinical professionals and families have tried to obtain a signal from severely disabled patients with demented disorders or ALS on a mechanical ventilator with tracheostomy. However, these signals have been too subtle on occasion, especially at the advanced stage, to determine delivery of suitable care and to evaluate care appropriateness to each patient. All's well that ends well. The question arises, "How can we judge whether each care is suitable or not without an accurate signal?"

Two considerations may be supposed. First, the technology can be applied to tools. For example, for advanced-stage ALS without dementia, regardless of how subtle the signal is, even if it is detectable, the signal can be connected to an augmentative and alternative communication (AAC) device [3,4]. For another example, regardless of how demented a patient is, if we can apply a tool to accumulate their facial signals for good or no-good expressions for a period of time, we may be reassured of what services we have provided.

Second, vocational education can be considered. We need to share knowledge and skills required for communicating with severely disabled patients with ALS among colleagues. However, in the clinical fields, health-care professionals and undergraduates are too busy to make sufficient time for acquiring knowledge and for becoming familiar with new skills.

Here, we present clinical desires to obtain signals of human expression, with the aim to ask opinions on communication of severely disabled patients from specialist members of the International Society of Affective Science and Engineering. We also discuss whether or not our desires to catch signals of human expression are too idealistic and infeasible.

2. Technology

2.1. Caring for the totally locked-in state of ALS

The totally locked-in state (TLS) has been defined as a state whereby a patient's thought has been well preserved, but surrounding people have no method to detect any signal of the patient's thought [5-8]. This situation occurs in 10% or more of advanced-stage ALS patients with tracheostomy and positive pressure ventilation (TPPV). The longer one lives with TPPV, the higher prevalence of TLS is estimated. Far less patients choose TPPV support in the USA or UK, while nearly 30 % of ALS patients currently live with TPPV in Japan [9,10]. The function of voluntary movement of extra-ocular muscles is well preserved even through to the latest stage of ALS. However, at the end of the trajectory, the function disappears in some cases [11]. Many kinds of tools have been invented to detect subtle voluntary signals, including detecting pattern changes on electroencephalography (EEG) or functional near-infrared spectroscopy (fNIRS) [11-14]. Regardless, the meaningful use of this tool among patients is extremely rare in clinical settings. Reports on brain-machine-interfaces (BMI) have failed to show good results for complete TLS patients with no applied method, including BMI [11-14]. In contrast, their caregivers have on occasion stated that they have been able to catch a positive or negative sign from the TLS patient. No clinician knows what factors contribute to this so-called "signal", even if the caregiver can describe it, because there are no objective methods to reconfirm such claims. A tool to objectively catch signals of human expression could therefore be useful.

2.2. To detect human expression

Ideally, a tool for catching signals of human expression would be able to detect a patient's voluntary expression, not only immediately, but even after collecting several factors over a period of time. Such signals could be in the form of good or no-good expressions on the patient's face or any part of their body. The tool might bring about reassurance not only for patients, but also for carers and health-care providers with regard to ensuring each patient's comfort and dignity. Severely ill patients, especially with dementia, seldom show constant good or no-good signals. Furthermore, palliative care for cancer patients has gradually become common. Regardless, for non-cancer patients, especially for demented patients, palliative care has just stood on the start, because no scale to detect patients' subjective comfort exists [2].

Another question to consider is, "How precisely are we able at present to evaluate normal people on their subtle change of human expression?" A tool that can detect and evaluate such change would be good for vocational education in terms of learning clinical skills.

For example, learning how to use letter boards for severely disabled patients with ALS is considered to be difficult among health-care professionals who have never had such knowledge and experience [15]. We therefore sought to measure the speed and emotional burden of nursing students' use of a letter board in a simulation of treating ALS patients. We attempted this via an educational trial about how to use letter boards at the school of nursing, the faculty of medicine, Mie university in 2016.

Participants: Five adult students (20–35 years of age, mean 24.2±4.9 years, comprising two men and three women) were selected among applicants after a call for paid participants from the school of nursing. The participants were taught how to play the role of a severe ALS patient without cognitive impairment. They followed the trial protocol of responding with only eye movements using three different types of letter boards (Grid type, Flick type and Kuchimoji).

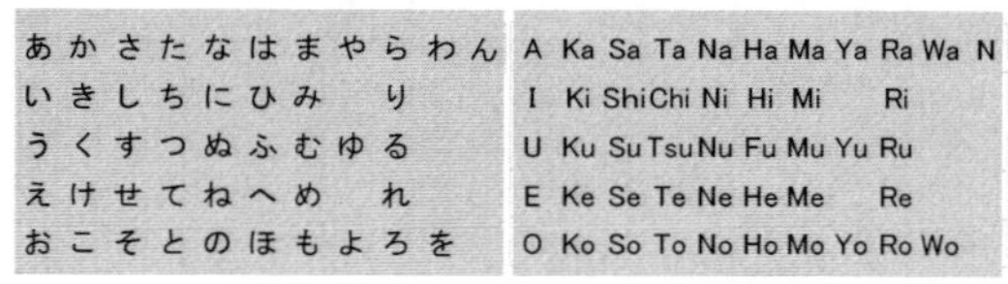

Fig. 1: Letter board: Grid type: 50-letter board (shown in original Japanese letters on the left and in translated alphabetical notations on the right)

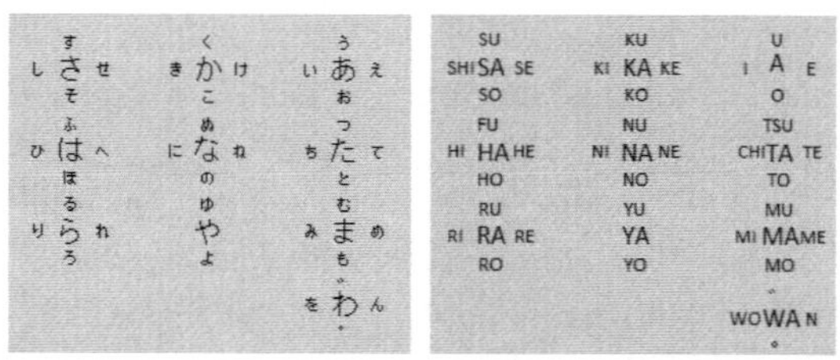

Fig. 2: Flick type: cross-shape board (shown in original Japanese letters on the left and in translated alphabetical notations on the right)

Kuchimoji comprises an oral shape and eye-blink method without a board. Participants acting as patients were allowed to express oral shapes for five different vowels in Japanese: "A", "I", "U", "E" and "O". Formerly even in Japan, there were many vowels with some differences especially in local accents. But only these 5 vowels have been converged and merged by the Ministry of Education after the WWII. There are subtle variances in expression of each vowel among people. But most of the oral shape (expression) would be identifiable in patients with moderate to severe disability. Intentional eye blink with sufficient length and times (twice or 3 times) is a good way to show "yes" or "no" in ALS patients even with severe disability. For example, when the patient tried to convey "Ke", the participant read the "E" shape with the patient's mouse, then the participant read aloud the "E" line, like "E", "Ke", "Se", "Te", "Ne" and so forth. The participant could catch the patient's signal of intentional eye blink at "Ke".

Protocol: Three students received letters from the participants acting as patients in a 60-minute session for 5 consecutive days. (fig.3)

During each session, a scenario composed using 200 Japanese letters was provided to the participant acting as a patient. They were shown the scenario for the first time during preparation for each session. They were told it was unnecessary to use sonant marks (dots added to kana symbols).

The passages were selected from the daily newspaper column "Tensei-Jingo" (the Asahi Shinbun) from 2015. One of the research member RM prepared all of the scenario passages without showing anyone else. No same passage was used twice.

Receivers consisted of 3 research members other than RM. They were MK, NN and TM. Each of them took the same part of the session through the trial. They kept away from the scenarios until the completion of each trial.

The trial was held in the practical room of fundamental nursing at the school of nursing in August 2016. Vital signs were checked, and questionnaires with visual analogue scales to measure the participants' emotional burden were completed before and after each session. The inter-beat (R-R) intervals of electrocardiogram and heart rate changes of each participant during the 60 minutes from the beginning to the end of the session were also measured by using MemCalc/BonalyLight (GMS Co., Ltd. Tokyo, Japan 2015). Participants replied only with eye movement and blinking.

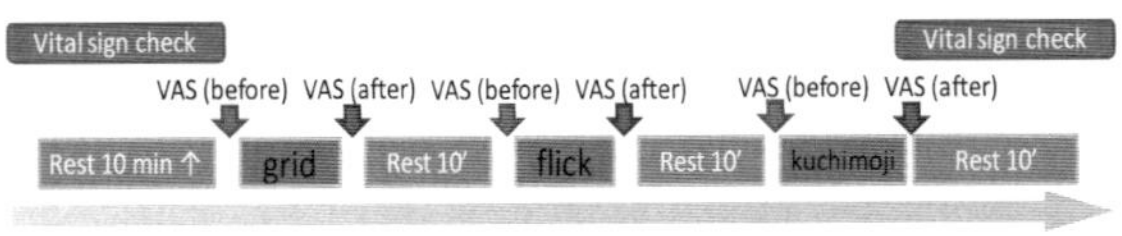

Fig. 3: Protocol. VAS = visual analogue scale.

The outcomes were the number of successful communicated Japanese kana letters in 5 minutes for each type of board. The emotional burden was measured by changing the R-R intervals of the electrocardiogram and visual analogue scale (VAS) before and after each session. The ratio of VAS values (after / before) was set as the stress ratio.

The IRB permission number was No. 3046 (August, 2016), Faculty of Medicine, Mie University.

Results

Kuchimoji, the oral shape and eye-blink method was faster than the grid-type 50-letter board and the flick-type cross-shape board. (fig.4) Accuracy was the same across all three modalities as of the second day. (fig.5) Subjective emotional burden (stress ratio) markedly decreased by the second day. (fig.6)

However, no significant difference among participants or sessions was found on the LF, HF, and LF/HF ratio of the heart rate variability data.

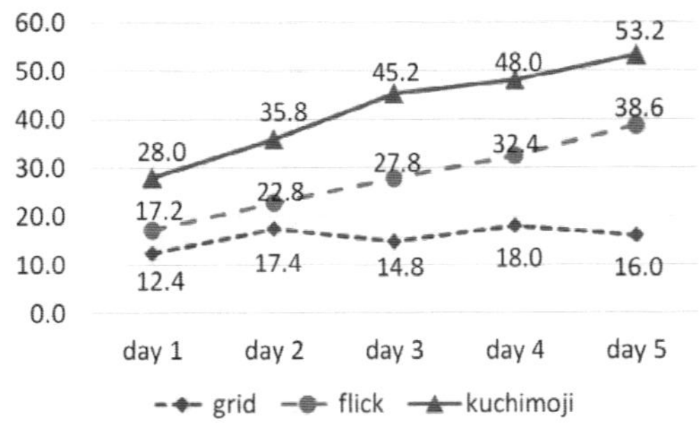

Fig. 4: Total number of received letters / 5 min. (average)

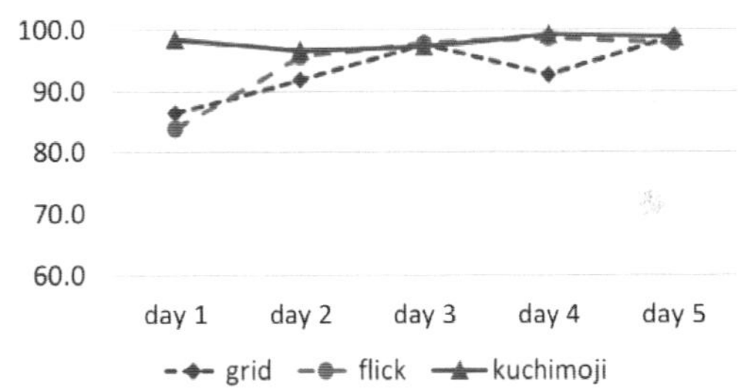

Fig. 5: Correct proportion of received letters (%)

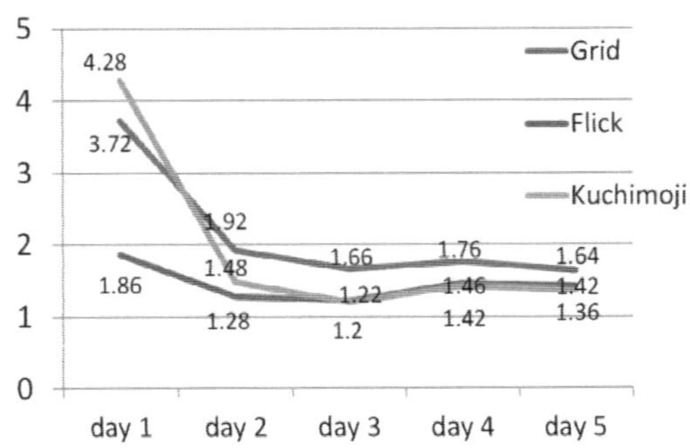

Fig. 6: Stress ratio

This trial was merely a pilot study, but it has potential in teaching knowledge and skills about communication for patients with ALS within a relatively short timeframe to students aiming to become health-care professionals. Additionally, the results of this investigation may apply to not only students but also people with ALS and health-care professionals. We need objective evidence on the effectiveness of such an education trial. We failed to show a significant difference of heart rate variability on this trial. We merely obtained subjective data of stress ratios from VAS values.

We pose an additional question, "Is there any possibility to catch signals of human expression in healthy people?" A tool to catch subtle changes in expressions may provide us with another chance to evaluate human stress.

3. Education

3.1. Trying to educate within a short timeframe

We are planning to design a half-day course for undergraduate students on methods and skills required for communicating with severely disabled patients with ALS. The effectiveness and maintenance of the course's effect will be evaluated only according to the number of letters received within 5 minutes and the VAS scale stress ratio. These approaches mirror the aforementioned methods and will include an interval after 6 months of intervention and the same contents as showing on figure 7.

The proposed scheme includes a point of weakness. That is, it lacks necessary objective data in addition to heart rate variability. To address this weakness, a tool to catch signals of human expression would be a good candidate as an evaluation method.

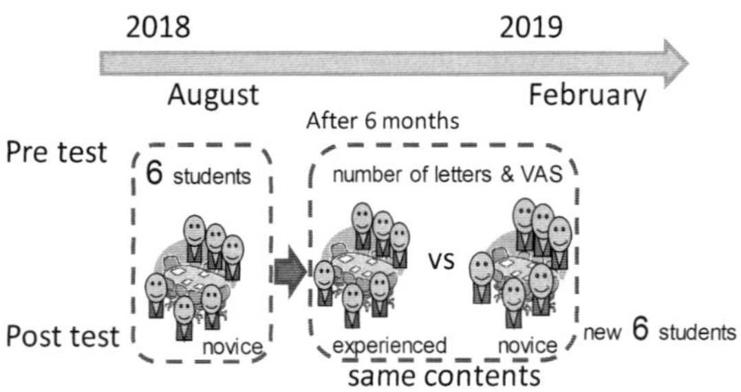

Fig. 7: Illustration of a half-day course for students to learn communication methods and skills and its evaluation strategy

4. Comments

In Japan, one third of ALS patients currently live with TPPV [9,10]. This high ratio alongside the Grant-in-Aid program for designated chronic diseases may be able to account for the high prevalence of complete TLS in Japan [1,9]. Therefore, communication support is essential for patients with ALS [2, 4-8]. Use of a letter board is the most common and convenient tool for communicating with severely disabled patients, even in situations where there is no access to electricity [4,15].

However, education is insufficient with regard to how to use a letter board or which AAC device should be applied, not only for undergraduate students but also for all health-care professionals who care for ALS patients [4,15]. Most patients and carers hope to maintain communication by use of tools such as BMI, even though ethical issues need to be considered [16]. However, in daily clinical and committee activity, we have never observed any model case in which BMI has been used meaningfully, with a successful attempt in patients. For this reason, we presented here an investigation into clinical desires to catch signals of human expression. Are our desires too idealistic and infeasible?

ACKNOWLEDGMENTS

This work was supported by Grant-in-Aid for Scientific Research (C) in Japan, 2017. We thank Edanz Group (www.edanzediting.com/ac) for editing a draft of this manuscript.

REFERENCES

1. Japan Intractable Disease Information Center. number of people with a grant-in-aid program for designated chronic diseases. (in Japanese) http://www.nanbyou.or.jp/entry/1356 (accessed on 17th January, 2017)
2. Y Narita; Neurodegenerative disorders, The Japanese Journal of Hospice and Palliative Care; 27 (supple), pp. 130-137, 2017. (in Japanese)
3. The Rehabilitation Engineering Society of Japan. The Guideline of AAC Introduction for severly disabled people 2012-2013. (in Japanese) http://www.resja.or.jp/com-gl/gl/index.html (accessed on 17th January, 2017)
4. Y Narita; Communication support for ALS patients under artificial ventilation : present and future perspectives, Shinkei Naika (Neurological Medicine) ; 87(5), pp. 539-544, 2017. (in Japanese & English abstract)
5. H Hayashi, EA Oppenheimer; ALS patients on TPPV:

totally locked-in state, neurologic findings and ethical implications, Neurology; 61, pp.135-137, 2003.

6. A Kawata, K Mizoguchi, H Hayashi; A nationwide survey of ALS patients on tracheostomy positive pressure ventilation (TPPV) who developed a totally locked-in state (TLS) in Japan, Rinsho Shinkeigaku; 48(7), pp.476-480, 2008. (in Japanese & English abstract)
7. T Doki, H Ueyama; care for totally locked-in patients with ALS, Nanbyou to Zaitakukea (intractable diseases and home care); 20, pp. 8-11, 2014. (in Japanese)
8. Y Nakayama, T Shimizu, Y Mochizuki, et al.; Predictors of impaired communication in amyotrophic lateral sclerosis patients with tracheostomy-invasive ventilation, Amyotroph Lateral Scler Frontotemporal Degener; 17, pp. 38-46, 2015.
9. F Kimura F; Tracheostomy and invasive mechanical ventilation in amyotrophic lateral sclerosis: decision-making factors and survival analysis, Rinsho Shinkeigaku; 56(4), pp.241-7, 2016. (in Japanese & English abstract)
10. G Christodoulou, R Goetz, M Ogino, et al; Opinions of Japanese and American ALS caregivers regarding tracheostomy with invasive ventilation (TIV), Amyotroph Lateral Scler Frontotemporal Degener;17(1-2), pp.47-54, 2015.
11. D De Massari, CA Ruf, A Furdea, et al.; Brain communication in the locked-in state, Brain; 136, pp.1989-2000, 2013.
12. G Gallegos-Ayala, A Furdea, K Takano, et al.; Brain communication in a completely locked-in patient using bedside near-infrared spectroscopy, Neurology; 82(21), pp.1930-1932, 2014.
13. U Chaudhary, B Xia, S Silvoni, et al.; Brain-Computer Interface-Based Communication in the Completely Locked-In State, PLoS Biol; 15(1), pp.e1002593, 2017.
14. R Spataro, A Chella, B Allison, et al.; Reaching and Grasping a Glass of Water by Locked-In ALS Patients through a BCI-Controlled Humanoid Robot, Front Hum Neurosci;11p.68, 2017.
15. M Yoshinaga, Y Abe, C Sato, et al; Is there any difference between accustoming and times of trials of communication drills using a transparent letter board, Kangojissen-no-Kagaku; 42, pp.68-73, 2017. (in Japanese)
16. M Ienca, RW Kressig, F Jotterand, et al.; Proactive Ethical Design for Neuroengineering, Assistive and Rehabilitation Technologies: the Cybathlon Lesson, J Neuroeng Rehabil;14(1), p.115, 2017.

ISASE-MAICS 2018

Holistic Framework for accelerated learning by Adapting & Personalizing lesson plan for children based on emotions

*Amarnath Dasaka, ** Bapi Raju Surampudi

** International Institute of Information Technology, Hyderabad IIIT · Centre for Cognitive Science , India*
Amarnath.d@research.iiit.ac.in
*** International Institute of Information Technology, Hyderabad IIIT · Centre for Cognitive Science , India*
Raju.bapi@iiit.ac.in

Abstract: Affective education is a formal curriculum designed to help children better understand their feelings and respond to challenging situations, thereby transforming themselves and the world around them. Emotions impact the learning ability at multiple levels (Attention, Memory and decision making etc.). Though they have been advancements in terms of the content (Rich multimedia-based lessons etc.) for **effective-learning**, proportionate advancements have not taken place in the **affective-learning** domain – for example "How to adapt the learning based on the current mood and situation?". **Can we mitigate the adverse effects of emotions?** This problem of learning is especially compounded for university students where each student has flood of information to absorb & assimilate and is constantly under stress, furthermore, Personalized & Real-time/continual mentoring by the teachers to students is not practical. We have developed a framework and prototype which can be used to adapt the learning-content based on the current mood of the student. We achieve this by capturing the real time gestures & facial expressions (based on universal facial expressions of seven emotions – anger, contempt, disgust, fear, joy, sadness, and surprise) and adapt the content shown to mitigate the negative & amplify the positive impacts of emotion.
The Task (Chess Puzzles) given to validate the effectiveness of Methods show significant Improvement on sample size of 80 students.

Keywords: *Affective education, Facial Expressions, Holistic Learning, Emotions and Learning, Personalized Feedback*

1. INTRODUCTION

Affect is a concept used in psychology to describe the experience of feeling or emotion. Affective computing is the study and development of systems and devices that can recognize, interpret, process, and simulate human affects. It is an interdisciplinary field spanning computer science, psychology, and cognitive science. Affective computing is also sometimes called emotion-AI [4].

Affective education is a formal curriculum designed to help students better understand their feelings and solve their problems, thereby transforming themselves and the world around them. [3]. Though it is recognized that emotions are very crucial there is lack of consensus regarding how to incorporate them into the existing frameworks.

The term affective computing involves the intention of Artificial Intelligence researches to model and incorporate emotions in intelligent systems. The aim of affective computing is to build an intelligent computing system which can recognize and understand human emotions, and can respond intelligently, sensitively, and friendly; like a human. This concept combines the perspectives of many disciplines, such as neuroscience, psychology, and philosophy.

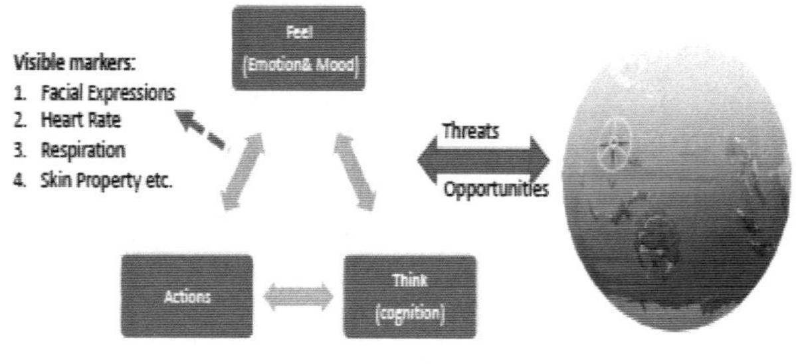

Figure 1: Human Behavior & Emotive Markers

The Main goal of this research is the following:

1. Develop an affordable system that will make learning a joyful experience & accelerate rate of

learning (especially for Students). To achieve this grand goal, we realized that incorporating emotions into the architecture was paramount. So, the sub-tasks are the following:

2. Study & Synthesize the existing literature related to emotions and its impact on the learning ability at multiple levels (Attention, Memory and decision making etc.).
3. Design and Develop a Framework where effective methods of learning (with respect to emotion) can be validated
4. Develop automated Facial emotion recognition system so that the different strategies to mitigate the negative effects of emotions can be studied precisely.
5. Test and Report the findings on "one strategy" and its effectiveness
6. Based on the findings develop a Road MAP for future experiments.

Procedure for collecting data:

a. Select an Appropriate Task & Prepare Data
b. Select appropriate users
c. Remove the outliers based on the expertise of the users with respect to the task.
d. Split the users into control group and test group in phase 1(counter balancing) and again reverse the role (Control become Test subjects and vice-versa) in phase 2.
e. Administer the tests
f. Remove outliers
g. Analyze results

2. Background

2.1 Intelligent Tutoring systems

Robert Gagne [5] proposed a taxonomy of learning outcomes based on the cognitive theory of learning. Robert Gange was a leading scientist regarding learning theory. He lists of nine instructional events for planning lessons:

1) Gaining attention, 2) Informing students about the objective, 3) Stimulating recall of prior learning, 4) Presenting the Content, 5) Providing learning guidance, 6) Eliciting performance, 7) Providing feedback, 8) Assessing performance and 9) Enhancing retention and transfer

As you can see from the above list, the starting point is "Gaining attention", any lapse in attention at the starting point and the learning will be sub-optimal.

Modeling emotion plays an important role for emotional computing because of the necessity of making human computer interaction more natural. [6].

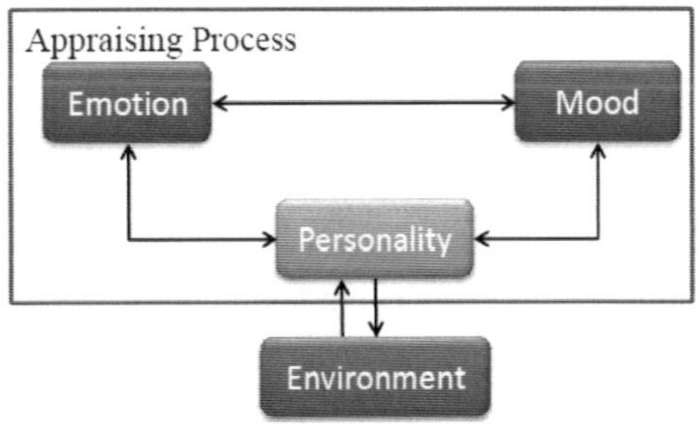

Figure 2: Relation between Personality Mood and Emotion [6]

Emotion is analogous to the state of the mind that is only momentary. It is influenced by personality and Mood.

2.2 Interrupts to Cognition due to emotions

1. Impact of Emotions on Judgement and Decision making: Range of cognitive dimensions (rather than just valence) usefully differentiates emotional experience and effects [1]
2. Emotion-related cognition interrupts ongoing cognitive processes and directs attention, memory, and judgement to address the emotion-eliciting event [1]
3. Appraisal tendencies are goal-directed processes through which emotions exert effects on judgement and choice until the emotion-eliciting problem is resolved [1].

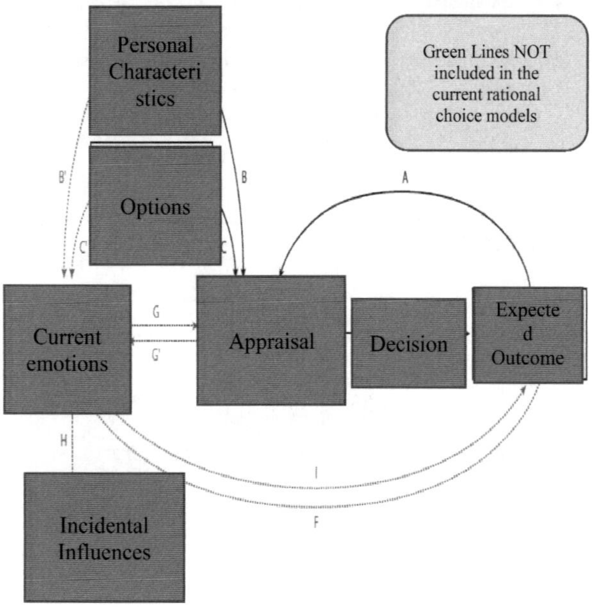

Figure 3: General Model that synthesizes Emotive and cognitive domains with respect to Decision making [1]

2.3 Perception is affected by bodily states

1. Perception: Perception is affected by the bodily states & this in turn effects judgement and cognition.
2. There is relationship between our emotional/cognitive state and our time perception
3. Time seems to flow fast when you expect something positive compared to when you expect negative
4. There is a promising application area with regards to the modification of the perception of time to take more rational decisions

Figure 4: Shades of Anger and Likely Responses [7]

2.4 **Universal Emotions** & Action Units

1. Facial Action Coding System (FACS) taxonomizes Facial movements by their appearance on face.
2. Atlas of Emotions Maps emotions based on 5 Universal Emotions.
3. These emotions are Sadness, Fear, Anger, Enjoyment and disgust (& Neutral)
4. The rest are Derived from these fundamental emotions

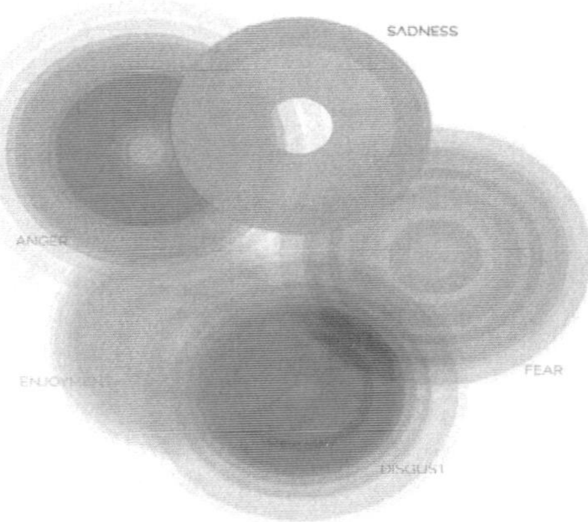

Figure 5: Universal Emotions and their Interaction [7]

Case Study: Consider the following hypothetical scenario [illustrated Figure 6 below:]

Your friend gets angry with you and you start arguing with him.

If you take a step back and see what contributed to the

1. [What is Apparent]
   i. 1[The Event /Trigger] (Friend gets angry) → 6 [Emotion] (You Feel anger) → 8 [Response] (You Argue)
2. [What is Not Apparent]
   i. Trigger occurs in a context and influenced by our Prior experience and world view.
2. [Response]
   i. Strategies can be employed to choose the best response – that help us respond in helpful and constructive ways, instead of the instinctive response

The essence of the above scenario is that taking a step back and being aware of the emotions- Step 3 gives enough room to mitigate the harmful effects of the emotion and then optimal decision can be taken (which may include 7 (take time out) or 9 (avoid it altogether)

Awareness of our emotions means understanding how they are triggered, what they feel like and how we

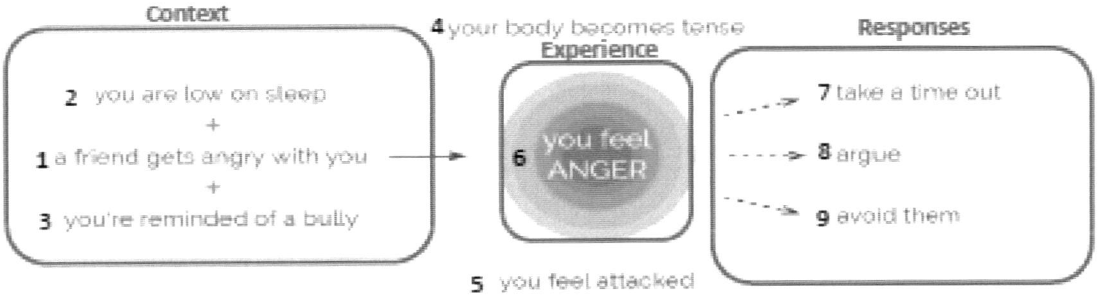

Figure 6: Anger – The genesis and Repercussions [7]

Researchers have also found that mindfulness meditation lead to slower perception of time (Kramer, et al. 2013)

3. Methods

The study aims to explore the strategies currently available to mitigate the negative impact of the emotions and quantify the effectiveness. We administered tests for Undergraduate students at IIIT Hyderabad, India. To avoid variation due to gender, context & in limited time available to conduct experiment, we selected students who were already familiar with chess (Familiarity with Chess rules and ability to evaluate - Value of pieces & familiar with Chess notation).

Why chess was selected for evaluating the cognitive skills?

Chess is a good model to study high-level human brain functions such as spatial cognition, memory, planning, learning and problem solving [11].

chess Puzzles were selected because it is one of the few fields that has a quantitative and reliable measure of skill (the Elo rating). It is, therefore, an ideal environment for studying expert performance and skill acquisition. [9]

According to Nobel Prize Winner Herbert Simon, the impact of chess on cognitive science is comparable to that of Drosophila (fruit fly) for the field of genetics.

One Review article published [9], spans 19 studies and more than 1,700 participants. This paper evaluated chess players' performance on cognitive tasks.

The findings show overall correlations between chess skill and four cognitive abilities: fluid intelligence (the ability of solving new problems and adapting to novel situations); processing speed (for example reaction time); short-term memory; and comprehension knowledge (knowledge and skills assimilated through experience, such as vocabulary and reading comprehension). [9]

1. Data Collection
   1. Chess Puzzles [10] we given one by one to the participants to be solved in 30 minutes. [When the participant completes the problem next one automatically appears]
   2. Scoring system: The ELO system is used, The ELO system rates players based on their current skill level. Initially, Problem with average difficulty (Generally starts at 1500) is given and if the participant is successful then his rating improves, and difficulty of the problem is accordingly adjusted. Opensource websites like lichess.org provides a platform and maintains the infrastructure and player profile along with historical data.
   3. ELO scoring system was very effective as we have noticed during our earlier experiments that tendency to just guess to get to the next problem without trying will result in penalty, in that way it acts as an effective deterrent for guessing.
   4. Overall score, Time spent on each problem etc. were noted.
   5. The duration and frequency of the Stimulus varies depending the emotional state observed (along with request to participants to be aware of their state)

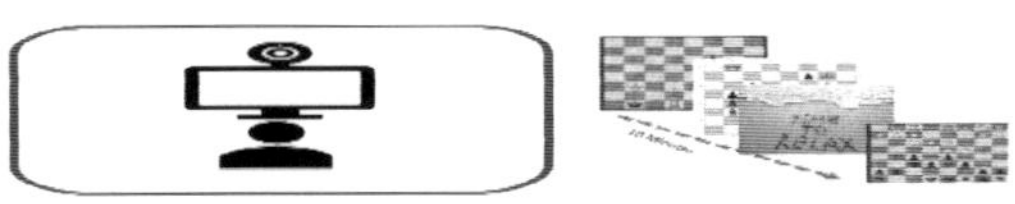

Figure 7: Experimental/Test Setup

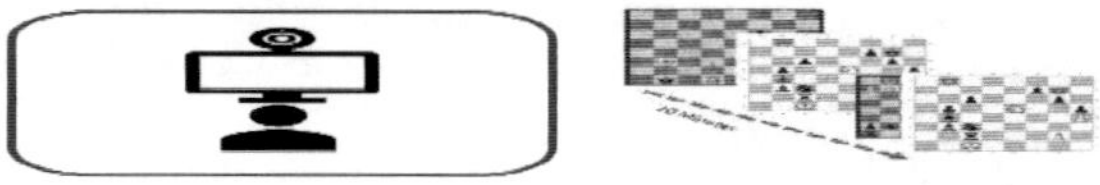

Figure 8: Control Setup

Please Note: Students were counter balanced.

i. 40 students worked on Experimental/Test setup first while another set of students (40) worked on Control setup.
ii. The roles were reversed in the next round. So, at the end of the tests, the set of 20 people participated in both the setups.

4. Results

The experiment was conducted during February-April 2018.

The results (control and Experimental setup) were analyzed and one strategy to mitigate the adverse impact of emotions was proven to be effective.

1. Participants

We did experiment with 92 students (Undergraduate Engineering students) after eliminating 12 of them (as they were outliers: Experts/Novices), we were left with 80 students. All the students were (All male, Mean 19.1 Years, SD 1.5; range 16-22 Years). (Reason for only Male: we wanted to limit the number of variables affecting our analysis we did not want to introduce gender/expertise into the results)

2. Results – Graphs and Tables

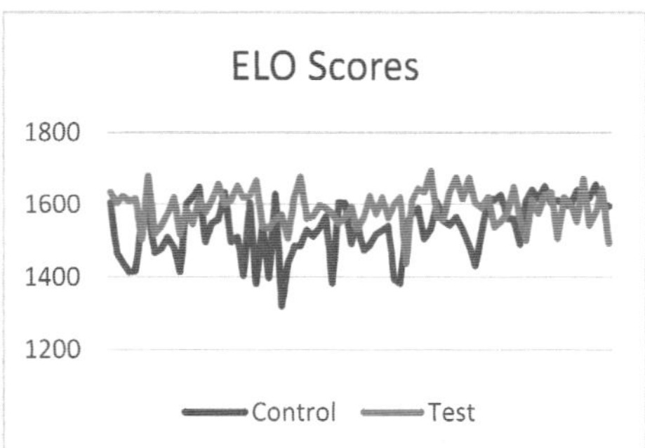

Figure 9: Chess Scores – Paired [ELO vs #Student-ID]

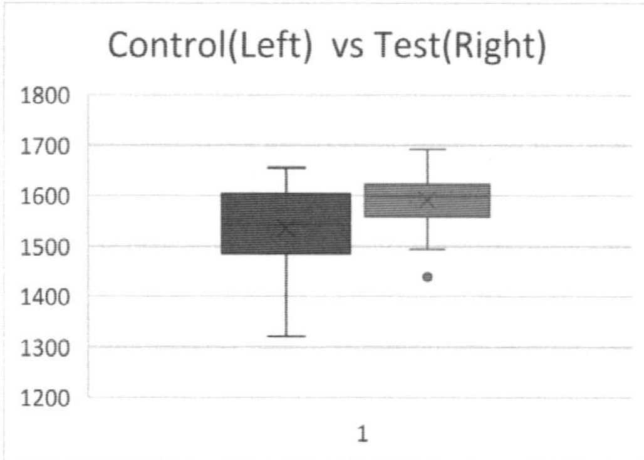

Figure 10: Box Plot of Scores (ELO rating [Y-Axis])

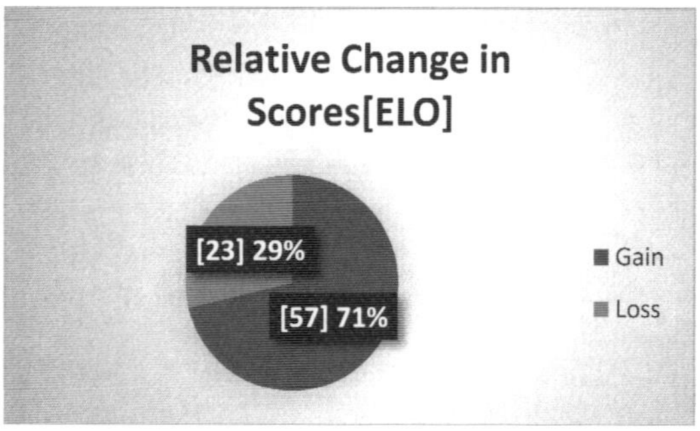

Figure 11: Relative change in Chess Scores

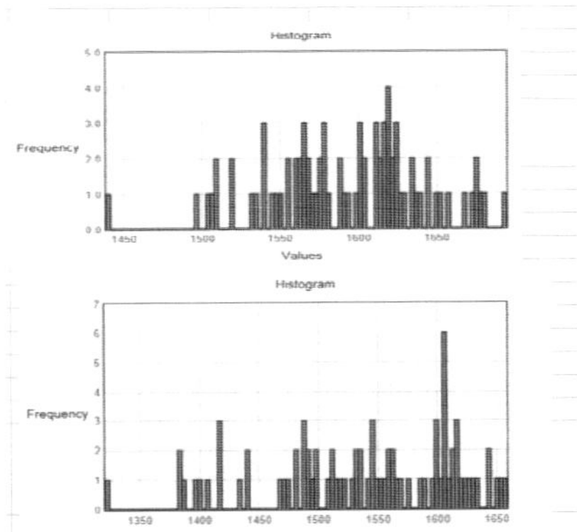

Figure 12: Distribution of Scores(ELO) - Test(Top) vs Control (Bottom) Chess scores

Normality Test for Changes in Scores(ELO): Shapiro-Wilk test was applied. P value = 0.233481. (Skewness = 0.184605 and Excess kurtosis: -0.628239)
Since p-value > α (.05), H0 was accepted. The data can be considered normal.

Table 1: Paired T-Test and Key Results

	Control	*Test*
Mean	1535.4	1591.1875
Variance	6086.572	2472.8125
Observations	80	80
Pearson Correlation	- 0.045438	
Hypothesized Mean Difference	0	
df	79	
t Stat	- 5.285617	
P(T<=t) one-tail	5.42E-07	
t Critical one-tail	1.664371	
P(T<=t) two-tail	1.08E-06	
t Critical two-tail	1.99045	

Wilcoxon Signed-Rank Test (For Difference In scores):

Significance Level: .05
Two-tailed hypothesis
Result Details
W-value: 703
Mean Difference: -67.6
Sum of pos. ranks: 703
Sum of neg. ranks: 2537
Z-value: -4.3982
Mean (W): 1620
Standard Deviation (W): 208.49
Sample Size (N): 80

Result - Z-value

The Z-value is -4.3982. The p-value is close to zero. The result is significant at $p \leq 0.05$.
Note: The W-value is 703. The distribution is approximately normal. Therefore, the Z-value above was used

5. Discussion

Though, on an average the results look promising (71.25% of participants have improved the score), individually analyzed there are some participants were the method did not prove to be effective [28.75%], Further experiments on a large scale and varied condition need to be conducted to establish conclusive results. Due to the time and resources available we were unable to conduct the experiment on larger scale/Different setups.

6. Conclusion

The results based on the experiments conducted indicate that understanding emotions by just being aware of them has a significant impact on the cognitive skills. The ability to detect emotions and being aware of them at the earliest has significant benefit. We believe that this is to some extent explainable as the test setup in the experimental setup facilitates for alternating between focused and diffused mode of brain and for problems like chess, taking a fresh look at the position by alternating between the Focused Mode(Depth) and Diffused mode (for alternate options) is extremely critical. Nevertheless, the method is very effective. This also could in part explain the promising results. The automated facial analysis serves to detect the emotions in un-biased way and real-time feedback helps student to re-focus on the current task saving valuable time. This we believe has tremendous potential for accelerated learning – which is essential in the current age of information overload. Our current study was limited due to resources available, we plan to extend the experiment to include larger & heterogenous group. We have collected the gaze data and gaze time, we need to analyze and find insights into the root cause which we believe can open doors to develop applications of immense benefit.

7. Acknowledgement

We thank the students of IIIT Hyderabad for participating in the experiment.

8. References

1. [1] Jennifer S. Lerner, Ye Li, Piercarlo Valdesolo,and Karim S. Kassam ;Annual Rev. Psychol. 2015. 66:799–823
2. [2] cognitive-appraisal theories (e.g. Lazarus,1991b; Ortony, Clore, & Collins, 1988; Roseman, 1984; Scherer, 1988; Smith & Ellsworth, 1985; Weiner, 1980, 1986)
3. [3] https://medical-dictionary.thefreedictionary.com/Affective+Education>
4. [4]https://en.wikipedia.org/wiki/Affective_computing
5. [5] R. M. Gagne, "The Conditions of Learning and Theory of Instruction," (4th Edition). New York: Holt Rinehart and Winston (1985).[57]
6. [6]Elbeh, Heba. "A personalized emotional intelligent tutoring system based on AI planning." (2012).
7. [7]http://atlasofemotions.org/#continents/anger
8. [8] Ekman, Paul "What Scientists Who Study Emotion Agree About", Perspectives on Psychological Science (2016): 31-34
9. [9] Burgoyne, Alex & Sala, Giovanni & Gobbet, Fernand & McNamara, Brooke & Campitelli, Guillermo & Hambrick, Zach. (2016). The relationship between cognitive ability and chess skill: A comprehensive meta-analysis. Intelligence. 59. 10.1016/j.intell.2016.08.002.
10. [10] Opensource Free and World's Biggest Chess Database 1,743,871 Problems collection of more than 6 million games from professional tournaments. https://chessblunders.org/training ([Randomly selected 3000 Mate in 2+ problems]
11. [11]https://www.nature.com/articles/sdata201544
12. Lichess.org[opensource online chess engine]

ISASE-MAICS 2018

Potential Tendency Differences between English and Japanese in Detecting Appropriate Respondents at Q&A Sites

Yuya YOKOYAMA*, Teruhisa HOCHIN ** and Hiroki NOMIYA **

* *Kyoto Prefectural University, 1-5 Hangi-cho, Shimogamo, Sakyo-ku, Kyoto 606-8522, Japan*
** *Kyoto Institute of Technology, Gosyokaidou-cho, Matsugasaki, Sakyo-ku, Kyoto, 606-8585, Japan*

Abstract: In order to eliminate mismatches between the intentions of questioners and respondents of Question and Answer (Q&A) sites, nine factors of impressions for Japanese and English statements have experimentally been obtained. Factor scores are then estimated by using the feature values of statements. So far the possibility of searching Japanese respondents capable of giving appropriate answers to a newly posted question has been established. It has been shown that the distance and the number of appearance may help us select users who can give appropriate answers to a question. In the similar fashion, this paper tries to find the possibility of detecting respondents who can appropriately answer a newly posted question at English Q&A sites. As a result of analysis, while there were several users who iteratively gave answer statements for Japanese, there are only a small number of respondents who only posted at most two answers for English.
Keywords: *Q&A Sites, Factor Score, Euclidean Distance*

1. INTRODUCTION

Recently, the number of people using Question and Answer (Q&A) sites on the Internet has been increasing. Q&A sites are online communities where users can manually post questions and answers. Thus, these sites are thought to be databases containing enormous amounts of knowledge to solve various problems. When a user posts a question, others may respond. The questioner selects the most appropriate response as the "Best Answer" (BA) and awards the respondent with a certain number of points that serve as a fee. The BA is the response statement the questioner subjectively finds most satisfying.

As the number of users of Q&A sites increases, and more questions are posted, it becomes harder for respondents to select questions that match their specialty and interests. Consequently, a question posed by a user may not be seen or answered by qualified respondents. Moreover, if an appropriate respondent is not encountered, mismatching may occur, causing the following problems:

- A questioner may acquire incorrect knowledge from inappropriate answers.
- Respondents may not have the necessary knowledge to properly answer the question, and thus the problem remains unsolved.
- Users may be offended by answers that contain abusive words, slanders, or statements against public order and standards of decency.

There have been a number of prior works investigating Q&A sites; introducing users to answer statements [1, 2], and inspecting the quality or tendency of answer statements [3-5], etc. These prior works have mainly used textual features or link analysis. However, some users may prefer a polite style, while others may write statements in a ruder style. Some commonly use abstract words, whereas others use more concrete words. These tendencies have not been considered. Meanwhile, our work focuses on using impressions as well as textual features. Moreover, although there are some prior works that introduce users to answer statements as described [1, 2], it is difficult to say that a way to introduce appropriate respondents to a questioner has yet been established. Therefore, with using the impression of statements, our work aims to introduce appropriate respondents to a questioner.

Our goal is to present questions to users who are qualified to properly answer them, thus avoiding the problems described above. The impressions of sixty statements posted on Yahoo! Chiebukuro (Y!C) [6] have been evaluated [7]. By applying factor analysis to the experimental results, nine factors were obtained.

Factor scores obtained through factor analysis represent the impressions of the statements, and this is necessary for estimating the factor scores of other statements. The statements were estimated using multiple regression on the feature values assigned to the statements [8]. The overall estimation accuracy for all nine factors was proved to be good.

The possibility of detecting respondents who can appropriately answer a newly posted Japanese question was examined [9]. Here we assumed that a respondent whose impression is similar to that of a questioner is thought to be adequate to give an adequate answer. We attempted a process of getting proper respondents to a question by using questions actually already posted at Y!C. As a result of analysis, it was shown that there were some nonresponding users who have a shorter Euclidean distance between the factor score of a questioner and that of a respondent. Those users were thought to be capable of appropriately answering that question. It was also shown that with the consideration of categories, more appropriate users could be detected [10].

Most of the feature values, however, are dependent on Japanese. Therefore, it is necessary to look into how extensive our method can be applied in other languages as well [11]. Experimental materials evaluated were the statements actually posted to Yahoo! Answers (Y!A) [12]. As a result, nine factors were obtained. It has been shown that some main factors could be obtained in English as well. It has also been shown that different type of factors could be obtained from English statements. Factor scores were then estimated from the feature values of English statements, such as words and characters, syntactic information, and appearance percentages through multiple regression analysis [13]. As a result of estimation, it has been shown that estimation accuracies of all of the factors are very good.

In this paper, in the similar fashion as Japanese, we try to find the possibility of detecting respondents who can appropriately answer a newly posted English question at Y!A. As a result of analysis, some different tendency could be observed between English and Japanese; among the 100 short distances between question and answer statements, while there are several users who iteratively posted answer statements for Y!C (Japanese), there are only a few respondents who give at most two answers for Y!A (English). This could result from customary or cultural difference between English and Japanese.

The remainder of the paper is organized as follows. Our previous works are summarized in Section 2. A method to find appropriate potential answerers is proposed and evaluated in Section 3. Considerations towards our analysis are provided in Section 4. Finally, Section 5 concludes the paper.

2. PREVIOUS WORKS

2.1 Obtaining Factors of Statements (Japanese)

An experiment was conducted to evaluate impressions of answers. There were forty-one evaluators, and they evaluated the style or content of statements and assigned labels from a group of fifty words [7]. Twelve sets of questions and answers were evaluated, and these included three from each of four major categories: Auction, PC, Love, and Political/Social Problems; the categories were chosen from those actually posted at Y!C in 2005 [7]. Factor analysis was applied to the experimental results, and nine factors were obtained. The factors indicate the nature of a statements, as explained by the various impression words assigned to that statement; they were named accuracy, displeasure, creativity, ease, persistence, ambiguity, moving, effort, and hotness.

2.2 Estimation of Factor Scores (Japanese)

2.2.1 Feature Values of Statements

The factor scores were obtained for only the sixty statements used in the experiment. To be able to estimate the factor scores of other statements, multiple regression analysis was applied to their feature values [8]. Overall, seventy-seven feature values were adopted; these are summarized, syntactic information, word imageability, expression in the closing sentence, word familiarity and notation validity.

2.2.2 Estimation Result

Multiple regression analysis was performed on the sixty questions and answers employed in the impression evaluation experiment. 281 quadratic terms (the product of two explanatory variables) were used according to seventy-seven explanatory variables, and the respondent variables with factor scores for the nine factors.

Multiple correlation coefficients, which show the goodness of the estimation, were above 0.9 for all nine factors [8]. As a result of analysis, it was shown that the estimation accuracies of all of the factors are very good.

2.3 Impression and Suitability of Q&A (Japanese)

2.3.1 Purpose

The differences are determined between the impressions of a given question and the answers already posted for it in Y!C, by calculating the Euclidean distance between their factor scores [9]. These differences could be used to identify those users who could appropriately answer that question.

2.3.2 Dataset

The differences between the impressions of the questions and those of the answers, and the suitability of the answers were examined in order to determine if it would be possible to use this information to find users who would be expected to give an appropriate answer [9]. One question was chosen from each of the following categories: Auction, PC, and Love. For the respondents who posted the answers to those questions, the factor scores for most of the answers they posted in 2005 are obtained, by using the multiple regression equations described in Section 2.2.2.

2.3.3 Result

Distances were calculated for a total of 66,238 answer statements, using the formula (1):

$$D = \sqrt{\sum_{k=1}^{9}\left(Fac_{Q_k} - Fac_{A_k}\right)^2} \qquad (1)$$

where Fac_{Q_k}, Fac_{A_k} are the score for the kth factor for a question and for an answer, respectively. The distances were then sorted in ascending order. The threshold rank is determined based on the irregular bump. Each threshold rank is set as 24, 18, and 22 for the Auction, PC, and Love statements, respectively.

The answer statements whose ranks are smaller or equal to each threshold one are shown in Table 1. Each row indicates a separate answer statement other than one actually posted to its question used for the analysis. Each column entitled is explained as follows:

- "No." means the ascending order rank of distance for each answer statement.
- "Answer" indicates whether the respondents gave an answer to the questions used for the analysis. Each answer statement is given either notation such as "A01" or "Others." How to interpret these notations are explained as follows:
  - "A," "P," and "L" are denoted if they answered the questions, standing for Auction, PC, and Love, respectively, regardless of the identical category.
  - Numbers are given from "01" to "09" ("06," respectively) for Auction (PC and Love).
    - The number "01" means the answer statement actually chosen as a BA by the questioner.
    - The numbers "03," "04," "05," "06," "07," and "09" indicate the answer statements of non-BAs denoted as actually posted in chronological order. The numbers "02" and "08" happen to be absent in Table 1.
    - "Others" is denoted if they did not actually answer the questions.
- "Distance" means the Euclidean distance between the factor score of the answer statement and that of a question one, obtained through Formula (1).
- "ID" means Q&A page IDs where each answer statement is posted and browsed. IDs consist of unique multiple digit numbers. Each page can be referred in the URL composed of "http://detail.chiebukuro.yahoo.co.jp/qa/question_detail/q" and a respective ID.
- "Overlap" indicates users who appear at least twice. Those users are denoted as (A) to (E). They are shaded in Table 1 to emphasize that they appear at least twice.

How to grasp the data in Table 1 will be explained by taking an example of answer statements denoted as "A01." The statements are posted by the same respondent (A) whose one actual answer to an Auction question was actually chosen as a BA. Among those answer statements other than the BA, the second (third, respectively) row of Auction indicates that the distance is 0.796 (0.805) between the Auction question and an answer whose ID is 111505126 (12961032) posted by (A).

An answer statement actually posted by a user who also answered a question of one category can appear in another dataset of a different category. Taking an example of (A), an answer statement denoted as "A01," whose distance is 0.999, appears in the PC dataset, though it was posted by (A), who answered an Auction question.

2.3.4 Analysis

The users denoted as (A), (C), and (E) in the column entitled "Overlap" appear many times for Auction, PC, and Love, respectively. Thus users who gave answer statements of the same categories appear in Table 1. From these results, with the consideration of categories of answer statements, particularly some users appear most in each dataset [10]. Therefore, users who have posted answers on a certain category can be thought to appropriately answer a question of the identical category. It can be regarded that a specific user who specializes in a particular category could be expected to give appropriate answers to questions of the identical category. It can be regarded that a specific user who specializes in a particular category could be expected to give appropriate answers to questions of the identical category.

2.4 Obtaining Factors of Statements (English)

Most of the feature values in our study are dependent on Japanese. Thus, it is required to see how extensive our study could be applied in other languages. As a first step, factors that describe impression of English statements were obtained in the similar fashion stated in Section 2.1.

In order to directly compare our English method with Japanese one, most of the impression words used are the same ones [11]. With using these fifty impression words,

Table 1 Answer statements whose factor scores are close to those of the question (Japanese)

(a) Auction

No.	Answer	Distance	ID	Overlap
1	A03	0.770	13228478	
2	A01	0.796	111505126	(A)
3	A01	0.805	12961032	(A)
4	A04	0.831	12402382	(B)
5	A01	0.834	12847837	(A)
6	A01	0.862	12617472	(A)
7	A09	0.899	114526801	
8	Others	0.910	1038895	
9	A01	0.913	126678687	(A)
10	A01	0.914	132071733	(A)
11	A01	0.933	143239349	(A)
12	A01	0.935	135925478	(A)
13	Others	0.939	1031505	
14	A04	0.943	11181606	(B)
15	A01	0.944	132089723	(A)
16	A01	0.946	13624073	(A)
17	Others	0.948	1036190	
18	A01	0.952	102620885	(A)
19	A01	0.955	121809722	(A)
20	A01	0.960	146442314	(A)
21	A04	0.966	10294125	(B)
22	A07	0.972	12350617	
23	A01	0.975	132702838	(A)
24	A01	0.976	132678538	(A)

(b) PC

No.	Answer	Distance	ID	Overlap
1	A01	0.999	135875548	(A)
2	Others	1.026	1027550	
3	P03	1.080	131088083	(C)
4	P03	1.141	106256660	(C)
5	Others	1.143	1014830	(D)
6	P03	1.161	113495966	(C)
7	L05	1.176	116358036	
8	Others	1.213	1018650	
9	A01	1.229	144533979	(A)
10	L05	1.239	111497381	(E)
11	Others	1.241	1032875	
12	Others	1.266	1026950	(D)
13	Others	1.282	1039765	
14	P03	1.283	113385486	(C)
15	P03	1.285	123741507	(C)
16	Others	1.303	1029145	
17	Others	1.308	1042750	
18	Others	1.322	1026710	

(c) Love

No.	Answer	Distance	ID	Overlap
1	L05	0.850	10937970	(E)
2	L06	0.864	131363453	
3	L05	0.875	11652216	(E)
4	L05	0.925	11795306	(E)
5	L05	0.930	136283433	(E)
6	L05	0.934	122611942	(E)
7	L05	0.939	13807818	(E)
8	L05	0.941	101124475	(E)
9	L05	0.944	111178621	(E)
10	Others	0.945	1029535	
11	L05	0.949	112562681	(E)
12	L05	0.953	102295340	(E)
13	Others	0.961	1046935	
14	Others	0.962	1046515	
15	L05	0.966	122938652	(E)
16	L06	0.990	131191763	
17	L05	1.004	101178825	(E)
18	L05	1.008	12382852	(E)
19	L04	1.015	133649808	
20	L05	1.020	131041513	(E)
21	A01	1.030	125454957	(A)
22	L05	1.030	12522997	(E)

impression evaluation experiment was conducted for four foreign subjects (3 males: Mexican, Vietnamese, and French, and 1 female: French). Experiment materials were six sets of Q&A English statements from Y!A (three each from "Computer & Internet" and "Auction ebay."). Similar as the previous experiment depicted in Section 2.1, each set consists of one question and four answer statements including the "BA."

Factor analysis was applied to the experimental results. As a result of the analysis, nine factors were obtained. Both similarity and difference were confirmed between the Japanese factors and English ones. Moreover, some factors could be obtained in one language while they failed to in another language.

2.5 Estimation of Factor Scores (English)

Similar as the estimation of Japanese factor scores explained in Section 2.2, multiple regression analysis was applied to the feature values in order to be able to estimate factor scores of all the statements [13]. Overall, twenty-six feature values were adopted. These are summarized, as follows:

- Word: The appearance number of word of each statement is extracted. Moreover, the ratio of word to sentence is taken into consideration as well.
- Part-of-Speech (POS): Syntactic information was extracted through morphological analysis applied to the statements of experimental materials used in Section 2.4. Similar as Word depicted above, the appearance number and ratio of POS of each statement is extracted.

As a result of analysis, the estimation of all the nine factors were very good.

3. IMPRESSION and SUITABILITY of Q&A (English)

3.1 Purpose

As explained in Section 2.3, the differences are determined between the impressions of a given question and the answers already posted for it in Y!C, by calculating the Euclidean distance between their Japanese factor scores [9, 10]. These differences could be used to identify those users who could appropriately answer that question. In order to see how this method could be extensive in English, the differences determined by impressions will be applied to English statements as well.

3.2 Dataset

The differences between the impressions of the English questions and those of the answers, and the suitability of the answers are examined in order to determine if it would be possible to use this information to

Table 2 Answer statements whose factor scores are close to those of the question (English)

(a) QEng01

No.	Distance	ID	Overlap
1	1.38	20100301190221AAHGC5Q	
…	…	…	…
47	2.79	20100221140530AAlcqiL	(A)
48	2.79	20100221140530AAlcqiL	(A)
…	…	…	…
79	3.09	20100223144245AAtS42Q	(B)
80	3.09	20100223144245AAtS42Q	(B)
81	3.11	20100225191231AAIiD6y	(C)
…	…	…	…
86	3.13	20100225191231AAIiD6y	(C)
…	…	…	…

(b) QEng02

No.	Distance	ID	Overlap
1	1.54	20100328095230AAhycCR	
…	…	…	…
27	2.50	20100328094946AAMZVxy	(D)
…	…	…	…
69	3.09	20100227123651AA21OkR	(E)
…	…	…	…
88	3.26	20100327093527AALC1du	(D)
…	…	…	…
92	3.27	20100227123651AA21OkR	(E)
…	…	…	…

(c) QEng03

No.	Distance	ID	Overlap
1	1.35	20100402143956AA21DNQ	
…	…	…	…
4	1.44	20100301134435AAVEcnX	(F)
5	1.46	20100226002840AADQ9Nb	(G)
…	…	…	…
33	1.98	20100301134435AAVEcnX	(F)
…	…	…	…
47	2.16	20100227052922AAZhN2X	(H)
48	2.17	20100328183909AAdCdgl	
49	2.17	20100326102809AA6bNLW	(I)
…	…	…	…
60	2.22	20100223144659AAJSycm	(J)
61	2.22	20100223144659AAJSycm	(J)
62	2.24	20100301070738AAncwRx	
63	2.24	20100226002840AADQ9Nb	(G)
…	…	…	…
68	2.28	20100326102809AA6bNLW	(I)
…	…	…	…
72	2.30	20100320160954AABgv54	(K)
…	…	…	…
80	2.37	20100227052922AAZhN2X	(H)
…	…	…	…
94	2.45	20100321153526AAu2Oyi	(K)
…	…	…	…

find users who would be expected to give an appropriate answer [9, 10]. Experimental materials are extracted from sourceforge [14], where data on Y!A are open to public so that research on Community Question Answering can be facilitated. Since the category of all the Q&A statements provided in sourceforge [14] is only "Computer & Internet," the category of three questions and answer statements used for the analysis is "Computer & Internet."

For the respondents who posted the answers to those questions, the factor scores for most of the answers they posted in 2013 are obtained, by using the multiple regression equations, as described in Section 2.5. Factor scores are calculated using Java programs. The factor scores calculated are three question and altogether 5,491 answer statements. Those statements extracted are as follows:

- Three question statements used for the analysis are randomly chosen. However, the statements are chosen that include as few grammatical errors and miswritten characters as possible so that morphological analysis can be applied without problems.
- The following total 5,491 answer statements are extracted from sourceforge [14].
  - Answer statements are chosen that are posted by the respondents who gave answers to each question statement used for the previous experiment depicted in Section 2.3.4. The total number of these answer statements is 313.
  - Answer statements are selected that are posted by the respondents who did not post answers to any question statements used in Section 2.3.4. The number of these answer statements is 5,178.

3.3 Results

Euclidean distances D between each question statement and 5,491 answer statements are calculated by using the formula (1), as explained in Section 2.3.3. The distances are then sorted in ascending order.

The answer statements whose distances are ranked in shorter 100 are shown in Table 2. A column "ID" that does not appear in previous result (Table 1) are explained as follows. Columns entitled "No.," "Distance" and "Overlap" are depicted in Section 2.3.3.

- "ID": IDs are composed of the mixture of alphabets numbers, starting from eight numbers consisting of the date of actual posted time. Each page can be referred and browsed in the URL comprising "http:// answers. yahoo.com/question/index?qid=" and a respective ID.

3.4 Analysis

From the results shown in Table 2, the numbers of users who actually answered each question are 3, 2, and 6, respectively. Unlike the previous result shown in Table 1, where particular users appear repeatedly in short distance, only a few users appear at most twice. Thus, differences of tendency can be observed between Japanese and English in finding appropriate respondents at Q&A site.

4. CONSIDERATIONS

Several certain respondents frequently appeared for Y!C, as shown in Table 1 (Japanese), while mere a handful of respondents appeared not more than twice for Y!A, as shown in Table 2 (English). There are two possible reasons. Firstly, the category used for those analyses and included in respective dataset are completely different. For Y!C dataset, provided by National Informatics of Institute [15], it covers most of the categories in Y!C. On the other hand, for Y!A dataset, provided as sourceforge [14], it includes only the category "Computer & Internet." Thus, it is required to add for other categories than "Computer & Internet" for Y!A.

Another possible reason is that there could be customary or cultural difference between English and Japanese. In calculating factor scores, the meanings of contents are not regarded. Therefore, in order to inspect the differences more profoundly, the contents of answer statements should be minutely regarded and examined. Further analysis could shed the light on customary or cultural difference between English and Japanese.

5. CONCLUSION

In this paper, in the similar fashion as Japanese, we tried to find the possibility of finding respondents who can appropriately answer a newly posted English question at Y!A. As a result, some different tendency could be observed between English and Japanese. While there were several users who iteratively gave answer statements for Y!C (Japanese), there are only a small number of respondents who only posted at most two answers for Y!A (English). This could result from customary or cultural difference between English and Japanese.

For future work, an additional experiment with more subjects and samples is required. Since all the foreign subjects were non-native English, an experiment with native English subjects must be conducted. The contents must be regarded so that customary or cultural difference between English and Japanese could be revealed. It is also required to use the estimated scores to estimate the BAs. To detect appropriate answerers, the characteristics of users must be revealed and used for investigation.

ACKNOWLEDGMENTS

This research was partially supported by the Japan Society for the Promotion of Science, Grant Number 26008587, and 2015-2016.

REFFERENCES

1. Pawal Jurczyk and Eugene Agichtein: Discovering Authorities in Question Answer Communities by Using Link Analysis, Proc. of 16th ACM Conference on Information and Knowledge Management (CIKM), pp. 919-922, 2007.
2. Fatemeh Riahi , Zainab Zolaktaf , Mahdi Shafiei and Evangelos Milios: Finding Expert users in Community Question Answering, Proc. of the 21st International Conference Companion on World Wide Web (WWW12), pp.791-798, 2012.
3. Eugene Agichtein, Castillo Carlos, Debora Donato, Aristides Gionis and Mishne Gilad: Finding High-Quality Content in Social Media, Proc. of the Int'l Conf. on Web Search and Web Data Mining (WSDM08), pp.183-194, 2008.
4. Yuanjie Liu , Shasha Li, Yunbo Cao, Chin-yew Lin, Dingyi Han, and Yong Yu: Understanding and Summarizing Answers in Community-Based Question Answering Services, Proc. of the 22nd International Conference on Computational Linguistics, pp.497-504, 2008.
5. Daphne Ruth Raban: Self-Presentation and the Value of Information in Q&A Websites, Journal of the American Society for Information Science and Technology Volume 60, Issue 12, pp.2465-2473, 2009.
6. Yahoo! Chiebukuro (URL, in Japanese), http://chiebukuro.yahoo.co.jp/, 2018.
7. Yuya Yokoyama, Teruhisa Hochin, Hiroki Nomiya, and Tetsuji Satoh: Obtaining Factors Describing Impression of Questions and Answers and Estimation of their Scores from Feature Values of Statements, Software and Network Engineering, pp.1-13, Springer, 2012.
8. Yuya Yokoyama, Teruhisa Hochin, and Hiroki Nomiya: Using Feature Values of Statements to Improve the Estimation Accuracy of Factor Scores of Impressions of Question and Answer Statements, International Journal of Affective Engineering, Vol. 13, No. 1, pp.19-26, 2014.
9. Yuya Yokoyama, Teruhisa Hochin, and Hiroki Nomiya: Towards Detecting Appropriate Respondents to Questions Posted at Q&A Sites by Disregarding and Considering Categories of Answer Statements, International Journal of Affective Engineering, Vol.15, No.2, pp.167-175, 2016.
10. Yuya Yokoyama, Teruhisa Hochin, and Hiroki Nomiya: Improvement of Obtaining Potential Appropriate Respondents to Questions at Q&A Sites by Considering Categories of Answer Statements, International Journal of Affective Engineering, Vol.16, No.2, pp.63-73, 2017.
11. Yuya Yokoyama, Teruhisa Hochin, and Hiroki Nomiya: Factors Describing Impression of English Question and Answer Statements, Proc. of 11th Spring Conference of Japan Society of Kansei Engineering, G12-3, 2016.
12. Yahoo! Answers (URL), https://answers.yahoo.com, 2018.
13. Yuya Yokoyama, Teruhisa Hochin, and Hiroki Nomiya: Estimation of Factor Scores from Feature Values of English Question and Answer Statements, Proc. of 15th IEEE/ACIS International Conference on Computer and Information Science (ICIS2016), pp.741-746, 2016.
14. sourceforge, Yahoo! Answers Datasets, Summary (URL), http://sourceforge.net/projects/yahoodataset/, 2018..
15. National Institute of Informatics (URL, in Japanese), http://www.nii.ac.jp, 2018.

ISASE-MAICS 2018

Proposal of a Recommendation Method by Direct Setting of Preference Patterns Based on Interrelationship Mining

Yasuo KUDO*, Masashi KURODA * and Tetsuya MURAI **

* *Muroran Institute of Technology, 27-1 Mizumoto, Muroran-shi, Hokkaido 050-8585, Japan*
kudo@csse.muroran-it.ac.jp
** *Chitose Institute of Science and Technology, 758-65 Bibi, Chitose-shi, Hokkaido 066-8655, Japan*
t-murai@photon.chitose.ac.jp

Abstract: In this paper, we introduce a recommendation method by directly setting of users' preference patterns of items for similarity evaluation between users. Yamawaki et al. proposed a recommendation method based on comparing users' preference patterns instead of directly comparing users' rating scores. However, Yamawaki et al.'s method for extraction of preference patterns has limitation of representation ability and this method is not applicable in the case that a user has "cyclic" preference patterns. Our method for extraction of preference patterns is based on partial pairwise comparison of items and it is applicable to represent "cyclic" preference patterns. A tourist spot recommender system is implemented as a prototype of recommender system based on the proposed approach and the implemented recommender system is evaluated by experiments.
Keywords: *Recommendation method, Preference pattern, Interrelationship mining, Rough set, Tourist spot recommender system*

1. INTRODUCTION

Nowadays, with the rapid growth of the amount of information on internet, recommender systems (RSs) become popular in various aspects of our daily life. There are various approaches of recommender systems, however, difficulty of providing recommendations with both high accuracy and high diversity is pointed out [1], and there are many approaches that aims at providing recommendations with high accuracy and high diversity (e.g. [2-6]). For example, Yamawaki et al. [7,8] proposed a recommenddation method that is based on similarity of preference patterns between the active user and other users instead of directly comparing rating scores in the framework of collaborative filtering.

In this paper, instead of making active user's preference patterns from rating scores of the active user, we introduce a recommendation method that the active user inputs her/his preference patterns directly.

2. BACKGROUND

2.1 Recommender systems

Recommender systems use the opinions of a community of users to help individuals in that community more effectively identify content of interest from a potentially overwhelming set of choices [9]. Collaborative filtering is one of the most popular methods of recommender systems and is used in various commercial or research recommender systems. In general, inputs of collaborative filtering is a user-item rating matrix. In the case of user-based collaborative filtering, similarity score of an active user and other users is measured by some similarity criterion (e.g., Pearson correlation coefficient, cosign similarity, etc.) and the top k users with the highest similarity scores with respect to the active user are selected. The set of the most similar users, called the neighborhood, of the active user is used for predicting rating scores of items that the active user has not rate, and the top t items become the candidate of recommendation to the active user.

2.2 Rough set theory

Rough set theory, originally proposed by Z. Pawlak [10,11], provides a mathematical basis of data analysis of nominal datasets. Targets of data analysis by rough set theory is described by decision tables. Here, we use an extended formulation of decision tables by Yao et al. [12] instead of Pawlak's original definition. A decision table DT is defined by the following quintuple:

$$DT = (U, C \cup \{d\}, \{V_a | a \in AT\}, \mathbf{R}_{AT}, \rho), \quad (1)$$

where U is a finite and nonempty set of objects, C is a finite and nonempty set of condition attributes, $d \notin C$ is the decision attribute, $\{V_a | a \in AT\}$ is a family of sets V_a of attribute values for each attribute $a \in AT = C \cup \{d\}$, and $\rho: U \times AT \to V$ is an information function that assigns a value $\rho(x, a) \in V_a$ of the object $x \in U$ at the attribute $a \in AT$, where $V = \cup_{a \in AT} V_a$. For each attribute $a \in AT$, various relationships defined on the domain V_a are available, e.g., equality relation, order relation, similarity relation, etc., and $\mathbf{R}_{AT} = \{\{R_a\} | a \in AT\}$ is a set of families $\{R_a\}$ of binary relations defined on V_a for every attribute $a \in AT$. Note that usual decision tables are implicitly assumed that the family $\{R_a\}$ consists of only the equality relation $=$ defined on V_a [12]. We also assume that every family $\{R_a\}$ includes the equality relation $=$ defined on V_a.

2.3 Rough-set-based interrelationship mining

Rough-set-based interrelationship mining was proposed by Kudo and Murai [13] and it aims at extracting characteristics based on interrelationships between different attributes in a given decision table [14]. To explicitly treat interrelationships between different attributes, the given decision table defined by (1) is reformulated as follows:

$$DT_{int} = (U, AT_{int}, V \cup \{0,1\}, \mathbf{R}_{int}, \rho_{int}), \qquad (2)$$

where U and V are identical to the original decision table DT.

The set $\mathbf{R}_{int}$ of families of binary relations is defined by

$$\mathbf{R}_{int} = \mathbf{R}_{AT} \cup \left\{\{R_{a_i \times b_i}\} \middle| \exists a_i, b_i \in C\right\} \cup \left\{\{=\} \middle| For\ each\ aRb\right\}, \qquad (3)$$

where each family $\{R_{a_i \times b_i}\} = \left\{R^1_{a_i \times b_i}, \cdots, R^{n_i}_{a_i \times b_i}\right\}$ consists of n_i ($n_i \geq 0$) binary relations defined on $V_{a_i} \times V_{b_i}$. The expression aRb is defined later.

The set AT_{int} of attributes is defined by

$$AT_{int} = AT \cup \{aRb | \exists R \in R_{a \times b}, R(a,b) \neq \emptyset\}, \qquad (4)$$

and each expression aRb is called an interrelated condition attributes that describe an interrelationship between two condition attribute a and b explicitly. The set $R(a, b)$ is the set of objects that supports the interrelationship between two condition attributes a and b by the binary relation R and called the support set of the interrelationship between a and b. The support set $R(a, b)$ is defined by

$$R(a,b) = \{x \in U | (\rho(x,a), \rho(x,b)) \in R\}. \qquad (5)$$

The set $AT = C \cup \{d\}$ is identical to the original decision table.

Finally, the information function ρ_{int} is defined by

$$\rho_{int}(x,c) = \begin{cases} \rho(x,c), & if\ c \in AT, \\ 1, & c = aRb\ and\ x \in R(a,b), \\ 0, & c = aRb\ and\ x \notin R(a,b). \end{cases} \qquad (6)$$

2.3 Yamawaki et al.'s recommendation method

In this subsection, we briefly review Yamawaki et al.'s recommendation method [7,8].

This method is an extension of collaborative filtering and it mainly consists of the following three parts: (1) Extraction of users' preference patterns as interrelated condition attributes in interrelationship mining, (2) Evaluation of the similarity of preference patterns between the active user and other users, and (3) Prediction of active user's rating scores and making a list of recommended items to the active user.

Suppose that $U = \{u_1, \cdots, u_l\}$ is a finite set of users and $P = \{p_1, \cdots, p_m\}$ is a finite set of items. Let R be a user-item rating matrix, where R is an $l \times m$ matrix and the element $r_{i,j} \in Range \cup \{*\}$ at the i-th row and the j-th column of R is the rating score of the j-th item by the i-th user. The symbol * means that the user does not rate the item. Yamawak et al.'s method is as follows [7]:

(Extraction of preference patterns)

1. Construct n pairs of items $(a_1, b_1), \cdots, (a_n, b_n)$ by randomly selecting items from the set of items that the active user $x \in U$ has rated.
2. For each pair (a, b) constructed in step 1, make an interrelated attribute $a \leq b$ by using a binary relation $\leq$ defined on $V_a \times V_b$.
3. For each user $u \in U$, set the values of the interrelated attributes $a \leq b$ as follows:

$$\rho_{int}(u, a \leq b) = \begin{cases} 0, & if\ \rho(u,a) > \rho(u,b)\ , \\ 1, & \rho(u,a) \leq \rho(u,b), \\ *, & \rho(u,a) = *\ or\ \rho(u,b) = *\ . \end{cases} \qquad (7)$$

The value of the interrelated attribute $a \leq b$ for the active user $x \in U$ represents a preference pattern of the active user. The value of $a \leq b$ is 0 means that the user prefers the item a to the item b. The value of $a \leq b$ is 1 mean that either the user prefers b to a or the user likes (or dislikes) both a and b at the same level.

(Evaluation of similarity of preference patterns)

4. Compare the preference patterns between the active user $x \in U$ and the other users $u \in U$ as follows:

$$sim(x,u) = \frac{|\{a \leq b \in AT_{int} | \rho(x, a \leq b) = \rho(u, a \leq b)\}|}{n}, \qquad (8)$$

where $|X|$ means the cardinality of the set X. The similarity score $sim(x, u)$ represents the ratio of the user

u's preference patterns that is consistent with the active user's preference patterns.

(Prediction of active user's rating scores and recommendation)

5. Select top k users with highest similarity scores as the neighborhood N of the active user $x \in U$.
6. For each item $p \in P$ that the active user $x \in U$ does not have the rating score, estimate active user's rating score of the item p as follows:

$$pred(x,p) = \bar{r_x} + \frac{\sum_{u \in N_p} sim(x,u) \times (r_{u,p} - \bar{r_u})}{\sum_{u \in N_p} sim(x,u)}, \quad (9)$$

where $\bar{r_x}$ and $\bar{r_u}$ are the average rating scores of the active user x and the user u, respectively, and the set

$$N_p = \{u \in N | r_{u,p} \neq *\}$$

is the set of users in the neighborhood N that the user has rated the item p.

7. Select top t items with highest estimated rating scores and make a list of recommended items to the active user.

Yamawaki et al. [8] also proposed a revised method of extraction of preference patterns. This method considers not only the order relationship between rating scores but also the difference of rating scores.

3. PROPOSED METHOD

In this section, we introduce a method to directly set user's preference patterns, and report a prototype of tourist spot recommender system based on the proposed method.

3.1 Direct setting of preference patterns

As we reviewed in Section 2.3, Yamawaki et al.'s method makes users' preference patterns from the users' rating scores of items. However, this extraction method of preference patterns has limitation of representation ability and the following situation is not representable.

Suppose that a, b, and c are three items and a user has the following preference patters:

- The user prefers the item b to the item a,,
- The user prefers c to b, and
- The user prefers a to c.

We think that this kind of "cyclic" preference patterns also represent user's *Kansei* evaluation of items. To treat such characteristics of preference patterns, we introduce a method to directly set preference patterns by users.

Our method is based on partial pairwise comparison. In the traditional pairwise comparison (e.g., Thurstone's pairwise comparison [15]), all possible pairs of items are required to evaluate by a subject, however, it is actually impossible if there are many items. We then propose the following method to directly set users' preference patterns:

1. Set the number n of constructed preference patterns.
2. $PP = \emptyset$
3. Create a set of pairs of items
$$Q = \{(a_1, b_1), \cdots, (a_n, b_n)\},$$
where there are no pairs that both (a_i, b_i) and (b_i, a_i) are in the set Q.
4. For each pair (a_i, b_i) $(1 \leq i \leq n)$, the user selects either a_i or b_i intuitively. If a_i is selected, add the preference pattern $a_i > b_i$ to the set of preference patterns PP. Otherwise, add $a_i < b_i$ to PP.
5. Output PP as the set of the user's preference patterns.

3.2 Recommendation method by directly setting of preference patterns

Our recommendation method is based on Yamawaki et al.'s recommendation method in Section 2.3. Extraction of preference patterns, steps 1-3 in Section 2.3, are replaced to the proposed method in Section 3.1. For evaluation of similarity between the active user $x \in U$ and the other user $u \in U$, we use the following criterion instead of the equation (8):

$$sim(x,u) = |PP_x \cap PP_u|, \quad (10)$$

where PP_x and PP_u are the sets of preference patterns of the active user x and the other user u, respectively. Step 5 for selection of the neighborhood is identical to the one in Section 2.3.

Because our method does not use the rating information, selection of recommended items to the active user, steps 6 and 7, are different from the ones in Section 2.3. Therefore, these two steps are replaced by the following two steps:

6. For each user $u \in N$ in the neighborhood of the active user, make a set of items P_u that are most frequently selected by the user u.
7. Select t items randomly from the set $\bigcup_{u \in N} P_u$.

3.3 A prototype of recommender system

We implemented a prototype of recommender system based on the proposed approach. This system recommends tourist spots in Hokkaido prefecture, Japan, from 43 tourist spots that we inputted to the system. For each tourist spot, we selected one photo from two web pages [16,17] that open various photos of many tourist spots in Hokkaido.

Figure 1 shows a screenshot of the implemented system.

The user of this system is presented a pair of photos and is asked which tourist spot she/he wants to visit. For example, in Figure 1, the user is asked which tourist spot (left: Sapporo Clock Tower, right: Night view of Hakodate city) the user wants to visit. The user answers intuitively by clicking one of the two photos. By repeating this question-answering 10 times, the user's preference patterns are obtained and at most 5 tourist spots are recommended by comparing the user's preference patterns and other users' preference patterns that have already inputted in the system.

Figure 1: Screenshot of the recommender system

4. EXPERIMENTS

We conducted a pre-experiment and an evaluation experiment to evaluate usefulness of the proposed method. Note that all experiments were organized with respect to Ethics Regulations related to Research with Human Subjects in Muroran Institute of Technology.

4.1 Pre-experiment

The purpose of the pre-experiment is to collect other users' sets of preference patterns in the recommender system. 31 subjects attended to the pre-experiment. In the pre-experiment, each subject was presented 50 pairs of photos and answered intuitively which tourist spot in the pair she/he wants to visit. By this pre-experiment, the sets of preference patterns of 50 subjects were obtained and these sets were used as the other users' sets of preference patterns in the evaluation experiment.

4.2 Evaluation experiment

In the evaluation experiment, 10 subjects who did not attend the pre-experiment attended. In this experiment, the number of the subject's preference patterns was $n = 10$, the number of neighborhood users was $k = 3$ as almost $1/10$ of the users in the system, and the number of recommended tourist spots was $t = 5$. In the case that the number of candidates of recommended tourist spots is less than five, all candidates were recommended.

For comparison, a recommender system that randomly provides at most 5 tourist spots as the recommendation result was used. To avoid the effect of difference of presented pairs and the order effect, after 10 times question-answering by the subject, recommendation results by the two systems were presented simultaneously without informing which result is by the proposed system. For each result, the subject evaluated the recommended tourist spots by 5-point scale rating score (1: tourist spot that the user does not want to visit, 3: neither, 5: tourist spot that the user wants to visit).

As the result, the average evaluation score of the proposed system was 3.87 and the average score of the random recommender was 3.28. Note that the average similarity score between the subject and other user in the proposed system was 2.57, which means that, on average, the set of preference patterns for each subject has 2 or 3 common patterns with other users in the system.

The score of the proposed system was higher than the score of the random recommender; however, there was no statistically significant difference by paired samples t-test (p=0.08>0.05). One reason of this result is that the number of subjects was small and further evaluation experiments with many subjects are needed.

5. CONCLUSION

In this paper, we introduced a recommendation method that the active user inputs her/his preference patterns directly. The proposed method is an improvement of Yamawaki et al.'s method to extract users' preference patterns and our method is applicable even though the user has a kind of "cyclic" preference patterns. We also implemented a tourist spot recommender system as a prototype of recommender system based on the proposed approach.

For future works, we need to conduct evaluation experiments again with many subjects and users in the system. It is expected that the number of subjects and users will strongly affect the experiment results. In the prototype system, the number of tourist spots was 43 and it is very small as a recommender system. Increasing the number of tourist spots is also important for improving the prototype system. Moreover, effects of parameter setting (the number of presented pairs, the size of neighborhood, the number of recommended items, etc.), similarity criterion, and selection method of recommended items are also considered for revision.

ACKNOWLEDGMENTS

This work was supported by JSPS Grant-in-Aid for Scientific Research (C) Grant Number 16K00365.

REFFERENCES

[1] K. Bradley and B. Smyth, Improving recommendation diversity, In: Proc. 12th Nat. Conf. Artif. Intell. Cogn. Sci. (AICS-01), Maynooth, Ireland, pp. 75–84, 2001.

[2] M. X. Gan and R. Jiang, Constructing a user similarity network to remove adverse influence of popular objects for personalized recommendation. Expert Systems with Application, 40, pp.4044-4053, 2013.

[3] M. X. Gan and R. Jiang, Improving accuracy and diversity of personalized recommendation through power law adjustments of user similarities, Decision Support Systems, 55, pp. 811-821, 2013.

[4] M. G. Vozalis, A. I. Markos, and K. G. Margaritis, A Hybrid Approach for Improving Prediction Coverage of Collaborative Filtering, In: Proc. of AIAI 2009, pp. 491-498, Springer, 2009.

[5] Z. P. Zhang, Y. Kudo, and T. Murai, Neighbor selection for user-based collaborative filtering using covering-based rough sets, Annals of Operations Research, 256(2), pp. 359–374, 2017.

[6] T. Zhou, Z. Kuscsik, J. G. Liu, M. Medo, J. R. Wakeling, and Y. C. Zhang, Solving the apparent diversity-accuracy dilemma of recommender systems, Proceedings of the National Academy of Sciences of the United States of America, 107(10), pp. 4511-4515, 2010.

[7] J. Yamawaki, Y. Kudo, and T. Murai, Proposal of a Recommendation Method Based on Interelationship Mining and Collaborative Filtering, In: Proc. of JSKE12S, Osaka, Japan, 1B-07, 2017 (in Japanese).

[8] J. Yamawaki, Y. Kudo, and T. Murai, An Improved Recommendation Method Based on Interelationship Mining and Collaborative Filtering, In: Proc. of JSKE19, Tokyo, Japan, B26, 2017 (in Japanese).

[9] P. Resnick and H.R. Varian, Recommender systems, Communications of the ACM, 40, 56–58, 1997.

[10] Z. Pawlak, Rough Sets, International Journal of Computer and Information Science, 11, pp.341-356, 1982.

[11] Z. Pawlak, Rough Sets: Theoretical Aspects of Reasoning about data, Kluwer Academic Publisher, Dordrecht, 1991.

[12] Y. Y. Yao, B. Zhou, and Y. Chen, Interpreting Low and High Order Rules: A Granular Computing Approach, Proc. of RSEISP 2007, LNCS 4585, Springer, pp. 371–380, 2007.

[13] Y. Kudo and T. Murai, A Plan of Interrelationship Mining Using Rough Sets, In: Proc. of the 29th Fuzzy System Symposium, pp. 33-36, 2013 (in Japanese).

[14] Y. Kudo and T. Murai, A Review on Rough Set-Based Interrelationship Mining, In: V. Torra. A. Dahlbom, and Y. Narukawa (eds.), Fuzzy Sets, Rough Sets, Multisets and Clustering, pp. 257-275, Springer, 2017.

[15] L. L. Thurstone, A Law of comparative judgment. Psychological Review, 34, pp. 273-286, 1927.

[16] Hokkaido Muryo Shashin Sozai-Shu DO PHOTO, http://photo.hokkaido-blog.com (in Japanese).

[17] Hokkaido Prefecture Free Photos, https://www.photock.org/list/pr/hokkaido/

ISASE-MAICS 2018

Performance Evaluation of Interactive Evolutionary Computation Applying Gaze Information

Hiroshi TAKENOUCHI* and Masataka TOKUMARU **

** Fukuoka Institute of Technology, 3-30-1 Wajiro-higashi, Higashi-ku, Fukuoka-shi, Fukuoka 811-0295, Japan*
*** Kansai University, 3-3-35 Yamate-cho, Suita-shi, Osaka 564-8680, Japan*

Abstract: We present an Interactive Evolutionary Computation (IEC) system that applies user gaze information. Historically, IEC systems have faced the problem of heavy user evaluation loads. Therefore, to solve this issue, we apply a user gaze information approach to solve such issues. When user gaze information is applied to the evaluation of candidate solutions, IEC systems can obtain user evaluation information while they view multiple candidate solutions. In this paper, we verify the effectiveness of the eye tracking IEC system using evaluation experiments with real users. In the experiment, we use a normal IEC system as a comparison method where users evaluate candidate solutions by 10-stage evaluation manually. The experimental results show that the eye tracking IEC method can generate solutions that offer results equivalent to the compared system.
Keywords: *Gaze information; Interactive evolutionary computation; Eye tracker*

1. INTRODUCTION

Interactive evolutionary computation (IEC) is used to support product development. While users require products which are functional, IEC systems help designers develop products that can also satisfy their subjective and emotional preferences [1]. Systems using IEC include image retrieval [2], voice generation [3], and so on.

Traditional IEC based system suffer from large user evaluation loads of candidate solutions. Previously, we attempted to use a tournament evaluation method that uses paired comparison method to simplify user evaluation [4]. However, this method forces users to evaluate candidate solutions expressly. To solve this problem, some researchers have proposed to apply the biological information of users in their evaluation of candidate solutions. By exploiting the user's biological information such as heartbeats or brainwave, system can obtain user evaluation information as the user is viewing the candidate solutions. Previous studies have verified the effectiveness of this method for obtaining candidate solutions that satisfy user preferences [5, 6]. However, users must wear special devices such as a heart rate meters or electroencephalographs to measure their biological information. For these researches, such IEC systems have been difficult to popularize.

Thus, to solve such issues, we apply user gaze information in the evaluation of candidate IEC solutions. Gaze information includes user's potential preferences and applies various systems for determining user preferences [7]. For applying user gaze information to the evaluation of candidate solutions, IEC systems can obtain user evaluation information by merely having users view multiple candidate solutions. Such a technique is effective for marketing applications that require a good understanding of user's potential preferences. Moreover, the system can learn the user's preferences and recommend various goods that are likely to satisfy them based only on a viewing of the catalog.

Previous IEC systems with user gaze information have been proposed [8, 9]. While their results achieved a certain level of effectiveness, such studies have failed to clearly verify the overall effectiveness of a user gaze information-based method. Moreover, user motivation is thought to be an issue in the evaluation of objects used in these aforementioned systems. Therefore, we verify the effectiveness of the method with gaze information in terms of the evolutionary performance of candidate solutions. Moreover, we use a genetic algorithm (GA) within an evolutionary algorithm of IEC.

In this paper, we perform an evaluation experiment to verify the effectiveness of the method. We use two methods: eye tracking IEC (E-IEC) and normal IEC (NIEC). In the first method, users see the presented designs by the system. In the second one, they evaluate all designs by 10-stage evaluation manually. The experiment uses the NIEC method for comparison in which users evaluate candidate solutions by 10-stage evaluation and demonstrate satisfactory levels of system generated designs and user evaluation loads.

2. E-IEC SYSTEM

2.1 Schematic of the E-IEC system

Figure1 shows the schematic of the E-IEC system. First, the system generates the initial candidate solutions which are then presented to the user. Then, the user views all candidate solutions, while the system measures user gaze information. When the user finished to evaluate candidate solutions, the system obtains user evaluations. Finally, the system operates GA processing that results in new designs being generated and presented to the user again. The system repeats these operations and creates user preference design.

In the E-IEC system, each candidate solution is evaluated using user gaze information. We use a Tobii Pro X2-30 eye tracker to obtain user gaze information. This device can measure user gaze information at a rate of 30 [Hz].

Figure 2 shows candidate evaluation of the E-IEC. In Figure 2, the E-IEC system divides the interface into eight areas. First, the E-IEC system measures user gaze positions for each sample (black circles in Figure 2) and then counts the number of user gaze positions of each candidate solution. If the gaze position is out of the interface, the system does not measure and count the number of user gaze positions.

For example, when the number of user gaze position samples of each candidate solution are $s_1 \sim s_8$, each s_i is equals to 3, 2, 2, 1, 3, 3, 2, and 2. Next, the E-IEC system normalizes these s_i in a range from 0 to 100. Then, the evaluation values of each candidate solution v_i, are 100, 50, 50, 0, 100, 100, 50, and 50. The system uses these evaluation values v_i for GA processing.

2.2 User evaluation

Figure 3 shows the interface of the E-IEC system. First, a user starts the system and evaluates the presented designs by viewing them. The system receives user gaze information while the designs are being viewed. When a user finished watching the designs, they click the "Next" button and new designs are presented. A user repeats these operations until his/her preference designs generated. Finally, when a user finished using the system, they click the "End" button.

Figure 4 shows the experimental setting of the E-IEC system. The user sits in front of the screen and views the presented designs. Conversely, in the NIEC system (the compared system), the subjects input their evaluation values of the candidate solutions using the mouse.

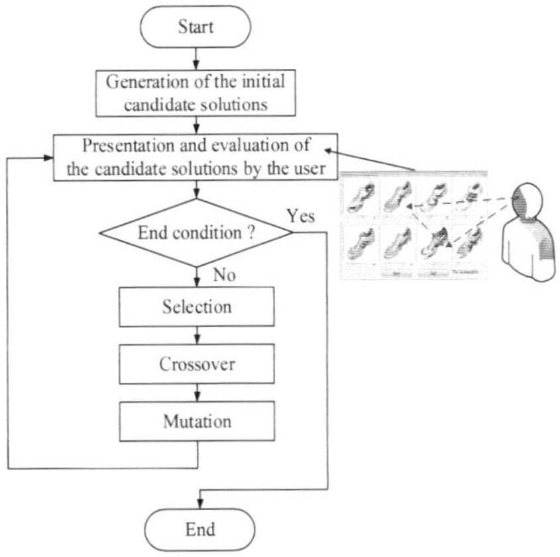

Figure 1: Outline of the E-IEC system

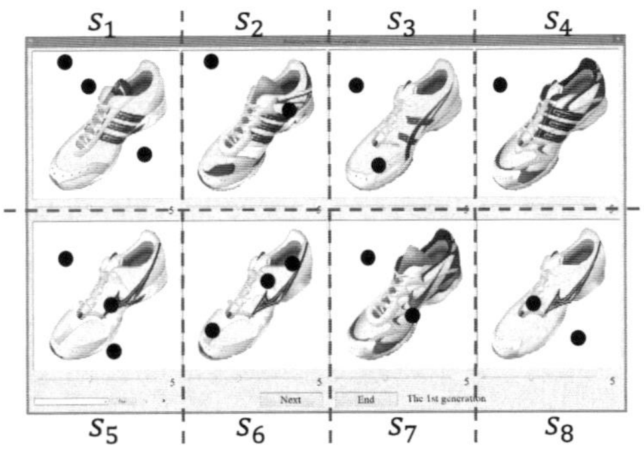

Figure 2: Candidate evaluation of the E-IEC

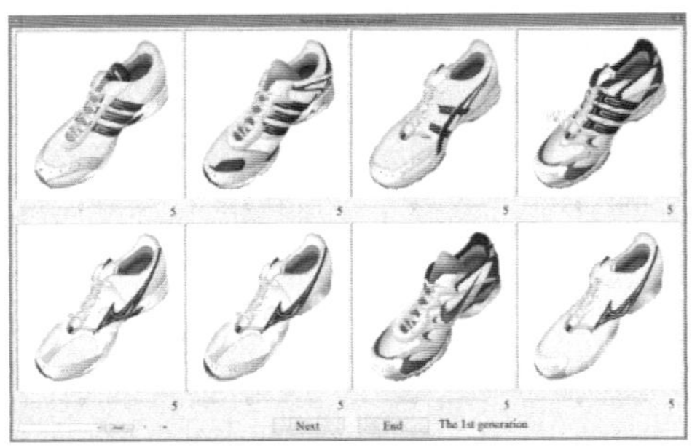

Figure 3: Interface of the E-IEC system

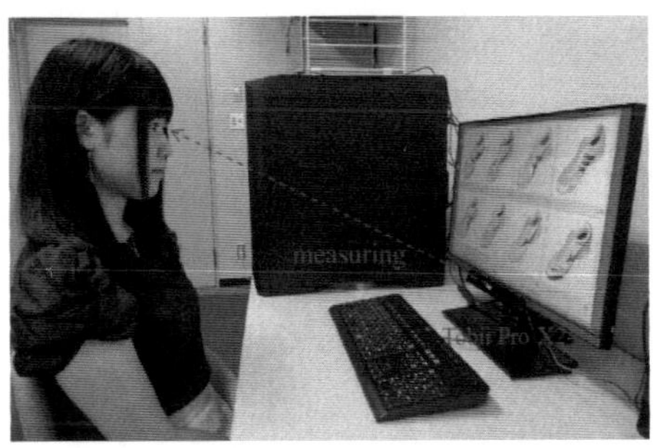

Figure 4: Experiment environment

3. EVALUATION EXPERIMENTS

We performed an evaluation experiment to verify the effectiveness of the E-IEC method in the view point of evolutionary performance of candidate solutions and the evaluation loads of users. We employ 16 subjects in their 20s university students (6 men and 10 women). In the experiment, the compared system also uses normalized evaluation values of the 10-stage evaluations for GA operations.

Moreover, subjects use the E-IEC system in two patterns (E-IEC 1 and E-IEC 2). In the case of the E-IEC 1, subjects see as many of their favorite designs as they wish after watching all the designs freely. In the case of the E-IEC 2, they see all designs freely while evaluating them. Subjects finished using the system when 80% of the presented designs became satisfactory.

Table 1 shows the experimental parameters. The subjects used each system based on the concept that customers will select running shoes designs that they will want to wear to enjoy running. We use running shoes designs as an evaluation object [4]. Each design consists of five parts. Each part has eight designs expressed by 3 bits (gene length: 15 bits). The system can generate 32,768 running shoe designs. We performed questionnaires to survey the satisfaction levels of the generated candidate solutions and usability (i.e., the level of evaluation load) for each system and measured the time by users evaluating the designs for each system. Moreover, we considered the effect of the order in which each system was used, so the use order of the three systems was set randomly for each subject.

4. EXPERIMENTAL RESULTS

4.1 Satisfaction level of generated designs

Figure 5 shows the average and standard deviations of satisfaction levels of the generated designs from each system. The satisfaction levels of the two systems except the E-IEC 2 were approximately 4, whereas the E-IEC 1 was able to generate designs that users can satisfy. We performed the statistical test to confirm whether there were statistically significant differences in the satisfaction levels of each system. However, we made no confirmations when the significance level was 5%. Therefore, the results showed that the three systems were able to generate designs that satisfied the preference of the subjects.

Table 1: Experimental Parameter

Parameters	E-IEC systems	NIEC system
Candidate solutions	8	
Gene length	15 bits	
Selection	Roulette selection + Elite preservation	
Crossover	Uniform crossover	
Mutation rate	20 %	

4.2 Usability of the systems

Figure 6 shows the average and standard deviations of the usability of each system. The usability of the E-IEC 1 and E-IEC 2 were higher than that of the NIEC. While using the NIEC, subjects had to manually evaluate the designs. However, in the E-IEC system, they can more easily evaluate the designs because they only view the designs. The operation loads of the E-IEC system were smaller than that of the NIEC. Moreover, the usability of the E-IEC 2 was slightly higher than that of the E-IEC 1. This was caused that subjects using the E-IEC 2 system by seeing designs freely. Lastly, psychological loads of the subjects when using the E-IEC 2 were smaller than those of the E-IEC 1. From the results of the statistical test, we confirmed statistically significant differences when the significance level was 5%. The usability of the E-IEC 1 and 2 were significantly higher than that of the NIEC.

However, some subjects commented that "he/she felt the fatigue with the E-IEC systems because they see the presented designs with a fixed stare." The fixed stare has no difference in the normal gaze for measuring the gaze information. Then, we will revise the experimental conditions.

As a result, the E-IEC system is effective for reducing evaluation loads of users and can generate designs suiting their preferences.

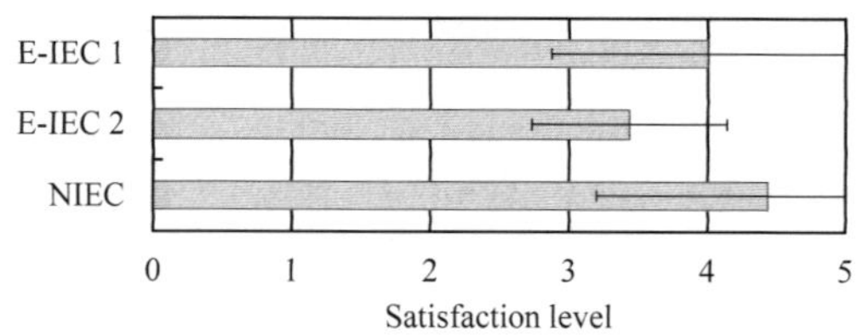

Figure 5: Results of the satisfaction levels

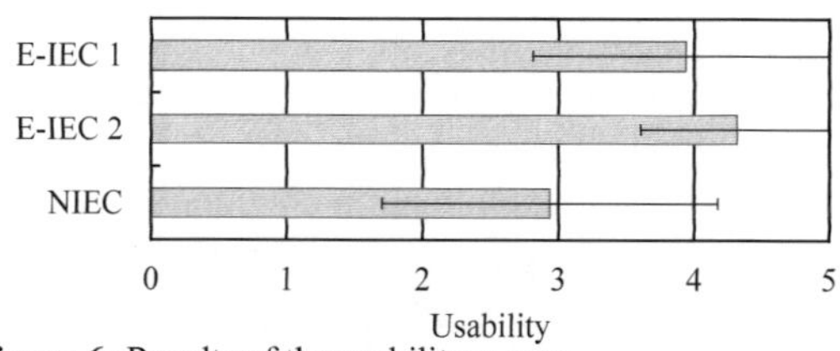

Figure 6: Results of the usability scores

4.3 Evaluation time for using the systems

In an IEC system, the time spent evaluating designs is a significant factor to reduce the evaluation load of users.

Figure 7 shows the average and standard deviations of the time spent evaluating the designs for each system. The evaluation time is measured from the point of initial presentation of designs to finishing the evaluations in the final generation. The evaluation times required for the E-IEC 1 and 2 systems were shorter than those required for the NIEC system. This was because subjects evaluated the designs manually in the NIEC. In the E-IEC system, they only view the presented designs or their favorite one.

The statistical testing results showed that when the significance level was 5%, the statistically significant differences of the evaluation times of the system were confirmed. The evaluation times for the E-IEC 1 and 2 were significantly shorter than that of the NIEC.

From the all results, we have confirmed that the E-IEC system can not only generate designs that satisfy users but can also reduce their evaluation loads. Moreover, the evaluation times using the E-IEC system were significantly shorter than that of the NIEC. Therefore, the E-IEC system is effective for creating an easy-to-use and effective IEC system.

5. CONCLUTION

We presented an IEC system applying user gaze information in evaluating candidate IEC solutions. We performed the evaluation experiments to verify the effectiveness of the E-IEC system. The experimental results show that the E-IEC system is effective for reducing the evaluation loads of users. In future study, we will demonstrate a more effectiveness of the E-IEC system.

ACKNOWLEDGMENTS

This research was partially supported by MEXT.KAKENHI (16K16141).

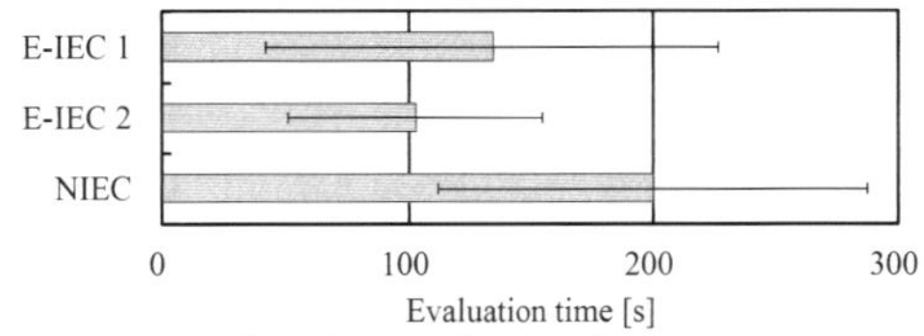

Figure 7: Results of the evaluation time

REFFERENCES

1. H. Takagi, "Interactive Evolutionary Computation: Fusion of the Capabilities of EC Optimization and Human Evaluation," Proceedings of the IEEE, 89(9), pp.1275–1296, 2001.
2. C. C. Lai, Y. C. Chen, "A User-Oriented Image Retrieval System Based on Interactive Genetic Algorithm," IEEE Transactions on Instrumentation and Measurement, 60(10), pp.3318–3325, 2011.
3. V. M. Marques, C. Reis, J. A. T. Machado, "Interactive Evolutionary Computation in Music," 2010 IEEE International Conference on Systems Man and Cybernetics (SMC), pp.3501–3507, 2010.
4. H. Takenouchi, M. Tokumaru, N. Muranaka, "Tournament-style Evaluation using Kansei Evaluation," International Journal of Affective Engineering, 12(3), pp.395–407, 2013.
5. M. Unehara, K. Yamada, T. Shimada, "Subjective Evaluation of Music with Brain Wave Analysis for Interactive Music Composition by IEC," Joint 7th International Conference on Soft Computing and Intelligent Systems and 15th International Symposium on Advanced Intelligent Systems (SCIS&ISIS 2014), pp.66–70, 2014.
6. M. Fukumoto, S. Nakashima, S. Ogawa, J. Imai, "An Extended Interactive Evolutionary Computation Using Heart Rate Variability as Fitness Value for Composing Music Chord Progression," Journal of Advanced Computational Intelligence and Intelligent Informatics, 15(9), pp.1329–1336, 2011.
7. M. M. Moniri, F. A. E. Valcarcel, D. Merkel, D. Sonntag, "Human Gaze and Focus-of-Attention in Dual Reality Human-Robot Collaboration," 2016 12th International Conference on Intelligent Environments, pp.238–241, 2016.
8. D. Pallez, P. Collard, T. Baccino, L. Dumercy, "Eye-Tracking Evolutionary Algorithm to Minimize User's Fatigue in IEC Applied to Interactive One-Max Problem," GECCO '07 Proceedings of the 10th annual conference on Genetic and evolutionary computation, pp.2883–2886, 2007.
9. T. Holmes, J. Zanker, "Eye on the Prize: Using Overt Visual Attention to Drive Fitness for Interactive Evolutionary Computation," GECCO '08 Proceedings of the 10th annual conference on Genetic and evolutionary computation, pp.1531–1538, 2008.

ISASE-MAICS 2018

Eye Movement Detection Using k Nearest Neighbor Method

*Daisuke Tamaki, **Hiromi Fujimori, *Hisaya Tanaka

** Kogakuin University, 1-24-2 Nishi-Shinjuku, Shinjuku-ku, Tokyo 163-8677, Japan*
***Ochanomizu University, 2-1-1 Otsuka, Bunkyo-ku, Tokyo 112-8610, Japan*

Abstract: Switch using bio-signal are researching for communication of a physically disabled person such as ALS. We have researched bio-signal device for daily life support of ALS patients using ocular potential. We suggested Doubled Constant to RMS (DCR) method that is dynamic calculate the threshold value using RMS to detect to intentional action. However, DCR method has problem that the threshold increase from signal fluctuation, and cannot be detected large electrooculography change by intentional action. We need research better method for detection to intentional action. In recent years, it has been found that classification by pattern recognition in intentional action gives high accuracy for EMG. We compared the DCR method and the k neighborhood method which is one of the pattern recognition. It is because, Bio-signal switch has need better detection method. In result, each method has different detect conditions. In future, DCR method and knn method are combined for improved accuracy, and consider online analysis on EOG.

Keywords: *Bio-signal switch, EOG, ALS*

1. INTRODUCTION

Bio-signal switch is control device used bio-signal such as Electromyography (EMG), Electrooculography (EOG) and Electroencephalogram (EEG). Intractable neurological disease patients have been report who can use home appliances by Bio-signal switch. It is because they can use bio-signal switch by remaining body function [1].

ALS is one of intractable neurological diseases that is making it difficult to move the body by a disorder of motor neurons. However, ALS patients are said can do eye move when terminal symptoms [2]. EOG is eye potential charged retina and cornea that is changed by eye move. ALS patients can use EOG.

We have been researching bio-signal switch, assumed daily life. Long wearing bio-signal switch in real life is assumed. In case of patients use bio-signal switch long time, we assume reactive depression. Kaneko reported out the reduction of EOG when long time VDT work [3]. There is also a problem of individual differences in the response of the EOG. For that reason, patients have possibilities who can't use detection method of intentional motion using fixation threshold. Therefore, we proposed Doubled Constant to RMS (DCR) method that is dynamically calculated threshold using RMS [4]. In result, DCR method has detected EOG over 70% of all subjects who used bio-signal switch for the first time. However, we ascertained RMS uprising by eye potential fluctuation. DCR method is calculated using RMS. Therefore, the threshold was uprising when increased RMS. For that reason, DCR method had a case that is not detected intentional eye motion. In this report, it is to Identify characteristics of detection method to intentional eye move that to conduct a study of detection method for bio-signal switch. We comparison DCR method and knn method. The knn method is one of pattern recognition. By comparing the two methods, we have clarified the detection characteristics to the EOG by the intended eye movement in the bio-signal switch.

2. Detection Method

2.1 Measurement data

In this research, Detection result recorded offline both methods count detection as shown in the table 1. It was set to Hit if it was detected during action intention, or Miss if not detected. False Alarm (FA) is miss detection during no intentional action, or Correct Rejection (CR) if not detect. We decided input method that is raise the eyeball with closing eyes from previous research [5] (Figure 1). Amplification of EOG occurs twice when does intentional eye movement. It is because, Subjects move "raising and returning" the eyeballs. The electrode for signal measurement was attached to the reference electrode to the right ear, the electrode for EOG measured to 1 cm below the right eyeball, and the GND for filter to the left earlobe. We measured EOG by OpenBCI that is multi-sensor. The sensor setting is that sampling rate is 250Hz and bandpass filter to 1-50Hz. The measured flow shown in Figure 2. The measure start 20 seconds are rest section. 10 sets were performed with one set including a total of 10 seconds in which the motion section was 5 seconds and the rest section was 5 seconds. Subjects were 14 people healthy male and female.

Table 1: Record matter

	Detection	No detection
Action intention	Hit	Miss
No action intention	False Alarm	Correct Rejection

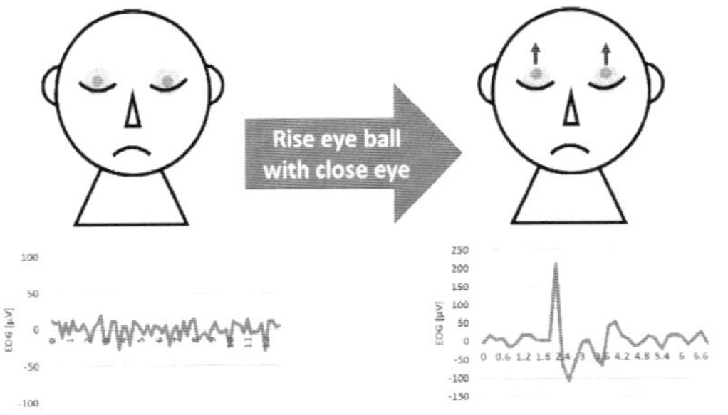

Figure 1: Intention action and EOG

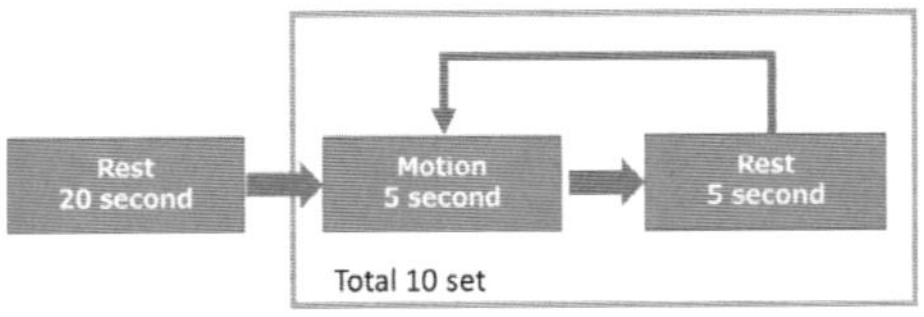

Figure 2: Measurement Flow

This experiment has been approved by the Research Ethics Review Committee for human subjects Kogakuin University Human (Approval No. H 28-22).

2.2 k nearest neighbor (knn) method

The knn method is one of pattern recognition that is a method of classification. Learning data are plotted on the vector space, and k pieces of learning data are acquired in order of distance from unknown data. The result of taking a majority vote by the obtained learning data is a classification result. In this study, classification was performed by using the Euclidean distance which is the usual distance between two points for distance calculation. The knn method can operate stably even with small learning data and can obtain relatively high classification performance [6].

2.3 Doubled Constant to RMS (DCR) method

We proposed "Doubled Constant to RMS (DCR)" method that use threshold method. The threshold calculated by multiply RMS by constant (formula (1)). EOG (t) is the value of the EOG at time t. RMS (t) indicates the value of RMS of time t. The RMS was dynamically calculated using the formula (2) using the eye potential during the last 2 seconds. "a" is a changeable parameter for multiplied to RMS. When the absolute value of EOG (t) exceeds RMS (t) multiplied by a, it is determined that the switch has been input. In this experiment a = 3.5 was set parameter [3].

$$\begin{cases} |\boldsymbol{EOG(t)}| \geq \boldsymbol{RMS(t)} \times \boldsymbol{a} \cdots \textbf{switch on} \\ |\boldsymbol{EOG(t)}| \leq \boldsymbol{RMS(t)} \times \boldsymbol{a} \cdots \textbf{switch off} \end{cases} \quad (1)$$

$$RMS(t) = \sqrt{\frac{1}{n}\sum_{k=t-w}^{t} EOG(k)^2} \quad (2)$$

3. Result

3.1 Result of knn method

We did classification that used one of 14 subjects for test data and other subjects are used for training data. This classification applied while changing test data to all subjects. The classification result shown in Table.2. It was possible to detect more than 80% in 12 out of 14 subjects. Although it was possible to obtain a detection for many subjects, it was very low as 1 for Sub.9. Although it is not as much as Sub.9, only about half of the whole of Sub.5 could be detected. Regarding misdetection, they were all related to noise generated in the rest section of 20 seconds.

Table.2: Result of knn method (total 10 times)

Sub	Hit	Miss	FA	CR
1	10	0	0	10
2	10	0	0	10
3	10	0	1	9
4	8	2	0	10
5	8	2	0	10
6	8	2	1	9
7	10	0	0	10
8	5	5	0	10
9	1	9	0	10
10	10	0	1	9
11	10	0	0	10
12	10	0	0	10
13	9	1	0	10
14	10	0	0	10

Table.3: Result of DCR method (total 10 times)

Sub	Hit	Miss	FA	CR
1	8	2	0	10
2	8	2	1	9
3	8	2	1	9
4	10	0	1	9
5	7	3	1	9
6	8	2	2	8
7	10	0	0	10
8	5	5	0	10
9	2	8	0	10
10	7	3	0	10
11	8	2	3	7
12	10	0	3	7
13	9	1	2	8
14	10	0	1	9

Keywords: Bio-signal switch, EOG, ALS

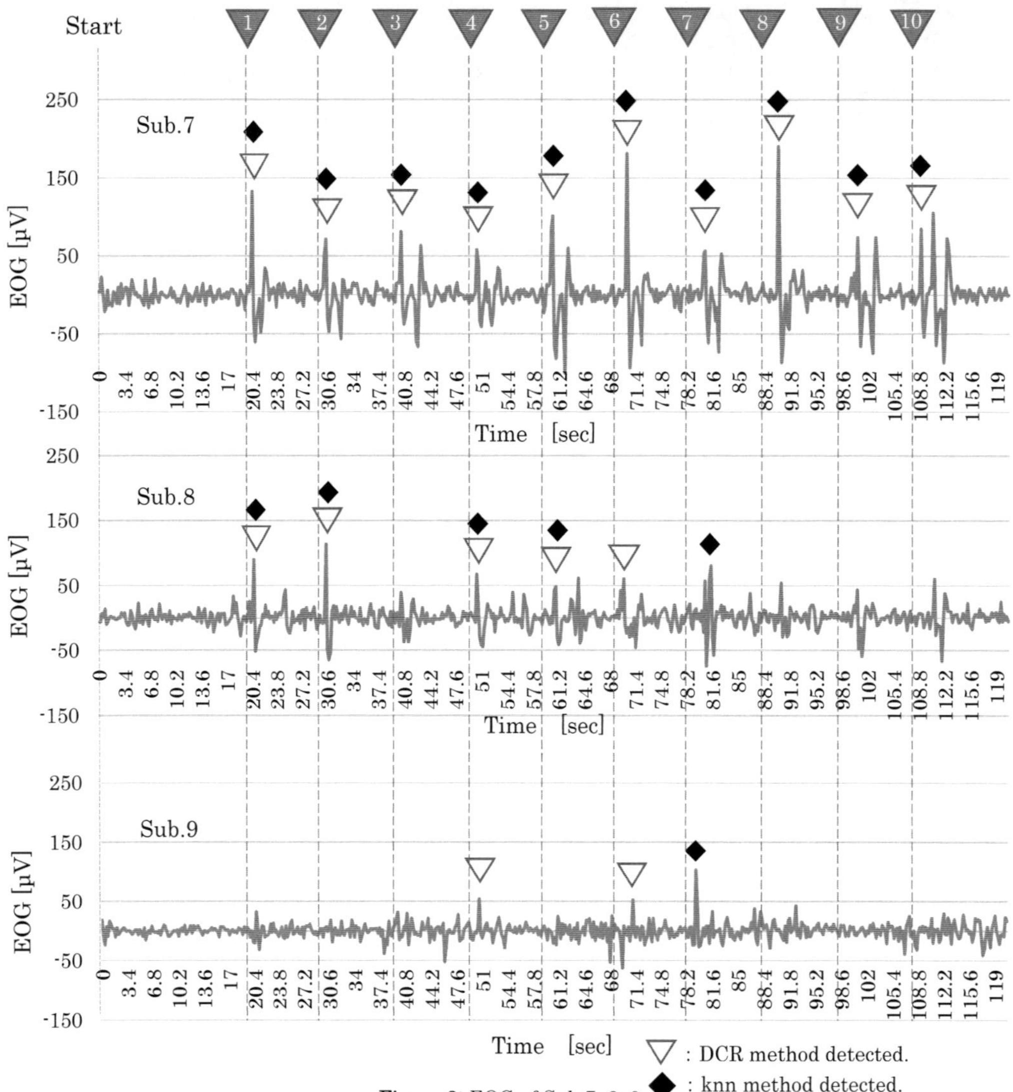

Figure 3: EOG of Sub.7, 8, 9

3.2 Comparison of each methods

The Table 3 is result of detection for the same data by DCR method. knn method is better than the DCR method about Hit and FA. Sub7 was the most detect in each method. Sub.9 was the least in each method. Sub.9 was the least in each method. It can be seen that the DCR method has more detected than knn method in Sub.9. Looking at the detected timing of Sub.9, knn method and DCR method were detected different move timing. This could be seen by other subjects. Figure 3 is Sub.9's EOG in measure section include rest time. The vertical axis represents the potential [µV] of the EOG, and the horizontal axis represents time (second). The timing indicated by the portion indicated by the broken line indicates the eye move, and the number at the upper portion indicates the number of the interval.

EOG of Sub.9 was less change than other subjects. In the EOG of Sub.9, it was the 4th and 6th sections detected by the DCR method, and the 7th section detected by the knn method. Sub.9 had little change in EOG as a whole, and knn method detected the 7th section was highest in his section. Also, the detected section potential of DCR method was comparatively higher than other section in Sub.9. In the first section, although the potential higher than the other sections can be confirmed, the intended motion was not detected. For FA, each method was not detected noise that observed the 3rd section and the 10th section. And, each method has detected different section in Sub.4 and Sub.8. Notably, EOG of Sub.8 was low change like Sub.9 when he did intentional eye motion. The Only DCR method has detected 6th section in Sub.8. This section EOG was small. However, this EOG change was larger than shortly before waveform.

Keywords: Bio-signal switch, EOG, ALS

4. Discussion

4.1 Detect Count

knn method is better than the DCR method for Hit and FA when it compared each method. Here, we calculated Hit rate and FA rate of each method from detection count. Formula 3,4 are used for calculating Hit rate and FA rate. The Result of average Hit rate and average FA rate show in Figure 4. Even in this case. knn method is better than the DCR method. It is because, knn method is higher than the DCR method for average Hit rate, and knn method is lower than the DCR method for average FA rate. However, each method has detected different section like Sub.9. Therefore, we investigated patterns that could not be detected for each method.

$$\textbf{Hit rate}(\%) = \frac{\boldsymbol{hit}}{\boldsymbol{hit + miss}} \times \mathbf{100} \quad (3)$$

$$\textbf{FA rate}(\%) = \begin{cases} \dfrac{\boldsymbol{FA}}{\boldsymbol{FA + CR}} \times \mathbf{100} \cdots (\boldsymbol{FA > 0}) \\ \dfrac{\mathbf{0.5}}{\boldsymbol{FA + CR}} \times \mathbf{100} \cdots (\boldsymbol{FA = 0}) \end{cases} \quad (4)$$

4.2 Waveform that could not be detected

As a result of the study, it was found that the waveform which could not be detected was almost three patterns.

In Sub.4, 8, 9, there was a section that could not be detected by each method. In Sub.4, each method did not detect of 6th section. This section was the lowest amplitude in his EOG. In other, Sub.8 and Sub.9 was lower EOG than other subjects. Figure 3 is EOG of Sub.7, 8, 9. Sub.7 EOG was larger than Sub.8, 9. Also, Sub.8's detection count is better than Sub.9. Looking at the waveform of Figure 3, the change in EOG can be seen in Sub.8 rather than Sub.9. DCR method has detected intentional eye motion in Sub.8 that is section 1, 2, 4, 5, 7 and detected section 1, 2, 4, 5, 7 by knn method. Each method had not detected in section 3, 8, 9, 10 of Sub.8 that was changed little of EOG than rest section. From these, we think each method is not detected when a change EOG potential is little or EOG power is low.

4.3 knn method

Shown in Figure 5 is the 10th section of Sub.4. This section was detected by only DCR method. Sub.4's EOG potential was about 100μV in his measurement section. However, the 10th section EOG potential is lower than other his section. For that reason, it is can think that knn could not detected this section. On the other, DCR method could detect this section when even EOG small. We think it is because EOG was change than his rest section. DCR method is considered that have characterized that can detect intentional eye motion when EOG was changed even if EOG is small.

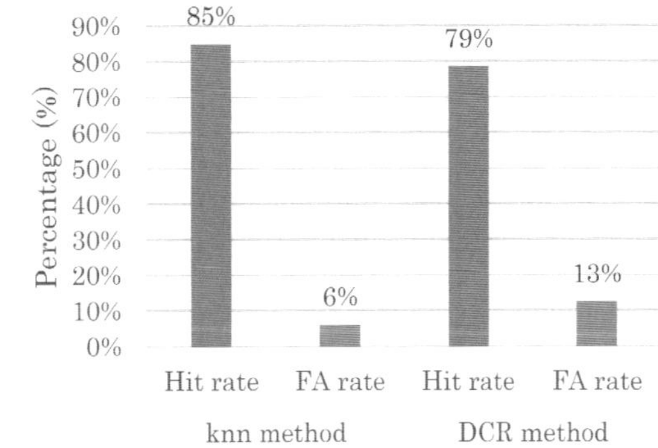

Figure 4: EOG that only DCR method detect

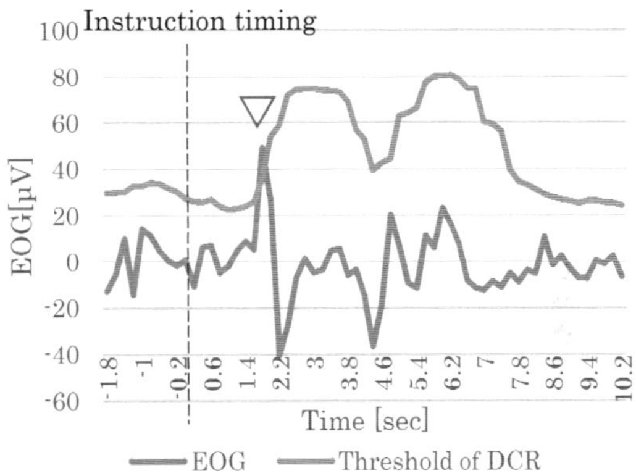

Figure 5: A typical waveform that is detected by DCR method

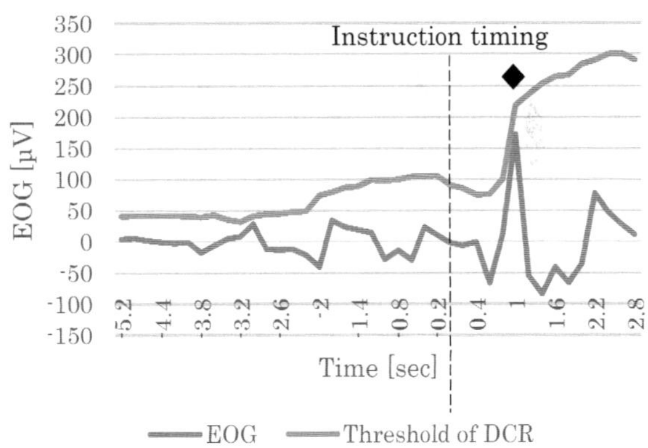

Figure.6: A typical waveform that is detected by knn method

4.4 DCR method

Waveform fluctuation before intentional eye motion is characteristic that can detect motion by only knn method. The threshold of DCR method was corresponded change EOG. It is because, the threshold is a constant multiple of RMS. The threshold increases due to fluctuation, and it is considered that it could not be detected because the potential further increased due to the intended operation. Figure 6 is the 5th section of Sub.5. The vertical axis represents the potential [μV] of the EOG, and the horizontal axis represents time (second) when 0 is instruction timing. The timing indicated by the portion indicated by the broken line. Look at Figure 6, the threshold is rises by EOG fluctuation before intentional eye motion and after eye motion when 95 seconds time point. DCR method did not detect this section. This feature occurred 14 times among all subjects.

4.5 In a section containing noise

Also, knn method has not detect section including noise. It is meant, knn method is stronger than a DCR method for FA. Figure 7 is the 10th section of Sub.6. This section was mixed in noise. DCR method has detect eye motion using RMS. For that reason, DCR method would falsify detect noise. knn method is using distance of the vector for detecting. Large noise is considered not detected because the vector distance is far away.

The section that is detected by an only knn method had characteristic of EOG fluctuation. Since the DCR method is strongly influenced by waveform fluctuation, it is considered that only the knn method could be detected. knn method did not detect when EOG is small. However, DCR method can detect when EOG was changed even if EOG is small. For these reasons, each method has different detect the condition. We think accuracy improvement when combined each method.

5. Conclusion

In this study, we studied the detection characteristics of intentional motion detection method using EOG to support daily living. We compared the detection accuracy with the DCR method which dynamically calculates threshold using RMS proposed so far and the knn method which is one of pattern recognition. In result, the average Hit rate of knn method is 85% that is higher than 79% of DCR method. However, we found each method has different detect the condition. In the knn method, it is difficult to be affected by the fluctuation of the waveform, and in the DCR method, it was possible to detect even a small waveform change which can't be detected by the knn method. DCR method and knn method are detect different conditions, we think accuracy improvement when combined each method. In EMG, Ichikawa et al. proposed a combination of pattern recognition and threshold method [7]. From now on, we will study methods to combine each method for the purpose of improving detection accuracy. Also, all experiments by the knn method were done offline this time. We need to consider online analysis on EOG by knn method.

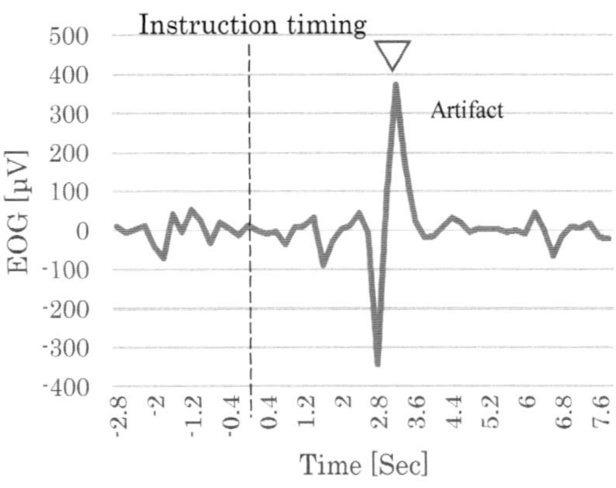

Figure 7: EOG included noise

ACKNOWLEDGMENT

This work was supported by a Grant-in-Aid for Scientific Research (C) 15K00762.

Reference

1. Chisima, Nara, Hashimoto, Itou, : "Current State of Communication Support for Amyotrophic Lateral Sclerosis (ALS) Patients and Development of Brain-Computer Interface (BCI) for P300 Event-Related Potentials"; JSMBE 47(2),190-198,2009.
2. Abe, "To actual state-of-the-art treatment and welfare of symptoms and diagnosis - all of the nerve intractable disease" ; Shinkoh Igaku Shuppansha, p28, 2007.
3. Kaneko, Sakamoto, "Observations on the spontaneous blinks during the prolonged VDT works" ; JES, p.400-401 , vol.36, 2000.
4. Tamaki, Tanaka, "EOG Analysis Algorithm for Biological Switches" ; Human Interface Symposium 2017, 6D2-2, Human Interface Society, 2017.
5. Ohya, Kawasumi,"Development of an Input Operation for the Amyotrophic Lateral Sclerosis Communication Tool Utilizing EOG", JSMBE,Vol.43(1), pp.172-178, 2005.
6. Harada, "Image Recognition", Kodansha, pp.142-143.
7. Ichikawa, Hori, "Development of Interface System using Electromyograms of Face Movements" ; FIT 10(2), 559-560, IPSJ, 2011.

ISASE-MAICS 2018

Real-Time Grayscale Dehazing Scheme For Car Vision

Zhi WANG*, Daishi WATABE* and Jianting CAO*

**Saitama Institute of Technology, FukayashiFusaiji1690, Saitama, Japan*
{t7001vuk, dw, cao}@sit.ac.jp

Abstract: To improve the safety of autonomous cars, their obstacle detection capability in bad weather must be substantially improved. Haze is a major factor that degrades outdoor images. Although various dehazing schemes have been proposed, a dehazing scheme designed to improve obstacle detection capability has not been reported. Hence, we present a dehazing algorithm that enhances the safety of an autonomous car. This algorithm should be able to work in real time, even using edge computers typically installed as car electronics. Furthermore, this algorithm should work on grayscale images, as systems dependent on color images are often unaffected by environmental color changes caused by factors such as a setting sun. We developed this algorithm based on the following three existing dehazing algorithms: dark channel prior, median dark channel prior, and the parameter tuning scheme for dark channel prior. We extend these methods based only on grayscale images. In terms of object detection capability, structural similarity index measure, and peak signal-to-noise ratio, the empirical results showed that our grayscale image-based proposed algorithm is comparable to the results of current cutting-edge methods, and operates in real time.

Keywords: *Dehazing, Object detection, Autonomous cars*

1. INTRODUCTION

Outdoor image-processing systems required for car vision or security surveillance are inevitably affected by poor weather, such as haze, fog, or smoke, which is then considered as noise. Under such conditions, photos captured outdoors often yield low contrast and appear blurred. Thus, this is an important challenge for autonomous (self-driving) car design and development, as poor visibility in bad weather conditions can lead to traffic accidents. Systems providing car vision naturally operate more effectively in good, rather than poor, weather conditions. To improve the recognition rate of object detection, it is necessary to solve the problem of visibility degradation. Therefore, we propose a fast dehazing method for car vision, and test it using Faster R-CNN [1]. In the area of object detection, the current study could prove significant, because the improvement of the obstacle detection capability of a car could allow it to effectively detect the front of obstacles and thus ensure safe driving.

However, dehazing is a challenging problem in the field of image processing. We cannot obtain the depth of haze if the input is only a single image. Several dehazing methods have been proposed to estimate the object depth by using multiple images or additional information. For example, object depth could be determined from two images of the same location taken under different weather conditions [2], or from various degrees of polarization [3], [4]. Kopf et al. [5] performed dehazing of outdoor images by using known 3D models. These methods estimated the depth by enabling effective dehazing of images. However, these vision algorithms have limited applicability in a large number of situations when considering car vision alone.

In recent years, single-image dehazing has made great progress, as the methods have been developed as based on prior knowledge or assumptions. Tan [6] observed that haze-free images must have more contrast than hazy images. By maximizing the contrast in hazy images, the visual result was found to be better than expected. However, the restored images appear with unnatural edges. Moreover, for target recognition, these new edges are detrimental, as they compromise recognition.

Tarel [7] proposed a novel algorithm and variants for restoring scene visibility. The main advantage of this method is its speed, which enables the application of visibility restoration; the study was noted for being the first to perform this task in real time. Furthermore, the complexity of this algorithm depends only linearly on the number of image pixels.

In [8], Tarel proposed an extended algorithm as based on previous work [7]. As it was designed for the visibility enhancement of road images, this model demonstrated that a large portion of the image can be assumed as a planar view of the road, but with visibility distance above 50 m.

He et al. [9] proposed a dark channel prior (DCP) method to calculate the transmission map. The dark channel prior indicates that, in nature, haze-free outdoor images contain some pixels that have very low intensities, or are close to zero in at least one color channel. Additionally, they implemented soft matting to reform restored images. Although the method is simple, the result proved to be quite significant. Since this time, many other algorithms based on DCPs have been adopted and improved. However, rapid processing has remained difficult to achieve in real time.

Gibson et al. [10] proposed a DCP-based method. The method uses a median filter to replace a minimum filter, and saves time in forming restored images. Although less time expensive, this method produces reconstructed images with low luminance, low peak signal-to-noise ratio (PSNR), and a low structural similarity index measure (SSIM).

Liu et al. [11] proposed a parameter that can automatically adjust the amount of haze to be removed, and can be rapidly processed; however, the restored images are often distorted in the form of pixels appearing completely white or black in the restored image.

2. METHOD

2.1 He et al. DCP-based dehazing principle

Haze Physical Model

The haze physical model has been widely implemented in computer graphics and computer vision to describe haze in images, and is based on Narasimhan's atmospheric model [12]:

$$I(x) = J(x)t(x) + A(1 - t(x)) \tag{1}$$

where $I(x)$ is defined as the observed RGB color intensities at pixel position x, $J(x)$ represents the intensities of the original image, which is viewed as the haze-free image, A is defined as the global atmospheric light, and $t(x)$ is called a transmission map. Once A and $t(x)$ are given, we obtain the haze free image $J(x)$ by solving Eq. (1).

Estimation of dark channel-based transmission map

He et al. [9] defined a dark channel of color image I as follows:

$$I^{DC}(x) = \min_{y\in\Omega(x)} \left(\min_{c\in\{R,G,B\}} I^c(y) \right) \tag{2}$$

where $I^c(y)$ represents the pixel value of channel c at coordinate y , and $\Omega(x)$ denotes a small squared region of interest of fixed size around x.

He et al. [9] developed an algorithm as based on observations of outdoor haze-free images in which at least one color channel comprised pixels with very low and close to zero intensities for most of the non-sky patches.

$$J^{DC}(x) = \min_{y\in\Omega(x)} \left(\min_{c\in\{R,G,B\}} J^c(y) \right) \approx 0 \tag{3}$$

They referred to this assumption as a DCP. Using this observation, computing the dark channel for both hand sides of Eq. (1), we have the following:

$$I^{DC}(x) \approx A(1 - t(x)) \tag{4}$$

Hence, the transmission map $t(x)$ can be obtained as

$$t(x) \approx 1 - \frac{I^{DC}(x)}{A} \tag{5}$$

Estimation of atmospheric light

He et al. [9] first selected the top 0.1% brightest pixels in the dark channel; these pixels are typically the most haze-opaque. Among these pixels, the pixels with the highest intensity A_0 in the input image I are selected as the atmospheric light.

$$A = A_0 \tag{6}$$

Haze removal parameter ω

He et al. [9][13] introduced a parameter ω $(0 \le \omega \le 1)$ for Eq. (6) to control haze removal.

$$t(x) \approx 1 - \omega\frac{I^{DC}(x)}{A} \tag{7}$$

Note that this parameter ω is application-based and must be manually determined.

Obtaining a haze-free image

By substituting Eqs. (6) and (7) into Eq. (1), the final restored haze-free image $J(x)$ can be obtained as follows:

$$J(x) = \frac{I(x) - A_0}{t(x)} + A_0 \tag{8}$$

In order to avoid zero division, He et al. [9] introduced a small positive number t_0 to compute $J(x)$, as follows:

$$J(x) = \frac{I(x) - A_0}{\max(t(x), t_0)} + A_0 \tag{9}$$

He et al. [9] used $t_0 = 0.1$.

Refinement Restored Image

In order to improve the distortion near edges in the recovered image, He et al. [9] applied soft matching and a bilateral filter to the transmission maps. Although this process improves the recovered image, it is very time expensive.

2.2 Extending the DCP developed by He et al.

Median DCP (MDCP)

In order to increase the efficiency of the algorithm developed by He et al. [9], Gibson et al. [10] implemented a median filter instead of a minimum operation (as is shown in Eq. (2)) to omit the soft matching process; it was designated as the median dark channel. Similar to Eq. (3), Gibson et al. [10] assumed that this median dark channel of the haze-free image is near zero; the resulting assumption was referred to as the median DCP (MDCP).

$$J^{\mathrm{MDC}} = \operatorname*{med}_{y\in\Omega(x)} \left(\min_{c\in\{R,G,B\}} J^c(y) \right) \approx 0 \tag{10}$$

Consequently, the transmission map $t(x)$ can be obtained as

$$t(x) \approx 1 - \frac{I^{MDC}(x)}{A} \qquad (11)$$

The use of a median filter has the two following advantages: 1) it preserves edges while smoothing out the flat regions, and 2) it has a fast running speed owing to the omission of the soft matching process.

Estimation of parameter ω

Liu et al. [11] proposed a method that can automatically optimize the parameter ω in Eq. (7) for various images as follows:

$$\omega = pm \qquad (12)$$

where m is the average of the maximum and minimum intensity values, and p is an experimentally determined value.

2.3 Proposed method

The use of grayscale images

It is known that a system dependent on color image processing is unreliable in outdoor computer vision. Because environmental colors, as is observed in a setting sun, can easily alter system performance, we aimed to develop a dehazing algorithm as solely based on grayscale images. Hence, we evaluated the resulting algorithm on grayscale images. In the preliminary experiment, we found that Gibson's method was moderately effective, even on grayscale images. Thus, we assumed the following as a starting point for the proposed method:

$$t(x) = 1 - \omega \frac{\underset{y \in \Omega(x)}{\text{med}}\, Y(y)}{A_0} \qquad (13)$$

Estimation of parameter ω

We assume ω has the following form:

$$\omega = \min(pm(m + 0.5), 0.95) \qquad (14)$$

where m is the average of the maximum and minimum grayscale image intensity values. In the preliminary experiment, when the p value belongs to [1.2, 1.5], a good result is obtained. In this study, we used $p = 1.3$ in all experiments.

Mask size

We selected a 5 × 5 mask size for the median filter. Choosing 3 × 3 yields a low PSNR, whereas a mask size of 7 × 7 results in a degraded restored image and a low SSIM.

Restored Image Refinement

DCP method-based dehazing has the disadvantage of low luminance in the restored images. However, we solved this problem by introducing gamma correction to the transmission map.

Flow of the proposed algorithm

Figure 1 shows the flow of the proposed algorithm.

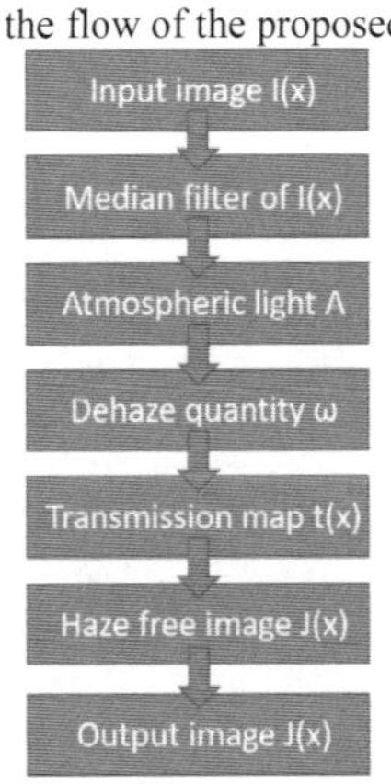

Figure 1: Flow of the proposed algorithm

Genealogy of the proposed algorithm

The genealogy of the proposed algorithm is given in Fig. 2.

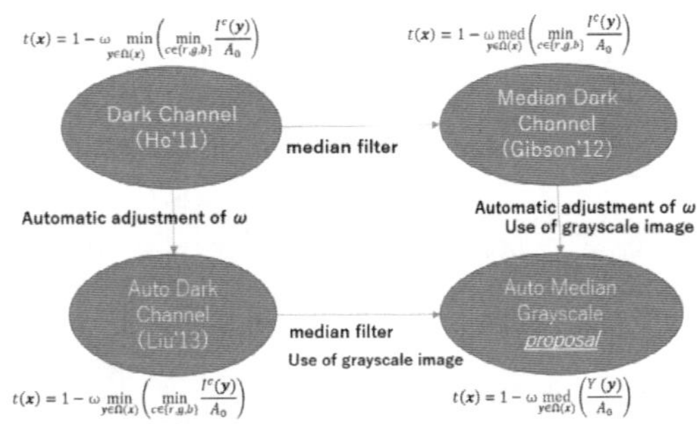

Figure 2: Genealogy of the proposed algorithm

3. EXPERIMENT

To verify the effectiveness of our proposed method, we performed the following five experiments:

A) First, we compared our results to those obtained via the methods proposed by Gibson et al. [10] and Liu et al. [11], because our method is an extension of their methods. Note that the comparisons were performed using benchmark images.

B) Second, we compared the detection accuracy of the proposed method (softmax probability of Faster RCNN) to those of the other two methods (i.e., [10] and [11]) by using a hazy car image [12].

C) Next, by using benchmark images, we compared the PSNR and SSIM of all the images, the results of which are listed in Tables I and II.

D) Finally, to evaluate the processing time, we randomly selected 30 images of different sizes, and measured the processing time averaged over three trials.

Keywords: Dehazing, Object detection, Autonomous cars

4. RESULTS AND DISCUSSION

4.1 Comparison of softmax probability

Figure 3: Object detection system running on Faster RCNN. The top image is the original image, followed by the image obtained via the method proposed by Liu et al. [11], and then the method proposed by Gibson et al. [10]. The bottom-most image is obtained via the proposed method.

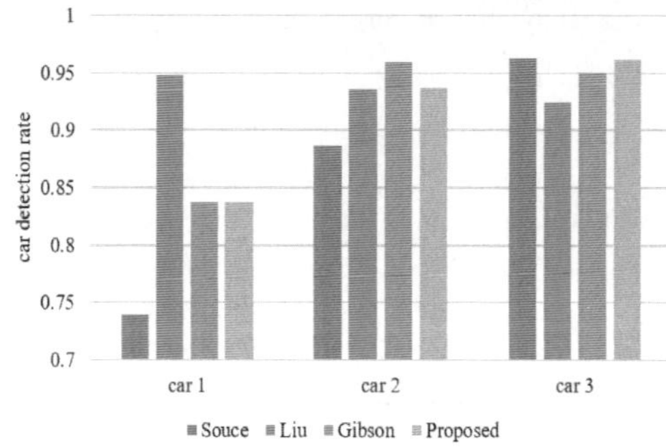

Figure 4: Softmax probability of car detection rate for source image obtained via the method proposed by Liu et al. [11], Gibson et al. [10], and the proposed method.

In terms of the softmax probability for true positives, a higher value is better. We first performed the dehazing operation, and then tested the recognition rate of object detection by using the Faster R-CNN-based detection system. The detection result is illustrated in Fig. 3, and the softmax probability is summarized in Fig. 4. It can be seen that our grayscale image-based method is comparable to the current state-of-the-art methods.

4.2 Comparing human visibility by using benchmark images

Some dehazing results based on benchmark images are shown in Figs. 5 and 6.

Figure 5: Comparison of dehazing results. (a) Original image and results of (b) Liu et al. [11], (c) Gibson et al. [10], and (d) the proposed method.

Figure 6: Comparison of dehazing results. (a) Original image and results of (b) Liu et al. [11], (c) Gibson et al. [10], and (d) the proposed method.

As is shown in Figs. 2 and 3, all methods removed a noticeable amount of haze in the benchmark image. However, the proposed method yields an image that is slightly brighter than those of the other methods, especially that of [10]. The amount of removed haze is slightly less than that achieved via the method proposed in [11]. In addition, due to the remaining part of the fog in the output image, we think that such a result with better authenticity. On the other hand, in the case of a grayscale image being used as the input image, because the MDC is merely a median-filtered grayscale image, the approximation given in Eq. (10) is not consistently true. This may be one reason for the slightly inferior performance in this area. However, considering that our proposed method only uses the grayscale image, the result is satisfactory.

4.3 Comparison of the PSNR and SSIM using benchmark images

Tables I and II show the verification of the PSNR and SSIM results, where the proposed method is observed to achieve the best performance. For the PSNR and SSIM, a higher value corresponds to better performance. It can be seen that our method is comparable to the conventional methods.

Table 1: PSNR results

	He[9]	Tan[6]	Tarel[7]	Tarel[8]	Gibson[10]	Proposed
ny12	14.675	11.710	16.978		13.459	15.031
ny17	17.263	12.763	13.513		12.075	15.114
y01	13.173	12.143	17.369		13.568	13.814
y16	13.568	12.403	14.510		12.398	13.992
G000	9.821	11.974	18.404	13.763	12.714	16.971
G001	9.457	10.892	16.348	12.020	11.864	16.320
G002	10.302	12.739	18.552	14.226	12.915	17.130
G003	10.326	12.387	18.572	14.290	12.793	17.022
G004	10.445	12.404	18.719	14.108	12.748	16.979
canon3	13.000				15.649	19.255
canyon2	10.019				12.050	15.417
forest1	16.652				13.807	15.384
train	13.430				12.813	13.046

Table 2: SSIM results

	He[9]	Gibson[10]	Tan[6]	Tarel[7]	Proposed
y01	82.59%	79.53%	73.73%	85.07%	85.52%
y16	89.16%	82.48%	76.41%	83.58%	91.05%
ny12	86.61%	81.76%	63.34%	85.79%	88.03%
ny17	84.96%	77.94%	77.72%	85.24%	89.47%
G000	52.58%	70.44%	67.46%	69.87%	89.82%
G001	50.89%	69.62%	60.08%	68.21%	89.62%
G002	53.63%	70.16%	70.06%	71.15%	89.68%
G003	53.78%	69.54%	68.97%	71.41%	89.41%
G004	53.94%	69.21%	68.56%	70.44%	89.29%

4.4 Processing time

The processing time results are shown in Fig. 8. Regarding hardware, a Core i5-6300HQ 2.3 GHz unit is used. The code is written by using OpenCV 2.4.9 in Visual Studio 2013. The processing speed can reach more than 70 frames per second, and the pixel and processing time are linearly related.

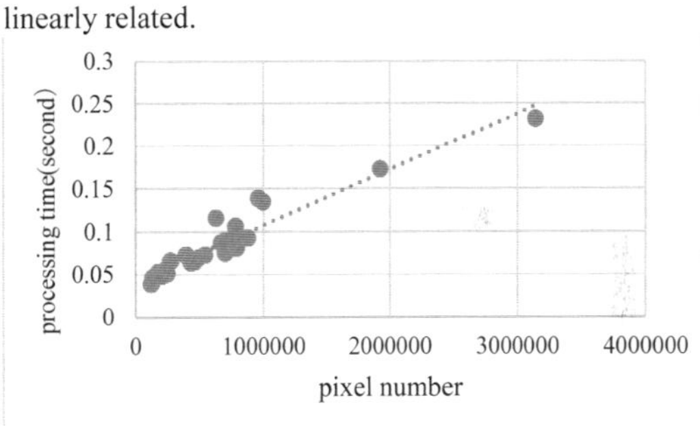

Figure 7: Linear relationship between processing time and pixel number

5. CONCLUSIONS AND FUTURE WORK

The current paper is an extension of [14]. Thus, in this paper, we have included a reason for the use of grayscale and new evaluation approaches based on softmax probabilities.

We proposed a dehazing algorithm that can achieve the following tasks:

A) Work on grayscale images (unaffected by color illumination change)
B) Operate in real time.

The empirical results indicate that our proposed algorithm is comparable to the currently implemented algorithms [10][11] in terms of object detection capability, structural similarity index measure, peak signal-to-noise ratio, and real-time operability; the favorable performance is primarily attributed to the fact that the proposed algorithm was derived as based on only grayscale images.

The impact of this algorithm is as follows: since it can be applied to edge devices common to car electronics such as a drive image recorder in autonomous cars, and because this algorithm is based on grayscale images, which are unaffected by color illumination change, the proposed algorithm can improve car safety.

In the case of a grayscale image being used as an input image, the MDC is simply a median-filtered grayscale image. Thus, approximation of Eq. (10) is not consistently true. However, our finding is that the proposed method is applicable to various images. As the results reported here are mainly purposed to verify and validate the proposed method, the number of images used in this study may not be sufficient. Thus, future work should focus on identifying and analyzing cases in which the proposed approach does not yield adequate results.

REFERENCES

[1].S. Ren, K. He, R. Girshick, J. Sun; Faster R-CNN: Towards Real-Time Object Detection with Region Proposal Networks, IEEE Transactions on Pattern Analysis and Machine Intelligence; 39(6), pp. 1137-1149, 2017.

[2].S. G. Narasimhan, S. K. Nayar; Contrast Restoration of Weather Degraded Images, IEEE Transactions on Pattern Analysis and Machine Intelligence; 25(6), pp. 713-724, 2003.

[3].S. Shwartz, E. Namer, and Y. Y. Schechner; Blind Haze Separation, IEEE Computer Society Conference on Computer Vision and Pattern Recognition (CVPR), New York, 2006.

[4].Y. Y. Schechner, S. G. Narasimhan, and S. K. Nayar; Instant dehazing of images using polarization, IEEE Computer Society Conference on Computer Vision and Pattern Recognition (CVPR), Kauai, 2001

[5].J. Kopf *et al.*, Deep photo: model-based photograph enhancement and viewing, ACM Transactions on Graphics; 27(5), pp. 1-10, 2008.

[6].R. T. Tan, Visibility in bad weather from a single image, 26th IEEE Computer Society Conference on Computer Vision and Pattern Recognition (CVPR), Anchorage, 2008.

[7].J. P. Tarel and N. Hautiere; Fast visibility restoration from a single color or gray level image, IEEE 12th International Conference on Computer Vision (ICCV), Kyoto, 2009.

[8].J. P. Tarel, N. Hautière, A. Cord, D. Gruyer, and H. Halmaoui; Improved visibility of road scene images under heterogeneous fog, IEEE Intelligent Vehicles Symposium, La Jolla, 2010.

[9].K. He, J. Sun, and X. Tang, "Single image haze removal using dark channel prior," in IEEE Conference on Computer Vision and Pattern Recognition, 2009.

[10].K. Gibson, D. Võ, and T. Nguyen; An investigation in dehazing compressed images and video, OCEANS 2010: MTS/IEEE Seattle, Seattle, 2010.

[11].Q. Liu, M. Chen, and D. Zhou; Fast haze removal from a single image, 25th Chinese Control and Decision Conference, Guiyang, 2013.

[12].S. G. Narasimhan and S. K. Nayar; Vision and the Atmosphere, International Journal on Computer Vision; 48(3), pp. 233-254, 2002.

[13].K. He, J. Sun, and X. Tang; Single Image Haze Removal Using Dark Channel Prior, IEEE Transactions on Pattern Analysis and Machine Intelligence; 33(12), pp. 2341-2353, 2011.

[14].Z. Wang, D. Watabe, and J. Cao; Improving visibility of a fast dehazing method, World Automation Congress (WAC), Rio Grande, 2016.

ISASE-MAICS 2018

Motor Imagery Multi-task Classification Method

Ryo TAKAHASHI*, Hisaya TANAKA*

** Informatics Major, Kogakuin University, 1-24-2 Nishishinjuku, Shinjuku-ku, Tokyo 163-8677, Japan*

Abstract: We studied on the MI-BCI (Motor Imagery Brain-Computer Interface). MI-BCI is an interface that operate a computer using changes in brain activity that appear when imaging moving a body part. For example, MI-BCI is possible to assign the left-hand motor imagery to the power ON/OFF command. A problem of MI-BCI is a few number of the command. Currently, MI-BCI commands are four commands using "left-hand", "right-hand", "legs" and "tongue" motor imagery. Therefore, we attempted to add the number of MI-BCI commands by classifying eight kinds of motor imagery brain activity "no movement", "left-hand", "right-hand", "legs", "both-hands", "left-hand + legs", "right-hand + legs", "both-hands + legs". Motor imagery by multiple body parts "both-hands", "left-hand + legs", "right-hand + legs", "both-hands + legs" are called multi-task. Multi-task are combination of simultaneous motor imagery of left-hand, right-hand, and legs. This makes it possible to add the number of commands to $2^N - 1$ (N is number of body part). We used LDA to classify motor images. As a result of classification, the correct classification rate was 26.9%. It was shown that multitask motion recall can be classified, and it was suggested that it is possible to add the number of MI-BCI commands to$2^N - 1$.
Keywords: *MI-BCI, Short-Time Fourier Transform, Multi-Class Classification, Multi-task*

1. INTRODUCTION

BCI (Brain-Computer Interface) is an interface for operating a computer by detecting a specific signal in EEG (electroencephalogram). BCI don't need body movement. Therefore, it is expected to apply to patients who cannot move the body. There are two types of BCI, Synchronized BCI and Desynchronized BCI. Synchronized BCI operate a computer by detecting EEG by external stimulation. However, Synchronized BCI needs an equipment for stimulating the user. Furthermore, user cannot operate a computer at the user's voluntary timing, because the subject is given the stimulus at the timing unintended. Therefore, and the use of the BCI is limited. On the other hand, Desynchronized BCI can operate the computer at the user's voluntary timing. One of Desynchronized BCI is called MI-BCI. MI is a mental task of moving the body. MI-BCI operates computer by motor imagery. For example, it is possible to assign the left-hand motor imagery to the power ON/OFF command. However, the MI-BCI has the problem of a few command. Currently, one command is made by one body part motor imagery. Kawato's research classified EEG at the time of right-hand, left-hand, legs, and tongue motor imagery [1]. However, in this research, the number of MI-BCI commands of are only four.

Adding the number of MI-BCI commands makes possible to give complex commands to the computer. It expands the range of activities in the lives of patients who cannot move the body. The researches are being made to add the number of MI - BCI commands by combining motor imagery. Wang's research made 8 commands using right-hand, left-hand, and foot motor imagery [2]. There are 4 command groups of 2 selections determined by left or right-hand motor imagery. Switching of the command groups is done by leg motor imagery. However, it takes time to control the computer, because it needs two-step motor imagery. Geng's research classified 4 EEG states "no movement", "left-hand", "right-hand", "both-hands" by combining left and right-hand motor imagery [3]. His research used "Parallel classification method" for classification of motor imagery.

Therefore, we attempted adding MI-BCI commands by classification of 8 EEG states "no movement", "right-hand", "left-hand", "legs", "both-hands", "right-hand + legs", "left-hand + legs", "both-hands + legs" by combining left-hand and right-hand, legs motor imagery (Figure 1). Content of tasks are image to hold at hand motor imagery, and image to walk at legs motor imagery. This makes it possible to add the number of MI-BCI commands to $2^N - 1$ (N is the number of body parts). We

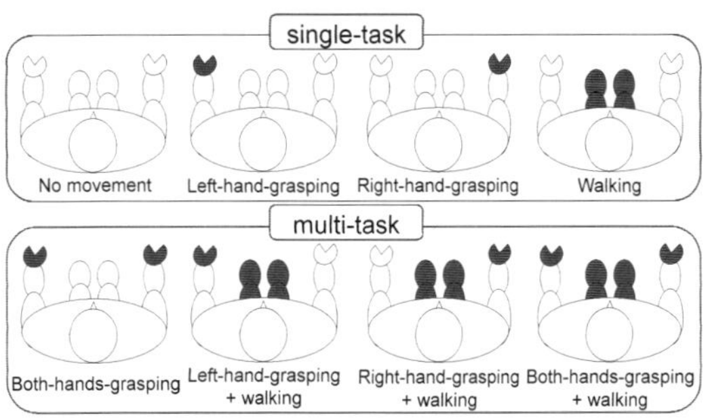

Figure 1: Motor imagery mental tasks

call single motor imagery as single task and combinations of motor imagery as multi-task.

Multi-task motor imagery is a psychologically complicated task because it simultaneously performs multiple mental tasks. Therefore, it is considered that the CCR (Correct Classification Rate) of multi-task will be lower than the CCR of single-task. We compared the CCR of single-task and multi-task to examine the possibility of multi-task motor imagery classification. As to the examination of multi-task discrimination, how much CCR is the chance level (12.5%) as a minimum basis rate of multi-task and how much CCR changes compared with single-task.

There are two classification methods in multitask classification. The one is OVR (One-Versus-Rest) classification method which is often used in multi-class classification. The other one is Parallel classification method which Geng proposed. In the Geng's research, there was no difference in CCR between the two classification methods. However, the 8 classes classification that added the leg motor imagery has not been clarified. Therefore, we compared the two classification methods, OVR classification method and parallel classification method.

2. MEASUREMENT

2.1 Subject

The subjects were 6 healthy males (mean age:22.3 $\pm$ 0.56). The subjects were asked to explain the contents of the experiment beforehand and experimented after gaining consent. 4 subjects had MI-BCI experience, and the other two had no experience.

2.2 Measurement environment

Figure 2 shows the measurement environment. The subject was seated in a chair in a relaxed state and tasked according to the PC screen. At that time, the subjects were covered an electrode cap and measured an EEG by electroencephalograph. Figure 3 shows the electrode

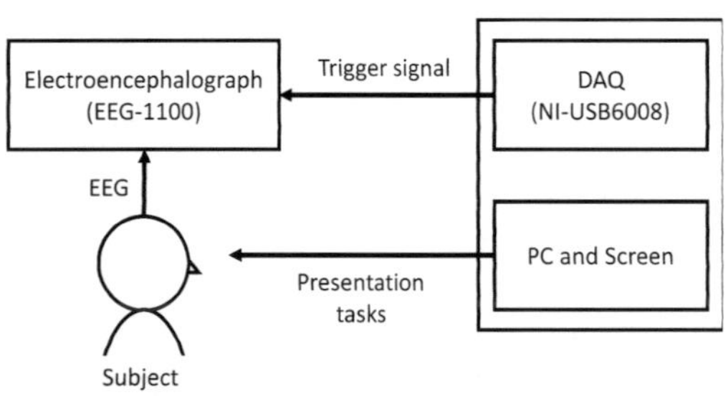

Figure 2: Measurement environment

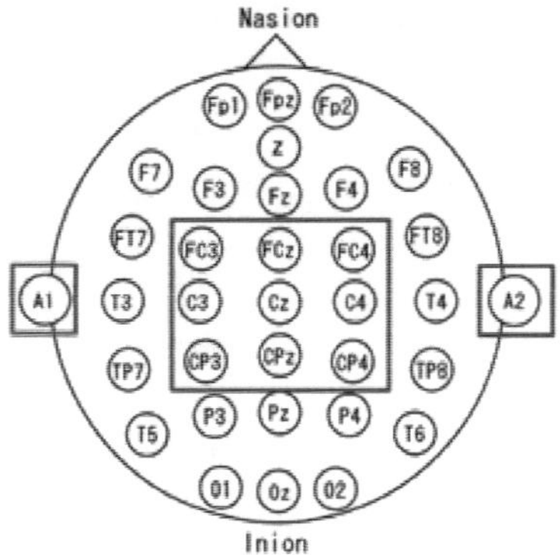

Figure 3: Electrode arrangement

arrangement used. According to the international 10-20 method, the reference electrodes were A1 and A2, and the remaining 9 electrodes were used as probe electrodes.

In addition, DAQ was connected to an electroencephalograph and a PC to retrieve the time of the MI task.

2.3 Content of task

Figure 4 shows the content of task. Subjects were made resting state for 15 seconds after starting measurement. After that, subjects were repeated motor imagery task for 3 seconds and resting state for 6 seconds 30 times. Figure 5 shows the presentation image given to the subject and the corresponding motor imagery. Subjects were

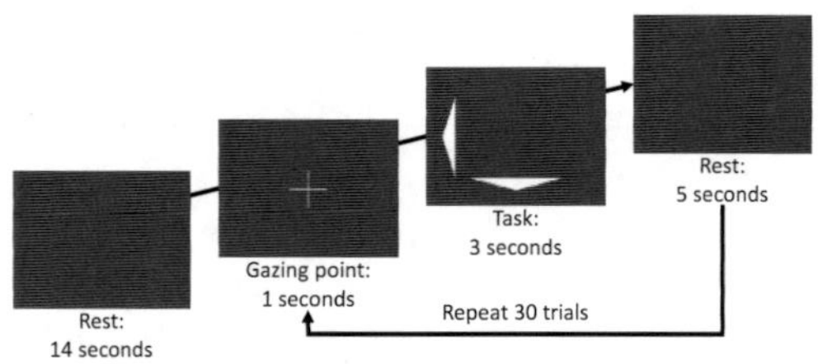

Figure 4: Measurement flow

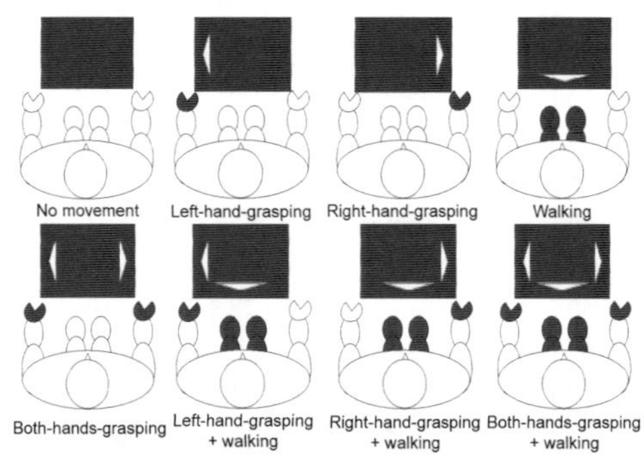

Figure 5: Presentation task and mental task of motor imagery

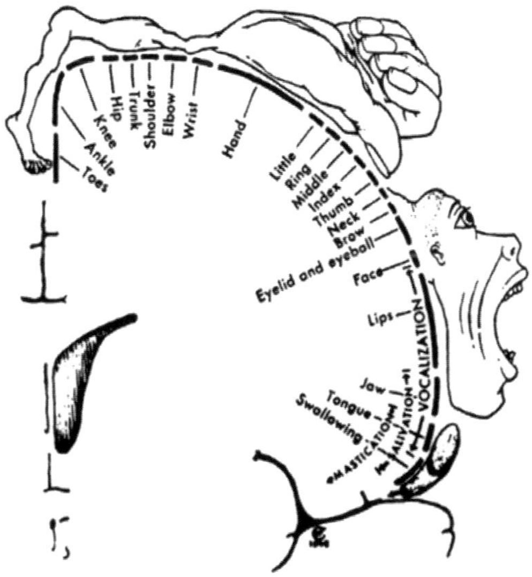

Figure 6: Hemisphere of brain map in motor cortex [4]

performed the left-hand motor imagery in the case of left-pointing triangle, right-hand motor imagery in the case of right-pointing triangle, legs motor imagery in case of down-pointing triangle. The contents of the task were in order of "no movement", "left-hand", "right-hand", "legs", "both-hands", "left-hand + legs", "right-hand + legs", "both-hands + legs" motor imagery. Subjects were instructed to imagine gripping motion at time of hand motor imagery and walk motion at time of legs motor imagery.

The figure 6 shows the hemisphere of brain map in motor cortex created by Penfield et al. This shows the corresponding activation place of each body part. The left half of the body has a part corresponding to the right cortex and the right half of the body has a part corresponding to the left cortex. The activation place of the legs cannot be separated spatially, because it located in longitudinal fissure of cerebrum. Therefore, subjects were performed walking motor imagery by both legs motor imagery.

3. EEG ANALYSIS / CLASSIFICATION

We classified EEG using feature value extracted from measured EEG data. The feature value used frequency information extracted using STFT (Short-Time Fourier Transform). In the classification, two kinds of parallel classification method and OVR classification method were used to classify the multi class. The OVR classification method is based on the idea that multi-task

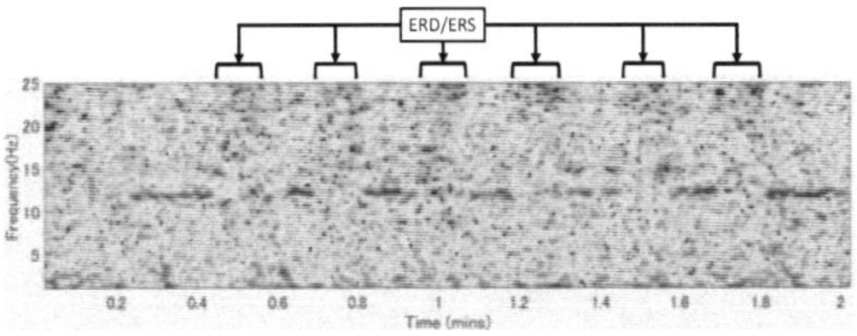

Figure 7: Occurrence of ERD / ERS

specific EEG appears in multi-task motor imagery. The parallel classification method is based on the idea that multi-task EEG are a superposition of single-task EEG of left hand, right hand, and legs.

3.1 Feature value extraction

It is confirmed that EEG's 8-13 Hz power decreases in the corresponding motor cortex by motor imagery [5]. The frequency power is decreased when motor imagery is performed, and the frequency power is increased when motor imagery is stopped. It is called ERD/ERS (Event Related Desynchronization / Synchronization). The spectrogram of figure 7 shows the occurrence of ERD / ERS. The more red, the stronger the frequency power. ERD / ERS occurs at 12 Hz. Therefore, we focused on ERD / ERS and feature value was used frequency power by STFT. Feature value was averaging powers of 8-13 Hz at the time of motor imagery task. The size of the time window was set to 3000ms, and the movement width of the time window was set to 300ms. The number of dimensions of the feature value was D=90 by 10 time-series frequency powers at the time of motor image tasks, measured with 9 electrodes.

3.2 Multi-class classification

OVR (One-Versus-Rest) classification method and Parallel classification method were used for multi-class classification. Both classification methods are based on a binary classification. LDA (Linear Discriminant Analysis) was used for binary classification. LDA is a kind of discrimination method of supervised learning. Eq.1 shows the discriminant function of LDA. $\boldsymbol{x}$ is a feature value extracted from EEG data, $\boldsymbol{a}$ is a discrimination coefficient, and b is a constant term. The discrimination class is determined by the sign of the discrimination function z. The discrimination coefficient $\boldsymbol{a}$ is a vector that maximizes $f\ (\boldsymbol{a})$ (Eq.2). $\boldsymbol{S_B}$ is the covariance matrix between the classes and $\boldsymbol{S_W}$ is the sum of the covariance matrices in the class. Twenty out of 30 motor imagery tasks were taken as teacher data and the remaining 10 times were taken as test data. The verification was used 3-fold cross-validation, and the average classification accuracy of the test data was taken as the CCR.

$$z = \sum_{n=1}^{D} a_n x_n + b \qquad \text{(Eq.1)}$$

$$f(\boldsymbol{a}) = \frac{\boldsymbol{a}^T S_B \boldsymbol{a}}{\boldsymbol{a}^T S_W \boldsymbol{a}} \qquad \text{(Eq.2)}$$

3.2.1 One-Versus-Rest classification method

OVR classification method is a method of creating a plurality of discriminant functions for classifying a target class or other classes. Test data is classified based on the discriminant function created. Figure 8 shows an outline of OVR classification method. In this research, 8 discriminant functions were created. The test data was fitted to these discriminant functions, and the discriminant score taking the maximum value was used as the classification result. An advantage of OVR classification method is possible to exclude motor imagery tasks that cannot be classified.

3.2.2 Parallel classification method

Parallel classification method is a multi-class classification method used by Geng's research [3]. Parallel classification method is to combine classification as to whether or not motor imagery by a single body part. Figure 9 shows the outline of parallel classification method. Eq.3 shows the relationship between the discriminant score z and the signal output by each classifier. Each classifier outputs $signal = 1$ as motor imagery is performed when $z \geq 0$, and outputs $signal = 0$ as motor imagery is not performed when $z < 0$. We created three classifiers, left-hand classifier, right-hand

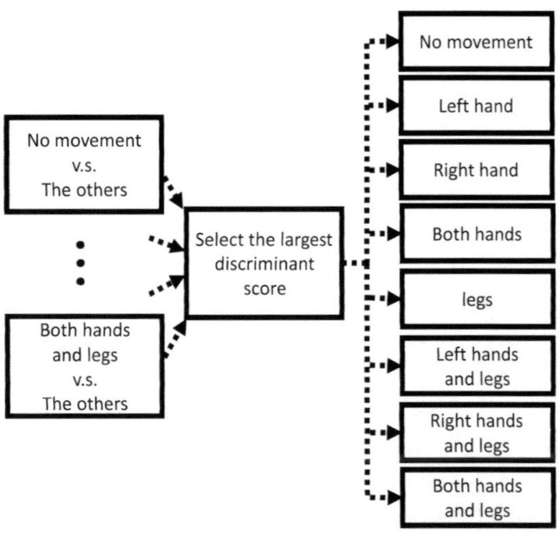

Figure 8: One-Versus-Rest classification method

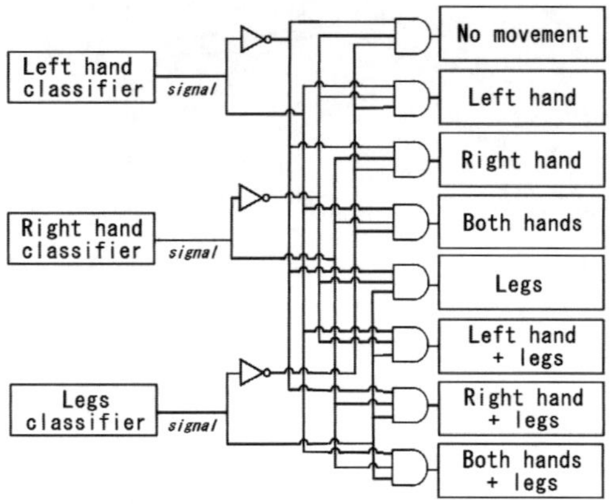

Figure 9: Parallel classification method

classifier, legs classifier. EEG is estimated based on *signal* by three classifiers. For example, EEG is estimated "left-hand + legs" motor imagery when $signal = 1$ in the left hand classifier, $signal = 0$ in the right hand classifier, and $signal = 1$ in the foot classifier. An advantage of Parallel classification method is that the computational cost is low because the number of discriminant functions is small.

$$signal = \begin{cases} \mathbf{1}, & z \geq 0 \\ \mathbf{0}, & z < 0 \end{cases} \qquad \text{(Eq.3)}$$

4. CLASSIFICATION RESULTS

4.1 CCR of 8 EEG states

Figure 10 shows the CCR of 8 EEG states using the two classification methods. The average CCR of OVR classification method was 2.1% higher than CCR of Parallel classification method. All motor imagery tasks exceeded the chance level. However, in the parallel classification method, CCR of the "left-hand + legs" motor imagery was low near the chance level. Focusing on CCR of the multi-task, the OVR classification method showed higher CCR than Parallel classification method.

4.2 Comparison of single-task and multi-task CCR

Figure 11 shows the difference between CCR of the single-task group and CCR of the multi-task group. In Parallel classification method, it was shown that CCR of multi-task group was 5.3% lower CCR the single-task group. On the other hand, in the OVR classification method, it was shown that the CCR of the multi-task group was 1.4% higher than the single-task group.

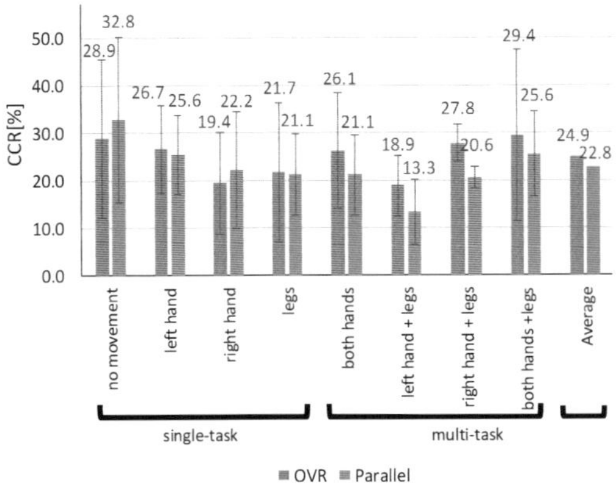

Figure 10: CCR of each motor imagery

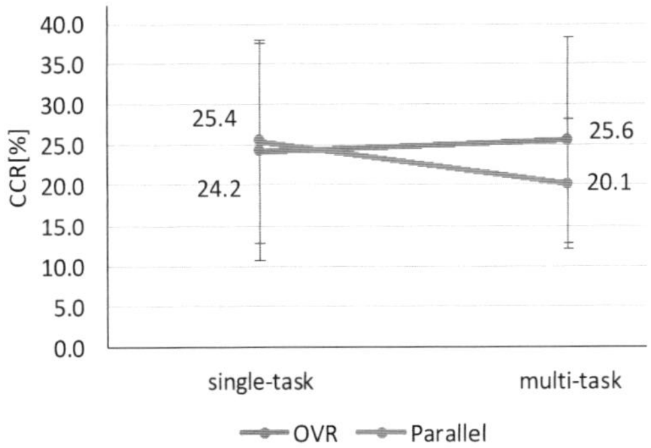

Figure 11: Difference between single-task and multi-task CCR

5. DISCUSSION

5.1 Possibility of multi-task classification

From Figure 10, the CCR of "left hand + leg" motor imagery by the parallel classification method was the lowest as 13.3%. This research classified EEG of 8 states. This was shown to be above the chance level 12.5%. Therefore, it is considered that classification is possible at least in any recall task / classification method.

5.2 Suitable classification method

We discuss two classification methods of OVR classification method and parallel classification method. Regarding the characteristics of the classification method, The OVR classification method is based on the idea that multi-task specific EEG appears in multi-task motor imagery. Also, the parallel classification method is based on the idea that multi-task EEG are a superposition of single-task EEG. In CCR of multi-task motor imagery, Figure 11 shown that the OVR classification method was 5.5% higher than the Parallel classification method. It is suggested that EEG occurring at multi-task motor imagery is not superposition of single-task EEG but EEG peculiar to multi-task motor imagery. Therefore, it is better to use the OVR classification method when classifying EEG of multi-task motor imagery.

5.3 Validity of feature value

We discuss the feature value to improve the CCR. In this research, feature value was used based on the occurrence of ERD/ERS at 8-13 Hz power during motor imagery. Figure 12 shows the change in frequency power in "right-hand" motor imagery tasks by subject 2. The frequency power at the time of motor imagery task is shown by a red line, and the frequency power of 3 seconds before and after motor imagery task is shown by a blue line. The values were the average values after normalized frequency power of each trial. In the FC3, C3, CP3, C4 electrodes, it has transitioned to 0 or more at no motor imagery task, and it has transitioned to 0 or less at motor imagery task. This is ERD / ERS. The feature value was extracted only the frequency power at the motor imagery task. However, the extracted feature quantity is already in a state where the power has been transitioning to 0 or less. Therefore, it is impossible to confirm the variation of the frequency power. It is considered to be due to motor imagery performed even outside the task time.

Therefore, we classified EEG using not only the frequency information of the task presentation time but

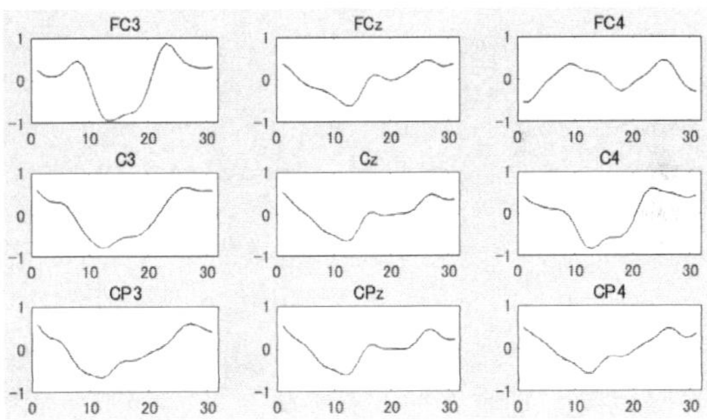

Figure 12: "right-hand" frequency change in subject 2

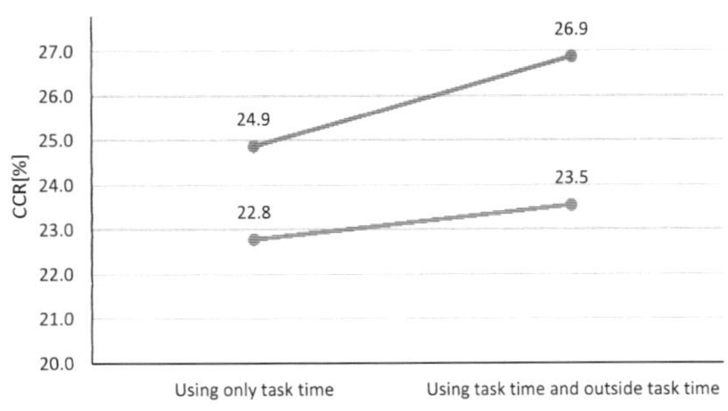

Figure 13: Difference in CCR due to changing feature value

also the frequency information of 3 seconds before and after the task presentation time. Frequency information of 30 samples was taken out from one electrode and task. Then, in order to make the number of dimensions D = 90, 30 samples were downsampled to 10 samples. Figure 13 shows the classification result. CCR was improved 2% in the OVR classification method and 0.7% CCR in the parallel classification method. To improve the CCR, we consider that it is necessary to use not only the frequency power during motor imagery but also that one during other than motor imagery time.

6. CONCLUSION

In this research, we attempted to classify a multi-task motor imagery to add the number of MI-BCI commands. Multi-task classification was used two kinds of classification methods OVR classification method and Parallel classification method. As a result, multi-task classification has been shown to be possible, because the CCR was 26.9% using OVR classification method and 23.5% using Parallel classification method.

In using OVR classification method, CCR of multi- task didn't decrease to compare with that of single-task. Therefore, it was suggested that it is useful to use OVR classification method for multi-task classification.

In the future, it is necessary to improve CCR toward practical application. In this research, the frequency power at the presenting task was used as the feature value. However, it was impossible to extract the variation of the frequency power. Therefore, improvement of CCR is expected by using the frequency power before and after motor imagery by changing the time window. In the future, we need to examine feature value used for classification.

REFFERENCES

[1] Tatsuya OKABE, Kentaro YAMADA, Masahiro KIMURA, Akihiro TODA, Masaaki SATO, Okito YAMASHITA, Yusuke TAKEDA, Mitsuo KAWATO.: Brain Machine Interface Technology Enabling Control of Machine by Human Thought Alone, Honda R&D Technical Review Vol.22 No.2 (October 2010).

[2] B. Xia, D. Xiao, J. Li, H. Yang, C. Wang.: Motor imagery BCI-based robot arm system, Proceedings on Seventh International Conference on Natural Computation, pp. 181–184(2011).

[3] Geng T, Gan JQ, Dyson M, Tsui CS, Sepulveda F.: A novel design of 4-class bci using two binary classifiers and parallel mental tasks, Computational Intelligence and Neuroscience (2008).

[4] Penfield W, Rasmussen T. The cerebral cortex of man: a clinical study of localization of function, New York: Macmillan (1950).

[5] G. Pfurtscheller, F. H. Lopes da Silva.: Event related EEG/MEG synchronization and desynchronization, basic principles (1999).

ISASE-MAICS 2018

Visualization of ERD/ERS on leg Motor Imagery

Ryo MACHIDA*, Hisaya TANAKA **

* *Kogakuin University, 1-24-2 Nishi-Shinjuku, Shinjuku-ku, Tokyo 163-8677, Japan*
em17017@ns.kogakuin.ac.jp
** *Kogakuin University, 1-24-2 Nishi-Shinjuku, Shinjuku-ku, Tokyo 163-8677, Japan*
hisaya@cc.kogakuin.ac.jp

Abstract: Brain computer Interface (BCI) is the interface that is able to control the computers or machines without physical movement by reading User's intent from specific electroencephalogram (EEG) pattern. Event Related Desynchronization (ERD) / Event Related Synchronization (ERS) is one of the specific EEG pattern. ERD is caused the decrease of EEG frequency power in alpha (8-12Hz) and beta (12-30Hz) bands on the motor area related to the body parts by preparing movement, actual movement, or Motor Imagery (MI). In contrast to ERD, ERS is caused the increase of EEG frequency power in a similar way and bands. There are many researches of BCI using ERD/ERS because this is useful as rehabilitation and logical switch information in the controller, etc. We also have the research significance to realize the interface for patients can't walk or VR-walking machine using BCI, therefore, leg MI was used about the kind of MI. The BCI related to leg get close to realize by enhancing the detection accuracy on leg MI. To enhance the detection accuracy, we focused on quantifying ERD/ERS. However, current quantifying is not suitable for online analysis because analysist need to set reference data by selecting the data ERD/ERS appeared. Therefore, ERD/ERS detection algorithm was proposed for online analysis in this research. On the proposing that algorithm, we used alpha band (8-12Hz).

Keywords: *BCI, ERD, ERS, Motor Imagery, ERD/ERS*

1. INTRODUCTION

Brain computer Interface (BCI) is the interface that is able to control the computers or machines without physical movement by reading User's intent from specific electroencephalogram (EEG) pattern. Event Related Desynchronization (ERD) / Event Related Synchronization (ERS) is one of the specific EEG pattern. ERD is caused the decrease of EEG frequency power in alpha (8-12Hz) and beta (12-30Hz) bands on the motor area related to the body parts by preparing movement, actual movement, or Motor Imagery (MI). In contrast to ERD, ERS is caused the increase of EEG frequency power in a similar way and bands [1] [2]. There are many researches of BCI using ERD/ERS because this is useful as rehabilitation and logical switch information in the controller, etc. We also have the research significance to realize the interface for patients can't walk or VR-walking machine using BCI, therefore, leg MI was used about the kind of MI. The BCI related to leg get close to realize by enhancing the detection accuracy on leg MI that man imagine one's movement like walking.

Currently, it's known how to quantify ERD/ERS as the standard calculation of Pfurtscheller and Aranibar [3] [4]. ERD/ERS calculation to quantify is following. EEG is squared after filtering to become alpha (8-12Hz) or beta (12-30Hz) band, and the obtained-squared EEG frequency power is averaged in all sections that subjects trying MI as subject's data. Similarly, subjects' EEG frequency power is also averaged as reference data in only the selected sections from all subjects trying MI sections that ERD/ERS is observed clearly. After that, ERD/ERS is quantified by the calculation of Relative Amplitude (RA) using the calculated subject's data and reference data [3] [4].

However, ERD/ERS quantification (In this research, calculating RA is called quantifying ERD/ERS or ERD/ERS quantification.) is not suitable for online analysis because analysist must set reference data for the calculation of RA beforehand. Therefore, in this research, we aimed to propose auto ERD/ERS detection algorithm in arbitrary sections, this enable to detect the reference data. We proposed ERD/ERS detection algorithm, and compared to the results by simple algorithm using half of subjects' maximum value. On the proposing that algorithm, we used alpha band (8-12Hz) because the latency of ERD/ERS in beta band (12-30Hz) is longer than that in alpha band (8-12Hz) [3], short latency speed is so important for online.

2. EEG MEASUREMENT

2.1 Measurement environment

Our experiment was conducted according to the "Kogakuin University Research ethics review for human subjects H25-6". Eight healthy subjects (mean age 23 years) participated in the EEG measurement.

Figure 1 shows BCI configuration. The system (BCIsys) that is created by MATLAB and SIMULINK was used for measurement and analysis. The sampling frequency was 256Hz. On the recording, active dry electrodes (g.tec, g.SAHARAelectrode) was used. Measured EEG on each electrode were rounded up and treated as individual by channel box (g.tec, g.GAMMAbox), and amplified by biological amplifier (g.tec, g.USBamp). EEG electrodes arrangement is based on International 10-20 system. A1(left ear lobe) was used as the standard electrode, FPz was used as the ground electrode, Cz was used as the exploring electrode.

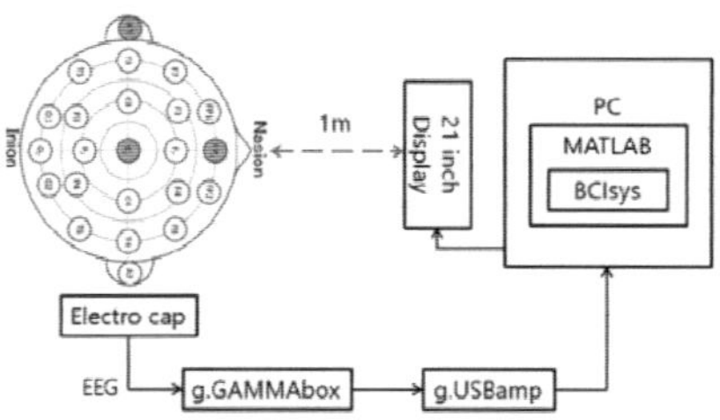

Figure 1: BCI Configuration

2.2 MI-mental task

The subjects were required to repeat relax and MI states according to the task information shown on the PC display while sitting in a chair. Figure 2 shows MI-mental task that subjects were required. Subjects conducted MI of knee up and down having the imagination they are walking. Figure 3 shows the flow of mental task information. As shown in Figure 3, the subjects waited for 10 seconds at first, after that, they repeated MI and relax states respectively every 10 seconds for 110 seconds. Total record time was 120 seconds, this record was conducted twice for all subjects. Relax task and MI-mental task were displayed blue and red color respectively to subjects.

To avoid blink artifact in the sections of MI-mental task, the subjects resisted blink during the MI state by the instruction before experiment. For the same reason, they looked at the display without moving their eyes around.

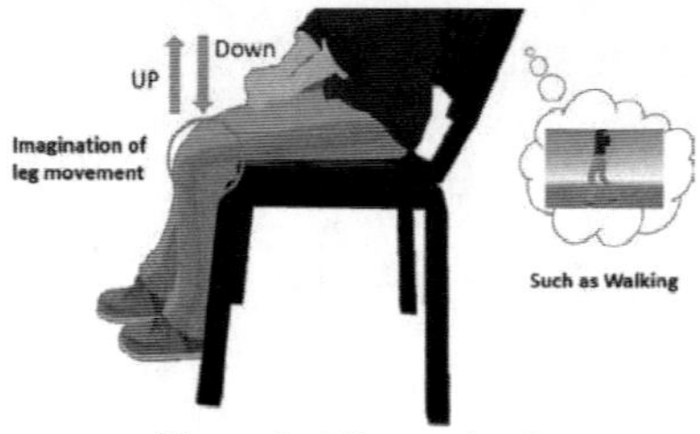

Figure 2: MI-mental task

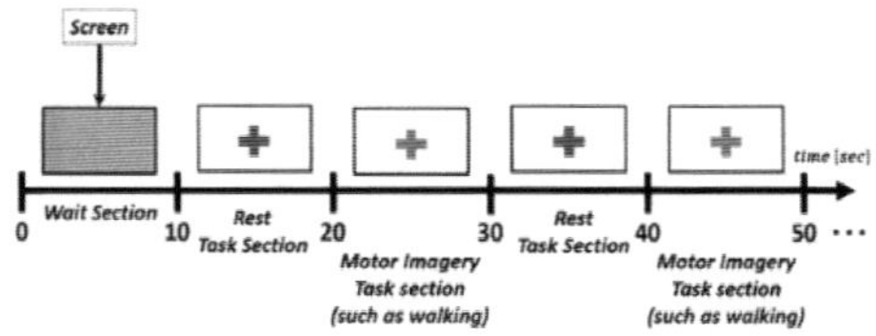

Figure 3: Time flow of mental task information

3. ERD/ERS DETECTION ALGORITHM

3.1 Time-frequency analysis

To observe EEG power spectrum, short-time Fourier transform (STFT) that is the one of time–frequency analysis method, and Band Power Method (BPM) were used. BPM calculates the average of power in a given frequency band after STFT [5].

Table 1 shows STFT parameters setting. Rectangular window was used as window function. Equation (1) shows the feature quantity that EEG frequency power: $EP(t)$ is obtained at time t using the BPM.

$$EP(t) = \sum_{f=f_1}^{f_2} Power(t,f)\ [\mu V^2] \quad (1)$$

t is time, and f is frequency. Here, f_1 is 7, f_2 is 13. Further, $Power(T,f)$ is a function for calculating the power of f (Hz) at time t.

Table 1: STFT parameters

Parameter	Setting
Window function	Rectangular window
Window length (samples)	256
Window displacement (samples)	1

3.2 ERD/ERS detection method for online

ERD and ERS is detected alternately in online. In this part, ERD and ERS detection algorithm is shown.

3.2.1 ERD detection algorithm

The flow of the algorithm is shown on the following.

1. Renewing Maximum of $EP(t)$: $MAP(t)$
2. ERD detection using $MAP(t)$
3. Loop (1~2) until ERD is detected

Mathematically, these are shown as follows.

$$MAP(t) = \begin{cases} EP(t) \\ (\textit{if } MAP(t) < EP(t)) \\ MAP(t) \\ (\textbf{\textit{otherwise}}) \end{cases} [\mu V^2] \quad (1)$$

$$ERD(t) = \frac{MAP(t) - EP(t)}{MAP(t)} \quad (2)$$

In this research, ERD was detected when $ERD(t)$ is more than 1/2. The initial value of $MAP(t)$ was decided to $EP(t)$ on the time just detected ERS. First initial value of $MAP(t)$ was decided to 0.001.

3.2.2 ERS detection algorithm

4. Renewing Minimum of $EP(t)$: $MIP(t)$
5. ERS detection using $MAP(t)$ and $MIP(t)$
6. Loop (4~5) until ERS is detected

Mathematically, these are shown as follows.

$$MIP(t) = \begin{cases} EP(t) \\ (\textit{if } MIP(t) > EP(t)) \\ MIP(t) \\ (\textbf{\textit{otherwise}}) \end{cases} [\mu V^2] \quad (3)$$

$$ERS(t) = \frac{EP(t) - MIP(t)}{MAP(t)} \quad (4)$$

In similar to ERD, ERS was also detected when $ERS(t)$ is more than 1/2. The initial value of $MIP(t)$ was decided to $EP(t)$ on the time just detected ERD.

4. RESULTS

4.1 Evalutation

To evaluate the Proposed Method, Proposed Method was compared to the simple ERD/ERS detection algorithm. Simple that algorithm detect ERD when measured EEG frequency power exceeded the half of maximum that power on the whole in each subject's data. Similarly, ERS is also detected when measured EEG frequency power fall behind maximum that power in each subject's data. This algorithm is called Half Maximum Method in this research. Note that Half Maximum Method is not able to use online analysis because we can't know maximum that power in subject's data until the measurement finish.

To compare to Half Maximum Method, EEG frequency power was averaged in each MI-mental task section and in each 5 seconds before and after MI-mental task section on Proposed Method and Half Maximum Method, in case that Detected MI time in MI-mental task section [sec] that is the time during the section from the detected ERD to ERS in MI-mental task section exceeded arbitrary set value [sec]. As the set value, 0, 1, 2, 3, 4, 5, 6, 7, 8, 9, and 10 [sec] were used in this research.

4.2 Analysis

Figure 4 shows the analysis process on Proposed Method using one of the subjects' data. Horizontal axis in all plots is time [sec]. First plot is the filtered EEG after using alpha band filter (8-12Hz). Second plot is EEG frequency power calculated by using STFT and BPM, and the moving average was used for the calculated that power on the window length is 3 seconds to visualize in this research. Third plot is the detected timing ERD/ERS. ERD detection timing become 1, ERS detection timing become -1, and normal time is 0. The section from the detected ERD to ERS in MI-mental task become Detected MI time in MI-mental task section. Fourth plot is the decided results on the data, these results are decided when Detected MI time in MI-mental task section exceeded arbitrary set value (On figure 4, set value is 8 sec). After the analysis of all subjects' data, each decided results were averaged over all subjects every set value. Note that, before average on Proposed Method and Half Maximum Method, the normalization was conducted using maximum value in each decided results.

As the example, Figure 5 shows the averaged-decided results over all subjects in case that set value is 8 [sec]. Vertical axis is EEG frequency power (normalized before average), horizontal axis is time [sec]. Table 2 shows the decided results in each MI-mental task section in each subject's data. Because each subjects conducted MI-mental task twice in measurement, the data was shown as Sub[Subject's Name]-[Number of times]. The data that background color is gray were not used in analysis because it is observed that data has noise clearly. Decided results were marked by ○, and not decided results were marked by × in Table 2.

Figure 6 and Figure 7 show the averaged EEG frequency power in the decided results for all set value (0-10 [sec]) on Proposed Method and on Half Maximum Method respectively. Vertical axis and horizontal axis is similar to Figure 5. Table 3 and Table 4 show averaged EEG frequency power during MI or not MI-mental task on each set value in Proposed Method and in Half Maximum Method respectively. Table 5 shows ERD/ERS detection rate in MI-mental task over all subjects' data every set value (0-10 [sec]). ERD/ERS detection rate : DR calculated from the number of the decided results and the number of MI-mental task by equation (5). Comparison to Half Maximum Method was conducted by these figures and tables.

$$DR = \frac{\textit{number of the decided results}}{\textit{number of MI mental task}} * 100 \quad (5)$$

Table 2: Decided results in each MI-mental task
(Decided : ○, Not Decided : ×, Set value: 8 [sec])

	1st try	2nd try	3rd try	4th try	5th try
SubA-1					
SubA-2	○	×	○	○	○
SubB-1					
SubB-2	×	×	○	×	○
SubC-1					
SubC-2					
SubD-1	×	○	○	○	×
SubD-2	×	×	○	○	×
SubE-1					
SubE-2					
SubF-1	×	×	×	×	×
SubF-2	○	×	×	×	×
SubG-1	×	○	○	×	○
SubG-2					
SubH-1	×	×	×	○	○
SubH-2	○	×	×	×	○

Table 5: ERD/ERS detection rate in MI-mental task over all subjects' data every set value (0-10 [sec])

		Proposed Method	Half Maximum Method
Set value (0-100 [sec])	0	100.00%	100.00%
	1	91.11%	95.56%
	2	82.22%	82.22%
	3	82.22%	77.78%
	4	71.11%	68.89%
	5	68.89%	57.78%
	6	60.00%	48.89%
	7	53.33%	44.44%
	8	48.89%	42.22%
	9	44.44%	31.11%
	10	No decided results	No decided results
AVERAGE		70.22%	64.89%

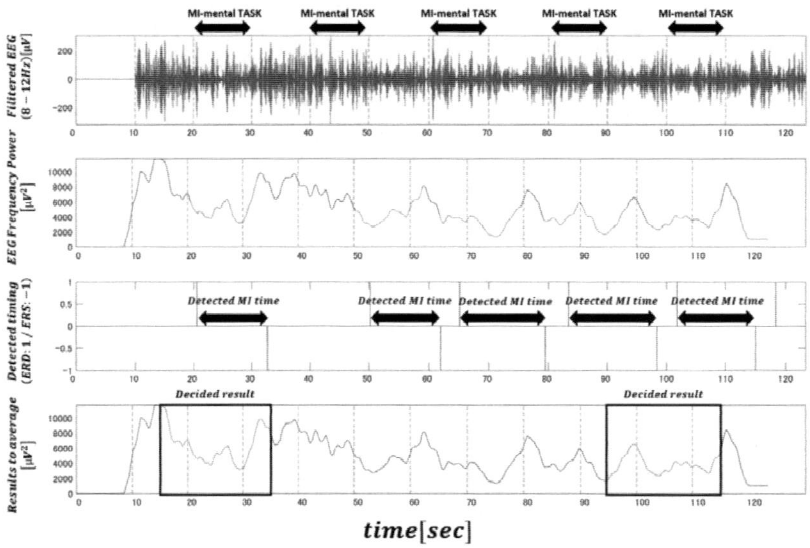

Figure 4: Analysis process on Proposed Method using one of the subjects' data (In case that set value is 8 [sec])

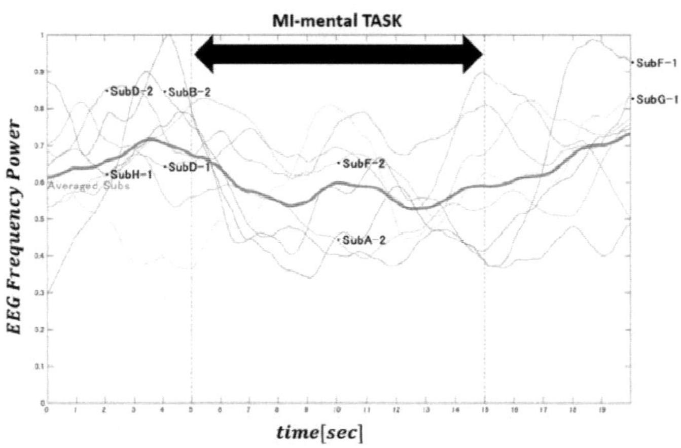

Figure 5: Averaged-decided results over all subjects

(In case that set value is 8 [sec])

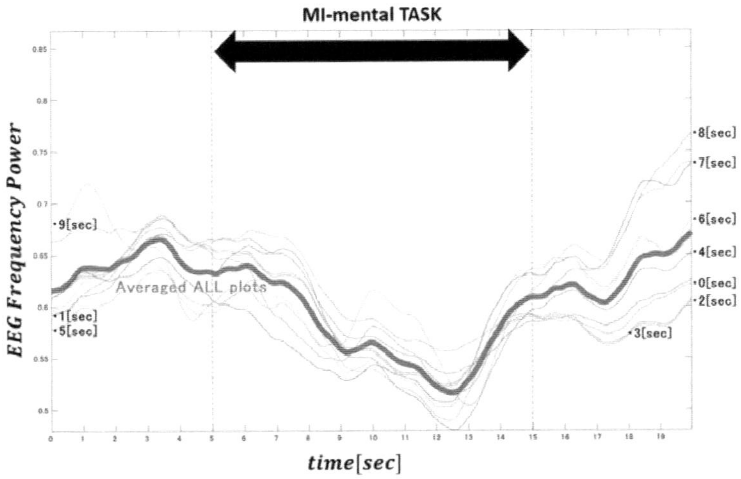

Figure 6: Averaged EEG frequency power in the decided results over all subjects for all set value (0-10 [sec]) on Proposed Method

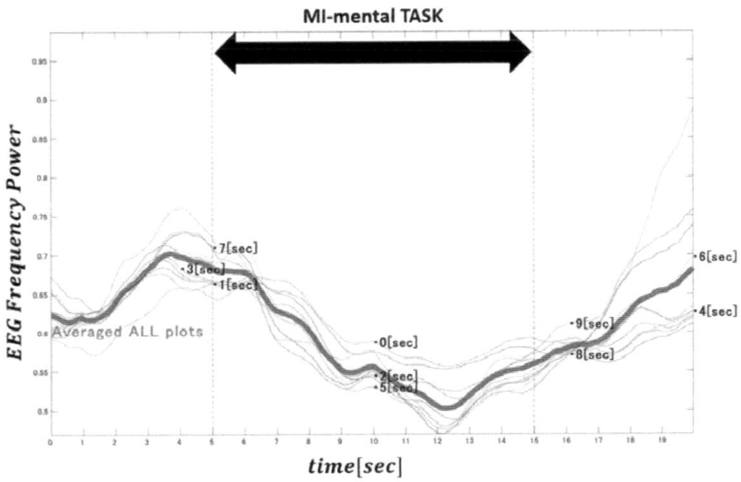

Figure 7: Averaged EEG frequency power in the decided results over all subjects for all set value (0-10 [sec]) on Half Maximum Method

Table 3: Averaged EEG frequency power during MI or not MI-mental task in each set value on Proposed Method

	Averaged EEG frequency power [μV^2] for set value [sec] in MI or not MI										
Set value	0	1	2	3	4	5	6	7	8	9	10	S.D.
MI-mental task	0.616	0.617	0.615	0.617	0.629	0.626	0.631	0.652	0.672	0.666	No decided results	0.022
Not MI-mental task	0.606	0.591	0.580	0.582	0.571	0.567	0.568	0.558	0.573	0.579	No decided results	0.014
Difference	0.010	0.026	0.035	0.035	0.058	0.059	0.063	0.093	0.100	0.087		

Keywords: BCI, ERD, ERS, Motor Imagery, ERD/ERS

Table 4: Averaged EEG frequency power during MI or not MI-mental task in each set value on Half Maximum Method

	Averaged EEG frequency power [μV^2] for set value [sec] in MI or not MI										
Set value	0	1	2	3	4	5	6	7	8	9	10	S.D.
MI-mental task	0.616	0.612	0.618	0.626	0.632	0.606	0.639	0.654	0.662	0.686	No decided results	0.026
Not MI-mental task	0.606	0.598	0.575	0.574	0.570	0.557	0.564	0.559	0.553	0.572	No decided results	0.017
Difference	0.010	0.014	0.042	0.052	0.062	0.049	0.076	0.095	0.110	0.114		

5. DISCUSSION

Figure 6 and Table 3 indicate that the difference of EEG frequency power between MI-mental task and not MI-mental task become larger as set value gets higher. Similarly, Figure 7 and Table 4 also indicated that. This shows ERD/ERS was caused surely by that subjects conducted MI, and detected by Proposed Method and Half Maximum Method.

As shown in Table 5, the difference between Proposed Method and Half Maximum Method was appeared on that rate more than 4 [sec], although ERD/ERS detection rate is almost same to 3 [sec]. Therefore, the averaged ERD/ERS detection rate on Proposed Method and Half Maximum Method was 70.22% and 64.89% respectively. This fact indicated the Proposed Method has potential to detect much more ERD/ERS than Half Maximum Method. Additionally, as mentioned in 4.1 Evaluation, Half Maximum Method is not able to use online analysis because we can't know maximum EEG frequency power in subject's data until the measurement finish.

It is thought that Proposed Method would be useful as reference extracting reference data, ERD/ERS is quantified by the calculation of Relative Amplitude (RA) using the calculated subject's data and reference data as mentioned 1. INTRODUCTION [3] [4].

6. CONCLUSION

We have the research significance to realize the interface for patients can't walk or VR-walking machine using BCI, therefore, leg MI was used about the kind of MI. The BCI related to leg get close to realize by enhancing the detection accuracy on leg MI. Therefore we focused on quantifying ERD/ERS.

The primary aim of this research is proposing ERD/ERS detection algorithm is enable to serve the problem that analysist must set reference data by selecting the data ERD/ERS appeared to quantify ERD/ERS. In this research, we proposed ERD/ERS detection algorithm, and compared to the results by simple algorithm (called Half Maximum Method) to evaluate. On the proposing that algorithm, we used alpha band (8-12Hz).

As the results, it was demonstrated that Proposed Method is possible to detect ERD/ERS in online analysis and Proposed Method has potential to detect much more ERD/ERS than Half Maximum Method. Averaged ERD/ERS detection rate on Proposed Method and Half Maximum Method was 70.22% and 64.89% respectively.

.

ACKNOWLEDGMENTS

This work was supported by Grant-in-Aid for Scientific Research(C) 15K00762.

REFFERENCES

[1] Pfurtscheller, Gert, et al. "Separability of EEG signals recorded during right and left motor imagery using adaptive autoregressive parameters." IEEE transactions on Rehabilitation Engineering 6.3 (1998): 316-325.

[2] Pfurtscheller, G., et al. "EEG-based discrimination between imagination of right and left hand movement." Electroencephalography and clinical Neurophysiology 103.6 (1997): 642-651.

[3] Sandhya, B., C. Shendkar, and M. Mahadevappa. "Single channel event related (de) synchronization (erd/ers) analysis of motor execution in stroke affected foot drop subjects." Medical Imaging, m-Health and Emerging Communication Systems (MedCom), 2014 International Conference on. IEEE, 2014.

[4] Pfurtscheller, Gert, and A. Aranibar. "Evaluation of event-related desynchronization (ERD) preceding and following voluntary self-paced movement." Clinical Neurophysiology 46.2 (1979): 138-146.

ISASE-MAICS 2018

Electronic Medical Record Visualization for Patient Progress Tracking

Chau VO[1], Tru CAO[1,2], Nam DOAN[1], Son TU[1], Anh NGUYEN[3], Binh NGUYEN[3], and Bao HO[3]

[1] *Ho Chi Minh City University of Technology, Ho Chi Minh City, Vietnam*
chauvtn@hcmut.edu.vn, tru@cse.hcmut.edu.vn, nhatnam.hcmut@gmail.com, ttson.cse@gmail.com
[2] *Eastern Washington University, Spokane, Washington State, United States of America*
tcao2@ewu.edu
[3] *John von Neumann Institute, Vietnam National University, Ho Chi Minh City, Vietnam*
anhngd93@gmail.com, nvbmed@gmail.com, bao.ho@jvn.edu.vn

Abstract: Patient progress tracking is important to a doctor in a treatment process. In order to have enough information about a patient and the treatment made for the patient, a doctor has to view a lot of medical data about symptoms, test results, drugs and their dosages in a period of time. With electronic medical records, it is convenient for the doctor to view and search for any information he/she needs as compared to paper medical records. It would be even better if all the related electronic medical records over time of each patient are visualized appropriately to support the doctor in patient progress tracking. Therefore, our EMRVisualization system is proposed as a web-based application on tablet computers for visualizing all the related medical data in an integrative manner. The system provides an interactive visualization with accurate data at different detail levels, quick access and convenience for a doctor to keep track of the progress of each patient over time. Its demonstration with the real data of gastroenterological Vietnamese patients in Thong Nhat Hospital, Ho Chi Minh City, Vietnam, has been conducted and showed that every interaction of a doctor can be accomplished in at most two steps.

Keywords: *Medical Treatment, Temporal Data, Interaction Method, Tablet Computer, User-Computer Interface*

1. INTRODUCTION

Medical data visualization has received much attention all over the world due to its usefulness and significance as discussed in [12]. The existing visualization systems are often divided into two groups: the systems in [1, 2, 5, 7, 9-11] for single patient-related visualization, and the ones in [3, 4, 6-8] for patient group-related visualization.

Those systems have been proposed with a diversity of purposes. For example, [2] provided a general practitioner with a mobile electronic medical record (EMR) application for house visits; [3] supported a doctor to find frequency trends of keywords in unstructured texts of nursing narratives; [5] generated communication facilities about prostate cancer health risk for patients and doctors; [6] discovered patient groups for better patient care; [7] supported clinical decision making in psychotherapy; [9] aimed at visual analytics; [10] supported the therapy of diabetic patients; [11] analyzed clinical notes for clinical preparation task; [16] supported patient progress tracking using group-based tracking graph analysis.

In the aforementioned systems, a web-based interface was often developed. Desktop or laptop computers for end-user's operations were used for system deployment except for tablet computers in [1, 11] and mobile phones in [2]. Although tablet computers and mobile phones are more portable than desktop computers, their small screens require an efficient user interface's design.

In our work, a visualization system named EMRVisualization is proposed with medical data visualization on tablet computers for patient progress tracking. Our system provides doctors with the functionalities for extracting and visualizing clinical symptom data, test results, and drugs and their dosages over time in a treatment process in an integrative manner. More calculation is also made for derived information about the patient progress, via calculating differences in test results and about the drugs and dosages that the patient has taken for a certain period. A demonstration has been conducted for doctors on the real data of gastroenterological Vietnamese patients in Thong Nhat Hospital, Ho Chi Minh City.

Compared to the existing works, the domain and tracking purpose of our system are different from those of the systems in [1, 2, 5, 7, 9, 10, 11]. Such differences lead to our distinct visualization design for presentation and interaction on tablet computers. Besides, our work considers and visualizes unstructured symptom data, which are common in healthcare, in a quantitative approach, instead of a keyword-based approach in [3]. Moreover, in our system, medical data are supported in various types.

2. USER REQUIREMENTS

Closely working with the gastroenterological doctors in the hospital, we discover both functional and non-functional user requirements about the need of visualizing EMRs for patient progress tracking.

For functional user requirements, the medical laws and regulations in the hospital are examined. The treatment process and the duty of a doctor in the process are studied. Expectations of a doctor who is using a computer-based health information system are considered. Particularly in a treatment process, a doctor has to record all of the clinical symptoms of a disease that a patient is being diagnosed with. The doctor may have some tests done for the patient so that more information can be obtained and analyzed for the disease and medication. Drugs and their dosages can be then decided.

After the patient takes the prescribed medicine, the doctor visits the patient and repeats the treatment process with recording the symptoms, giving some further tests if needed, and medication accordingly. The patient progress is tracked over time so that the doctor can make sure that the drugs can be prescribed for the disease adaptively and effectively until the patient gets better.

As a result, symptoms, test results, and medication need to be visualized in that sequential and integrative manner. In addition, the doctor wants to know how better the patient can get if the drugs are used in a certain time period and how much the drugs should be taken in that period. Besides, information extraction on demand is desired so that the doctor can have a particular view on the status of the patient in treatment over time.

With these functional requirements, our system focuses on visualizing the data related to symptoms, test results, and medication of each patient. Their temporal aspect is also considered. Furthermore, the system concentrates on interaction to provide medical information on demand via selection, search, panel collapsing, chart collapsing, and closing commands. Derived information via calculation on test results, drugs, and their dosages is also prepared.

For non-functional requirements, accuracy with different detail levels, quick access, and convenient operations are given and discussed. Different detail levels imply the data of each patient in the collection level and in the individual level. At both levels, the visualized data must be the same as those in the real medical records. For this requirement, our system needs data extraction from the real medical records correctly. It also needs to visualize the extracted data at these different detail levels.

Quick access means that a doctor can have access to any element of interest as fast as possible. Thus, from the perspective of system development, every interaction between a doctor and our system needs to be designed with the minimum number of required steps.

Convenient operations enable a doctor to use the system in a treatment process in an easy manner with no distraction. It shows the usability of our system in practice and, at the same time, the feasibility of a computer-based application in the medical domain. In order to meet this requirement, all of the factors of a standard information system have been considered. They are hardware, software, information, network, and people.

Particularly, we choose an implementation on a tablet computer on the end-user's side. This application is connected via the Internet with the application and database server for any request on demand. With a tablet computer and wireless connection, a doctor can carry the tablet computer to anywhere at anytime, and has access to any information of each patient during a treatment process, instead of a collection of paper medical records. Moreover, the interface needs to be familiar to doctors so that they can operate the system smoothly. Thanks to the participating gastroenterological doctors at Thong Nhat Hospital in Ho Chi Minh City, our system's design is completed with their considerable assistance.

3. THE PROPOSED SYSTEM

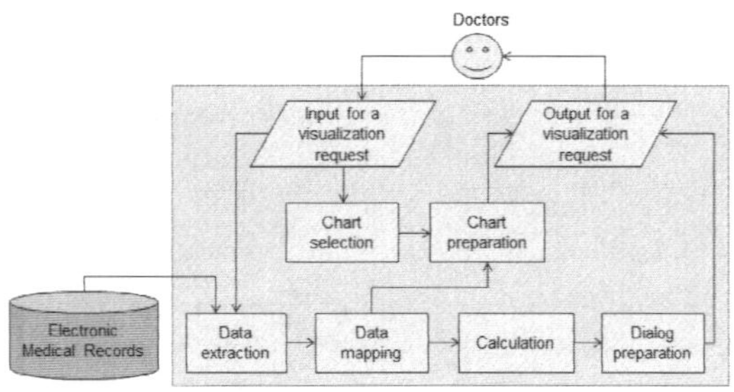

Figure 1: Architecture of our EMRVisualization system

In this section, we propose the EMRVisualization system to support doctors to keep track of patient progress in their treatment process. By tracking, a doctor can figure out the treatment effectiveness as soon as possible. For this purpose, our system development starts with user requirements in the real world so that its design can be made as a bridge between doctors and computers with EMRs.

Figure 1 shows the architecture of our system with its main modules. In our system, doctors are end-users. EMRs are assumed to be available in the database for data extraction.

3.1 Data and their types

Treatment notes are rich of medical data that are important and suitable for being used in tracking the progress of each patient. They contain the details of clinical symptoms, test results, and medication that a doctor gave a patient. These data are stored in a database.

As typed in the database, medical data of symptoms can be classified into the following groups:

- Discrete data: binary, categorical, ordinal, or
- Continuous data: numeric.

For test results, a numeric value of each variable in a test is provided with its normal range. Medication is given by a doctor. Drugs and their dosages are temporally prescribed. The doctor wants to see the relatedness between such medical data and the changes of symptoms and test results in patient progress tracking.

3.2 Visualization design

a. Layout of the system's single screen interface

In our system, single screen interface is used to give doctors effortless access to integrated data of symptoms, tests, and medication on a tablet computer. Figure 2 shows the layout of our single screen interface in English.

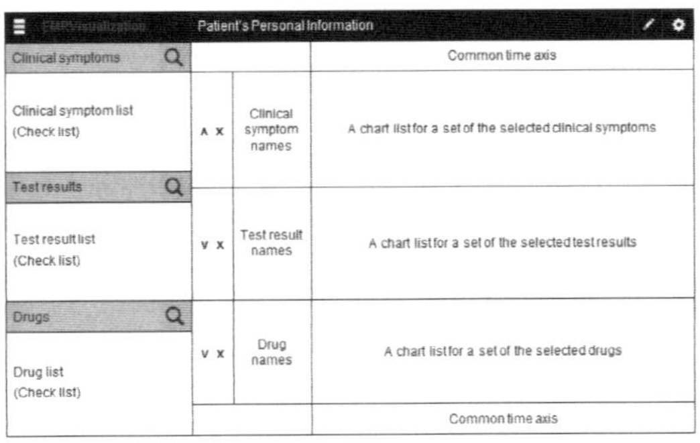

Figure 2: Layout of our system's single screen interface

In this single screen interface, on the right side is the largest main panel for visualization of clinical symptoms, test results, and drugs and their dosages over time. On the left side is the smaller panel for selection with check lists and searching for the clinical symptoms, test results, and drugs. We also have a list of icons for different interactions presented in Section 3.3.c.

b. Charts

For specific visualization, line and bar charts are used by default. Both symptom and test data are essential signals for a treatment process. Their changes inform the effectiveness of a treatment. In order to present their values and changes, line charts are chosen.

Besides, different marker types are used. Filled circles (•) are used for numeric data, filled triangles (▲) for binary data, and filled squares (■) for categorical data. They have a textual description for each numeric value. By contrast, bar charts are chosen for medication so that what medicine and how much the patient took can be clarified. Nevertheless, other charts can be selected alternatively upon user's desire using the setting control.

The time axes of all the charts are united into common time axes. We place one common time axis on the top and another one at the bottom of the right panel. They are with explicit time points at the finest time granularity up to the temporal aspect of visualized medical data. For each chart, a grid is embedded so that data points can be aligned with their values and time axes.

c. Interaction

In our design, interaction is important to the system's usability. It enables and then motivates doctors to communicate with the system. Characteristics of a tablet computer's screen are thus examined and the design is optimized with the best practices.

For a tablet computer with a limited touchable screen space, our system avoids using its keyboard as much as possible. Instead, click events are exploited for interaction by touching. In order to catch doctors' attention, popular icons with conventional meanings are used as follows:

- Icon: a collapsing control to hide the left panel and enlarge the right panel for larger charts of medical data. This is useful for doctors to view data in a limited space.
- Icon: a note control to open the note dialog and provide a place where a doctor can take a note on the patient's status, after viewing medical data in treatment.
- Icon: a setting control to open the chart setting dialog and allow changing the default design choices.
- Icon: a checking control in a check list to select an item of interest in a symptom, test, or drug list. A chart corresponding to the selected item is then visualized in the right panel. If the list is long, a scrollbar appears and helps a doctor to explore all items over the list.
- Icon: an un-checking control in a check list to de-select an item in a symptom, test, or drug list. This control makes the existing chart of the item disappear in the right panel and the item de-selected from the list.
- Icon: a search control for an item of interest in a symptom, test, or drug list. This control provides a quick access to a shorter list of items of interest if the original list is long. Only the items that contain the search string inputted by a doctor are in the check list for selection.
- Icon: a hiding control, aka a chart collapsing control, to hide a selected chart temporarily in the right panel. This is useful for an application on a tablet computer as providing more space for viewing other charts.

- Icon ✔: an un-hiding control to unhide a selected chart and make it appear in the right panel for being reviewed.
- Icon ✖: a closing control to remove a selected chart from the list. This control is equivalent to the un-checking control in the left panel. However, it provides a quick access to de-select an item of interest and remove its chart after its data have been viewed.

In addition to the interactions behind the icons, interactions are also integrated into charts and caught via click events. By default, time series data for each symptom, each variable in a test, or each drug are visualized in a chart at the collection level.

In order to make each chart less complicated with data labels, no detail of each value is shown in a chart. Therefore, visualization at the individual level is provided by a single-click event on a chart. Touching a data point in a chart brings the details of that point, which consist of its timestamp, marker, value, unit, and description if any.

For more derived information, a doctor can interact with a test or drug chart using a double-click event and a single-click event. For a test chart, a difference between two points in time in test results is calculated and shown in a pop-up dialog. For a drug chart, drug amount in a period of time is computed and shown in a pop-up dialog.

Our system's design is made as simple as possible. Therefore, doctors do not have to remember any sequence of operations. Indeed, all the main interactions are placed on the main dialog with the single screen interface. The others are designed as pop-up, additional for derived information and for other actions of low use frequency.

In summary, our system's design aims at interactive data visualization. It is kept simple but informative for a treatment process. Simplicity makes the system feasibly deployed in practice, while rich information makes the system helpful for doctors, i.e., its end-users.

3.3 System prototype

In our system's demonstration on a Samsung tablet, we use the real data of gastroenterological patients at Thong Nhat Hospital, Ho Chi Minh City, from the treatment notes entered by doctors. They are in Vietnamese with English medical terms and drug names.

a. Single screen interface with different detail levels

When visiting a patient, a doctor can look at patient's medical data, namely, symptoms, test results, and medication made so far. A corresponding screen is turned on for a given patient shown in Figure 3, with three sections on the right panel, namely, "Triệu chứng lâm sàng" (symptoms), "Kết quả xét nghiệm" (test results), and "Thuốc điều trị" (drugs and dosages). This screen matches the single screen interface layout in Figure 2.

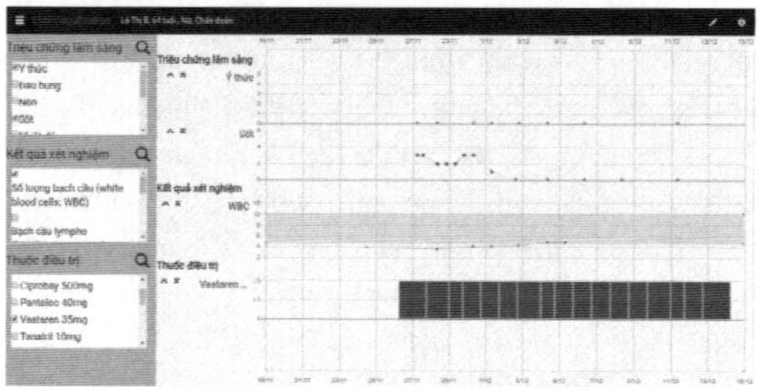

Figure 3: A screen shot on a tablet computer

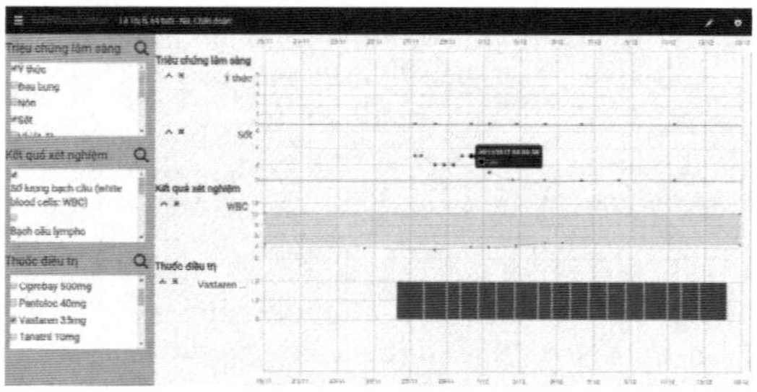

Figure 4: Clinical symptom details

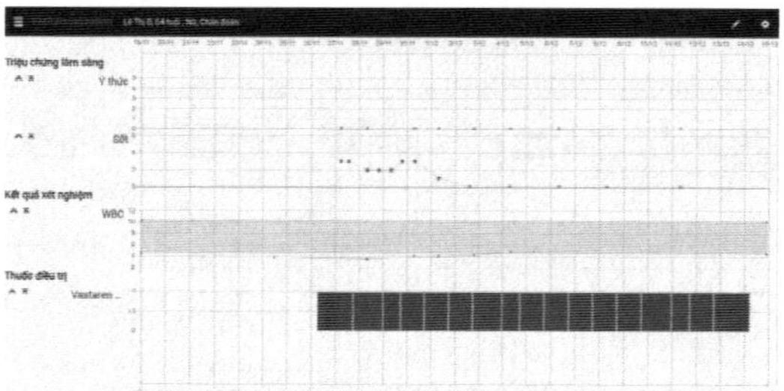

Figure 5: Screen collapsing to enlarge the right panel

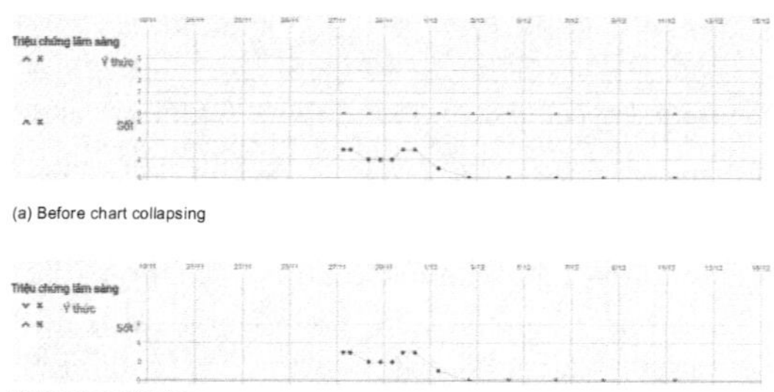

(a) Before chart collapsing

(b) After chart collapsing

Figure 6: Chart collapsing to switch the focus

For more specific values at a certain point in time, a doctor can touch a data point on a chart. Demonstrated in Figure 4 by touching a data point on "Sốt" (fever) chart, the details of "Sốt" (fever) symptom on 30/11/2017 are presented. At 08:00 on that day, the patient had a high fever ("Cao"). Similarly, the details of test results, drugs and dosages can be presented by touching on demand.

b. Reconfiguration for more space on a tablet computer

Touching the collapsing icon in the header allows the left panel to be hidden and the right panel to be enlarged. Figure 5 shows the interaction result for more space in the horizontal view. By contrast, the chart collapsing icon in the right panel brings more space in the vertical view. In addition, interaction with this icon makes the current display less detailed. It also allows a doctor to switch the focus to other items. Demonstrated in Figure 6, (a) shows two charts for "Ý thức" (Consciousness) and "Sốt" (Fever), while (b) shows only one chart for "Sốt" after chart collapsing for "Ý thức".

c. Search for more specific items of interest

(a). Before filtering test results

(b). After filtering test results with the keyword "hồng" ("red")

Figure 7: Keyword-based search for test results with the keyword "hồng" (red)

In case of a long list of symptoms, test results, or drugs, keyword-based search can generate a shorter list of more specific items. In Figure 7, we use a keyword-based search for test results with the keyword "hồng" (red). Before this search, the test variable names with this keyword are not on top of the list. That makes a doctor hard to find the related test results. After this search, the test results are filtered and only the test variable names that contain "hồng" (red) appear in the list for further selection. This is also applied to symptoms and drugs.

d. Calculation for further data exploration

Introduced earlier in Section 2, a doctor may want to see if a patient gets better during a treatment process. For this purpose, our system calculates test results and dosages. The doctor can obtain the results by a combination of a double-click event and a single-click event. A double-click event is caught by double touching a starting data point and a single-click one by an ending data point.

In Figure 8, a difference between two test values of WBC at two time points is derived in value change and percentage. Such a difference alerts the patient status change and lets the doctor know if the current treatment is effective. Similarly, more information is calculated for each drug and its dosages. The doctor can have further analysis on such information with the corresponding symptoms and test results. This helps the doctor realize if drugs have sufficiently been used for treating the disease.

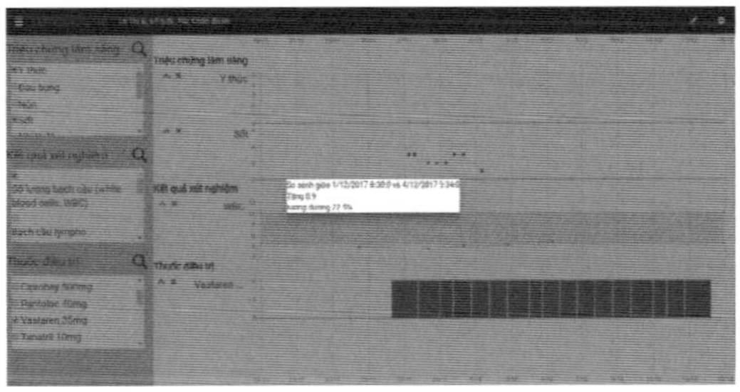

Figure 8: Calculation of the differences in test results

4. SYSTEM EVALUATION

As an evaluation, our system fulfills the requirements in Section 2. For functional ones, interactive visualization of all data required for patient progress tracking has been made. For non-functional ones, all system's factors have been analyzed and built under the doctor-centered view.

Medical data can be extracted accurately from the database of EMRs and then visualized in both set-based and individual-based forms. Quick access has been ensured with the single screen interface where each interaction requires at most two steps.

For the commercial systems in [1, 11] for tablet computers, their technology was not presented in details. According to their descriptions in [1, 11, 12], both systems did not visualize the temporal medical information of a patient in the sequence of clinical symptoms, test results, and then medications. By contrast, our system presents them in an integrative manner just like the data use sequence of doctors in their treatment.

Besides, their demonstration is not completed with the information of gastroenterological patients, while ours is done with those and aims at other chronic diseases. Among the supported data types, our system takes into account clinical text, normalizes and quantifies them for visualization, while [1] had no mention of such data type, and [11] handled unstructured medical records with entity-based relation graphs. That is also why only our system visualizes clinical symptoms, while the others mainly presented vitals over time as time series.

As for [1], the time axis and its granularity were not explicitly presented, while they are given on the top and bottom of the right panel in our system, so that doctors can quickly know the temporal aspect of any data. In addition, drugs and their dosages over time are visualized in bar charts by our system, while they were not in [1]. Furthermore, a normal range of each variable was not explicitly visualized in [1], while it is given in line charts by our system. So, our system provides quicker access to normal and abnormal values of each variable in treatment.

To the best of our knowledge, our EMRVisualization system, which exploits medical data of clinical symptoms, test results, and medications, in an integrative manner, is the first medical information visualization system on a tablet computer for patient progress tracking.

5. CONCLUSIONS

In this paper, we propose the EMRVisualization system as a solution to bridging the gap between medical doctors and computers as EMRs are created, stored and utilized. The proposed system can support doctors to view EMRs of their patients accurately, conveniently and quickly in a long treatment period. All the treatment history of each patient can be queried and visualized on a tablet computer when a doctor visits that patient. The patient progress can be easily tracked with visualized clinical symptoms, test results, and drugs in treatment over time. Every interaction can be made with at most two steps. This characteristic enables a doctor to communicate instantly with the system for required information. Thus, the system can assist the doctor significantly in practice.

As our future works, more interaction techniques on tablet computers will be examined including speech recognition. Extending the system with access to the data of multiple other patients during treatment is considered. Above all, largely deploying the system in practice for more evaluation and improvement is currently carried out.

ACKNOWLEDGMENTS

This work is funded by Vietnam National University at Ho Chi Minh City under the grant number B2016-42-01.

REFERENCES

[1] Allscripts; Allscripts Introduces iPad Application for EHRs; Health IT Outcomes, URL: https://www.healthitoutcomes.com/doc/allscripts-introduces-ipad-application-0001; Last Accessed by Feb 9th, 2018.

[2] R.D. Croon, J. Klerkx, and E. Duval; Designing a Useful and Usable Mobile EMR Application through a Participatory Design Methodology: a Case Study; The IEEE International Conference on Healthcare Informatics; pp. 1-10, 2014.

[3] S. Fang, M. Lwin, and P. Ebright; Visualization of Unstructured Text Sequences of Nursing Narratives; The 2006 ACM Symposium on Applied Computing; pp. 240-244, 2006.

[4] J.P. Ford, L. Huang, D.St.P. Richards, E.P. Ambinder, and J.L. Rosenberger; R.A.P.I.D. (Root Aggregated Prioritized Information Display): A Single Screen Display for Efficient Digital Triaging of Medical Reports; Journal of Biomedical Informatics; 61, pp. 214-223, 2016.

[5] A. Hakone, L. Harrison, A. Ottley, N. Winters, C. Gutheil, P.K. Han, and R. Chang; PROACT: Iterative Design of a Patient-Centered Visualization for Effective Prostate Cancer Health Risk Communication; IEEE Transactions on Visualization and Computer Graphics; 23(1), pp. 601-610, 2017.

[6] E.W. Huang, S. Wang, and C.X. Zhai; VisAGE: Integrating External Knowledge into Electronic Medical Record Visualization; Pacific Symposium on BioComputing; 23, pp. 578-589, 2018.

[7] K. Koerner, D. Dailey, M. Lipp, H. Connor, and R. Sharma; Data Visualization for Psychotherapy Progress Tracking; The 30th ACM International Conference on Design of Communication; pp. 213-218, Seattle, 2012.

[8] M.H. Loorak, C. Perin, N. Kamal, M. Hill, and S. Carpendale; TimeSpan: Using Visualization to Explore Temporal Multi-dimensional Data of Stroke Patients; IEEE Transactions on Visualization and Computer Graphics; 22(1), pp. 409-418, 2016.

[9] C. Plaisant, R. Mushlin, A. Snyder, J. Li, D. Heller, and B. Shneiderman; LifeLines: Using Visualization to Enhance Navigation and Analysis of Patient Records; American Medical Informatic Association Annual Fall Symposium, pp. 76-80, Orlando, 1998.

[10] M. Pohl, S. Wiltner, A. Rind, W. Aigner, S. Miksch, T. Turic, and F. Drexler; Patient Development at a Glance: an Evaluation of a Medical Data Visualization; The 13th International Conference on Human-Computer Interaction; IV, pp. 292-299, 2011.

[11] P. Ruchikachorn, J.J. Liang, M. Devarakonda, and K. Mueller; Watson-Aided Non-Linear Problem-Oriented Clinical Visit Preparation on Tablet Computer; The IEEE VIS 2014 Workshop on Visualization of Electronic Health Records; pp. 1-4, 2014.

[12] B. Shneiderman, C. Plaisant, and B.W. Hesse; Improving Health and Healthcare with Interactive Visualization Methods; IEEE Computer, Special Issue on Challenges in Information Visualization; 46(5), pp. 58-66, 2013.

ISASE-MAICS 2018

Expectation about contribution on comfortable nursing care from Affective Science and Engineering

Keiko FUKUROKU*, Yugo NARITA*,**, Hiroharu KAWANAKA***, Hiroshige HIBASAMI*

** Course of Nursing Science, Graduate School of Medicine, Mie University, 2-174 Edobashi, Tsu-shi, Mie 514-8507, Japan*
*** Department of Neurology, Mie University Hospital, Mie University, 2-174 Edobashi, Tsu-shi, Mie 514-8507, Japan*
**** Graduate School of Engineering, Mie University, 1577 Kurima-machiya, Tsu-shi, Mie 514-8507, Japan*

Abstract: We investigated the comfort in nursing care. First, we examined the use of "Vein Display" to observe variations in individuals' subcutaneous blood flow. We found the venipuncture site selection was significantly improved with "Vein Display", but did not evaluate the difficulty of students to perform venipuncture as there are currently no scales to reflect their affective fluctuations. Second, we verified the comfortability of MRI with limited body movement. We measured the affective and physical distress of patients in response to body positioning using various devices. Next, we aim to measure the physical ability and perception of the elderly with a high risk of sarcopenia to cope with daily activities. Here we will determine parameters used to predict the risk of sarcopenia and identify factors which worsen sarcopenia. We intend to use the tools available from Affective Science to measure the detectable emotional change.

Keywords: *comfort, nursing care, affect*

1. INTRODUCTION

We have been challenging education and researches on comfortable nursing care both for patients and for nurses including students. On this opportunity, we want to show you what topics we have tried, difficulties found there and what we are aiming next for comfortable nursing care. Something we expect your contribution from Affective Science and Engineering will be also presented here.

2. Utilization device

2.1 The use of "Vein Display" to observe the positioning of individual subcutaneous blood

The 1st use of Affective Science and Engineering at our nursing program in improving nursing care took place when teaching our nursing students how to accurately select venipuncture sites. Venipuncture is often painful for patients. And, some of the known complications from venipuncture include nerve injury, hemorrhage, infection, vasovagal reaction, and so forth.

It is not easy for novice students to learn such an invasive skill like venipuncture at the training room in the school. A vein visualization display system, "Vein Display", had been developed to observe individual subcutaneous blood running by near infrared light. We used "Vein Display" for students'education of the safe and proper selection of venipuncture sites in the forearm (Figure1).

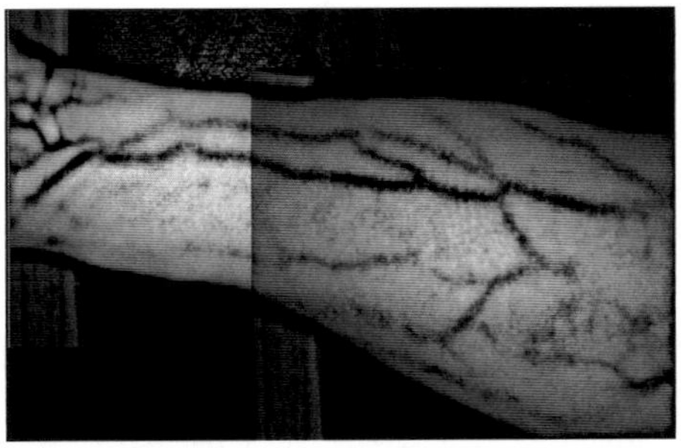

Figure1 Shot image : Left forearm

The protocol of the series of the trials was set as a part of scenario to get a suitable route for drip infusion by a needle with wings at the forearm.

We evaluated whether the sites selected by the students were consistent with safe and appropriate venipuncture, as defined by the 3-point-based scale on the following 4 adverse criteria: 1) meandering site of the vein, 2) branching site of the vein, 3) near the common site of cutaneous nerve, and 4) less than 4cm from the cubital crease or the most distal crease of the wrist. In order to maximize butterfly needle safety even during joint motion, the following 3 levels were evaluated: "yes" meant the site selected represented a clear risk and was scored as 0, "ambiguous" meant the site selected represented a potential risk and was scored as 1, and "no" meant free from any risk and was scored as 2. The total possible score ranged from 8 (highest) to 0 (zero), except in the case of "extravascular" site selection (defined as site selection more than 2mm away from the target vein), which was not scored, regardless of any other criteria (Table1).

We found that venipuncture site selection time was significantly improved with the "Vein Display", particularly in the case of "difficulty to see" subcutaneous veins (1). But at that time, we could not evaluate how difficult the nurse-role students felt during the trial, because of no scale to reflect their affective fluctuation. Just we expect a tool on emotional change while students are doing not so easy tasks.

Table 1 vein selection score to keep a butterfly needle safely at the forearm

	item	score		
		yes	ambiguous	no
1	meandering site of the vein	0	1	2
2	branching site of the vein	0	1	2
3	near the common site of cutaneous nerv	0	1	2
4	less than 4cm from the cubital crease or the most distal crease of the wrist	0	1	2
*	extravascular : (site selection of more than 2mm from blood vessels on the image)		not scored	

highest score 8
lowest score 0 *except for the selection of extravascular

2.2 Whether people can stay still comfortable in the MRI without movement of the focused body parts or not?

To avoid any nerve injury on venipuncture is mandatory. Variation of cutaneous nerve running causes sometimes complication on venipuncture. Some patients insist that they are suffering from causalgic pain caused by venocentesis. Now we may be able to detect some of large cutaneous nurves by electro-physiological methods like nerve conduction studies. It also causes another uncomfort due to electric stimulation. And the method is different from imaging. Magnetic resonance images (MRI) itself has no pain except for forced staying in very narrow space without movement. MRI may be able to let us accumulate precice data on alive human cutaneous nerves. A dangerous zone map may be shown from the data. Once we had a good experience to have felt effectiveness of visualizing tool on superficial veins, then we wanted to visualize cutaneous nerves at the forearm by MRI. However, it was very difficult for any type of MRI sequences to visualize small peripheral nerves like a cutaneous nerve (2). We tried to make an educational navigation system to avoid the high risk area of nerve injury at venipuncture with the partial support from the national Grants-in-aid for Scientific Research "Challenging Exploratory Research (2015-2019)", depending on the published variation of cutaneous nerves at the forearm (3,4,5). During waiting for development of new MRI sequences to show fine nerves, a topic rose: whether people can stay still comfortable in the MRI without movement of focused body parts or not?

The reason: first of all, such nerves are too fine to be delineated. The second, it is not easy to keep the object site at the center of the gantry.

To take fine images of MRI, people include healthy persons are supposed to be supine or slightly lateral decubitus position and to keep the examining part of body in the center of the gantry for 20 minutes or longer without movement in the narrow space. This positioning can create distress for people include health persons. No article was found that focused on measurement about affective and physical distress on patients as a result of the body positioning requirement in MRI, and body motion in the limited space of MRI.

Then, we made a simulated model MRI out of wood and acrylic boards, precisely tracing the actual Philips INGENIA 3.0T Omega HP. No movement of the object is necessary for fine MRI images. So, we want to measure the total amount of the movement by the 3 axis acceleration sensors and a small video camera and participants feeing. (Figure2, 3).

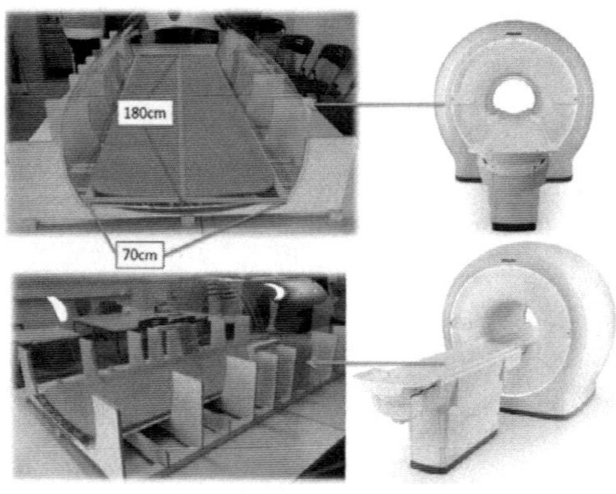

Figure2 Simulated model MRI out of wood and acrylic boards

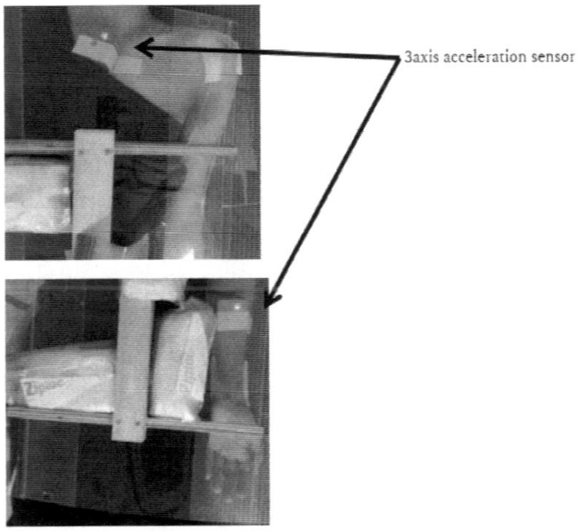

Figure 3 Mounting site of 3axis acceleration sensor

Participants: Eighteen adult students (20-40 years of age, mean 25. 3±6.3 years, comprising 8 men and 10 women) were participated with the written consent among applicants after a call for paid volunteers from the school of nursing and the faculty of industry. Mie University's IRB approved this study. (No.3090 13, January, 2017, Faculty of Medicine, Mie University).

Methods: Each subject's physical data was collected beforehand on height, weight, and body-mass index (BMI). The forearm motion was recorded by the 3 axis acceleration sensors on the forearm and the chest wall (just above the sternal body), both ①during 15 minutes on supine without any restriction before entering the model and ② during 20 minutes on keeping the subject's dominant forearm as center and motionless as possible in the model gantry. The small camera installed inside the acrylic transparent board was used as a supplemental tool to check their motion after the trial. The autonomic nervous reaction was simultaneously monitored as to heart rate variability and LF/HF (the ratio of low frequency / high frequency) by the MemCalc/Bonaly Light (GMS Co., Ltd. Tokyo, Japan 2015) (Figure4).

The subjective pain of areas of the body and mental & physical fatigue were collected by using the questionnaire with visual analogue scales (VAS). VAS 0 means "free" and 100means "extreme".

To test the significance of the differences, we used a non-parametric Mann-Whitney test for comparison of coefficient of variation between the forearm and sternum, and distress on hold state of dorsal position by BMI, and Wilcoxon signed-rank test for comparison of the heart rate variability analysis on LF/HF between before and during the gantry. For the analysis, SPSS Ver.20.0 was used and the significance level was set at <5%.

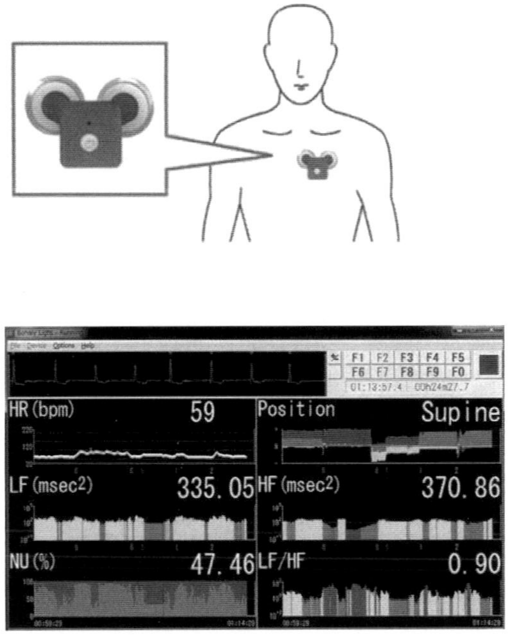

Figure 4 MemCalc/BonalyLight (GMS Co., Ltd. Tokyo, Japan 2015)

Results: The participants showed very little motion of their dominant forearm, keeping with suitable positioning for 20 minutes in the simulated gantry. The value of XYZ (Accx, Accy, Accz : acceleration, Gyrox, Gyroy, Gyroz: angular velocity) is used to calculate and detect the motions. There was no significant difference of coefficient of variation between the forearm and sternum. (Figure3, Table2). However one case of Gyroz was large variations.

Table 2 Coefficient of Variation (average value)

N=18

acceleration sensor item / mounting region	Accx	Accy	Accz	Gyrox	Gyroy	Gyroz
forearm	0.09	0.01	-0.01	-0.62	-1.46	135.76
sternum	0.19	-0.01	-0.01	-0.32	-8.24	-0.73

Mann-Whitney Test

The heart rate variability analysis on LF/HF was measured between before and during the gantry. Both of them the hold state (15-20min.) was significantly lower than the relaxed state (10-15min.) (Figure5, 6).

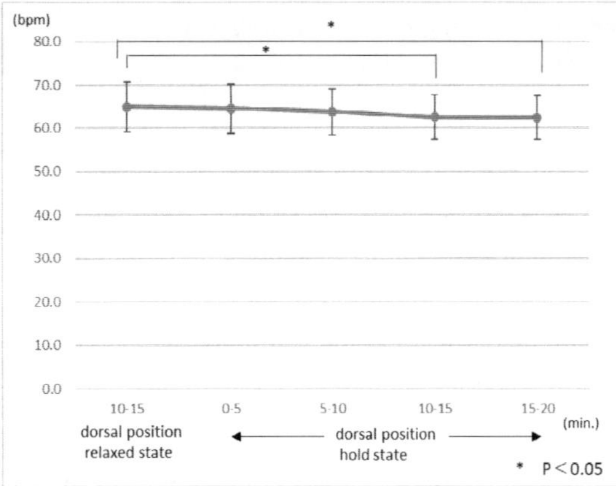

Figure 5 Heart rate variability **Wilcoxon signed-rank Test**

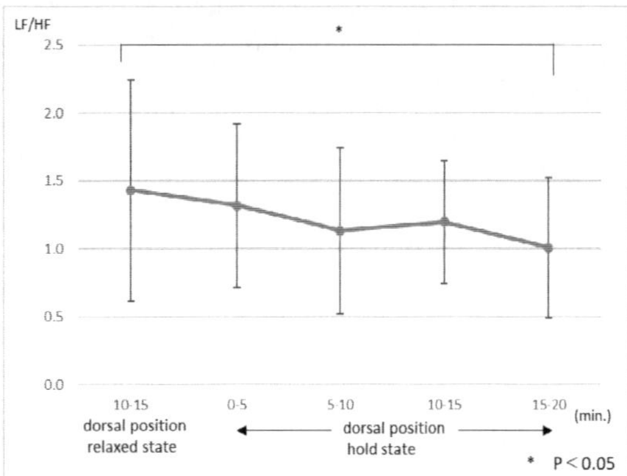

Figure 6 LF/HF variability **Wilcoxon signed-rank Test**

How was their pain or fatigue? The subjects with not more than BMI 18.5 scored the higher VAS values of fatigue and pain at staying in the gantry than the participants with more than BMI 18.5. The subjects with not more than BMI 18.5 showed pain in their finger tips on the dominant side, around their both side hips or uni-lateral hip, and unstable sense on their dominant (right) leg (Table3).

Table 3 Comparison of distress on hold state of dorsal position by BMI

distress \ BMI		under 18.5 (N=5)	over 18.5 (N=13)	P
fatigue		32.5±17.6	18.7±18.9	0.046*
pain	right finger	10.1±13.6	1.5±2.3	0.041*
	right waist	19.4±24.7	2.1±3.1	0.037*
unstable	right waist	22.2±23.3	5.3±12.5	0.008**
	left waist	18.9±24.8	5.9±12.0	0.033*
	right leg	19.0±26.3	2.2±4.4	0.02*

*P<0.05 **P<0.01

Mann-Whitney Test

Comments: We may be able to infer from the result that most people can stay 20 minutes in the MRI gantry keeping their forearm in the good position, probably without significant discomfort. Although we have waited for advanced MRI sequences, we have never got any good solution to delineate the cutaneous nerve at the forearm until now. Only subjective VAS values showed us the difference, while heart-rate variability analysis failed to show us any difference. We need something else to catch affective and physical distress from the participants objectively (6).

3. To measure of sense and the evaluation of the comfortableness for elderly of high risk of sarcopenia

Then, waiting for the next chance to delineate a fine cutaneous nerve, we have headed to the next topic on predicting and preventing of sarcopenia. Sarcopenia stems from the word "sarco" which means muscle and the word "-penia" which means reduction. Sarcopenia itself does not cause pain, unless fall or fracture occurs. But once elder people got such a fall or fracture, not only does sarcopenia create physical and emotional discomfort and pain for older adults, it is known to shorten their life expectancy. Japan's current "aging" society is forecasted to become even more "aging" with projected 31.8% of its population to be "older adults" in 2030. Of the older adults in 2013, over 45% of them are estimated to be single elder women's households. (7). Female's longevity means the increasing risk of sarcopenia and osteoporosis. One in 4 to 5 healthy elderlies in community was reported having sarcopenia in Japan (8). Decreased of muscle bulk in legs was reported even in the early stage of aging (9). Fracture, fall, and joint disorders are said to be the main reasons that people utilize the long-term care insurance in Japan (10,11). People with less movement tend to become more osteopolosis and sarcopenia as astronauts lost their bone density and muscle bulks under the state of zero-gravity. Three percent of muscle bulk is estimated to be lost a day in plaster fixation.

Therefore, we want to detect the effective parameters to predict the risk of and to find worsening factors of sarcopenia. Now we are thinking that it is natural and smooth for people to be checked in the activity of daily life: to acquire the data such as acceleration of the standing-up movement from the stool seat, the frequency of posture changes indoors, level of physical activities indoors and outdoors and so forth. Utilization of the technology of IoT seemed to be the most efficient tool for the elderly for its small size. Elderly tends to move a few times per hours. So collecting long time span would be good for the analysis. (12,13). The level of physical activity and measurements of physical strength of elderly are influenced by seasonal changes in physical condition (14). It may be well-known that hypertension control or parkinsonism reflects seasonal environments. In addition to this, the physical activity of elderly is greatly influenced by the degree of pain and fatigue. Therefore, it is important to capture the feeling or emotional change detectable by any objective tool in addition to the physical data (amount of muscle mass, grip, 10 m walking speed etc.), behavioral data (activity strength, walking distance, acceleration of posture change etc.) and environmental data (temperature, humidity, weather etc.). We would like to get the viewpoints from Affective Science such as the measuring of detectable emotional change using available tool.

REFFERENCES

1. K Fukuroku, Y Narita, Y Taneda, et al; Does infrared visualization improve selection of venipuncture sites for indwelling needle at the forearm in second-year nursing students? Nurse education in Practice; 18, pp1-9, 2016.
2. M Yoneyama; MR Neurography: Novel MR Imaging Techniques for Depiction of Peripheral Nerves. https://www.jsnt.gr.jp/Archive/pdf?gid=cq3neuro/2015/003202/029/0201-0204 (accessed on 17th January, 2018)
3. Singh S, Rani N, Kaushal P, et al; Anomalous cutaneous branch of median nerve in arm: a report of anatomical variation with clinical implications. Anat Cell Biol; 47(2), pp138-40, 2014.
4. Stylianos K, Konstantinos G, Pavlos P, et al; Brachial branches of the medial antebrachial cutaneous nerve: A case report with its clinical significance and a short review of the literature. J Neurosci Rural Pract. 7(3), pp443-6, 2016.
5. Yogesh A, Marathe R, Pandit S; Musculocutaneous nerve substituting for the distal part of radial nerve: A case report and its embryological basis. J Neurosci Rural Pract. 2(1), pp74-6, 2011.
6. Pedrazza M, Trifiletti E, Berlanda S, et al; Development and Initial Validation of the Nurses' Comfort With Touch Scale. J Nurs Meas; 23(3), pp364-78, 2015.
7. Cabinet Office, Government of Japan, Aging of society. (in Japanese) http://www8.cao.go.jp/kourei/whitepaper/w-2017/html/gaiyou/s1_1.html (accessed on 17th January, 2018)
8. Center for Gerontology and Social Science, sarcopenia practice guideline 2017 (in Japanese) http://www.ncgg.go.jp/cgss/news/20180117.html (accessed on 17th January, 2018)
9. M Ohni; Nutritional assessment in the elderly, The Journal of Japanese Society for Parenteral and Enteral Nutrition; 22(4), pp11-17, 2007. (in Japanese)
10. Oleksik A, Lips P, Dawson A, et al; Health-related quality of life in postmenopausal women with low BMD with or without prevalent vertebral fractures. J Bone Miner Res 15(7), pp1384-1392, 2000.
11. H Hagino, T Nakamura, S Fujiwara, et al; Sequential change in quality of life for patients with incident clinical fractures: a prospective study. Osteoporos Int. 20(5), pp695-702,2009.
12. K Ouchi, M Doi; Living Activity Recognition Technology Using Sensors in Smartphone. Toshiba Review.68(6), pp40-43, 2013. (in Japanese)
13. G Laput, Y Zhang, C Harrison; Synthetic Sensors Towards General Purpose Sensing. http://www.gierad.com/assets/supersensor/supersensor.pdf (accessed on 17th January, 2018)
14. K Fukuroku; The intervention of fall prevention exercise: physical fitness transition for 1year and follow-up survey after the intervention. J Japan Society of Nursing Research. 34(3) pp328, 2011. (in Japanese)

ISASE-MAICS 2018

Study of QOL Assessment Management Application

Yukiya FUNADA*, Shuji KURITA*, Jue ZHANG*, Emiko YAMAZAKI* and Takuro SAKURAI **

** Kogakuin University, 1-24-2 Nishi Shinjuku, Shinjuku-Ward, Tokyo 163-8677, Japan*

*** Bone soft tissue tumor · rehabilitation department, National Cancer Research Center Central Hospital, 5-1-1 Tsukiji, Chuo-Ward, Tokyo 104-0045, Japan*

Abstract: NCCN guidelines recommend conducting QOL assessments that display the score of a patient's quality of life, in addition tousing common assessment methods that simply diagnose the patient's medical conditions. Despite the effectiveness of these methods in determining the QOL for cancer patients, their paper answer sheets have always had a fixed format. As a result, there has been almost no progress in the efforts to digitize the questionnaires to effectively manage data, and clinicians have been required to invest inordinate amount of time and effort into collecting the EORTC assessment data in order to apply them to research. Accordingly, in this research, we used preliminary surveys to develop an application that calculates and manages data for EORTC QLQ-C30 which are the most popular QOL assessment methods. For future application, we have integrated functions to display acquired assessment data to patients using visual graphs for easy viewing and comparison, as well as a feature that allows the user to import the data from the answer sheet by simply taking a picture of it. Also, introduced a function to improve patients' motivation towards rehabilitation and encourage them to continue with rehabilitation. As a result, we succeeded in developing an application that reduces the burden of data input and analytical work on the clinician, that can present a graph that allows the cancer patient to immediately understand his or her medical condition while still showing consideration to the patient's mental state, and has a function that encourages improvement in motivation for rehabilitation.
Keywords: *Health care workers, QOL evaluation, Cancer rehabilitation, Application, Interface*

1. PREFACE

Nowadays, the survival rate of cancer has dramatically increased thanks to the development of anticancer drugs and advanced medical technology; cancer has become a treatable disease. So far antitumor effect and biochemical examination have become mainstream measures of the effectiveness of cancer treatments and their importance has been emphasized. However, in recent years evaluations of the mental state of the patient themselves – the mental distresses caused by various aspects of the treatment such as: the side effects of treatment, the cost of treatment, and leave or retirement from work – have become more and more important, rather than solely medical evaluations of the treatment itself [1]. NCCN guidelines (international cancer guidelines) recommend the implementation of QOL assessment – an assessment that is used to gauge the patient's quality of life and thus focuses not only on the medical condition but also on the mental state of the patient .

Although there are several methods of evaluating QOL, EORTC QLQ-C30 (henceforth known as C30) is the method typically used for cancer patients [2]. This QOL scale is a multidimensional evaluation method in which patients self-evaluate their daily functionality. While this is an effective method for evaluating the effect of cancer treatment on a patient's QOL, change in format of the answer sheet has not been approved and there has been no digitization of the survey or advancement of the data management system. As a result, it takes a huge amount of time to compile the results of the EORTC evaluation, which places a significant burden on clinicians.

we interviewed twenty healthcare professionals to understand the issues related to QOL. The investigations showed that, in order to obtain data for use in research, clinicians scan the answer sheets, and after compiling the data from the answer sheets stored on electronic medical records they directly input the answer number for each question heading into an Excel spreadsheet and use macro-functions to calculate the QOL score. Using Excel to calculate the score means that the score itself is calculated immediately; however, starting up the computer and using the macro-functions takes time. It became clear that tasks such as information compilation and management processing pose a huge burden for clinicians.

Furthermore, The supplemental question "Is it assumed that patients will be given their QOL evaluation results?" raised the opinion that the ability to present evaluation results instantly and visually to patients would affect their understanding of their own conditions. On the other hand, though it is up to healthcare providers to judge whether it would be appropriate to present such results to the patient in the first place, the opinion was also raised that it would be necessary to present the results in a way that would take into consideration the mental state of the cancer patient.

The opinion was also raised that, in situations in which a patient's desire to continue rehabilitation drops and they choose to not continue with rehabilitation and there is the chance that they may become bedridden, it is essential to promote a patient's motivation towards rehabilitation.

The issues related to QOL in the medical field and the requests of healthcare providers are summarized as follows: ①instantaneously calculating the QOL score and managing it as electronic data, ② displaying the results visually to the patient, ③ improving the patient's motivation towards rehabilitation.

Currently, due to the popularization of mobile phone and tablet terminals, the usage of mobile applications for medical treatment or health management has expanded, and it has become easy for individuals to personally confirm their healthcare data and monitor their own health.

In light of these circumstances, in order to solve the problems concerning the QOL by using a tablet terminal – a method which is popular in the medical field – and to test out the desires of healthcare providers in this research the following four features are implemented: ① "Calculation / Management Function" calculates the QOL score instantaneously and manages it as data, ② "Graph Presentation Function" displays the result visually to the patient in real time, ③ "Rehabilitation Activities Continuation Function" improves patient motivation for rehabilitation and encourages them to continue rehabilitation activities, ④ data input by camera, which further reduces the time required for data input. We then carried out comparative experiments and evaluation experiments for healthcare workers and general users and verified the effectiveness of the four kinds of functions. This research also aims to further improve user feedback obtained by user tests and evaluation.

2. ABOUT THE SUBJECT OF THIS STUDY

As described in previous studies relating to changes in QOL score [3], it has also been reported that QOL evaluation results are greatly affected by the specific medical condition of the patient in question and the timing of surgery. In this research it is not clear whether each implemented function was due to the influence of cancer patients or also due to the influence of general users.

Therefore, in this research, we incorporate the opinions of the healthcare professionals as much as possible, implement each function, and perform general user test and user evaluations.

Developing applications with a degree of stability and with effective functions has made conducting long-term experiments at clinical sites possible in the future.

3. DEVELOPMENT OF APPLICATION

3.1 Calculation and Management Functions

Our goal for this function was to calculate the QOL score instantaneously and manage it as electronic data. We used touch controls for data input in order to perform calculation quickly. In Figure 1A, the evaluation method is selected, and the evaluation value can be input as Figure 2B. Then, After inputting patient's personal data (ID, date of birth, gender, type of illness) in Figure 1C, the QOL score is calculated so that it can be stored as answer data in Figure 1D. Data storage uses SQLite, which is a database built into the application.

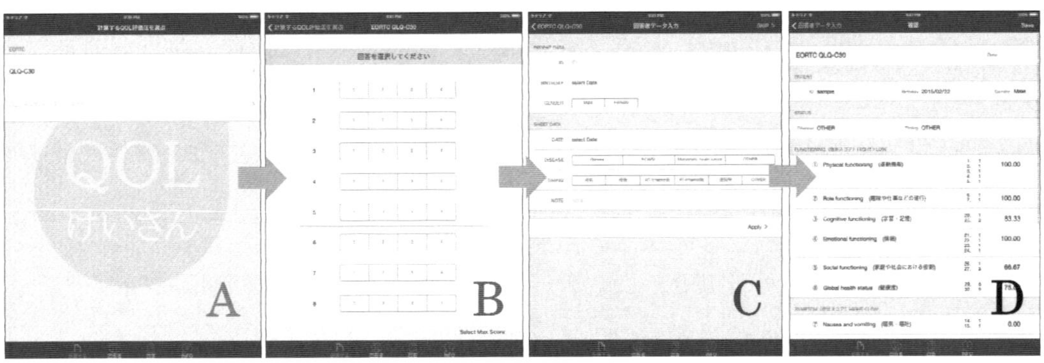

Figure 1: New response flow

3.2 Graph Presentation Function

In this function, we implemented a graph presentation function to present the evaluation results visually and to further understanding of the patient's condition. In presenting the results, the maximum value of the scale is set to the maximum value within scale the patient's own scores, intervals are widened, and it is filled in with the color green in order to make the display method easy to see, with emphasis on consideration to the patient's mental state (Figure 2). This function uses the PNChart library, and is based on radar charts, which are frequently used in the medical field.

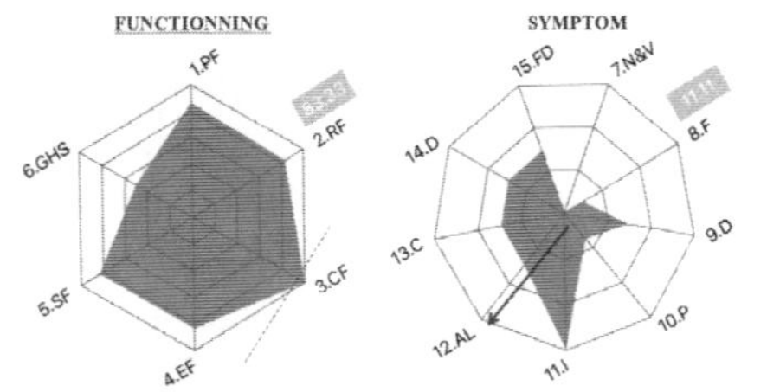

Figure 2: Graph presentation screen with emphasis on psychological consideration

3.3 Rehabilitation Activity Continuation Function

This function implements four kinds of functions based on the technique for enhancing patients' "motivation" for rehabilitation by Yamamoto et al [4] to improve motivation for rehabilitation of cancer patients and to encourage them to continue with rehabilitation.

Also, since there are different ways of solving each factor, we implemented two patterns for each function (Table 1) and combined four functions multiplied by two kinds of combined patterns to develop a total of sixteen patterns of application prototypes.

Table 1: Pattern implemented for the factor of each function

Function number	Function1	Function2	Function3	Function4
Factor	By illustration expression Visual stimulus	Depends on rehabilitation diary Linguistic instruction	Depending on the doctor's in charge Linguistic instruction	Due to alert sound Auditory stimulation
Pattern 1	Checkbox type	Positive case	Formal sentences	No alert sound
Pattern 2	Stamp type	Non positive cases	Substantive sentences	With alert sound

3.4 Data input function using a camera

In order to further reduce the time required for inputting calculation and management functions, we implemented the function of data input by camera. The user would take a photograph of the answer sheet and crop a specific range from the captured image. We created an image with red color extracted, and after acquiring the color on the y coordinate of the question item, we implemented to output the value corresponding to the answer number according to the x coordinate (Figure 3).

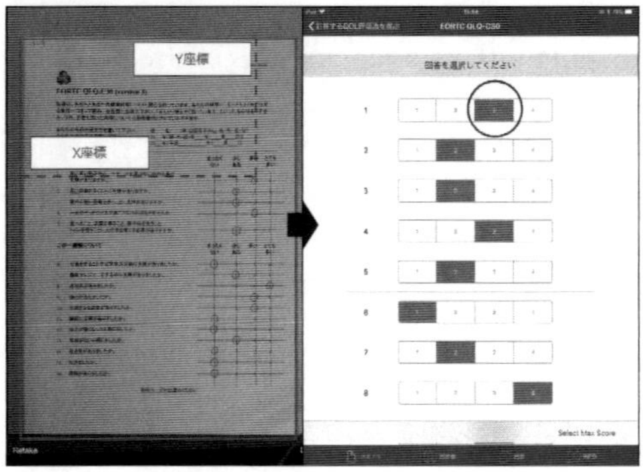

Figure 3: Flow of data input using a camera

4. VERIFICATION OF EFFECTIVENESS BY GENERAL USER TEST AND USER EVALUATION

4.1 Comparison of time required for Excel and calculation and management function

4.1.1 Outline of experiment and purpose

In order to verify the effectiveness of this application, we compared the calculation and management functions of this application with Excel, which the has macros of the QOL score calculation function used up until now.

In the experiment, which was conducted with twenty subjects, the answer number of each question item was input by two methods, the QOL score was calculated, and the time required to save the data was measured for each.

The subjects had ten answer sheets with answer numbers already checked, and they counted, and each measured the time required for counting.

4.1.2 Experiment Results

Excel requires an average time of about 10 minutes, and it turned out that this function took about 8 minutes in total to complete. The comparison results showed that it was possible to reduce the required time by an average of about two minutes, and the t test showed significance ($t(19) = 5.151$, $p < 0.01$).

In Excel, when subjects focused primarily on looking at the answer sheet, there were a significant number of subjects who input data incorrectly, which took time to correct, or subjects who finished without realizing that they had input the data incorrectly. In this application, on the other hand, incorrect inputs can be corrected by a simple tap. In addition, when there are un-input items, this application displays a warning on the screen; thus, we heard from subjects that correcting incorrectly input data was incredibly simple.

4.2 Rehabilitation activity continuation function evaluation experiment

Our goal for this function was to calculate the QOL score instantaneously and manage it as electronic data. We used touch control

Table 2: Time required to compile ten answer sheets

	Excel [sec]	App [sec]	Difference [sec]
Subject1	443	410	33
Subject2	635	517	118
Subject3	596	549	47
Subject4	694	494	200
Subject5	783	628	155
Subject6	492	404	88
Subject7	399	378	21
Subject8	594	529	65
Subject9	453	473	-20
Subject10	834	526	308
Subject11	607	468	139
Subject12	427	425	2
Subject13	481	439	42
Subject14	651	513	138
Subject15	589	433	156
Subject16	495	476	19
Subject17	731	420	311
Subject18	1009	702	307
Subject19	467	391	76
Subject20	603	476	127
Average	599	483	117

4.2.1 Outline of experiment and purpose

In the prototypes of all sixteen patterns a total of eight questionnaires were prepared based on the results of Tsukamoto et al.'s self-efficacy scale for cancer patients [5] – how the optimum combination and various functions affect the self-efficacy of cancer patients – and evaluation experiment was conducted on twenty general users.

The investigation was based on the result of the average value for each question of all prototypes, and consisted of obtaining the orthogonal sequence table (Table 4) using the experimental design method, performing conjoint analysis, and calculating the partial utility value and the contribution rate.

Subjects were asked to practice the training method "Locomo exercise [6]" which was created to prevent Locomo and is a rehabilitation exercise actually used by for rehabilitation patients and officially approved by the Japanese Orthopedic Surgery Society.

After that, for the prototype randomly presented, we asked eight questions (Table 3) to be evaluated in 5 stages.

Table 3: List of questions asked

Q1	Did you feel a sense of accomplishment after completing the task?
Q2	Have you experienced approval or evaluation from others?
Q3	Were you satisfied with the work itself?
Q4	Were you able to truly feel the degree of your medical condition or progress?
Q5	Do you want to continue rehabilitation in the future?
Q6	Did you understand and grasp the degree of your own medical condition?
Q7	Do you think that it seems that rehabilitation is should proceed reliably?
Q8	Did you feel like your feelings were considered?

Table 4: Partial utility value

Concept	Function1	Function2	Function3	Function4
1	Checkboxtype	Non positive cases	Formal sentences	No alert sound
2	Stamp type	Positive case	Formal sentences	With alert sound
3	Checkboxtype	Non positive cases	Formal sentences	With alert sound
4	Checkboxtype	Positive case	Substantive sentences	With alert sound
5	Stamp type	Positive case	Formal sentences	No alert sound
6	Stamp type	Non positive cases	Substantive sentences	With alert sound
7	Checkboxtype	Positive case	Substantive sentences	No alert sound
8	Stamp type	Non positive cases	Substantive sentences	No alert sound

4.2.2 Results of the Experiment

From the results of the partial utility value, the optimum combination for the following six questions - question ① the sense of achievement, question ② the approval or evaluation, question ③ the satisfaction of the work itself, question ⑤ the motivation to continue the rehabilitation, question ⑦ the sense of rehabilitation as reliable, question ⑧ the consideration of personal feelings - was visual stimulus of illustration in the form of a stamp, positive linguistic instruction by rehabilitation diary, linguistic instruction by formal comments from the attending physician, and auditory stimulation by way of an alert sound. The optimal solutions of questions ④ and ⑥ were changed with respect to function 1 and function 3, as opposed to the optimum solution for the above 6 questions.

Table 5: List of contribution rate for each question item of various functions

	Question 1	Question 2	Question 3	Question 4	Question 5	Question 6	Question 7	Question 8
Function1	14.6%	14.3%	7.6%	60.5%	13.9%	12.5%	17.3%	2.2%
Function2	12.2%	11.9%	12.7%	13.2%	8.3%	21.9%	13.5%	15.2%
Function3	34.1%	59.5%	36.4%	2.6%	66.7%	50.0%	51.9%	71.7%
Function4	39.0%	14.3%	43.2%	23.7%	11.1%	15.6%	17.3%	10.9%

Table 6: Average value of twenty subjects for each question in all prototypes

Type number	Type1	Type2	Type3	Type4	Type5	Type6	Type7	Type8	Type9	Type10	Type11	Type12	Type13	Type14	Type15	Type16
Question ①	3.95(0.97)	4.25(0.77)	3.70(1.05)	3.95(1.02)	3.80(1.08)	4.35(0.65)	3.15(1.24)	4.10(0.83)	4.00(1.05)	4.50(0.59)	3.75(0.94)	4.05(1.07)	4.05(0.97)	4.15(1.01)	4.00(0.63)	4.05(0.80)
Question ②	4.10(0.62)	4.15(0.85)	3.55(1.20)	3.75(1.18)	4.05(0.92)	4.50(0.74)	3.25(0.99)	3.50(1.24)	3.85(1.01)	4.20(0.93)	3.55(1.02)	3.75(1.26)	4.10(0.94)	4.20(0.60)	3.70(0.84)	3.60(0.97)
Question ③	3.60(0.92)	4.10(0.77)	2.60(1.24)	3.55(1.02)	2.90(1.30)	3.75(0.89)	2.70(1.14)	3.50(1.12)	3.65(0.79)	4.30(0.64)	3.00(1.05)	3.80(1.21)	3.50(1.07)	4.00(0.77)	3.00(0.84)	3.95(0.92)
Question ④	3.75(0.89)	3.60(1.07)	3.35(1.15)	3.60(1.28)	3.90(0.99)	3.95(1.16)	3.55(0.86)	3.70(1.00)	3.80(1.03)	3.70(1.14)	3.90(0.99)	4.10(0.89)	3.80(1.03)	4.00(1.14)	3.75(1.09)	3.85(0.79)
Question ⑤	3.75(0.89)	4.25(0.62)	3.40(0.80)	3.60(1.02)	3.85(0.73)	4.00(1.14)	3.15(1.15)	3.45(1.02)	3.75(0.89)	4.10(0.83)	3.60(0.92)	3.40(1.02)	4.10(0.70)	3.95(0.80)	3.55(0.92)	3.45(0.74)
Question ⑥	3.30(1.35)	3.60(0.97)	3.25(1.18)	3.45(1.24)	3.35(0.79)	3.25(1.04)	3.50(0.87)	3.85(1.11)	3.00(1.00)	3.50(1.16)	3.70(1.14)	3.80(1.03)	3.30(1.05)	3.05(1.12)	3.75(0.99)	3.55(1.12)
Question ⑦	3.85(0.85)	4.20(0.75)	3.55(0.97)	3.75(0.94)	3.80(1.03)	3.95(0.86)	3.55(1.02)	3.65(0.96)	3.95(0.80)	3.90(0.99)	3.80(1.03)	3.80(0.87)	4.05(0.74)	4.05(0.74)	3.75(0.77)	3.55(0.97)
Question ⑧	4.20(0.81)	4.40(0.66)	3.50(1.28)	3.85(1.15)	4.20(1.03)	4.30(0.78)	3.15(1.28)	3.45(1.02)	4.35(0.73)	4.70(0.46)	3.55(1.07)	3.45(1.12)	4.10(0.83)	4.20(0.83)	3.55(1.12)	3.35(1.01)

From the contribution rate results (Table 5), we found that the visual stimulus of the illustrative representation of function 1 has the most influence in helping patients realize their own degree of growth and progress. Difference in linguistic instruction through a rehabilitation diary function, function 2, was found to have less effect on self-efficacy. Differences in linguistic instruction by the attending physician, function 3, affected the most question items between all of the functions and among approval and evaluation from others, motivation for rehabilitation, understanding and grasp of the degree of the patient's own medical condition, sense of security toward rehabilitation, and the patient's belief that his or her feelings were considered. The presence or absence of auditory stimulation by the alert sound of function 4 has been found to have a high influence on the patient's sense of accomplishment after completion of the rehabilitation task as well as the satisfaction of operation of the application as a subsequent stimulus.

The results of the average value for each question from all of the prototypes (Table 6) show that the combination of prototype 10 – the visual stimulus of illustration in the form of a stamp, the positive linguistic instruction of the rehabilitation diary, the formal linguistic instruction by the attending physician, and the auditory stimulation of the alert sound – received a high evaluation for all questions.

The results of the partial utility value and the average value for each question of all prototypes showed that the combination of prototype 10 has the best effect on the formation of self-efficacy and may promote motivation for rehabilitation.

This application was therefore implemented based on the combination of prototype 10. Depending on the stage of treatment and the specific condition of the patient it should also be possible to make a custom setting to switch to the optimal solution, if there is a willingness to focus on self-efficacy based on the result of the partial utility value or the rate of contribution.

4.3 Experiment to measure identification rate

4.3.1 Outline of experiment and purpose

A stable identification rate is required to use data input function by camera. For this reason, we conducted an experiment to measure the identification rate of a method using a hand-held camera assuming normal usage conditions for twenty-five regular users.

We had subjects fill out the form with two types of red pen (ballpoint and felt-tip) to consider the influence of the thickness of the pen tip. Also, in taking into consideration individual differences in how the sheet would be filed out, we had subjects fill out the sheet using the following three methods: not specifying to "please fill out the sheet using a normal circle", specifying to "please fill out the sheet using a well-drawn circle", and specifying to "please cover over the numbers on the answer sheet" (unspecified, specified, and filled-in). The combination of each pattern is shown in Table 4. With regards to the method of photographing the sheet, we had subjects take photos using the following two methods: the method of displaying only the frame on the screen and shooting the paper so as to fit the specified frame, and the method of displaying the frame as well as grid-like auxiliary lines and taking the picture so that the intersections of the lines overlap the numbers on the paper.

There was a total of ten trial experiments. In addition, the experiment was carried out also with the fixed camera, as the hand-held camera method influenced the experimental

Table 7: Combination list of input method and photography method

Answer pattern	Types of pen	How to fill in	Shooting method
1	Ballpoint pen	Unspecified	Frame only
2	Felt pen	Unspecified	Frame only
3	Ballpoint pen	Designation	Frame only
4	Felt pen	Designation	Frame only
5	Felt pen	Fill	Frame only
6	Ballpoint pen	Unspecified	With auxiliary line
7	Felt pen	Unspecified	With auxiliary line
8	Ballpoint pen	Designation	With auxiliary line
9	Felt pen	Designation	With auxiliary line
10	Felt pen	Fill	With auxiliary line

4.3.2 Results of the experiment

Patterns that used felt-tip pens have an average identification rate of 76% or more, and the average discrimination rate of photographing methods displaying auxiliary lines was 90% or more.

The answer pattern with the highest average identification rate is pattern 9 which uses a felt-tip pen, the entry method is specified, and the auxiliary lines are displayed, and the average discrimination rate is 97.8%. The results of the T Test on the average identification number of the pattern using the felt pen for data input showed a significant difference in the response pattern with the auxiliary lines and the response pattern with only the frame.

From this fact, it was found that when photographing using a hand-held camera more accurate values can be acquired, and the rate of identification increases when the auxiliary lines are displayed on the screen. However, it was suggested that the hand-held camera shake could possibly influence the results, as there were some subjects with a low identification rate of answer sheets that used a felt-tip pen.

We conducted the T Test to find out the average identification numbers of the hand-held camera method and the fixed camera method, the results of which showed a significant difference in the response pattern in which the pen type is a felt pen, the shooting method is only the frame, and the entry method differs.

From this it was found that when photographing by hand, if the auxiliary line is not displayed, the identification rate decreases compared to the fixed method.

However, because a significant difference is not seen when the pen used for both the hand-held camera method and the fixed camera method is a felt-tip pen, the auxiliary line is displayed, and the response patterns differ, it was found that when the photography method uses an auxiliary line, the influence by camera shake is not so great, and we were able to obtain a stable, high identification rate.

5. CONCLUSION AND FUTURE ISSUES

In this research we implemented four types of functions - ① "Calculation / Management Function" calculates the QOL score instantaneously and manages it as data, ② "Graph Presentation Function" displays the result visually to the patient in real time, ③ "Rehabilitation Activities Continuation Function " improves patient motivation for rehabilitation and encourages them to continue rehabilitation activities, ④ data input by camera - using a tablet terminal, which is a medium popular in the medical field.

We conducted comparative and evaluative experiments for this application utilizing the four aforementioned functions and using healthcare professionals and general users as subjects and verified the effectiveness of these functions. We made further improvements using the feedback we obtained.

As a result, we succeeded in developing an application that reduces the burden of data input and analytical work on the clinician, that can present a graph that allows the cancer patient to immediately understand his or her medical condition while still showing consideration to the patient's mental state, and has a function that encourages improvement in motivation for rehabilitation.

It is suggested that this application has a certain degree of stability and effective function, as developers incorporated as much of the opinion of medical staff as possible and due to its utility made clear by the general user test and user evaluation.

In the future, it could be applied to the Ethics Committee and more detailed data could be obtained by conducting experiments with patients at the actual clinical site. In addition, if it is able to arbitrarily set question items and calculation formulas so that it can deal with multiple QOL evaluation methods, this application can act as a contribution to the whole medical industry.

REFFERENCES

[1] Shirojiro Shimousuji; QOL evaluation of anticancer drug, Drug-epidemiology, Vol.5,No.2, pp.88-89, 2011.

[2] Noriko Okita and Yoshitaka Narita; Current status and issues of QOL research, Neurosurgical journal, Vol.23, No.1, pp.46-58, 2014.

[3] Satori Ikeda; Literature Review on QOL Evaluation for Severely and Severely Handicapped Children, Bulletin of the Graduate School of Education Hiroshima University, Vol.63, No.1, pp.59-66, 2014.

[4] Junichi Yamamoto; Applied Behavior Analysis to Increase "Motivation" of Rehabilitation, Physical Therapy, Vol.8, No.41, pp.492-498, 2014.

[5] Naoko Tsukamoto; An attempt to create a self-efficacy scale for cancer patients, Vol.3, No.31, pp.198-206, 1998.

[6] The Japan Orthopedic Society; Locomotive syndrome, Locomo-pamphlet, pp.11-12, 2015.

ISASE-MAICS 2018

Fatigue Detection Using Facial Landmarks

Nafis IRTIJA, Mahsius SAMI, and Md Atiqur Rahman AHAD

Department of Electrical and Electronic Engineering, University of Dhaka, Bangladesh
irtija_nafis@yahoo.com, sami.apece@gmail.com, atiqahad@du.ac.bd

Abstract: Detection of fatigue in human face is crucial for medical and safety purposes. Although it is a simple task for a human observer, for a computer, it is a very challenging problem. That is why various attempts were made to successfully detect fatigue. In this paper, we tried to determine the presence of fatigue in a face using computer vision. Here we proposed a method for fatigue recognition by exploiting the facial landmarks. We used the OpenCV library for image processing, and dlib library for feature extraction. The whole method was tested on the extended Cohn-Kanade dataset and the Psychological Image Collection at Stirling (PICS) dataset where it provided a satisfactory level of accuracy.
Keywords: *Fatigue detection, Image processing, Machine Learning, Facial expression recognition, Support Vector Machine*

1. INTRODUCTION

Fatigue extreme tiredness and inability to work or maintain cognitive performance [1]. There are various physical and mental reasons that can induce fatigue. Fatigue Detection is of importance for various reasons. According to studies, fatigue can be the underlying cause of depression [2], aggressive behavior [3], inability to work [4] and last but not least, driving safety. Humans use their expressions to show emotions. Though fatigue is not exactly an emotion, it can be considered as a motivational drive to rest [5]. So, it can be deduced that fatigue will also show distinctive changes in facial features. Thus, it is logical to expect that an effective image processing algorithm can be designed that can detect fatigue from a human face using computer vision. But it is also natural that detecting fatigue is going to be much more challenging than recognizing emotions because of the subtlety of the facial changes.

In this research, we propose a method to detect fatigue from human faces using image processing and facial landmarks detection. According to studies [5], fatigue can cause hanging eyelids and droopy corner of the mouth. We aim to detect these symptoms from the faces in our work. The paper is structured as follows: section 2 gives a brief overview of previous related works. The proposed method is described in section 3. In section 4 we discuss the result and performance of our work. Finally, in section 5, we conclude our work and also discuss possible future improvements.

2. RELATED WORKS

Almost all of the works done regarding fatigue detection is concerned with driver drowsiness. But fatigue and sleepiness are not exactly the same [6]. This research targets detecting fatigue in general.

In fatigue detection, tracking and analysis of the specific facial feature points is the main challenge. The facial features of eyes, mouth, and head need to be located in the video sequence and then facial features can be tracked. Facial parameters are calculated using facial feature tracking in [7].

As the eye is the most important cue of fatigue, there have been a number of methods for fatigue detection based on eye tracking [8, 9, 10, 11, 12, 13, 14, 15]. In those approaches, the face is located first. A face can be located by analyzing the characteristics of skin color [11, 9]. Eye can be detected using edge detection [11]. By measuring the distances between the intensity changes in the eye area one can determine whether the eyes are open or closed [8] and one way of determining if a person is fatigued is to observe the change in the distance between the eyelids [9].

Slow closure of eyelids during critical performance tasks is a reliable sign of fatigue [15]. Yang et al. modeled the closure of eyes using a pair of parabolic curves and fit the model in each frame to maximize the total likelihood of the eye regions. An algorithm proposed by Liu et al. [14] can detect eye corners. With the eye corners restrictions, eyelids movement can be detected precisely.

In 2002, Gu et al. [16] showed that the simultaneous use of IR sensors (for pupil detection) and the Kalman filtering greatly increases the prediction accuracy of each facial feature position. Feature detection is accomplished in the Gabor space with respect to the vicinity of the predicted location.

Zhang et al. [17] managed to detect driver fatigue by tracking whether the eyes are closed over 5 consecutive frames using vertical projection matching. Faces are located using Haar algorithm and the projection technique detects the eye. A new real-time eye-tracking method is proposed based on unscented Kalman filter. Using SVM classifier they estimated the percentage of eye closure, a very strong cue of fatigue detection. This gave much better outcome compared to Naive Bayes classifier. The performance was further improved by fusing all four cues of fatigue using fuzzy rules [18].

Another method proposed by Azim et al. [19, 20] initially locates the face through Viola-Jones face detection. Then, a window containing mouth is extracted from the face region, spatial fuzzy c-means clustering technique is used to search for lips. The pupils are detected using radii of pupils, inter-pupil distance, and angle. These data are used to classify the true state of the driver. Later the result was improved using Fuzzy Expert System.

Yin et al. [21] used Gabor filters to get a multi-scale representation for image sequences and Local Binary Patterns are extracted from each multi-scale image. Another method is developed based on Infrared image processing and physiological feature-heart rate, which uses fuzzy neural network expert system to discern fatigue status [22].

Apart from facial feature-based methods for fatigue detection there are propositions based on grip force measurement [23, 24], monitoring Electrocardiography (ECG) indexes [25], Electroencephalogram (EEG) power spectrum analysis [26, 27], etc.

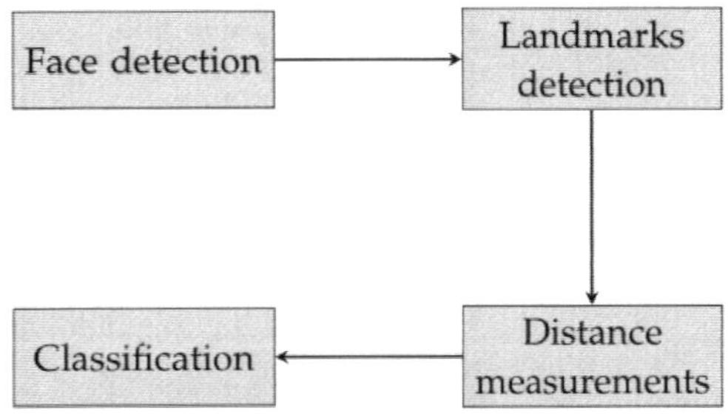

Figure 1: Flow diagram of Fatigue Detection

3. PROPOSED METHOD

We proposed a fatigue detection method based on changes in the eye and mouth region using facial landmark points. The method is summarized in Fig 1. The first step was detecting faces from the sample images. We used a Histogram of Oriented Gradients (HOG) based approach for this. Next, we detected 62 facial landmark points from all these faces. Then a central point was determined from which the distance of eye and lip corners are measured. The width of the eyes was also measured. Finally, all these distances were used as features to classify with a Support Vector Machine (SVM). In the following sections, the steps are described in details.

3.1 Face Detection

We used a classic face detector which is a combination of HOG features, a linear classifier, an image pyramid and moving window detection using the dlib library [28]. The dlib library implements the algorithm from [29]. In this method, an image is divided into small connected grids and for all the grids, the gradient is calculated. Then local histograms are determined from these gradients and combining these histograms a descriptor is formed. Finally, a linear SVM is used to detect faces. After detecting faces, the face area is cropped and resized to make all the images have the same size (see Fig. 3).

3.2 Facial Landmarks Detection

To find the landmarks on the faces, a shape estimator was used that is implemented in the dlib library based on the papers [30] and [31]. The estimator gives 68 landmark points including the corner of the eyes, the tip of the nose, etc. (Fig. 2). After detecting the landmarks are converted into coordinates.

Figure 2: Facial Landmark Points

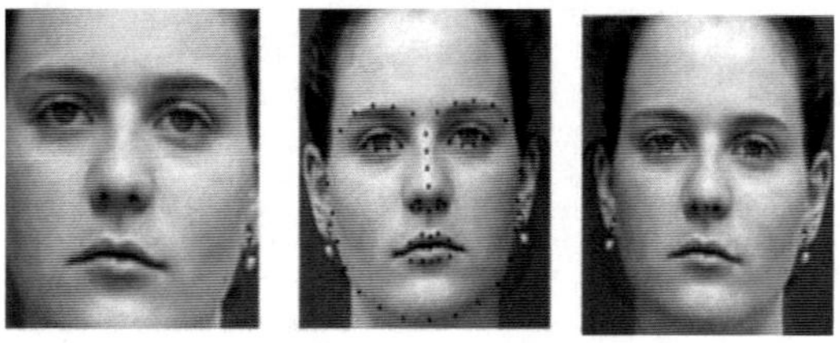

Figure 3: Three sample images for Subject 1

In the work of Kazemi and Josephine [30], a cascade of regression trees is used to detect the landmark points from a subset of pixel intensities. The sparse set of pixel intensities is determined using a gradient boosting algorithm. This method returns the landmarks accurately and efficiently. Ref. [31] proposed a semi-automatic annotation system to re-annotate most existing face databases using a unified protocol. The landmarks are from the multi-PIE 68 points mark-up in [33].

3.3 Distance Measurement

To detect the changes in the positions of the eye corner and lip corners, we computed a central point (green dot in Fig 3). The central point has the coordinates that is the mean of all the 68 coordinates [34].

$$\frac{\sum_{i=0}^{67}(x_i, y_i)}{68} \quad (1)$$

From this central point, the distance of the outer corners of the eyes (landmarks 37 and 46) and corners of the lips (landmarks 49 and 55) are measured. Also, the width of the eyes is also measured using landmarks 38, 39, 41, 42, 44, 45, 47, 48 (see Fig. 3).

3.4 Classification

All the measured distances were fed as features into a classifier. From the classifier, the accuracy and other metrics were calculated. For this experiment, an SVM classifier was used. SVM is a very powerful machine learning technique that can be used for classification [35]. For a training set of labeled examples $\{(x_i, y_i),\ i = 1,\dots,l\}$, where $x_i \epsilon R^n$ and $y_i \epsilon \{1, -1\}$, a new test example x is classified as:

$$f(x) = b + \sum_i \alpha_i k(x, x^{(i)}) \quad (2)$$

where b is a threshold parameter and α_i is a vector of coefficients. $k(x, x^{(i)})$ is called the kernel. The kernel is defined as, $k(x, x^{(i)}) = \phi(x).\phi(x)^{(i)}$. The relation between $f(x)$ and x is not linear, but $f(x)$ and $\phi(x)$ has a linear relationship. That is why SVM can take a dataset that is not linearly separable to a higher order where they are separable by a hyperplane [36].

4. RESULTS AND DISCUSSION

We used a total of 606 images from extended Cohn-Kanade [37] and Psychological Image Collection at Stirling dataset [38]. Among those 397 were of neutral faces. As there is no existing database of tired faces, we annotated 297 faces as tired and used in this experiment. These faces were mainly from sleepy, bored and sad faces. All the images were cropped and resized to be 350x350 pixels. After experimenting, the linear kernel with cost parameter c=10 was found to perform the best on the data.

Table 1: Results obtained from the landmark detection

	Accuracy	Precision	Recall	Support
Neutral	0.81	0.96	0.88	80
Fatigue	0.89	0.57	0.70	42
Average/ Total	**0.84**	**0.83**	**0.82**	**122**

This classifier gave an overall accuracy of 82.79%. The detailed performance report is given in Table 1. The Precision recall curve is shown in Fig. 4. Based on the complexity of the work, the results seem satisfactory. However, we need to explore smarter approaches for higher accuracy, especially from more realistic datasets.

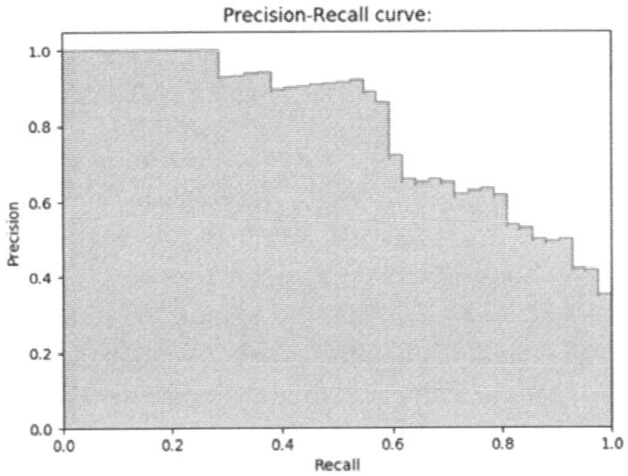

Figure 4: Precision versus recall curve for the achieved results.

5. CONCLUSION

In this paper, a method for fatigue detection is proposed based on facial landmarks detection. The main challenge of the method was to detect the subtle changes in features in a fatigued face in which respect the method achieves a satisfactory level of success. We used extended Cohn-Kanade dataset and Psychological Image Collection at Stirling dataset. We used the concept of landmark detection for feature extraction and then used SVM to detect fatigue from faces. Finally, we achieved an 82.79% accuracy.

There is a lack of datasets for fatigued faces. The performance of this research can be increased by building a strong and robust dataset for fatigued faces. This dataset can be built in some future research. Also, there are some other cases where the method can be further improved. For example, it can be modified so that it can be able to detect faces from live video streams and detect fatigued people.

REFFERENCES

[1] SC Gandevia. Some central and peripheral factors affecting human motoneuronal output in neuromuscular fatigue. Sports medicine, 13(2):93–98, 1992.

[2] P Skapinakis, G Lewis, and V Mavreas. Temporal relations between unexplained fatigue and depression: longitudinal data from an international study in primary care. Psychosomatic Medicine, 66(3):330–335, 2004.

[3] F Kuo and WC Sullivan. Aggression and violence in the inner city: Effects of environment via mental fatigue. Environment and behavior, 33(4):543–571, 2001.

[4] Samuele M Marcora, Walter Staiano, and Victoria Manning. Mental fatigue impairs physical performance in humans. Journal of applied physiology, 106(3):857–864, 2009.

[5] Tina Sundelin, Mats Lekander, Göran Kecklund, Eus JW Van Someren, Andreas Olsson, and John Axelsson. Cues of fatigue: effects of sleep deprivation on facial appearance. Sleep, 36(9):1355–1360, 2013.

[6] Jianhua Shen, Joseph Barbera, and Colin M Shapiro. Distinguishing sleepiness and fatigue: focus on definition and measurement. Sleep medicine reviews, 10(1):63–76, 2006.

[7] KP Yao, WH Lin, Chiung-Yao Fang, Jung-Ming Wang, Shyang-Lih Chang, and Sei-Wang Chen. Real-time vision-based driver drowsiness/fatigue detection system. In Vehicular Technology Conference (VTC 2010-Spring), 2010 IEEE 71st, pages 1–5. IEEE, 2010.

[8] Mandalapu Sarada Devi and Preeti R Bajaj. Driver fatigue detection based on eye tracking. In Emerging Trends in Engineering and Technology, 2008. ICETET'08. First International Conference on, pages 649–652. IEEE, 2008.

[9] Wenhui Dong and Xiaojuan Wu. Fatigue detection based on the distance of eyelid. In VLSI Design and Video Technology, 2005. Proceedings of 2005 IEEE International Workshop on, pages 365–368. IEEE, 2005.

[10] Liling Li, Mei Xie, and Huazhi Dong. A method of driving fatigue detection based on eye location. In Communication Software and Networks (ICCSN), 2011 IEEE 3rd International Conference on, pages 480–484. IEEE, 2011.

[11] Wen-Bing Horng, Chih-Yuan Chen, Yi Chang, and Chun-Hai Fan. Driver fatigue detection based on eye tracking and dynamk, template matching. In Networking, Sensing and Control, 2004 IEEE International Conference on, volume 1, pages 7–12. IEEE, 2004.

[12] Weiwei Liu, Haixin Sun, and Weijie Shen. Driver fatigue detection through pupil detection and yawing analysis. In Bioinformatics and Biomedical Technology (ICBBT), 2010 International Conference on, pages 404–407. IEEE, 2010.

[13] Zutao Zhang and Jiashu Zhang. A new real-time eye tracking for driver fatigue detection. In ITS Telecommunications Proceedings, 2006 6th International Conference on, pages 8–11. IEEE,

2006.

[14] Ang Liu, Zhichao Li, Lang Wang, and Yong Zhao. A practical driver fatigue detection algorithm based on eye state. In Microelectronics and Electronics (PrimeAsia), 2010 Asia Pacific Conference on Postgraduate Research in, pages 235–238. IEEE, 2010.

[15] Fei Yang, Xiang Yu, Junzhou Huang, Peng Yang, and Dimitris Metaxas. Robust eyelid tracking for fatigue detection. In Image Processing (ICIP), 2012 19th IEEE International Conference on, pages 1829–1832. IEEE, 2012.

[16] Haisong Gu, Qiang Ji, and Zhiwei Zhu. Active facial tracking for fatigue detection. In Applications of Computer Vision, 2002. (WACV 2002). Proceedings. Sixth IEEE Workshop on, pages 137–142. IEEE, 2002.

[17] Zutao Zhang and Jia-shu Zhang. Driver fatigue detection based intelligent vehicle control. In Pattern Recognition, 2006. ICPR 2006. 18th International Conference on, volume 2, pages 1262–1265. IEEE, 2006.

[18] Rajinda Senaratne, David Hardy, Bill Vanderaa, and Saman Halgamuge. Driver fatigue detection by fusing multiple cues. In International Symposium on Neural Networks, pages 801–809. Springer, 2007.

[19] Tayyaba Azim, M Arfan Jaffar, and Anwar Majid Mirza. Automatic fatigue detection of drivers through pupil detection and yawning analysis. In Innovative Computing, Information and Control (ICICIC), 2009 Fourth International Conference on, pages 441–445. IEEE, 2009.

[20] Tayyaba Azim, M Arfan Jaffar, and Anwar M Mirza. Fully automated real time fatigue detection of drivers through fuzzy expert systems. Applied Soft Computing, 18:25–38, 2014.

[21] Bao-Cai Yin, Xiao Fan, and Yan-Feng Sun. Multiscale dynamic features-based driver fatigue detection. International Journal of Pattern Recognition and Artificial Intelligence, 23(03):575–589, 2009.

[22] Chen Yong, Huang Qi, Liu Xia, and Zhang Changhua. All-weather detection method of driver fatigue [j]. Chinese Journal of Scientific Instrument, 3:034, 2009.

[23] Federico Baronti, Francesco Lenzi, Roberto Roncella, and Roberto Saletti. Distributed sensor for steering wheel grip force measurement in driver fatigue detection. In Proceedings of the Conference on Design, Automation and Test in Europe, pages 894–897. European Design and Automation Association, 2009.

[24] Thum Chia Chieh, Mohd Marzuki Mustafa, Aini Hussain, Edmond Zahedi, and Burhanuddin Yeop Majlis. Driver fatigue detection using steering grip force. In Research and Development, 2003. SCORED 2003. Proceedings. Student Conference on, pages 45–48. IEEE, 2003.

[25] YS Yang, ZQ Yao, ZY Li, and Kun JIAO. Investigation on correlation between ECG indexes and driving fatigue. Machinery Design & Manufacture, 5:048,2002.

[26] Shuyan Hu, Gangtie Zheng, and Björn Peters. Driver fatigue detection from electroencephalogram spectrum after electrooculography artefact removal. IET Intelligent Transport Systems, 7(1):105–113, 2013.

[27] Budi Thomas Jap, Sara Lal, Peter Fischer, and Evangelos Bekiaris. Using EEG spectral components to assess algorithms for detecting fatigue. Expert Systems with Applications, 36(2):2352–2359, 2009.

[28] Davis E King. Dlib-ml: A machine learning toolkit. Journal of Machine Learning Research, 10(Jul):1755–1758, 2009.

[29] Navneet Dalal, Bill Triggs, and Cordelia Schmid. Human detection using oriented histograms of flow and appearance. In European conference on computer vision, pages 428–441. Springer, 2006.

[30] Vahid Kazemi and Sullivan Josephine. One millisecond face alignment with an ensemble of regression trees. In 27th IEEE Conference on Computer Vision and Pattern Recognition, CVPR 2014, Columbus, United States, 23 June 2014 through 28 June 2014, pages 1867–1874. IEEE Computer Society, 2014.

[31] Christos Sagonas, Georgios Tzimiropoulos, Stefanos Zafeiriou, and Maja Pantic. 300 faces in-the-wild challenge: The first facial landmark localization challenge. In Computer Vision Workshops (ICCVW), 2013 IEEE International Conference on, pages 397–403. IEEE, 2013.

[32] Facial point annotations. https://ibug.doc.ic.ac.uk/resources/facial-point-annotations/. Accessed: April 18, 2018.

[33] Ralph Gross, Iain Matthews, Jeffrey Cohn, Takeo Kanade, and Simon Baker. Multi-pie. Image and Vision Computing, 28(5):807–813, 2010.

[34] Paul Van Gent. Emotion recognition using facial landmarks, python, dlib and opencv. http://www.paulvangent.com/2016/08/05/emotion-recognition-using-facial-landmarks/, 2016. Accessed: April 18, 2018.

[35] Corinna Cortes and Vladimir Vapnik. Support-vector networks. Machine learning, 20(3):273–297, 1995.

[36] Ian Goodfellow, Yoshua Bengio, Aaron Courville, and Yoshua Bengio. Deep learning, volume 1. MIT press Cambridge, 2016.

[37] Patrick Lucey, Jeffrey F Cohn, Takeo Kanade, Jason Saragih, Zara Ambadar, and Iain Matthews. The extended cohn-kanade dataset (ck+): A complete dataset for action unit and emotion-specified expression. In Computer Vision and Pattern Recognition Workshops (CVPRW), 2010 IEEE Computer Society Conference on, pages 94– 101. IEEE, 2010.

[38] Peter Hancock. Psychological image collection at Stirling (pics). Web address: http://pics.psych.stir.ac.uk, 2008.

ISASE-MAICS 2018

A Kernel *k*-Means-based Method for Diabetes Diagnosis

Tru CAO[1,2], Chau VO[1], Son NGUYEN[1], Atsushi INOUE[2], Duanning ZHOU[2]

[1] *Ho Chi Minh City University of Technology, Vietnam National University, Ho Chi Minh City, Vietnam*
tru@cse.hcmut.edu.vn, chauvtn@hcmut.edu.vn, tsonnguyen95@gmail.com
[2] *Eastern Washington University, Spokane, Washington State, United States of America*
tcao2@ewu.edu, ainoue@ewu.edu, dzhou@ewu.edu

Abstract: Diabetes diagnosis is important due to the death and complication consequences caused by the disease. It thus has attracted much research attention and effort in Artificial Intelligence to support human decisions. Our work proposes a kernel *k*-means-based predictive method and explores attribute selections for effective and robust diabetes diagnosis. This method uses homogeneous subclusters in the high dimensional kernelized feature space to compute the distance of a new instance to those subclusters and classify it accordingly. The PIMA and MIMIC data sets are respectively used for training and testing. Our experimental results could identify the best effective attribute groups and show that the proposed method outperforms existing ones for the task.
Keywords: *Disease diagnosis, feature selection, clustering, PIMA data set, MIMIC database*

1. INTRODUCTION

As reported in [20], diabetes is considered to be the seventh leading cause of death in 2030. It has risen from 108 million diabetic people in 1980 to 422 million ones in 2014. It is also a major cause of blindness, kidney failure, heart attacks, stroke, and lower limb amputation.

Diabetes diagnosis is thus important and has attracted much research effort in Artificial Intelligence to support doctors' decisions, as recently surveyed in [4]. In particular, machine learning methods were proposed, such as decision trees [6, 19], *k*-nearest neighbors [1], logistic regression [10, 14], neural networks [3, 5, 6, 7, 10, 11, 17], and support vector machines [12, 15]. In [2], electronic medical records were exploited for personalized diabetes management.

Besides prediction, [6, 8, 16] provided interpretable rules for decision making support in the disease diagnosis. Also, most of the above-mentioned works combined machine learning with other methods for data preprocessing such as genetic method [3], self-organizing maps [11], *k*-means [12], fuzzy c-means [16], random forests [14], and principal component analysis [11, 19].

Consequently, there were many different groups of attributes (i.e., feature) used for diabetes diagnosis as a machine learning task. However, to the best of our knowledge, there has been no extensive examination of attribute groups to identify the most effective ones for prediction. Meanwhile, doctors have relied on their medical knowledge to examine a patient's clinical and paraclinical information to diagnose diabetes.

In this paper, we propose a novel method and explore various attribute groups for diabetes diagnosis. Our method is a kernel *k*-means-based one that classifies a new instance, i.e., as positive or negative, depending on its distances to the homogeneous subclusters obtained from a training dataset in a high dimensional kernelized feature space. We use the PIMA dataset [17] for training our model and diabetes cases from the MIMIC database [9] for testing it in comparison to some existing ones.

Next, Section 2 formulates the diabetes diagnosis problem and presents our proposed method. Section 3 presents our experiments evaluating the effectiveness of different attribute groups and the performance of the proposed method. Finally, Section 4 gives some concluding remarks.

2. THE PROPOSED METHOD

2.1 Problem definition

Given the information of a person, the problem is to predict if the person potentially has diabetes. The information includes his/her lab test results, current and past personal diseases, medication history, and family medical history. The prediction is binary, i.e., 1 if positive with diabetes, or 0 if negative.

2.2 Attribute groups

We summarize and name the attribute groups used in the corresponding works based on the attributes in the

PIMA data set, as presented in Table 1 below. The description of each attribute can be found in [17].

Group 8 was originally proposed for diabetes diagnosis in [17]. Group 2 in [6] was found in the extracted rules. Group 3_1 in [14] contained the top ranked attributes. Group 6_2 in [1] was the best case among several selected groups. Especially, Group 5 is what doctors rely on to diagnose diabetes, as provided in the decision support medical information visualization system [13].

Table 1: Different attribute groups in the existing works

Related Work	Named Group	Number of Attributes	Attributes
[6]	2	2	Glucose, BMI
[14]	3_1	3	Glucose, Insulin, BMI
[15]	3_2	3	Pregnancies, Glucose, Age
[3]	4	4	Glucose, Insulin, BMI, Age
[13]	5	5	Glucose, BloodPressure, Insulin, BMI, Age
[12]	6_1	6	Pregnancies, Glucose, Insulin, BMI, DiabetesPedigreeFunction, Age
[1]	6_2	6	Pregnancies, Glucose, BloodPressure, Insulin, BMI, DiabetesPedigreeFunction
[17]	8	8	Pregnancies, Glucose, BloodPressure, SkinThickness, Insulin, BMI, DiabetesPedigreeFunction, Age

3.2 The proposed kernel *k*-means-based method

Firstly, diabetes shares some symptoms and has common medical attribute values with some other diseases. This leads to data overlapping for diabetic people and non-diabetic people, as shown in [11] via visualization. Therefore, we propose to use a kernel to map the original diabetes data space to a higher dimensional one, so that instances can be more discriminated.

Secondly, in medical research, the *k*-nearest neighbor method has recently been used for personalized diabetes management in [2]. However, if *k* is small, this method is ineffective with noises and, if *k* is large, it causes class heterogeneity of the *k* returned nearest neighbors. To overcome it, in this work we propose to use the 1-nearest neighbor method at the prediction step but on the derived homogeneous subclusters, rather than on the main clusters obtained from the training step using kernel *k*-means [18].

Details of our proposed method for diabetes prediction are as follows:

Input:

- D_t is a training set of instances X_i with classes y_i,
- D_u is a set of new instances X_j,
- k is a predefined number of clusters,
- *sigma* is a bandwidth of the Gaussian kernel function.

Output:

- Predicted class y_j of X_j for every $X_j \in D_u$.

Process:

Step 1: Construct a clustering model in the feature space of the training data

1.1. Compute a kernel matrix KM from the instances in D_t:

$$KM(X_r, X_q) = K_{rq} = e^{-\frac{\|X_r - X_q\|^2}{2*sigma^2}}$$

where $\| X_r - X_q \| = \sqrt{\sum_{d=1..p} (x_{rd} - x_{qd})^2}$

for r=1..n_t and q=1..n_t

1.2. Establish a membership matrix γ between k clusters C_o and n_t instances X_i in D_t, for o=1..k, i=1..n_t. Each cell in γ is 1 if X_i belongs to C_o; or 0, otherwise. This matrix is initialized with the traditional k-means method on D_t.

1.3. Repeat the following substeps until the membership matrix γ is unchanged:

1.3.1. Update the distance between each cluster C_o and each instance X_r in D_t in the feature space as follows:

$$\|\phi(X_r) - C_o\|^2 = K_{rr} - \frac{2\sum_{q=1..n_t} \gamma_{oq} K_{rq}}{\sum_{q=1..n_t} \gamma_{oq}} + \frac{\sum_{v=1..n_t} \sum_{z=1..n_t} \gamma_{ov}\gamma_{oz} K_{vz}}{\sum_{v=1..n_t} \sum_{z=1..n_t} \gamma_{ov}\gamma_{oz}}$$

for o=1..k and r=1..n_t

1.3.2. Update the membership γ_{or} between the instance X_r and the cluster C_o as follows:

$$\gamma_{or} = \begin{cases} 1, \text{if } \|\phi(X_r) - C_o\|^2 = argmin_{o'=1..k}(\|\phi(X_r) - C_{o'}\|^2) \\ 0, otherwise \end{cases}$$

for r=1..n_t and o=1..k

Step 2: Construct a predictive model

2.1. Derive homogeneous subclusters $HC_{o'}$ from the main clusters C_o in Step 1 for o'=1..k*$|Y|$, o=1..k

A homogeneous subcluster $HC_{o'}$ is defined as a smaller group of the instances in C_o that belong to the same class in Y. For each main cluster C_o, the maximum number of homogeneous subclusters $HC_{o'}$ is $|Y|$ when only one instance in C_o belongs to each class in Y. The minimum number is 1 when all of the instances in C_o belong to the same class.

2.2. Assign the common class $y_{o'}$ of all of the instances in a homogeneous subcluster $HC_{o'}$ to that homogeneous subcluster $HC_{o'}$ for o' = 1..k*$|Y|$

Step 3: Predict a class y_j of a new instance X_j for every $X_j \in D_u$

3.1. Calculate the kernel-induced Euclidean distance between X_j and each homogeneous subcluster $HC_{o'}$ via its mean vector:

$$distance(X_j, HC_{o'}) = 2 - 2*K(X_j, HC_{o'})$$

where $K()$ is the Gaussian kernel function, j=1..n_u, o'=1..k*|Y|.

3.2. Based on the smallest distance in the previous substep, assign the class $y_{o'}$ of the nearest homogeneous subcluster $HC_{o'}$ to the new instance X_j for prediction, i.e., $y_j = y_{o'}$.

4. EVALUATION

The evaluation of our proposed method is to answer the following questions:

Question 1: Given a data set and a method, which attribute group is more effective for diabetes diagnosis?

Question 2: Given a data set and an attribute group, which method is more effective for diabetes diagnosis?

Question 3: Given a data set, which method is more robust to missing values of attributes of instances?

The effectiveness is measured by the Accuracy, Recall, Precision, and F measures. In this context, Accuracy is the percentage of correctly predicted people to be either positive or negative with diabetes. Recall is the percentage of all true diabetic patients that are predicted. Meanwhile, Precision is the percentage of positively predicted people who are truly diabetic patients.

The robustness is addressed because, without preprocessing, there are many instances in the training and testing data sets that miss some attribute values. Table 2 presents the details of the two data sets PIMA and MIMIC that we use for training and testing, respectively.

We compare the proposed method with the following typical baseline methods: *k*-nearest neighbors (*k*-NN) [1], logistic regression (LR) [10, 14], neural networks (NN) [3, 5, 6, 7, 10, 11, 17], and support vector machines (SVM) [12, 15].

Table 2: Data descriptions for training and testing

Data set	Role	Number of Instances	Percentage of Positives	Percentage of Negatives	Percentage of Missing Values
PIMA	Training	768	34.9%	65.1%	12.1%
MIMIC	Testing	180	38.9%	61.1%	15.4%

For parameter settings, we use k in {1, 3, 5} for *k*-NN; feedforward multiplayer perceptrons with the default network configuration, learning rate = 0.01, and training time = 1,000 epochs for NN; the radial basis function as a kernel with *gamma* = 0.01 and C = 50 for SVM. As for the proposed kernel *k*-means-based method (KK), we use the Gaussian kernel function with the *sigma* computed from the attribute variances in {0.1, 0.09, 0.08, 0.07, 0.06, 0.05, 0.04, 0.03, 0.02, 0.01, 0.009, 0.008, 0.007, 0.006, 0.005, 0.004, 0.003, 0.002, 0.001, 0.0009, 0.0008, 0.0007, 0.0006, 0.0005, 0.0004, 0.0003, 0.0002, 0.0001} and k in {2, 4, 6, 8, 10, 12, 14}. The grid search scheme was used.

For the results, Accuracy is presented in percent (%) in the range [0, 100], while Recall, Precision, and F-measure are shown in the range [0, 1]. For Question 1, Table 3 and Table 4 respectively show the attribute group that gives a certain method the highest Accuracy or the highest F-measure. For each method and each attribute group, the highest measures are obtained with the best tuned parameters. In both cases, our proposed method has the best performance, with attribute group 3_1.

Table 3: The highest Accuracy for each method

Method	Attribute Group	Accuracy	Recall	Precision	F-measure
KK	3_1	**92.78**	0.81	1.00	0.90
k-NN	2	67.78	0.40	0.64	0.49
LR	2	69.44	0.46	0.65	0.54
NN	6_1	71.11	0.41	0.73	0.53
SVM	6_1	69.44	0.44	0.66	0.53
SVM	8	69.44	0.46	0.65	0.54

Table 4: The highest F-measure for each method

Method	Attribute Group	Accuracy	Recall	Precision	F-measure
KK	3_1	92.78	0.81	1.00	**0.90**
k-NN	3_2	60.00	0.56	0.49	0.52
LR	5	63.89	0.56	0.53	0.55
NN	3_1	67.78	0.49	0.61	0.54
SVM	5	62.22	0.59	0.51	0.55

For Question 2, Tables 5-7 respectively present the highest Accuracy, Recall, and F-measure of each method for each attribute group. For each measure, the highest values are obtained with the best tuned parameters. It shows that our proposed method outperforms all of the compared ones on every measure and every attribute group.

Note that group 3_1 consists of only three attributes, namely, Glucose, Insulin, and BMI. However, for our proposed method, it gives the same Recall as, but better Accuracy and F-measure than any other group, including group 8 (with 8 attributes) that doctors have used for diabetes diagnosis. For the other methods, it also give better results than, or comparable to, the other attribute groups. That is, machines can support doctors to have simpler but more accurate diagnosis.

Table 5: The highest Accuracy of each method for each attribute group

Attribute Group	KK	*k*-NN	LR	NN	SVM
2	**77.78**	67.78	69.44	68.33	68.33
3_1	**92.78**	67.22	68.33	67.78	67.78
3_2	**63.89**	60	63.33	60	62.22
4	**91.67**	65.56	66.67	67.78	64.44
5	**88.33**	66.67	63.89	66.67	62.22
6_1	**79.44**	62.78	68.89	71.11	69.44
6_2	**75.56**	60.56	67.22	68.89	68.89
8	**74.44**	63.89	67.78	70.56	69.44

Table 6: The highest Recall of each method for each attribute group

Attribute Group	KK	*k*-NN	LR	NN	SVM
2	**1.00**	0.40	0.46	0.47	0.49
3_1	**1.00**	0.39	0.46	0.49	0.49
3_2	**1.00**	0.59	0.54	0.57	0.51
4	**1.00**	0.34	0.51	0.44	0.54
5	**1.00**	0.34	0.56	0.47	0.59
6_1	**1.00**	0.14	0.41	0.41	0.44
6_2	**1.00**	0.13	0.39	0.43	0.43
8	**1.00**	0.30	0.44	0.41	0.46

Table 7: The highest F-measure of each method for each attribute group

Attribute Group	KK	*k*-NN	LR	NN	SVM
2	**0.78**	0.49	0.54	0.54	0.54
3_1	**0.90**	0.48	0.53	0.54	0.54
3_2	**0.60**	0.52	0.54	0.53	0.51
4	**0.88**	0.44	0.55	0.52	0.54
5	**0.84**	0.44	0.55	0.52	0.55
6_1	**0.76**	0.22	0.51	0.53	0.53
6_2	**0.73**	0.19	0.48	0.52	0.52
8	**0.68**	0.39	0.52	0.52	0.54

Table 8 and Table 9 focus on the proposed method. For each attribute group, Table 8 presents the corresponding Recall, Precision, and F-measure of the proposed method when it achieves the highest Accuracy. Meanwhile, Table 9 presents the corresponding Accuracy, Recall, and Precision of the proposed method when it achieves the highest F-measure. The results show that the proposed method has the highest values for the Accuracy at the same time as for the F-measure. Also, they are with groups 3_1, 4, and 5, which consist of only 3 to 5 attributes.

For Question 3, although there are respectively 12.1% and 15.4% of missing attribute values in the PIMA and MIMIC data sets, our proposed method still achieves high Accuracy and F-measure as compared to the baseline ones. This proves its robustness to such noises in the data.

Table 8: The Recall, Precision, and F-measure corresponding to the highest Accuracy of the proposed method for each attribute group

Attribute Group	Accuracy	Recall	Precision	F-measure
2	77.78	1.00	0.64	0.78
3_1	**92.78**	0.81	1.00	0.90
3_2	63.89	0.60	0.54	0.56
4	91.67	0.79	1.00	0.88
5	88.33	0.81	0.88	0.84
6_1	79.44	0.80	0.71	0.75
6_2	75.56	0.86	0.64	0.73
8	74.44	0.60	0.70	0.65

Table 9: The Accuracy, Recall, Precision corresponding to the highest F-measure of the proposed method for each attribute group

Attribute Group	Accuracy	Recall	Precision	F-measure
2	77.78	1.00	0.64	0.78
3_1	92.78	0.81	1.00	**0.90**
3_2	58.89	0.79	0.48	0.60
4	91.67	0.79	1.00	0.88
5	88.33	0.81	0.88	0.84
6_1	76.67	0.94	0.63	0.76
6_2	75.56	0.86	0.64	0.73
8	71.67	0.76	0.61	0.68

5. CONCLUSIONS

In this paper, diabetes diagnosis has been studied as a binary classification task with our new proposed method. The method generates the clusters of similar instances in a high dimensional feature space using the Gaussian kernel function. Homogeneous subclusters are derived from the main clusters. A new instance is then predicted to belong to the class of the instances in its nearest subcluster.

Besides, our work has also conducted the experiments with several attribute groups used the related works and one used by medical doctors in practice. A new diabetes data set from the MIMIC database has been built as a testing data set for evaluating these attribute groups and the compared methods. The results have showed that the proposed method outperforms the others on every attribute group, and that the group of 3 attributes Glucose, Insulin, and BMI are sufficient for diabetes diagnosis.

For future work, a parameter-free version of the proposed method is considered for its stability and friendliness in practical use. Enhancing a medical information visualization system with the findings of this work is also of our interest. Such an enhancement is helpful for bridging a gap between human experts and computer systems in disease diagnosis.

REFFERENCES

[1] S. Bahramian and A. Nikravanshalmani; Hybrid Method Based on K-Nearest-Neighbor Method and Adaboost with Selection of Feature by Genetic Methods for the Diagnosis of Diabetes, International Journal of Mechatronics, Electrical and Computer Technology, 6 (21), pp. 2977-2986, 2016.

[2] Dimitris Bertsimas, Nathan Kallus, Alexander M. Weinstein and Ying Daisy Zhuo; Personalized Diabetes Management Using Electronic Medical Records, Diabetes Care, 40, pp. 210-217, 2017.

[3] Dilip Kumar Choubey and Sanchita Paul; GA_RBF NN: a Classification System for Diabetes, International Journal of Biomedical Engineering and Technology, 23 (1), pp. 71-93, 2017.

[4] Dilip Kumar Choubey and Sanchita Paul; Classification Techniques for Diagnosis of Diabetes: a Review, International Journal Biomedical Engineering and Technology, 21 (1), pp. 15-39, 2016.

[5] Okan Erkaymaz, Mahmut Ozer and Matjaž Perc; Performance of Small-world Feedforward Neural Networks for the Diagnosis of Diabetes, Applied Mathematics and Computation, 311, pp. 22-28, 2017.

[6] Yoichi Hayshi and Shonosuke Yukita; Rule Extraction Using Recursive-Rule Extraction Method with J48graft Combined with Sampling Selection Techniques for the Diagnosis of Type 2 Diabetes Mellitus in the PIMA Indian Dataset, Informatics in Medicine Unlocked, 2, pp. 92-104, 2016.

[7] Nawaz Khan, Dhara Gaurav and Thomas Kandl; Performance Evaluation of Levenberg-Marquardt Technique in Error Reduction for Diabetes Condition Classification, Procedia Computer Science, 18, pp. 2629-2637, 2013.

[8] Stavros Lekkas and Ludmil Mikhailov; Evolving Fuzzy Medical Diagnosis of Pima Indians Diabetes and of Dermatological Diseases, Artificial Intelligence in Medicine, 50, pp. 117-126, 2010.

[9] MIMIC; MIMIC-III Database, URL: https://mimic.physionet.org/about/mimic/, Last Accessed by Feb 26th, 2018.

[10] Nongyao Nai-arun and Rungruttikarn Moungmai; Comparison of Classifiers for the Risk of Diabetes Prediction, Procedia Computer Science, 69, pp. 132-142, 2015.

[11] Mehrbakhsh Nilashi, Othman Ibrahim, Mohammad Dalvi, Hossein Ahmadi and Leila Shahmoradi; Accuracy Improvement for Diabetes Disease Classification: a Case on a Public Medical Dataset, Fuzzy Inf. Eng., 9, pp. 345-357, 2017.

[12] Ahmed Hamza Osman and Hani Moetque Aljahdali; Diabetes Disease Diagnosis Method Based on Feature Extraction Using K-SVM, International Journal of Advanced Computer Science and Applications, 8(1), pp. 236-244, 2017.

[13] Margit Pohl, Sylvia Wiltner, Alexander Rind, Wolfgang Aigner, Silvia Miksch, Thomas Turic and Felix Drexler; Patient Development at a Glance: an Evaluation of a Medical Data Visualization, IFIP Conference on Human-Computer Interaction, LNCS 6949, pp. 292-299, 2011.

[14] Sushant Ramesh, H. Balaji, N. Ch. S. N Iyengar and Ronnie D. Caytiles; Optimal Predictive Analytics of Pima Diabetics Using Deep Learning, International Journal of Database Theory and Application, 10(9), pp. 47-62, 2017.

[15] T. Santhanam and M.S. Padmavathi; Application of K-Means and Genetic Methods for Dimension Reduction by Integrating SVM for Diabetes Diagnosis, Procedia Computer Science, 47, pp. 76-83, 2015.

[16] Nesma Settouti, M. Amine Chikh and Meryem Saidi; Generating Fuzzy Rules for Constructing Interpretable Classifier of Diabetes Disease, Australas Phys Eng Sci Med, pp. 1-14, 2012.

[17] Jack W. Smith, JE Everhart, WC Dickson, WC Knowler and RS Johannes; Using the ADAP Learning Method to Forecast the Onset of Diabetes Mellitus, Annu Comput Appl Med Care, pp. 261-265, 1988.

[18] Grigorios Tzortzis and Aristidis Likas; The Global Kernel *k*-Means Clustering Method, The 2008 International Joint Conference on Neural Networks, pp. 1978-1985, 2008.

[19] Kamadi V.S.R.P. Varma, Allam Appa Rao, Thummala Sita Mahalakshmi and P.V. Nageswara Rao; A Computational Intelligence Technique for the Effective Diagnosis of Diabetic Patients Using Principal Component Analysis (PCA) and Modified Fuzzy SLIQ Decision Tree Approach, Applied Soft Computing, 49, pp. 137-145, 2016.

[20] World Health Organization (WHO); Diabetes, URL: http://www.who.int/mediacentre/factsheets/fs312/en/, Last Accessed by Feb 19th, 2018.

ISASE-MAICS 2018

Deep Learning of 2-D Images Representing n-D Data in General Line Coordinates

Dmytro Dovhalets, Boris Kovalerchuk, Szilárd Vajda, Răzvan Andonie*
Computer Science Department
Central Washington University, Ellensburg, WA, USA
{dmytro.dovhalets, boris.kovalerchuk, szilard.vajda, razvan.andonie}@cwu.edu
* *also with Electronics and Computers Department, Transilvania University, Brașov, Romania*

Abstract: While knowledge discovery and n-D data visualization procedures are often efficient, the loss of information, occlusion, and clutter continue to be a challenge. General Line Coordinates (GLC) is a rather new technique to deal with such artifacts. GLC-Linear, which is one of the methods in GLC, allows transforming n-D numerical data to their visual representation as polylines losslessly. The method proposed in this paper uses these 2-D visual representations as input to Convolutional Neural Network (CNN) classifiers. The obtained classification accuracies are close to the ones obtained by other machine learning algorithms. The main benefit of the method is the possibility to use the lossless visualization of n-dimensional data for interpretation and explanation of the discovered relationships besides the classical classification using statistical learning strategies.
Keywords: *Machine learning, CNN, General Line Coordinates, lossless visualization, multidimensional data.*

1. INTRODUCTION

Many procedures for n-D data analysis, knowledge discovery and visualization have demonstrated efficiency in the past. However, the loss of information, occlusion, and clutter in visualizations of n-D data continue to be a challenge for visual knowledge discovery. The dimension scalability challenge for visualization of n-D data is present at a low dimension of $n = 4$. Since only 2-D and 3-D data can be directly visualized in the physical 3-D world, visualization of n-D data becomes more difficult with higher dimensions as there is greater loss of information, occlusion and clutter. General Line Coordinates (GLC) [Kovalerchuk, 2018] visualize multidimensional data losslessly. There is no dimension reduction or loss of information during the visualization process. The n-dimensional data points are projected onto 2-D graphs without losing any information in the process, in contrast to (for instance) Self Organizing Maps. One of the methods from GLC is the GLC-Linear (GLC-L) [Kovalerchuk, Dovhalets, 2017, Kovalerchuk, 2018].

GLC-L projects multidimensional data into polylines that allow seeing the high dimensional data in a regular 2-D space. The use of GLC-L to visualize a single n-D point at a time produces its polyline, which can be interpreted as an image. The process is repeated for every given n-D point creating a set of images of n-D points from different classes. Transforming numeric multidimensional datasets into 2-D graphs (images) using GLC-L provides a unique lossless transformation of data. Visualizing only one n-D data instance at a time eliminates clutter and provides a clean visualization for all the data points.

Those artificially created images can be used later for classification if needed. Users can compare these images side-by-side for extraction of possible rules, features and relations, --with the condition that the number of images is relatively small and the patterns are recognizable by humans. Feeding these images to a CNN in a supervised learning paradigm allows automating this classification task for even larger datasets.

The proposed *conversion* of a *numeric Machine Learning* (ML) *classification task* to an *image recognition* task opens a unique new opportunity for resolving long-standing ML challenges of: (1) giving *explanation* to the discovered ML models, and (2) controlling *overfitting* and *overgeneralization* of ML models. This opportunity follows from the advantages of the visual analysis of multidimensional data as outlined below.

Explainable models often are too complex for domain experts, e.g., a decision tree with 50 layers and hundreds of nodes. Such large trees way exceed the magical number 7±2 of the Miller's law that is a limit on human capacity for processing information [Miller, 1956]. Thus, complex numeric ML models such as CNN must be "degraded" to the level of human understanding.

In contrast, humans recognize images with much larger number of features than 7±2. The face recognition by humans is one of such examples. It is *quick* and often *preattentive* due to *parallel* processing capabilities of the human visual system, in contrast with the sequential processing of the numeric information.

Thus, we suggest *visual explanation* of ML models on numeric data as an alternative to the traditional explanation in natural language or mathematical forms, that we call *textual explanation*, for short.

Fig. 1 shows an example of a possible way of visual explanation. Here, 9-D breast cancer data [Lichman, 2013] of benign and malignant cases is linearly separated (with over 96% accuracy) with distinct visual patterns using the GLC-L visualization method [Kovalerchuk, Dovhalets, 2017]. While the natural language description of these distinct patterns is not obvious, their visual distinction is way more clear. The angles at the bottom of the figure (see **Fig. 1**) indicate the contribution of each of the 9 attributes (dimensions) to the separation of classes. For SVM (Support Vector Machines), visual explanation can be in the form of visualized support vectors from opposing classes that SVM algorithm finds on images and uses for classification. More examples of visual explainable patterns for numeric classification tasks are provided in [Kovalerchuk, 2018].

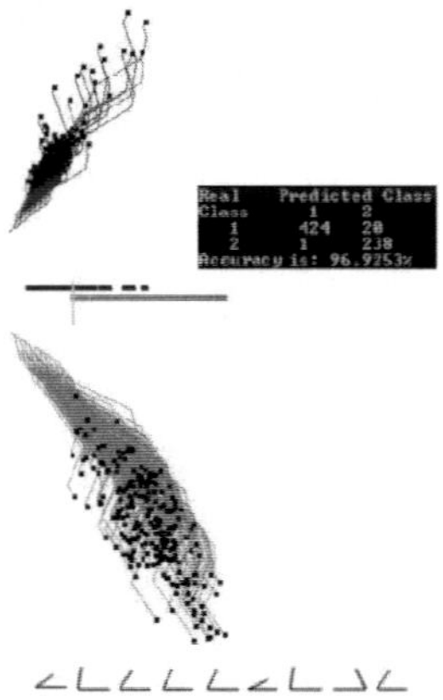

Figure 1: Wisconsin Breast Cancer dataset representation using GLC-L. Instances from one class are projected above in blue, while instances from the other class are below in red.

The visual explanation can be accompanied by a textual explanation, with an approximate linguistic description of differences of these visual patterns that can be generated by using fuzzy linguistic variables. Next, **Fig. 1** can be used to construct the exact linear discrimination model as it is generated in [Kovalerchuk, Dovhalets, 2017].

More generally, the visual explanation approach can be viewed as a part of the new paradigm of *Computing With Images* (CWI) [Kovalerchuk, 2013] that augments traditional *numeric computations* and Zadeh's Computing With Words (CWW) [Zadeh, 2012] concept.

Our goal is to combine visual representation of multi-dimensional data with the powerful deep learning technology. Our novel approach uses deep learning (CNN) architectures to classify not the original data points, but rather the 2-D images generated by the GLC-L method. In other words, we use lossless visualization of images as intermediary data representations. We apply this two-step process on standard data benchmarks to validate the proposed method. In our experiments, we compare our results with the ones obtained by applying the CNN model on the original data.

2. OUR METHOD: GLC-L + CNN

Originally, GLC-L was designed to visualize a linear function $F(\mathbf{x})$. Each attribute x_i from n-D point $\mathbf{x}=(x_1,x_2,..,x_n)$ is mapped to a line segment, and the line segments are stacked one on the top of each other with angles Q_i computed from the coefficients $C=(c_1,c_2,...,c_n)$ of the linear function F. The length of the line is the value of the attribute. A large value produces a longer line segment than a smaller one. The coefficients C are normalized in the range [-1,1], producing a new set of coefficients $K=(k_1, k_2, ...,k_n)$: $k_i = c_i/c_{max}$ producing a new linear function:

$$y = k_1x_1 + k_2x_2 + k_3x_3 + ... + k_nx_n \qquad (1)$$

In GLC-L the angles are, $Q_i = \arccos(k_i)$. For experiments with CNN, we can generate angles Q_i directly because the goal is wider than just a linear function. The segment is going to the right for positive k_i and to the left for the negative k_i.

Automatic search for the best coefficients can be optimized to separate better cases of opposing classes by a random search algorithm. It scans the search space for different sets of coefficients on the training dataset and the best coefficients are then evaluated on the test dataset.

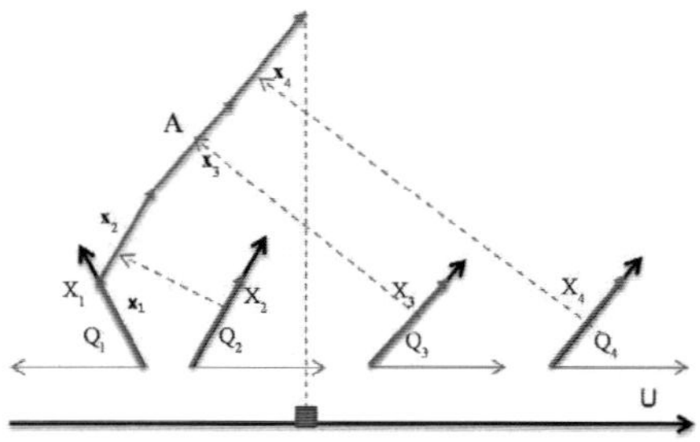

Figure 2: Visualization of 4-D data with GLC-L. The data attributes x_1-x_4 are all positive numbers with the value of 1. Having the same values for all attributes makes all of the line segments to be equally long. The first angle Q_1 is negative, which turns the line to the left, and the other angles Q_2-Q_4 are positive, turning the line to the right.

3. DATA TRANSFORMATION

The transformation process consists of (1) choosing a random set of coefficients (with respective angles), and (2) transforming the data using those coefficients. Using the same set of randomly chosen coefficients to visualize each data instance separately with GLC-L allows creating a set of artificial images. The image captures of the visualizations inherit their corresponding labels from the original data. Once the data are transformed and images are created, the newly rendered images are entered into a machine learning algorithm for training and testing. This process is repeated n times to find the best set of coefficients (angles) using a random search strategy for finding of the best coefficients set (angles).

For the best coefficient set, a second testing set is required to test properly them on independent data to avoid overfitting. For this purpose, the system takes in a dataset, shuffles it and splits it into two new sets for each iteration. The first set (set-1) is 80% of the original data and the second set (set-2) is the remaining 20% of the samples. For the experimental setup, a 10-fold cross validation is applied on set-1 during the search of best coefficients. Set-2 is used to test the system after the best coefficients are established.

The data transform has many parts, which could be optimized, including the architecture of the CNN itself. Optimization of hyper-parameters of the CNN are out of scope for this study. Experiments were focused on how different parts of the data transform system effect the data transformation while evaluating the artificially created images on the same CNN. Experiments were performed to understand how image size of the artificially created images, line thickness and the size of search of random coefficients affects classification. These experiments were all done on the same dataset using the same data split for training and testing subsets. The split for the subsets was 80% for the training set, 10% for the validation set and 10% for the testing set. For all experiments with different line thicknesses and sizes of the artificially created images, the same coefficients were used.

3.1 Line Thickness

The thickness of the line directly corresponds to how many pixels are being used in the created image. Having a thin line corresponds to a small number of pixels actually being used in the image representation. Having more pixels used corresponds to having more information in the image. We conducted experiments to test the last statement with different line widths and their effect on classification. The value *t*, which controls the width of the line, was the only variable being changed in these experiments. For each experiment, five different runs were performed, and their average is reported as the test accuracy. A run consists of selecting coefficients, transforming the data and classifying the transformed data with a CNN.

The experiments 1-3 conducted with line thickness at $t = 0.1$, $t = 1.0$ and $t = 2.0$, respectively. **Fig. 3** shows examples of how different *t* values change the line thickness and the visualization itself.

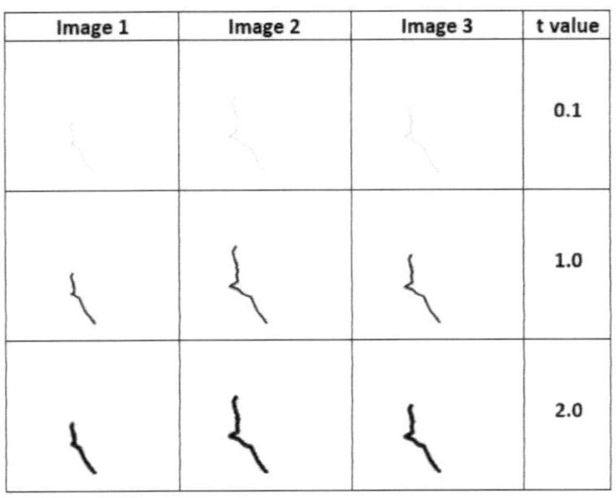

Figure 3: Projection Line Thickness with different *t* values. Image 1, 2 and 3 were randomly saved from the experiment. 4th column shows the *t* value used in the corresponding row.

Table 1: Accuracy results using different line thickness.

Run #	t=0.1	t=1.0	t=2.0
1	48.24%	71.92%	71.05%
2	72.80%	71.92%	73.68%
3	75.43%	70.17%	71.05%
4	48.24%	74.56%	72.80%
5	71.92%	76.31%	73.68%
Average	63.23%	72.97%	72.45%

Table 1 contains the results of experiments conducted to test the impact of the line thickness on the classification accuracy using a CNN. There is a dramatic improvement in accuracy going from $t = 0.1$ to $t = 1.0$. After that there is not much gain in classification accuracy going to $t = 2.0$. These experiments show that the thicker lines produce greater accuracy (see **Table 1** for more details).

3.2 Size of Artificially Created Images

Four different experiments were conducted to see the effect of the size of artificially created images on CNN classification accuracy. In these experiments, only the size of images was varied. The CNN input dimension was matched to the image size, but all other hyper-parameters remained unchanged. For each of the 4 experiments 5 different runs were performed, and the average of the 5 runs is reported on the test accuracy. Having images larger than 100x100 makes the accuracy drop significantly. Accuracy such as 51.75% and 48.24% is the result of the CNN not being able to converge during training. This is due to the hyper-parameters of the CNN. The hyper-parameters were tuned manually by trial runs and checking on much smaller images. Optimization of hyper-parameters for a CNN is out of scope for this study and it the topic of the future studies..

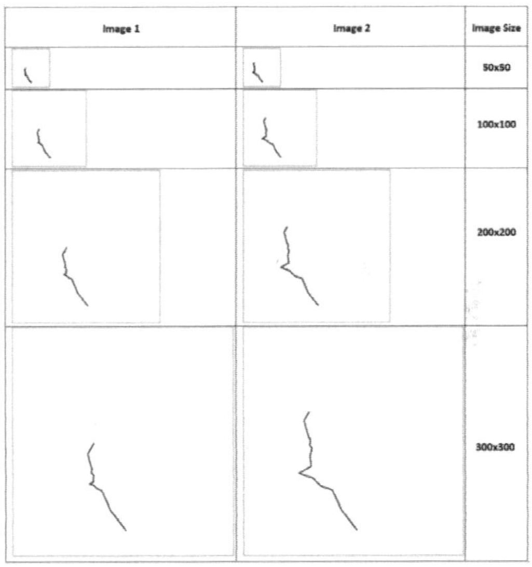

Figure 4: Examples of different image sizes used in experiments. Larger images produce much more detailed line.

Table 2: Accuracy dependence on the image size for data sets.

Run #	50x50	100x100	200x200	300x300
1	74.56%	71.92%	51.75%	51.75%
2	65.78%	71.92%	48.24%	51.75%
3	74.56%	70.17%	51.75%	51.75%
4	72.80%	74.56%	72.80%	51.75%
5	76.31%	76.31%	75.43%	48.24%
Average	72.80%	72.97%	59.99%	51.05%

Experiments were also performed to show that an extensive search is not needed for satisfactory results. For this set of experiments the number of epochs was the only variable being changed. Three different experiments were conducted with 5 runs for each experiment. In the first experiment, the number of epochs was set to 1, i.e., only one set of randomly selected coefficients was used to do the transformation and evaluation of the system. For the second and third experiments, the number of epochs was set to 20 and 100, respectively, i.e., 20 and 100 different sets of randomly chosen coefficients to transform the data were evaluated on producing the highest classification accuracy.

Table 3: The accuracy variation for different epochs and runs.

Run #	Epochs=1	Epochs=20	Epochs=100
1	64.03%	66.78%	66.78%
2	68.42%	71.05%	65.78%
3	68.42%	64.03%	69.29%
4	63.15%	73.68%	68.42%
5	67.54%	69.29%	65.78%
Average	66.31%	68.96%	67.21%

Table 3 contains the experimental results for the random search algorithm, which is used for selecting coefficients. The last row has the averages of the 5 runs for each of the experiments with different number of epochs used. There is a small improvement going from epochs 1 to epoch 20. Experiment with 20 epochs had CNN models trained on 20 different representations of data, rather than just 1. However, based on our experiments, going to 100 epochs does not further improve the results.

The random search experiments show that the search for coefficients does not have to be large. There is abundant amount of linear functions, which can be used for the transformation of data. While a linear function may exist, that produces the best separation of data, it is not required for data transformation.

4. DATA SETS

This section, describes the used datasets and preprocessing done to them. These datasets vary in number of classes, number of instances, and number of attributes per instance. Several of these datasets are from the UCI Machine Learning Repository [Lichman, 2013]. **Table 4** summaries these datasets.

Table 4: Quick overview of the datasets used in the experiments.

Dataset	Instances	Attributes	Classes
Swiss Roll 2-D	1600	2	4
Swiss Roll 3-D	1600	3	4
Wisconsin	683	9	2
Red Wine	1599	11	6
White Wine	4898	11	7
Diabetic	1151	18	2
MNIST-Subset	3000	484	3

The Swiss Roll dataset [Surendran, 2014] is a benchmark used to test dimensionality reduction algorithms. It has 1600 instances equally spread out among 4 classes. There are two subsets of the Swiss Roll Dataset: 2-D and 3-D.

The Wisconsin Breast Cancer (WBC) dataset is from the UCI ML repository. It consists of 699 instances with 11 attributes. We removed instances with missing values. The resulting 683 instances contain 444 benign cases and 239 malignant cases. The dataset is normalized to [0, 1] interval.

The wine quality data are also from the UCI ML repository. It is composed of red wine and white wine datasets with 1599 and 4898 instances, respectively. Both subsets have 11 attributes. Red wine quality has 6 unbalanced classes, with most of the instances belonging only into 2 classes. White wine quality dataset has 7 classes, and it is unbalanced too. Both subsets are normalized to [0,1] interval in each attribute.

Diabetic Rectionopathy Debrecen Dataset is also from the UCI ML repository. These data belong to two classes with and without signs of Diabetic Rectionopathy (DR, no DR). The data contain 1151 instances with 18 attributes. The classes are balanced with 540 instances with no signs of DR and 611 instances with signs of DR. Each attribute is normalized to [0,1] interval.

To test the robustness of the data transform method on high dimensional data, a subset of Modified National Institute of Standards and Technology (MNIST) database was used. This subset consists of 1000 instances from each digits 0, 1 and 2, totaling in 3000 instances. The original images are 28x28 pixels (784 dimensions). To avoid the curse of dimensionality, we removed the padding around the images by cropping only the digit portions, resulting in images of size 22x22 pixels (484 dimensions).

5. EXPERIMENTAL RESULTS

For classification, we used several CNNs to evaluate the transformation of numerical data with lossless visualization provided by the GLC-L considering CNN classifiers as one of the most powerful image classification tools [Zisserman, 2014]. For a fair comparison of performance of the data transform system on artificially created images, we conducted two sets of experiments for each dataset. In the first one, the raw numerical data are the CNN input. In the second one, the data transformed with GLC-L are the CNN input. All over the experiments, the hyper-parameters of the CNN remained the same. For the data transformation system, we used the following setting in final experiments:

- *t* value of 1.0;
- size of artificial images 50x50;
- 20 epochs with the data transformation system;
- 10-fold cross validation.

The experiments were carried out on the CWU supercomputer (IBM Power8), taking advantage of the GPU clusters. The system was implemented in Python, using the Keras CNN implementation. To compare the classification of the two sets of experiments two different CNN architectures had to be used. We used a regular CNN architecture to classify artificially created images and constructed 1-DC convolutional neural network to classify vectorial (non-image data). They use the same Adam optimizer [Kingma, 2017] with the learning rate set to 0.0001. Both networks were set for 1000 training epochs with an early stopping checkpoint. The training will stop if the validation accuracy for training is not improved over 100 epochs. The 1-DC CNN architecture used to numerical data is the following:

- 1-D Convolutional Layer with 64 output channels, filter length of 2 and rectified linear unit (RELU) activation
- Drop out layer with fraction of input units to drop set to 0.4
- Fully Connected Layer with 1024 output nodes and RELU activation
- Fully Connected Layer with number of output nodes equal to the number of classes, with a softmax activation

The architecture of the CNN used for classification of images is the following:

- Convolutional Layer with 64 output channels, a kernel shape of 2x2, stride of 2x2 and RELU activation
- Convolutional Layer with 64 output channels, a kernel shape of 2x2, stride of 2x2 and RELU activation
- Pooling layer with pooling size of 2x2
- Drop out layer with fraction of input units to drop set to 0.4
- Convolutional Layer with 128 output channels, a kernel shape of 2x2, stride of 2x2 and RELU activation
- Convolutional Layer with 128 output channels, a kernel shape of 2x2, stride of 2x2 and RELU activation
- Pooling layer with pooling size of 2x2
- Drop out layer with fraction of input units to drop set to 0.4
- Fully Connected Layer with 256 output nodes and RELU activation
- Drop out layer with fraction of input units to drop set to 0.4
- Fully Connected Layer with number of output nodes equal to the number of classes, with a softmax activation

The selection of these settings are the results of several trial runs. As we mentioned above, the optimization of the network architecture is out of the scope of the current research.

The original MNIST-Subset was not used in the 1-DC CNN because they are already images. Instead, they were evaluated with the CNN architecture used for classification of the artificially created images. **Table 5** contains results for 7 datasets for the raw input data with 1-DC CNN and for transforming numerical data with GLC-L and classifying images with a regular CNN. The results for 1-DC CNN are reported using 10-fold cross validation. The results for "Transform + CNN" are the average of 20 runs using the data transformation system with CNN trained in 10-fold cross validation.

Table 5: Comparison of the results considering several data collections and two types of CNNs.

Dataset	1-DC CNN	Transform + CNN
Swiss Roll 2-D	72.50%	97.43%
Swiss Roll 3-D	96.18%	97.55%
Wisconsin	96.92%	97.22%
Red Wine	60.65%	60.93%
White Wine	55.91%	60.76%
Diabetic	73.75%	69.04%
MNIST-Subset	99.53%	92.93%

For CNN classification, the angles between lines in polylines that represent n-D points were selected as follows. We generated ten different sets of angles $\{Q_i\}$ to produce polylines, and computed the accuracy of CNN classification of polylines for each $\{Q_i\}$. The best accuracy among these $\{Q_i\}$ is reported. We also conducted an experiment with WBC data and MNIST-subset polyline images contracted to 25x25 pixels, in order to test if the low resolution of image would be sufficient to get high accuracy scores. This experiment has shown that CNN is capable to find patterns with significant noise produced by lowering the image resolution. The resulting accuracies of 98.54% for WCB and 89.83% for MNIST-subset are similar to the accuracy rates obtained for the higher resolutions. Next, it opens the opportunity to get CNN model faster by decreasing images to 25x25 pixels.

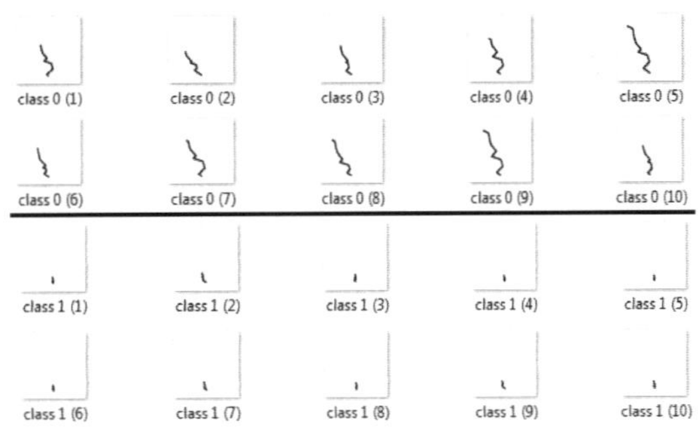

Figure 5: Random samples of WBC data visualized in GLC-L for the CNN model with the best accuracy.

Fig. 5 shows samples of polylines found for the CNN with the best accuracy on WBC polylines. In **Figure 5**, humans immediately discover two related features: length and height of the top point of the curve as discrimination features. These features help to explain the high accuracy of CNN on WBC data, even with the drastic decrease of the resolution to 25x25 pixels. These features are robust to the decrease of resolution. The high accuracy and presence of such simple features gave us an insight to search for a simpler classification rule understandable by a human. The first idea is to check the accuracy of classification using only the Y coordinate of the top point of each polyline.

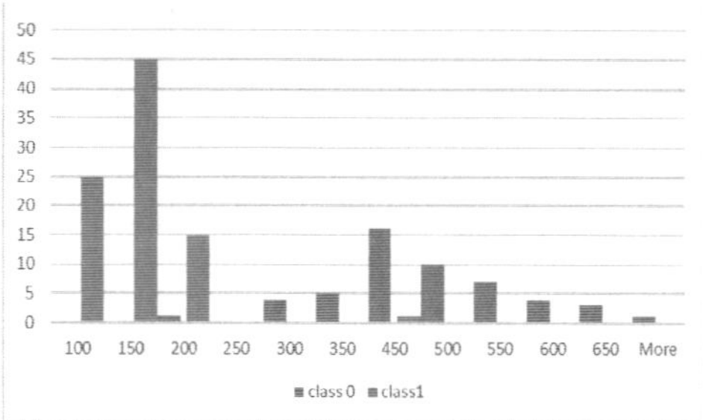

Figure 6: Distribution of values of Y coordinate of the top points of all polylines for WBC data.

Fig. 6 shows the distribution of this feature. It confirms this simple hypothesis. With a threshold at 250, practically all cases below this threshold are in class 0 and all the rest are in class 1. It means that attributes of WBC data with larger values and located more vertically in the figure contribute more for the sample to be in class 1. This classification rule is similar conceptually to the linear classification rule described in [Kovalerchuk, Dovhalets, 2017] for WBC data.

It shows that when complimentary simple rules exist they can be found by multiple methods. It allows getting more confidence in such discovered rules and making ensembles of them in the attempt to improve the total accuracy. For data with more complex models, CNN and other neural networks on artificial images open the opportunity to discover such models in images. It also allows tracing the network to find understandable features that led to the model similar to described in [Mao et al, 2014].

6. CONCLUSION

Our proposed approach shows how to use lossless 2-D visual representation of multi-dimensional data for deep learning on CNN architectures. It allows getting: (1) classification accuracy comparable with those obtained by the CNN on data non-converted to images as **Table 5** shows, (2) visual insight on efficient classification features as **Fig. 5** shows, and (3) visual insight on simplification and explanation of the discovered models for the domain experts who are not data scientists as **Figure 6** shows.

In addition to classification and visualization, GLC-L allows better understanding of the data, which a dataset in its raw representation is lacking. It is reached by interpreting vector data as an image. The benefits of using the image classifiers such as CNN are that they exploit the spatial representation of the pixels in the image (via convolution) by mimicking the human visual cortex.

In the future, this conversion opens a new opportunity for resolving long-standing ML challenges of model explanation, controlling model overfitting and overgeneralization. Both can come from the combination of computational tools suggested in this paper and the unique human perceptual abilities to digest easier a larger number of features and outliers in the visual form than in the numeric form. The idea of GLC visual approach for controlling over-fitting and overgeneralization in ML is to allows a domain expert to see n-D data in 2-D as it is shown in **Fig. 1** and then to limit the areas where the possible n-D points can be located in these visualizations [Kovalerchuk, 2018]. The combination of GLC-L and CNN can expand this possibility by visually controlling the areas around the polylines uses by CNN for classification.

REFERENCES

[1] Kingma DP, Ba J. Adam: a method for stochastic optimization, arXiv:1412.6980, 2017.
[2] Kovalerchuk B. Visual Knowledge Discovery and Machine Learning, Springer Nature, 2018
[3] Kovalerchuk, B., Dovhalets, D., Constructing Interactive Visual Classification, Clustering and Dimension Reduction Models for n-D Data, Informatics, 4(23), 2017, http://www.mdpi.com/ 2227-9709/ 4/3/23,
[4] Kovalerchuk, B., Quest for rigorous intelligent tutoring systems under uncertainty: Computing with Words and Images, In: IFSA/NAFIPS-2013, 685- 690.
[5] Lichman, M. UCI Machine Learning Repository, http://archive.ics.uci.edu/ml, 2013.
[6] Mao J, Xu W, Yang Y, Wang J, Yuille AL. Explain images with multimodal recurrent neural networks. arXiv:1410.1090. 2014 Oct 4.
[7] Miller, G. A. The magical number seven, plus or minus two: Some limits on our capacity for processing information. Psychological Review. 63 (2): 81–97.
[8] Simonyan K, Zisserman A. Very deep convolutional networks for large-scale image recognition. arXiv:1409.1556. 2014.
[9] Surendrani, D. Swiss Roll Dataset, 2014. http://people.cs.uchicago.edu/~dinoj/manifold/swissroll.html
[10] Zadeh L. A. Computing with words: Principal concepts and ideas, Springer, 2012.

ISASE-MAICS 2018

A Computational Framework for Identity Based on Situation Theory

Janelle MASON*, Kofi KYEI *, Darrion LONG**, Hannah FOSTER***, William NICK*, James MAYES***, and Albert ESTERLINE *

* *Department of Computer Science, North Carolina A&T State University, 1601 East Market Street, Greensboro, NC 27411 USA*
{jcmason, kkyei, wmnick}@aggies.ncat.edu, esterlin@ncat.edu
** *Dept. of Computer Science, Technology & Mathematics, Lincoln Univ. of Missouri, 820 Chestnut St, Jefferson City, MO 65101 USA*
darrion.long687@my.lincolnu.edu
*** *Department of Criminal Justice, North Carolina A&T State University, 1601 East Market Street, Greensboro, NC 27411 USA*
hnfoster@aggies.ncat.edu, jpmayes@ncat.edu

Abstract: This paper presents a computational framework for identity (initially about the culprit in a crime scene) based on Barwise's situation theory. Situations support information and can carry information about other situations. An utterance situation carries information about a described situation thanks to the constraints imposed by natural language. We are concerned with utterance situations in which identity judgments are made about the culprit in a crime scene, which is the corresponding described situation. The id-situation and crime scene along with various resource situations make up a case in the legal sense. We have developed OWL ontologies to provide concepts and principled vocabularies for encoding our scenarios in RDF, and we present an example of a SPARQL query of one of our encodings that spans situations. To follow how evidence supports hypotheses on the identity of the culprit in a crime scene, we use Dempster-Shafer theory. We tightly integrate it with our ontologies by having the representation of a case per our ontologies present a network containing situations and stitched together by objects; evidence "flows" along this network, diminishing and combining. We review the modifications of Dempster-Shafer theory required when one goes from a closed-world assumption to an open-world assumption. We review our plans regarding equational reasoning based on identities established in our id-cases, and we review the related issues regarding the meanings of URIs.
Keywords: *Situation Theory, Ontologies, Dempster-Shafer theory, Identity*

1. INTRODUCTION

The state of the art in frameworks for identity has been the SuperIdentity Project [2], which begins with some known information or element of identity, for example, a username, and transforms that element into another. For example, we use a username to determine an address. The elements are grouped according to the type of information, e.g., all email addresses, into characteristics. This creates multisets of elements of the same type. The set of all characteristics is a person's superidentity, an organized version of all known information about the individual.

An element of identity on its own, however, lacks the context needed to carry information useable as evidence. From the legal perspective, one must understand how a case is put together from various situations. Our work addresses this information and how it can be used as evidence (for the identity of an agent). We are concerned not just with the crime scene, but also with all the situations where information (e.g., fingerprints) was gathered and the processes by which its integrity is validated. For a concrete basis for information used in providing evidence, we base our framework on situation theory as developed by Barwise and his colleagues [14], the principal concern of which is how a situation supports information and carries information about other situations. Our examples have been from physical crime scene investigations because our colleagues' work with biometrics, the centuries-old legal norms, and our collaboration with the Criminal Justice Program at North Carolina A&T State University, however we are moving into the cyber world.

The topics of the remaining sections are as follows. Section 2 presents situation theory. For representing and reasoning about identity cases, we have developed OWL (Web Ontology Language) ontologies (which roughly provide schemas for data and inference); Section 3 presents these ontologies. Our approach uses Semantic Web standards (including OWL) for representing and reasoning. We encode cases in RDF (Resource Description Framework, another Semantic Web standard), using the concepts defined in our ontologies; Section 4 presents examples of this encoding. We are interested primarily in how the evidence supports hypotheses on the identity of the culprit in a crime scene, and for this we use Dempster-Shafer theory tightly integrated with our ontologies, as explained in Section 5. Identity is an equivalence relation and supports equational reasoning. Section 6 presents our plans regarding such reasoning and discusses the meaning of URIs (Uniform Resource Identifiers, which are the primary means in the Semantic Web for "naming" individuals). Section 7 concludes and discusses future work.

2. SITUATION THEORY

Once we refer to or quantify over scenes modeled by first-order substructures representing visual parts of the actual world as Barwise did initially, it is natural to quantify over other substructures, i.e., over representations of other parts of the world, that is, situations. (The standard reference for situation theory is Barwise and Perry's [1]; we also refer to [3], a formalization by Devlin) According to situation semantics (situation theory applied to linguistic meaning, Barwise's main concern), the meaning of an expression is conceived as a relation between an utterance situation and a described situation. There are also resource situations to fill out references. In general, one situation can carry information about another situation by virtue of constraints. For example, this is the gist of "Smoke means fire." The constraints by which an utterance situation carries information about a described situation are the conventions of natural language.

We consider making an identity judgment (as in a crime scene investigation) to be an utterance situation (which we call an id-situation), part of a constellation of situations making up a case. The crime scene is the described situation. Resource situations include such things as where a fingerprint was filed and where one took a facial image used to train a classifier. In cases where machine learning is involved, there could be a huge number of resource situations, and we propose to use summary metadata in such cases to introduce levels of evidence.

3. OUR ONTOLOGIES

We utilize the Semantic Web standards to express cases in our framework. OWL is the most popular language that is used to express ontologies. Our framework consists of OWL ontologies that are used to encode information on a case in an RDF triple store. We use the query language SPARQL (SPARQL Protocol and RDF Query Language) to execute queries per each case [8], [9]. RDF expresses simple propositions as triples of the form subject property object, stating that subject and object are related by binary relation property. An example might be Fred brotherOf Ed, meaning that Fred is the brother of Ed, but in fact, the subject must be a URI or a bnode (a placeholder, like a pronoun, local to the RDF document), the property must be a URI, and the object must be a URI or a bnode or a literal.

Triples may share subject, they may share an object, and the object of one may be the subject of another. Abstractly, an RDF document presents a graph, where a triple is a directed edge from the subject to the object, labeled by the property.

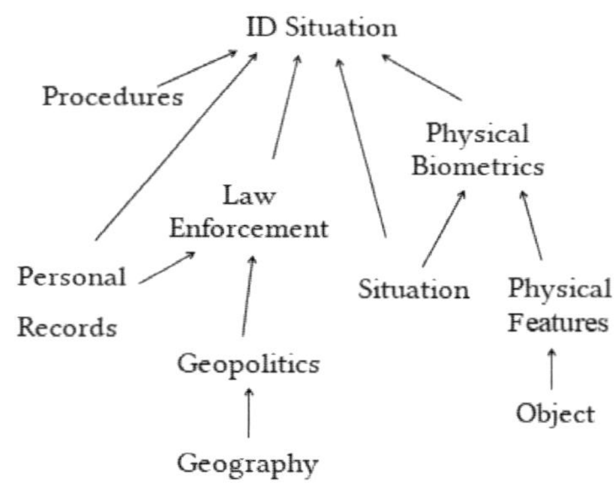

Figure 1: Framework Ontologies.

We have ontologies that are created specifically for our framework. Figure 1 depicts the relationships within our framework. Each ontology inherits from the ontology below. The Id Situation ontology is primarily focused on id-situations and constellations of situations (i.e., id-cases) that support id-situations. We assign the namespace prefix **`id`** to the Id Situation ontology. The Id Situation ontology is constructed on the Situation ontology. We assign the prefix **`sit`** to the Situation ontology. The Situation ontology contains two major classes, Situation and Infon, denoted as **`sit:Situation`** and **`sit:Infon`**, respectively. In Devlin's presentation of situation theory [15], an infon is an elementary item of information, a relation among objects at a time and place. A situation supports infons and may thereby carry information about other situations. Property **`sit:supports`** has domain **`sit:Situation`** and range **`sit:Infon`** (i.e., a situation supports an infon).

Our system of ontologies has the flexibility to include

other ontologies that relate to the structure of a case as well as to the specific type of information (such as biometric artifacts) and procedures that are required for evidence to support id-actions (judgments of identity). We created a Physical Biometric ontology to handle biometric artifacts. The biometric artifacts are images of suspects' physical features that are registered for usage by forensic professionals. We created the Physical Features ontology to account for the information captured regarding physical biometrics. It relates specific surface features to specific persons, which lets biometric images serve as identifiers.

Our Law Enforcement ontology is the most significant of our supporting ontologies. We import the standard FOAF ontology into this ontology. At the top-level, we use the `foaf:Agent` class with children `foaf:Organization` and `foaf:Person`. There is an affiliation property to associate agents with organizations and a certification property to associate professionals with certificates.

4. EXAMPLE ENCODING

We consider two crime scenes for our examples, one takes place at a party and another occurs at a tollbooth. During the party, someone stole the family jewels from their closet. We have a list of potential suspects by reviewing the guest list. The evidence that we are able to collect from the crime scene is a group photograph from a security camera that has a guest's hand on the closet door

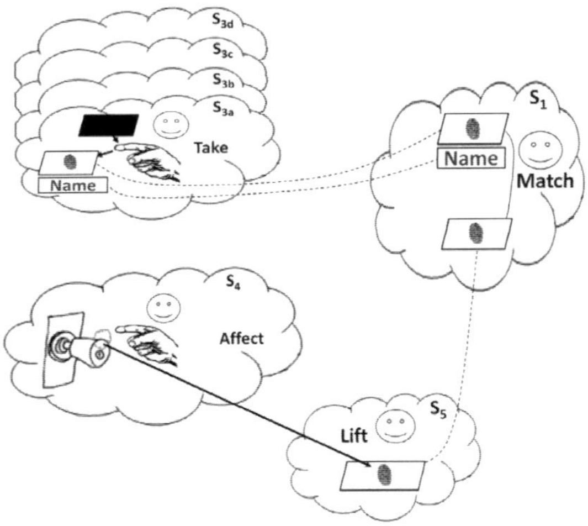

Figure 2: The fingerprint id-case.

and a fingerprint from the door knob of that door. This case targets two separate but coordinated id-situations for two pieces of evidence, the fingerprint and the snapshot. As a result, we have two coordinated id-cases.

Figure 2 depicts the fingerprint id-case with situation s_1 as the id-situation. This is where the forensic analyst compares fingerprints on file to the forensic evidence collected at the crime scene. For the results to be legally compelling, each fingerprint, from the police department or crime scene, must be taken and handled according to protocol in its respective situation. In each situation s_{3a}-s_{3d}, a suspect has their fingerprint taken and recorded on file by a forensic professional. In situation s_4 (part of the crime scene), the criminal touches the doorknob, which provides a forensic fingerprint. The Crime Scene Investigation team lifts the fingerprint from the doorknob in situation s_5 so that it can be compared against the fingerprints on file.

Figure 3 depicts the mugshot id-case with id-situation s_2. In situations s_{6a}-s_{6d}, a forensic professional takes a mugshot of each suspect. Each mugshot is compared to the photo captured by the security camera in s_7. In situation s_7, the group is recorded by the camera, which acts as an utterance situation producing a photo as a persistent description of situation s_8, with the group standing near the door with someone touching the doorknob during the party. Situation s_4 (where a fingerprint is left by touching the doorknob) is a part of situation s_8, the larger scene of what occurred at that moment during the party. In this scenario, there might be sufficient evidence in each id-case on its own to identify the culprit, but perhaps the fingerprint on the doorknob is indistinct and the group photo is blurred so neither is compelling. Combining the evidence from the two cases, however, might suffice. In Section 5, we present our application of Dempster-Shafer theory, which shows how combining evidence may strengthen our case.

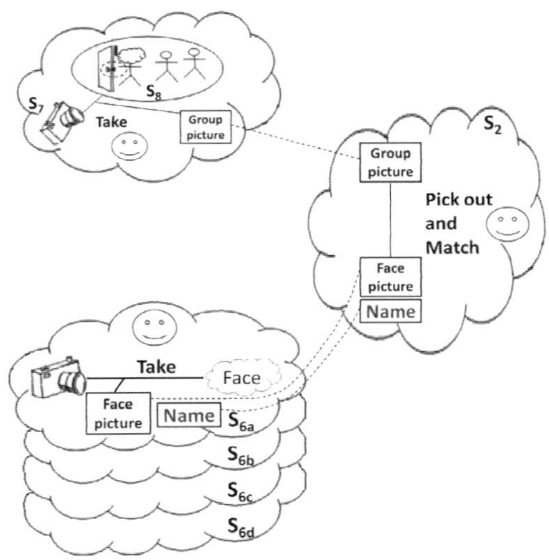

Figure 3: The mugshot id-case.

The second crime scene takes place where a guy runs a tollbooth, depicted in Figure 4. One security camera has taken a picture of the driver's face; call this situation $\mathbf{s_f}$.

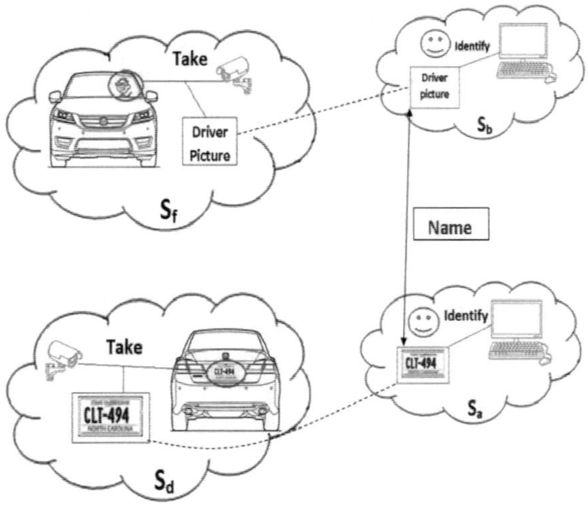

Figure 4: The tollbooth id-case.

Another camera has taken a picture of the license plate with the last digit obscure, it is clearly a North Carolina (NC) plate. Call this situation $\mathbf{s_d}$. Both $\mathbf{s_f}$ and $\mathbf{s_d}$ are parts of the crime scene. They are contemporaneous but spatially disjoint.

There is an id-situation, $\mathbf{s_b}$, where an investigator tries to match the license plate number from the photo from $\mathbf{s_d}$ with a number on file with the NC Department of Motor Vehicles (DMV). There is probably more than one valid matching license number; there could be up to 36. Even if there were only one, we might not have a closed case since there is no guarantee that the driver is the owner of the car. The investigation can take a multitude of turns, and many different situations might contribute. One could contact the owner and ask who was driving.

Critical situations here are where the DMV associates the license number with the owner: up to 36 such situations may be relevant. All these situations go together as the plate-matching id-case.

There is another, coordinated id-situation, $\mathbf{s_a}$, where an attempt is made to match the photo of the driver from $\mathbf{s_f}$ against mugshots the DMV has of all those with NC driver's licenses. This is central to another id-case, the face-matching case. This can cross over to the plate-matching case, for example, as confirmation when the owner is asked who was driving the car already identified by plate number. On its own, this case is difficult. For one thing, the DMV may not have a mugshot of the driver. Even if it has, the number of mugshots on file is so large that the chance of an unambiguous match is very small. In any case, relevant situations will include those where mugshots are taken. If the entire set of mugshots is accessed, this is a huge number of situations. In such a case, using our computational approach, rather than encoding information on the situations themselves, one would record meta-information that summarizes the set of mugshots. Even if we reduce the set of likely mugshots to a reasonable number, we still have to allow that the person is outside the set of people represented by the selected mugshots. Allowing an unbounded set of candidates is an instance of the open-world assumption, which requires special treatment when we apply Dempster-Shafer theory. We pick this up in Section 5.

5. EVIDENCE: DEMPSTER-SHAFER THEORY

We use Dempster-Shafer Theory (DST) [10], [5] to provide numerical values for evidence-based confidence one should have in our identities. The set of all possible elements is the frame of discernment. Mass, representing the strength of evidence, is assigned to subsets of the frame of discernment in such a way the sum of all assigned mass is 1.0. Note that mass may be assigned to singleton sets but also to non-singleton sets without being distributed over singleton components, which contrasts with the treatment of probabilities. Mass assigned to the frame of discernment itself represents ignorance. A focal element is any set assigned non-zero mass. A refinement is an analysis leading to a more detailed frame of discernment. Given a mass function, the belief function for a set that is a subset of the frame of discernment is the lower bound for likelihood, which is calculated by adding the masses of all subsets of the set, while the plausibility is the upper bound for the likelihood, which is calculated by adding the masses of the sets that overlap the set. The belief associated with a set is determined by adding the masses of all of its subsets. DST allows for the combination of multiple mass functions for different kinds of evidence to produce a new mass function for the combined evidence. There are many combination rules, appropriate for various conditions.

The structure of a case allows us to apply DST in a novel way [11], [12]. Think of the representation of a case (per our ontologies) as a network containing situations and stitched together by objects (e.g., a fingerprint is taken in one situation and used in a match in another). For DST, evidence flows through the network, diminished or combined on its way to a situation where an id-judgment is made. The links are constraints that allow the evidence to "flow". For example, if protocol (conventional constraints) is followed on taking the fingerprint on file, the similarity found in the id-situation can provide a certain level of evidence. We have considered combining mass functions, expanding the situation and so refining the frame of discernment, and modifying the main mass function in light of considerations such as reliability.

Zadeh showed that Demspter's rule gives counterintuitive results (Zadeh's paradox) when the two mass functions have different focal elements [7]. Smets [13] addresses such problems with his transferable belief model. He considers the frame of discernment as a set of atomic propositions rather than a set of corresponding individuals. (E.g., instead of Ed, Al, Ken, we have "It's Ed," "It's Al," and "It's Ken.") The atomic propositions are assumed disjoint. Instead of subsets of the frame of discernment, we have disjunctions of atomic propositions. Instead of a subset relation, we have implication. Smets defines three sets of propositions: *KP* (propositions known to be possible), *UP* (those not considered, "unknown"), and *KI* (those known to be impossible). The classical Dempster-Shafer and Bayesian approaches assume that *UP* is empty; this is a closed-world assumption (CWA) the truth is necessarily in *KP*.

The open-world assumption (OWA) allows a non-empty *UP* set (where the truth might be), and non-zero mass may be assigned to its elements. The content of the three sets gets redistributed as evidence accumulates. Proposition *A* is transferred from *KP* to *KI* if the evidence shows that *A* is impossible and from *UP* to *KP* if the evidence has us recall *A* and consider it possible. Transfer from *KI* to *KP* or *UP* and from *KP* to *UP* is not possible, and transfer from *UP* to *KI* has no practical effect since masses relate only to *KP*. If A is transferred from *KP* to *KI*, its mass is transferred either to the propositions in *UP* or to a more specific disjunction over the atomic propositions in *KP*. This "conditioning" forms the basis for the transferable belief model and a version of Dempster's rule that avoids Zadeh's paradox. The key notions are the OWA and that the empty subset of the frame of discernment may have non-zero mass. As mentioned, the OWA is natural for our second scenario.

Haenni [4] shows that the effect of the OWA can be achieved by adjoining to the frame of discernment an individual standing for anything else, so that the new frame is truly exhaustive. He shows that any degree of belief computed under the OWA is also obtained under the CWA and using Dempster's rule.

6. REASONING ABOUT IDENTITY AND THE MEANING OF URIS

We are developing software to exploit the logical nature of identity statements. We view an id-situation as involving an id-judgment, which is an assertion of an identity statement, where identity is a binary relation. The two denoting devices in an identity statement need not be verbal, as when, pointing to Fred, we say "He did it." Identity is an equivalence relation that partitions a set of denoting devices into equivalence classes; any such class provides our version of a superidentity. Asserting an identity between denoting expressions from different classes fuses the identities.

OWL provides the **`owl:sameAs`** property for identity and **`owl:differentFrom`** for its negation. OWL also supports inverse functional properties (such as the relation that makes id cards work): if P is an inverse functional property and we have triples $x\ P\ z$ and $y\ P\ z$, we can infer $x = y$. As mentioned, the Semantic Web was designed with identity in mind. The non-unique name assumption (a consequence of the open-world assumption) hold that two distinct names (URIs on the Web or more recently IRIs) are not assumed to denote distinct individuals unless we are told otherwise. We are developing SWRL rules for equational reasoning (substituting identical terms) on RDF triples that use the vocabulary defined in our ontologies.

URIs are the fundamental denoting expressions ("names") on the Semantic Web, and an account of identity using Semantic-Web resources must be clear on what is required for a URI to denote something. Halpin addresses the question of how agents can determine what a URI identifies (or denotes, refers to, or means) [6]. On the pre-Semantic Web, a URI just identifies the web-page its protocol accesses, but on the Semantic Web, URIs are used to identify all resources, causing confusion between a thing and a page about it. The 'logical position' on the meaning of a URI on the Semantic Web is that it is given by whatever things satisfy the model(s) given by the formal semantics of the documents in which that URI occurs. This position is generally held by logicians, who see the Semantic Web as entirely distinct from the hypertext Web. Halpin sees this position as identical to the 'descriptivist theory of reference' popular among logic-oriented philosophers from the first half of the 20th century and according to which the referent of a name is restricted to those things that make assertions involving it true. The descriptivist theory of reference was challenged by the 'causal theory of reference,' according to which an agent fixes a name to a referent known through direct acquaintance, and a causal chain to a current user of the name from past users allows its referent to be known across time. This philosophical position (according to Halpin) is the same as the 'direct reference position' on the meaning of a URI, that it is whatever was intended by the owner, a viewpoint generally held by many Web architects, who see no difference here between the Semantic Web and the entire Web. The referent of a URI is established by fiat by the owner and then communicated to others in a causal chain by creating web pages and Semantic-Web statements containing the URI. Halpin states that both positions ignore the notion of 'sense,' something that is objective in being a shared part of a public language. He thus presents a third position, the 'public language position,' where he grounds the notion of sense in Wittgenstein's analysis of "meaning as use" in a community. Here what a URI means is "the set of search terms that leads multiple users to discover the URI in the context of satisfying a particular information need."

URIs in our RDF encodings are clearly covered by the direct reference position as legal professionals have the task of assigning URIs to suspects, equipment, fingerprints, and so on. But there is still some aspect of the public language position since, in assigning URIs, the professionals follow conventions common to their profession. And there is also some aspect of the logical position since certain logical rules must be followed if the URIs will actually denote things: e.g., the same URI cannot be assigned twice, and certain type restrictions must be obeyed. The logical position is behind the development of ontologies (where, however, most of the terms are for universals). Still, as most ontologies formalize concepts and terms already used in their domains, there is a strong aspect of the public language position in forming ontologies.

7. CONCLUSION

We present a computational framework for identity based on Barwise's situation theory. Situations support information and can carry information about other situations. An utterance situation carries information about a described situation thanks to the constraints imposed by natural language. We are concerned with utterance situations in which identity judgments are made about the culprit in a crime scene, which is the corresponding described situation. The id-situation and crime scene along with various resource situations make up an id-case. In an investigation, there may be several coordinated id-cases that use different means in search of the same judgment. We have developed OWL ontologies to provide concepts for encoding our scenarios in RDF.

To follow how evidence supports hypotheses on the identity of the culprit, we use Dempster-Shafer theory tightly integrated with our ontologies. We focused on cases where the set of candidates is unbounded and reviewed the modifications of Dempster-Shafer theory required when one goes to an open-world assumption (OWA). We have the challenge of encoding OWA scenarios for our framework. The scenarios will contain OWA for Dempster-Shafer theory, OWL, and partiality with situation theory. In regards to Dempster-Shafer theory, we will develop the proper rules to determine how to handle evidence in the OWA. For OWL, we will determine how to represent the structure of OWA in a legal case.

As mentioned, the causal theory of reference fits quite naturally into our approach. In fact, we generalize this causal theory beyond linguistic reference. In a legal setting, Chain of Custody theory addresses what is needed "to ensure the integrity of evidence" all along the chain of those possessing the evidence and perhaps passing it along [17]. A chain of custody involves a sequence of what we call information-relevant actions. Barwise recognized one kind of information-relevant action, utterances (of declarative statements), but we recognize a multitude of kinds, for example, taking and duplicating a fingerprint. While a legal perspective emphasizes what authority was in control, a more general perspective adds the existence of a causal chain from the physical feature in question to where the information is used. (See [16] for further discussion of this point.) As also mentioned, there is some aspect of the logical position on the meanings of URIs as certain logical rules must be followed. The logical position also extends to the broader realm, beyond linguistic reference, since, for information to count as evidence, the physical processes making up the causal chain must occur in a setting where conventions are followed. Note that the links in the causal chain and in the chain of custody are where, in the application of Dempster-Shafer theory, mass may be discounted (for example, because the professional taking the fingerprint on file had not renewed her certification recently). Future work will include working out principled ways to represent causal chains and chains of custody to allow mass functions to be modified in consistent ways.

A major challenge for equational reasoning is the existence of so-called referentially opaque contexts [18], where substituting identicals does not preserve the truth of a statement. The scope of a verb of propositional attitude (e.g., "believe") is typically referentially opaque. For example, suppose that the statement "John believes that Jupiter is the fourth planet from the sun" is true, and "Jupiter is the fifth planet from the sun" is true. From the truth of these two statements, it does not follow, however, that "John believes that the fifth planet from the sun is the fourth planet from the sun." Other contexts that are typically referentially opaque include modal contexts (within the scope of, e.g., "It is necessary that ..."). Whenever we have access to a set of statements from another source (say, on the Web), we can ask whether these statements are within a referentially opaque context. We need a principled way to address this. We also reviewed the related issues regarding the meanings of URIs.

ACKNOWLEDGMENTS

This research is based upon work supported by the U.S. Government including the National Science Foundation. The views and conclusions contained herein are those of the authors and should not be interpreted as necessarily representing the official policies or endorsements, either expressed or implied, of the U.S. Government. The U.S. Government is authorized to reproduce and distribute reprints for Governmental purposes notwithstanding any copyright annotation thereon.

REFFERENCES

[1] Jon Barwise and John Perry. 1998. Situations and Attitudes (new ed.). Center for the Study of Language and Information, New York, NY.

[2] S. Creese D. Hodges and M. Goldsmith. 2012. A model for identity in the cyber and natural universes. In European Intelligence and Security Informatics Conf. (EISIC). 115–122.

[3] Keith Devlin. 1995. Logic and Information. Cambridge University Press.

[4] Rolf Haenni. 2006. Uncover Dempster's rule where it is hidden. In Information Fusion, 2006 9th International Conference on. IEEE, 1–8.

[5] Joseph Y Halpern. 2005. Reasoning about uncertainty. MIT press.

[6] Harry Halpin. 2011. Sense and Reference on the Web. Minds & Machines 21 (2011), 153–178.

[7] Zadeh L. (Ed.). [n. d.]. A mathematical theory of evidence (book review). ([n. d.]).

[8] M. McDaniel, E. Sloan, S. Day, J. Mayes, W. Nick, K. Roy, and A. Esterline. 2017. Situation-Based Ontologies for a Computational Framework for Identity Focusing on Crime Scenes. In Proc. IEEE Conf. on Cognitive & Computational Aspects of Situation Management (CogSIMA '17). Savanna, GA.

[9] M. McDaniel, E. Sloan, W. Nick, J. Mayes, and A. Esterline. 2017. Ontologies for Situation-Based Crime Scene Identities. In Proc. IEEE SoutheastCon. Charlotte, NC.

[10] Glenn Shafer. 1976. A mathematical theory of evidence. Vol. 42. Princeton University Press.

[11] E. Sloan, M. McDaniel, W. Nick, J. Mayes, and A. Esterline. 2016. Structure and Evidence in Identity Cases. In Proc. IEEE SoutheastCon (IEEE Symp. Series on Computational Intelligence (IEEE SSCI 2016)).

[12] E. Sloan, M. McDaniel, W. Nick, J. Mayes, and A. Esterline. 2017. Marshalling Situation-based Evidence in Identity Cases. In Proc. IEEE SoutheastCon. Charlotte, NC.

[13] Ph Smets. 1993. An axiomatic justifiaction for the use of belief function to quantify beliefs. In IJCAI, Vol. 93. 598–603.

[14] J. Barwise and J. Perry, Situations and attitudes, Reissued. Stanford, CA: CSLI Pubs., 1999.

[15] Devlin Keith. Logic and Information. Cambridge University Press. 1995.

[16] A. Esterline, W. Nick, and J. Mason, "Situations, Information, and Evidence," accepted for the 2018 IEEE Conference on Cognitive and Computational Aspects of Situation Management (CogSIMA).

[17] P. C. Giannelli, "Chain of custody," School of Law, Case Western Reserve University, Report, 1993. [Online]. Available: http://scholarlycommons.law.case.edu/faculty_publications/309.

[18] W. V. O. Quine, *Word and Object*, the MIT Press, 1960.

ISASE-MAICS 2018

A Self-Developing Computational System of Full Awareness and Understanding of Reality

Ben Khayut, Lina Fabri and Maya Avikhana

Intelligent Decisions Technologies Systems at IDTS, Department of AI, 106/5 Mezada street, Ashdod 77711, Israel

Abstract: The manuscript represents an approach to create a self-developing computational system of full awareness and understanding of reality through of the perception, processing, memorization and reproduction of languages, images, signals, sounds, feelings and emotions. This system is oriented on using in Kansei Engineering systems as a plug-in. The functionality of this system is realized by its processes of processing of data, information, knowledge, objects, models and modules in current situation. These processes are self-controlled and self-organized themselves under uncertainty of the changing environment with using of computational modeling of the: a) Memory, b) Fuzzy Control, c) Fuzzy Inference, d) Decisions Making, e) Knowledge Representation, f) Knowledge Generalization, g) Knowledge Explanation, h) Reasoning, i) Systems Thinking, j) Awareness, k) Cognition, l) Machine Learning, m) Computational Systemic Mind, and n) Intelligent User Interface. These processes are functioned and managed by the computational subsystems of "Memory", "Brain", "Cognition", "Nervous", "Knowledge Discovery", "Cyber-physics" and "Communication". These subsystems provide the functionality of the computational Self-Developing System of Full Awareness and Understanding in Kansei Engineering systems.

Keywords: *Awareness, Understanding, Cognition, Kansei, Engineering*

1. INTRODUCTION

The Kansei Engineering (KE) is defined in [1] as "translating the technology of perception and image of the consumer for the product into design elements". In other words (Wikipedia), the KE or Affective Engineering (AE) leads to the development of products and services by translating the psychological feelings and needs of the client into the product design area. In computer science, AE systems are intelligent and emotional systems, that help people to solve their problems in a timely manner, for example, in the conditions of lack of knowledge about the environment, its uncertainty and the extreme of the situation. The urgency and necessity of solving the problem of the Full Awareness of reality in AE systems is noted in [13] by the fact, "that both implicit and explicit affective and semantic categorization is dependent on visual awareness, and that affective recognition follows semantic categorization".

In this manuscript, KE technology is considered as a systemic computational model of reasonable perception, awareness, comprehension, cognition, machine learning and systemic deep mind. This model is used in the proposed Self-Developing Computational System of Full Awareness and Understanding of Reality (SDCSFAUR) with the aim to identify of their state and degree of change of properties, needs, aspirations, behavior and the relationship of the consumer to the product, being designed in the mode of continuous real-time, in conditions of uncertainty, environmental influences and in dissimilar subject domains. These properties, needs and aspirations, behavior and consumer attitudes to the product are used by the SDCSFAUR to generate control actions on the organizational objects with aim to orient of their design of products towards on the consumer's preferences.

The SDCSFAUR is designed to be used in AE systems as a plug-in with the aim of intellectualizing their functionality and solving their problems on basis of modern methods of Machine Intelligence (Fig. 1) [11].

The interaction of SDCSFAUR with systems and their users is carried out through Intelligent User Interface (IUI) on the basis of their preferred languages, signaling, gestural, images and sound fragments of communication.

In SDCSFAUR the data and information are pre-processed by Cyber-physical system and System of Situational Control and transmitted to computational Brain system by the Nervous computational system. The computational Brain system detects, percepts and analyzes of the data about objects of reality, forms new information and knowledge, and memorizes them in the repositories. Further, this system uses the previously accumulated knowledge provided with the methods of the Situational fuzzy control of data, information, knowledge, objects and subsystems [2], [3] for implementation of Fuzzy Inference [4], Decision Making [5], Reasoning, Systems Thinking [7], Situational Awareness, Cognition, Machine Learning and Computation of the Mind [8].

Based on the results, obtained from the operation of these subsystems are generated of control actions, which are transmitted through the computational Nervous and Cyber-physical systems to the Computational Brain as a responsiveness to the perception of the reality for generation of new decisions (Fig. 1). These new target solutions transform and shift the entire system of Machine Intelligence into a new state in accordance with the changed situation in the surrounding its reality. The Intelligent User Interface [9], Fig. 1. provides interaction (if necessary) of SDCSFAUR with AE systems and users.

According to [10], the "Situation Awareness" refers to "the perception of the environment elements, time, space, meaning and status future prediction".

Hence, as per [11], (Fig. 1), the problem of computational perception and comprehension of reality object meaning consists of computation of the previous, current (new) and future states of situation awareness and events associated with it. This process is implemented by computational fuzzy modeling and situational fuzzy control [3] of data, information, knowledge, objects and agents, fuzzy inference [4], decision making [5], generalization knowledge [12], reasoning, thinking [7], [10], cognition and machine learning [8], in continuous real time and under uncertainty of the environment.

The modeling of data, information, knowledge, objects, languages, images and signals is implemented by analysis and identification of the previous, current and predicted in future states of the situations awareness with the use of models, methods, subsystems and SDCSFAUR in general.

The SDCSFAUR contains computational models and subsystems (agents), which provide: a) perception of the objects of the reality, extraction and generalization of knowledge, cognition, deep learning, machine learning and full understanding of the languages, images, signals and their essences in the current situation, b) extraction, determination, conversion, representation and memorization of the states and of the object relationships in the memory on basis of internal and external representations of the language of thought, c) comparison of current and previous states of the degree of situational awareness of the reality and relationships between these states, and forming of their new state, taking into account the impact on them of the environment, which is vary in time, d) analysis of regularities and conditions of generation of the previous and current states of the degrees of situational understanding and predicting of their future states, e) computational actualization of these generalized states and relationships, and f) reproduction of the current states and relationships, represented in machine representation and transformation of them in the form of external presentation for their perception and understanding by the human and AE systems.

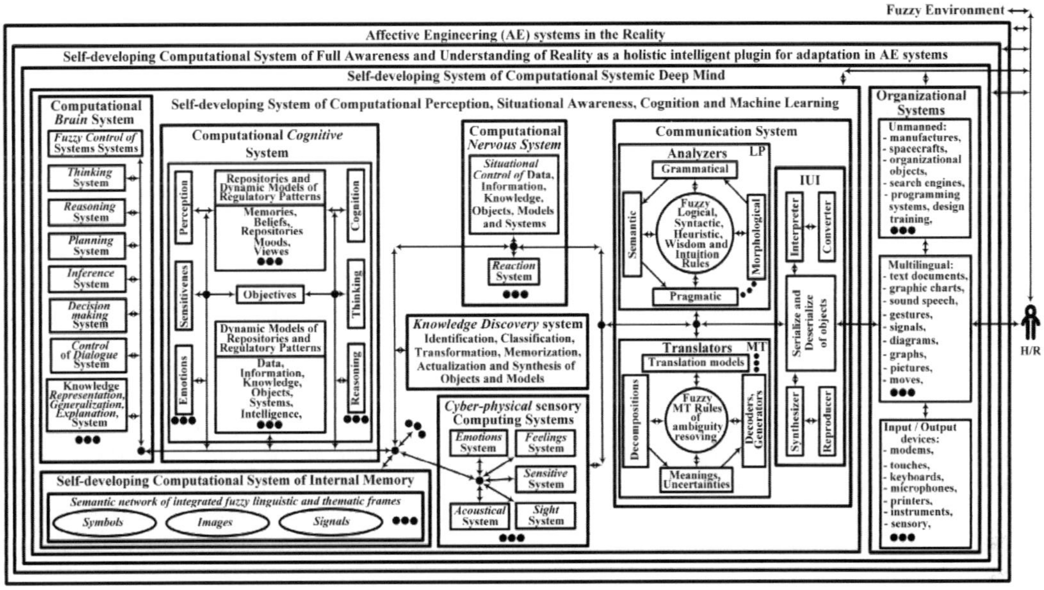

Figure 1: Main components of System of Full Awareness and Understanding of Reality for their adaptation as a holistic intelligent plugin in Affective Engineering systems.

2. ANALYSIS

There are many ideas, methods, algorithms and systems to resolve the problem of Awareness and Understanding in the AE systems. For example, some of them:

▪ In [14] is considered a system of automatic generation of the emotional movement of the robot with the use of its reference movement by establishing a correlation between of movement and the expressed emotion. This work is interesting in terms of expanding in this system the opportunities of situational awareness and understanding of emotions in the process of the robot's movements with the aim of solving AE problems.

▪ In [15] is proposed a moral judgment system using distributed representation and associative information from the predictive structure of the British National Corpus database. In our opinion, the effectiveness of the conducted studies in the field of computational judgment and reasoning would be more significant if for the solution of this problem would be used the functions of computational inference, decision-making, systems thinking, situational awareness, understanding and mind.

▪ In study [16], a method is proposed for determining student performance, based on affective factors of students when learning English using fuzzy sets. A model of understanding of students' progress and a system of fuzzy inference of students' success in learning English are considered. The state of the method, model and system are supported by the human intelligence, that means when a new situation arises, it becomes necessary of their reprogramming. We solve this problem by realizing a computational situational systemic perception, thinking, cognition, generalization of knowledge and machine learning on base of fuzzy inference and decision-making in continuous real time.

The novelty and efficiency of our approach to solving the problem of full Awareness and Understanding of the Reality in Affective Engineering systems is that we:

▪ Used the theories of Fuzzy Logic [17-18], Situational Control [19] and Cognition [8].

▪ Generalized and applied the concept of a Linguistic Variable of Fuzzy Logic [4].

▪ Developed the models, modules, subsystems and system of Perception and SDCSFAUR as a whole [8].

▪ Developed interrelated Memory structures, Functional methods and Components, that implement the following modeling processes in the system subsystems: a) Fuzzy Situational Control of data, information, knowledge, objects and processes [2], b) Presentation [7], Generalization [12] and Explanation of Knowledge, c) Fuzzy Inference [4], e) Control of Dialog [20], f) Reasoning [7] and Systems Thinking [6], g) Computer Systemic Mind [11], h) Perception, full Awareness [8] and Understanding of reality.

3. MEMORY, METHODS, MODELS, MODULES AND SUBSYSTEMS

This section provides a brief description, designed by us, of a dynamically changing Memory structure, Methods of processing, Models, Modules and Subsystems, that determine a holistic Model, a Method, a Functionality and a SDCSFAUR as a whole. The SDCSFAUR comprises of the methods of Perception of reality, full Situation Awareness, Cognition under uncertainty, realized using Machine Learning and Computational Mind methods.

3.1 Memory organization

The model (3), reflects a dynamically changing and growing structure of data, information and knowledge in form of graphical hypothetical convex (or nonconvex) polyhedron [8], which comprises a network of interrelated computational semantic frames. Each of the frame is an integrated set of semantic codes, that identifies a group of atomic objects (up to the level of the elementary symbol) and controlled by Situational Fuzzy Control module (1), [2-3], (Fig. 1).

3.2 Computational model of Module of the Systemic Situational Fuzzy Control

The model of this module is represented in [11] by (1) as

$$M = < A_n^G, K_n^G, F, (S_i : Q_j \overset{x,u,w}{\Rightarrow} Q_l : I) > \quad (1),$$

where:

$$A_n^G(G_n^D, G_n^Z, G_n^Y) \quad (2)$$

is a computational model of a mental Concept of *generalized linguistic variable*, which defines dictionary entries of linguistic and thematic objects in generalized thesauri, where: G_n^D, G_n^Z, G_n^Y, respectively, are determined by the segments of *accumulation* of linguistic and thematic data, information, knowledge and objects in the system of Computational Deep Mind [11] at whole,

$$K_n^G(R_n^D, R_n^Z, R_n^Y, A_n^N) \quad (3)$$

is a computational *Model* [11] of Systemic *Knowledge Module*, used for *fuzzy modeling* and situational fuzzy control of inhomogeneous linguistic and thematic *data, information, knowledge, objects, models* and *processes*, where:

A_n^N are *Concepts* (generalized linguistic variables and situations),

R_n^D, R_n^Z, R_n^Y, respectively, define in [11] the mental rules of modeling of *linguistic*, *thematic* and *mental* data, information, knowledge and objects,

$$F = u(x, w) \quad (4)$$

is an *objective* function, which defines in (1) the

objectives of modeling and situational fuzzy control by the linguistic, thematic and mental data, information, knowledge, objects, models and processes,

$$C =< (S_i : Q_j \overset{x,u,w}{\Rightarrow} Q_l : I) > \quad (5)$$

is a *Computational Sub model of Module of Situational* Fuzzy *Control* [11] in SDCSFAUR.

3.3 The model of Module of Systemic Situational Perception of Reality Under Uncertainty

The model of this Module is presented in [11] by (1) as

$$\mu^P =< M,(\mu_R^P(\mu_R^C(\mu_R^H(\mu_R^T(\mu_R^M(\mu_R^D(\mu_R^Z(\mu_R^L(\mu_R^F(\mu_R^Y(,...,)))))))))) > \quad (6),$$

where:

- M is a Computational Model of Module of Computational Systemic Situational Fuzzy Control of the data, information, knowledge, objects and processes.
- μ_R^Y is a *Cyber-physical module of perception* of reality.
- μ_R^F is a module of *generation of Systemic target computational rules* and *Situational Fuzzy Control* of the *actions* by the *actualization, coordination* and *communication* processes.
- μ_R^L is a module of *computational Systemic Fuzzy Logic Inference*.
- μ_R^Z is a module of *computational Systemic Presentation, Generalization* and *Explanation of Knowledge*.
- μ_R^D is a module of *computational Fuzzy Control* of the *Dialogue* and *Communication* with users and systems.
- μ_R^M is a module of *computational Systemic Decision-making* and their *Planning*.
- μ_R^T is a module of *computational mental Systemic Reasoning*.
- μ_R^H is a module of *computational mental Systemic Thinking*.
- μ_R^C is a module of *computational mental Systemic Cognition*.
- μ_R^P is a module of *computational Systemic Perception*.
- ... is a designation *of the Modules, which implement additional functionality of the Module of the Systemic Situational Perception, presented on its embedded levels.*

3.4 The model of Module of Systemic Full Situational Awareness in Reality

The model of this Module is presented in [11] by (6) as

$$\mu^A =< M,(\mu_R^A(\mu_R^C(\mu_R^P(\mu_R^H(\mu_R^T(\mu_R^M(\mu_R^D(\mu_R^Z(\mu_R^L(\mu_R^F(\mu_R^Y(,...,))))))))))) > \quad (7),$$

- where the difference from model (6) in [11] is the following presented model μ^A (7) of Module μ_R^A of *Systemic Full Situational Awareness in Reality*.

3.5 The model of Module of Systemic Cognition

The model of this Module is presented in [11] by (6) as

$$\mu^C =< M,(\mu_R^A(\mu_R^C(\mu_R^P(\mu_R^H(\mu_R^T(\mu_R^M(\mu_R^D(\mu_R^Z(\mu_R^L(\mu_R^F(\mu_R^Y(,...,))))))))))) > \quad (8),$$

- where the difference from model (6) in [11] is the following presented model μ^C (8) of Module μ_R^C of *Systemic Cognition*.

3.6 The model of Module of Computational Systemic Situational Machine Learning

The model of this Module is presented in [11] by (6) as

$$\mu^R =< M,(\mu_R^R(\mu_R^A(\mu_R^C(\mu_R^P(\mu_R^H(\mu_R^T(\mu_R^M(\mu_R^D(\mu_R^Z(\mu_R^L(\mu_R^F(\mu_R^Y(,...,)))))))))))) > \quad (9),$$

- where the difference from model (6) in [11] is the following represented model μ^R (9) of Module μ_R^R of *Machine Learning*, which is defined in [11] as

$$\mu_R^R =< P_{\min}^R(E_{\max}^T(T_n^S(\mu^R))) > \quad (10),$$

where:

- $P_{\min}^R$ is the value of property of *Time* in the property of *Productivity* of all subsystems (agents) of system of Computational Mind [11] at whole.
- $E_{\max}^T$ is the value of property of *Experience* of all subsystems (agents) of system of Computational Mind [11] at whole.
- T_n^S are *Tasks*, resolved by subsystems (agents) of system of Computational Mind [5] at whole.
- μ^R is the model of the Module of *Machine Learning*.
- R is a function of computing of *Productivity* of all subsystems (agents) of *Learning* system and System of *Computational Systemic Deep Mind* [11], with the value of *Time* property, which seeks to *min*.
- T are a variety of *Tasks*, which are involved in processes of all subsystems (agents), with value of their property of *Experience* of work, which seeks to *max*.
- S are a variety of *Subject Areas* (domains), in which the all systems (agents) are operating jointly the system of Computational Systemic Mind [5] at whole.

3.7 The model of Module of Systemic Full Understanding of the Reality

The model of this Module is presented as

$$\mu^U =< M,(\mu_R^R(\mu_R^A(\mu_R^P))) > \quad (11),$$

where:

- M is a computational Model of Module of *computational Systemic Situational Fuzzy Control* of data, information, knowledge, objects and processes.

- μ_R^P is a Computational Model of Module of *computational Systemic Situational Perception* of Reality.
- μ_R^A is a Computational Model of Module of *Full Situation Awareness of Reality*.
- μ_R^R is a Model of Module of *Computational* Systemic Situational *Machine Learning*.

Thus, the technology of modeling of Computational Perception, Machine Learning, Systemic Deep Mind, Situational Awareness and Understanding of Reality are presented by way of application of Situational Control, Cyber-physical and Systems approaches and using the developed by us methods of the Fuzzy Logic Inference, Decision-making, Systems Thinking and Cognition, which are realized by Module of Knowledge (3).

The computer representation of one of computational

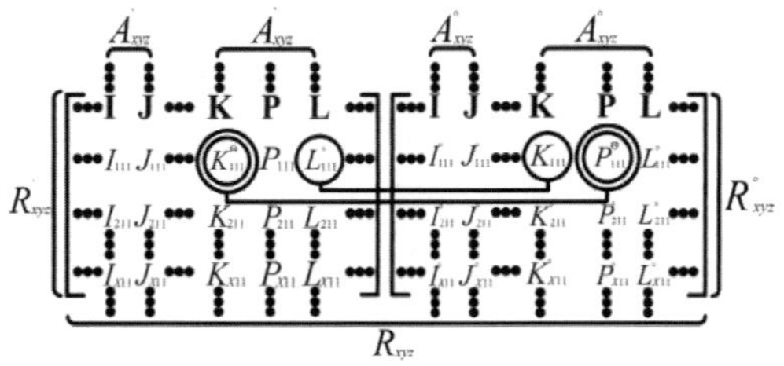

Figure 2: Fragment of semantic domain of fuzzy sets

Figure 3: Fragment of generalized linguistic variables in semantic network of frames

rules (12) of resolving lexical ambiguity in the process of modeling Systemic Deep Mind is given in [11] and is shown on the following Fig. 2, Fig. 3.

This process is functioning on the *external* and *internal* levels of representation and modeling of *Deep Mind*, using multivariate generalized *matrices*, obtained from model of semantic network of computational *frames*, organized in memory of the system of *Systemic Deep Mind.*

$$IF\ ((K^{\Theta} = P^{\Theta})\ AND\ (L^{\circ} = K^{\circ}))\ THEN\ ((I = I^{\circ})\ AND\ (J = J^{\circ})) \quad (12)$$

This rule (12) is interpreted by the computational model of the Module (3) for example, as follows: ***if*** two words, which are included in sentence in both languages and the code of *right compatibility* of word, which is located to the *left* from a group of two words in *another* language ***is equal*** to *conceptual* code of the word, located to the *right* of a group of two words of the *output* language and the code of *left compatibility* of word, located to the *right* of a group of two words of the *output* language ***is equal*** to *conceptual code* of word, located to the *left* of a group of two words of *input* language, ***then*** these *pairs* of words of *input* and *output* languages *correspond* and are *identical* each to other at the level of resolving the problem of conceptual *disambiguation* at the external and internal levels of their representations in machine translation process.

Through of using in a similar way of compositional rules of grammar, morphology, syntax, semantic, logical, psychological and other compositional rules and analyzing of languages, images and signals of reality we are implementing modeling of Computational Systemic *Deep Mind* and Full Awareness and Understanding of objects of Reality, represented on *internal* and *external* levels of their perception and cognition under uncertainty of environment.

Thus, the fuzzy control of the system of computational Mind performs a launch of the functional modules, which implement algorithms of Modeling of Computational Perception of reality, Situation Awareness, Cognition and Machine Learning under uncertainty. This process is iteratively performed continuously in real time by the successive call of following main group of nested, integrated, computational, interconnected and cooperated with each other of functional modules (agents) of *Perception* [11], *Data Mining* and *Fuzzy Inference* [4], *Decision-making* [5], *Reasoning* [7], *Systems Thinking* [6], *Cognition* [8], *Machine Learning* [11].

The *Situational Awareness and Understanding* are implemented as a system of interacting with each other of the processes of: a) Perception of reality, b) Computational Systemic Situational Fuzzy Control of data, information, knowledge and objects, and c) Computational Machine Learning in general.

CONCLUSION

This paper described a systemic, linguistic and cyber-physical (sensory) approach to modeling of SDCSFAUR through of Computational Perception of Reality, Cognition and Machine Learning under uncertainty. This system is oriented to introduction in the systems of KE as a plug-in with a view to their intellectualization, what will be considered in detail in our subsequent studies.

REFFERENCES

1. Misuo Nagamachi; Kansei Engineering: A New

ergonomic consumer-oriented technology for product development, International Journal of Industrial Ergonomics; 15, pp.3-11, 1995.

2. B. Khayut and Y. Pechersky; Situational Data Control; Deposited manuscript, VINITI, Moscow, p. 29, 1987.

3. B. Khayut, L. Fabri and M. Avikhana; Intelligent Multi-Agent Fuzzy Control System under Uncertainty, Journal of Computer Science & Information Technology (CS&IT); 4(18), pp.369-380, 2014.

4. B. Khayut; Modeling of Fuzzy Logic Inference in the Decision-making system; Institute of Mathematics of the Moldavian Academy of Science, Modeling Management systems, Vol.110, Shtiinca, Chisinau, pp. 134-143, 1989.

5. B. Khayut, L. Fabri and M. Avikhana; Planning, Decision-making and Control in Fuzzy Environment; Conference on Advance Trends in Soft Computing and Control in Fuzzy Environment, TX, San Antonio, Springer, pp.137-143, 2013.

6. B. Khayut, L. Fabri and M. Avikhana; Modeling of Intelligent System Thinking in Complex Adaptive Systems; Conference on Complex Adaptive Systems, PA, Elsevier, pp.93-100, 2014.

7. B. Khayut, L. Fabri and M. Avikhana; Knowledge Representation, Reasoning and Systems Thinking under Uncertainty; Conference on Computer Modeling and Simulation, UKSim-AMSS 16, Cambridge, pp.162-168, 2014.

8. B. Khayut, L. Fabri and M. Avikhana; Modeling of Computational Perception of Reality, Situational Awareness, Cognition and Machine Learning Under Uncertainty; Conference on Intelligent Systems IntelliSys 2017, IEEE, London, UK, pp.331-339, 2017.

9. B. Khayut, L. Fabri and M. Avikhana; Intelligent User Interface in Fuzzy Environment; International Journal of Artificial Intelligence & Applications (IJAIA), 2(1), pp.63-78, 2014

10. M. Endsley; Application Toward a Theory of Situation Awareness in Dynamic Systems; Journal on Human Factors, 37(1), pp.32-64, 1995.

11. B. Khayut, L. Fabri and M. Avikhana; Modeling of Computational Systemic Deep Mind under Uncertainty; Conference on Complex Adaptive Systems, CA, Elsevier, pp.135-144, 2016.

12. Y. Pechersky and B. Khayut; Generalization of Knowledge in Decision support systems, Conference on Questions of development computer facilities, Chisinau, pp.107-108, 1989.

13. M. Lahteenmaki, J. Hyona and M. Koivisto; Affective Processing Requires Awareness; American Psychological Association, Journal of Experimental Psychology, Vol.144, No.2, pp.339-365, 2015.

14. T. Takegoshi and M. Hagiwara; An Automatic Motion Generating System for Humanoid with Emotions; Transactions of Japan Society of Kansei Engineering, International Journal of Affective Engineering, (Accepted): 2017.

15. M. Yamamoto and M. Hagiwara; A moral Judgment System using Distributed Representation and Associative Information; Transactions of Japan Society of Kansei Engineering, International Journal of Affective Engineering, Vol. 15(4), pp. 493-501, 2016.

16. F.A. Bachtiar, E.W. Cooper, G.H. Sulistyo and K. Kamei; Student Assessment Based on Affective Factors in English Learning Using Fuzzy Inference; International Journal of Affective Engineering, Vol. 15(2), pp.101-108, 2016.

17. L. Zadeh; Fuzzy Sets; Information and Control, NY, Vol. 8, pp.338-359, 1965.

18. L. Zadeh; The Concept of a Linguistic Variable and its Application to Approximate Reasoning; Information Sciences, Vol. 14, pp.141-164, 1970.

19. D.A. Pospelov; Situational Control; Science, Moscow, pp.286, 1986.

20. Y. Pechersky and B. Khayut; An approach to the Control of Dialogue in Decision-making system; Conference on Tools in Automated Control Systems, Chisinau, pp. 145-146, 1988.

ISASE-MAICS 2018

Proposal for Molecular Affective Engineering

– Towards Innovation in Cosmetic Development –

Yoshiko NAKAO

NIHON L'OREAL K.K., KSP R&D D140, 3-2-1, Sakado, Takatsu-ku, Kawasaki-shi, Kanagawa 213-0012, Japan
ynakao@rd.loreal.com

Abstract: In the field of cosmetic development we have put our efforts mainly on Consumer interview and understanding of physical properties of products, to repeatedly obtain Consumer's purchase intent. However, we have recognized that the methodology contributes to confirmation of product benefit and to formulas screening, but it does not necessarily bring product innovation. Delivering innovation in cosmetic development requires more in-depth understanding of in-use performance of products at molecular level or from the chemical point of view.

This paper proposes a new approach of "Molecular Affective Engineering" which measures in-use product performance from macroscopic to microscopic levels in different order of magnitude, to sharply identify key elements to impact on an affective mind.

Keywords: *Molecular Affective Engineering, Chemical Character, in-use performance, Cosmetic Development, Kansei*

1. INTRODUCTION

In the field of Kansei/Affective Engineering (Kansei is Japanese but ISASE uses affective engineering. So, hereafter I will use affective engineering without mentioning it.), understanding of sensory experience driving emotion starts with consumer interview. Then the sensory experience is objectively measured by physical and mechanical methods, to translate the consumer's words into technical meanings. It helps us confirm the product benefit and screen formulas. However, the sensory experience is not discussed in chemical or molecular level, which is needed to deliver innovation in cosmetic development. Conversely, Instrumental Analysis has been well developed to dig into molecular and even atomic level phenomena for many years. But the application to Affective Engineering looks to be out of scope yet. If Affective Engineering is equipped with the field of Instrumental Analysis, we could sharply identify key elements to drive consumer's emotion in molecular level, bringing breakthrough innovation in Cosmetic development.

2. SENSORY EXPERIENCE AND MEASUREMENT SCALE (ORDER OF MAGNITUDE)

In case of skin care cream, the sensory experience in product usage includes the following 4 steps [1, 2];

1) Opening the package and the container

2) Pick-Up - the removal of the product from the container

3) Rub-Out – the application of the product to the skin

4) After Feel – the evaluation of the effect of the product on the skin.

We evaluate and feel the product by using the multiple human senses. The step 1 is the first touch point with the product. Appearance of the package and the container creates the first impression such as luxury and KAWAII. The usability of the container is another factor. The step 2 is the first interaction between the product and the finger. Appearance, smell and texture impact on the perception. The step 3 is the point of the interaction among the finger, the product and the face skin. It is the process of structure deformation of the product by spreading. In addition, absorption, penetration and evaporation take place in the step. In the step 4, stickiness, smoothness and bounciness of the skin are the key factors to be evaluated [3].

The phenomena taken place in each step impact on emotion and eventually on purchase intent, and they need to be understood and measured in various scales, to **reflect consumer preference into formulas.**

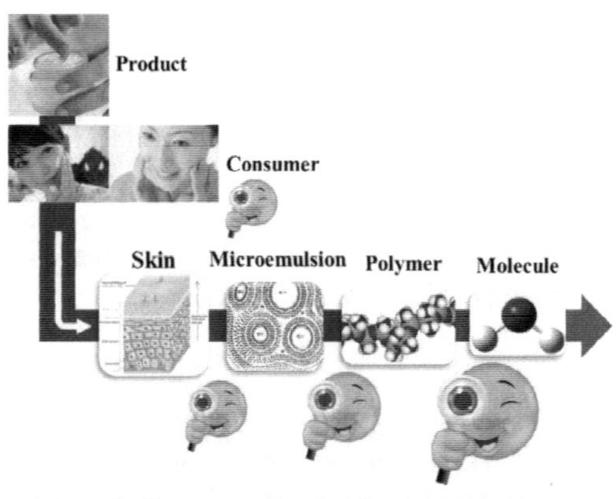

Figure 1: Measurement scale of sensory experience

Figure 1 shows how the sensory experience consists of the phenomena in various scales from centimeter to molecule.

The pick-up and the rub-out are mainly the processes of structure deformation of the microemulsion product via shear thinning or shear thickening defined as rheological properties [4]. The properties determine the application feel of the product such as spreadability and softness [5], greatly impacting on emotion.

After feel is evaluated by touching face. Smoothness or stickiness of skin is assessed by friction force or cohesion force at the interface between face and finger. The physical properties depend on deposition of the key ingredients, which is smaller scale phenomenon [6]. The skin bounciness is character of visco-elastic property of skin in millimeter-micrometer scale. But it is provided by penetration of moisturizing molecules.

3. MEASUREMENT TECHNOLOGIES

Here measurement technologies are introduced by order of magnitude.

3. 1 Centimeter – Millimeter

3. 1. 1 Friction Force

KES Surface Tester [7] was originally designed to measure hand touch feel on textile surface. It has been reapplied to surfaces of skin and hair for many years. I-Tester of Trinity-Lab Co., Ltd includes the specially designed finger probe [8] which allows us to measure surface friction in a way of actual finger stroke.

The field of haptic technologies has made a great progress along with the progress of VR (Virtual Reality) technologies in recent years [9]. For example, the finger sensor developed by Tanaka et.al., [10] enables us directly measuring tactile feel based on skin-propagated vibration. Techtile tool kit [11] measures sound generated by stroking and patting. We are able to differentiate tactile feel by the frequency profile among dry feel, wet feel and sticky feel, etc.

3.1.2 Cohesion Force

Stickiness corresponds to cohesion force between finger and face. The application feel method developed by TOYOBO [12] allows us to measure the stickiness as applied force to separate a finger from a face surface.

3.1.3 Elasticity

In-vivo tool to measure skin elasticity is very limited. YAWASA developed by Sakuma and Tec Gihan Co., Ltd. is the in-vivo tool to sensitively measure skin visco-elasticity [13].

3. 2 Millimeter – Nanometer

3. 2. 1 Rheology

Application of the product is the process of structure deformation of the microemulsion product. The increase or decrease of viscosity is measured as a function of shear force, which corresponds to shear thickening or shear thinning property [5]. Rigidity and recovery of the structure are also measured as visco-elasticity. These properties are highly related with the application feel. The area to measure in-use rheological properties of the cosmetic products is specifically called as psycho-rheology [14]. Rheometers which allow us to sensitively measure rheological behavior by mimicking in-use condition are produced by TA Instrument Inc., Anton Paar K.K. and Malven Instruments Ltd.

3. 2. 2 Surface Morphology

Confocal laser microscopy [15, 16] is applicable to the observation of topography of skin surface and cuticle gaps of hair in micrometer to angstrom spatial resolution.

3. 2. 3 Structure of Emulsion and Polymer

Polarizing microscopy [17] provides with information about packing, periodicity and molecular orientation. For example, if the micro-emulsion takes a lamella structure, Maltese Cross image is observed with a polarizing microscope. Cryo-SEM [18] technique provides with more detailed morphology of lamella in nano scale. Furthermore, Microscopy-FTIR [19] and Microscopy-Raman [20] are applicable to identification of molecular structure of the micro-emulsion. SAX (small angle X-ray scattering) and WAX (wide angle X-ray diffraction) provide us with the information of crystal structure and lamella space [21].

3. 3 Molecular Level

3. 3. 1 Adsorbed Molecules

FTIR-ATR [22] is a powerful tool for in-situ measurement of adsorbed molecules on skin and hair surfaces. Recently the in-vivo methods are developed to directly measure adsorbed molecules on skin [23]. It helps us clarify mechanism of skin feel. If SEWS technique [24] is combined, higher sensitivity can be achieved.

If the measurement is performed in UHV (Ultra High

Vacuum) for mimic skins, TOF-SIMS [25] provides elemental mapping of the adsorbed species.

Morphology of adsorbed molecules is obtained by AFM [26] in-situ and by SEM in UHV.

3. 3. 2 Penetrated Molecules

Confocal laser Raman spectroscopy [27] is the technique to enable us depth profiling of molecules. It detects penetration of key ingredients such as moisturizers and emollients as well as water content in epidermis.

Another technique is Nano-IR [28] which enables us molecular mapping with nano-level spatial resolution by combing FTIR with AFM. However, it is applicable only to cross-sectioned sample such as hair cross-section, not to in-vivo measurement of skin for now.

4. CONCLUDING REMARS

Here the proposal for the molecular affective engineering was explained by taking the 2 moments [29] of SMOT (the second moment of truth) and TMOT (the third moment of truth) in the sensory experience of the skin care cream. However, FMOT (the first moment of truth) is sometimes the most important moment to induce strong emotion and to accelerate the purchase intent. In the moment, information by eyes and nose is a more dominant factor to attract consumers. Package design and fragrance sound to be a matter of art or a matter of psychology. But introducing optical effect to the package and developing novel fragrance by molecular design are also the matters of the molecular affective engineering. So the molecular affective engineering plays key roles through whole the sensory experience, enabling us to develop innovative products.

The approach of the molecular affective engineering is also important in the other categories such as textile and paper products. The hand feels of the products; HARI (body/compressibility), KOSHI (bendability) and NUMERI (surface) depend on molecular structures and surface morphology of the fibers assembled. Appearance of the textiles is also a key factor to impact on perception. The textiles with the same color give us different impressions. It is explained by difference of the complex micro-components derived by the methodology of Mathematical Morphology [30].

Back to the1950s, Watson, Crick, Franklin and Wilkins co-discovered the double helix structure of DNA using X-ray crystallography [31], which formed the basis for modern biotechnology so called as molecular biology. The molecular level approach furthermore resulted in a significant progress in biology such as DNA cloning and genome analysis.

Lastly I emphasize the importance of this approach to equip Affective Engineering with the molecular level understanding by the Instrumental Analysis, to bring not only innovations into the development of the consumer products but also further evolution of Affective Engineering.

Affective Engineering is the science for emotion of human-beings, where tacit knowledge is translated into explicit knowledge. Connected research among multi-academic areas; psychology, physics, chemistry, VR, physiology and neuroscience is required in the process of unraveling emotion.

In this paper I sowed "seeds" of "**Molecular Affective Engineering**". I hope that buds will come out soon and hope to grow up to build a system of Kansei/Affective Engineering by raising it further in the future. Today, Kansei/Affective engineering is being discussed across various fields, and its unified academic system has not been constructed. In that sense as well, the development of Molecular Affective Engineering will be expected more and more from now on.

ACKNOWLEDGEMENTS

I would like to show my sincere appreciation to Professor Emeritus Hisao Shiizuka of Kogakuin University for great discussion and suggestions about the proposal. Dr. Setsuko Jitsukawa of NIHON L'OREAL K.K. supported me for this submission.

REFFERENCES

1. N. O. Schwartz; Adaption of the Sensory Texture Profile Method to Skin Care Products, Journal of Texture Studies, 6, pp.33-42, 1975.
2. I. V. Reeth, B. Courel and S.V. Doorn; Beyond Skin Feel: Innovative Methods for Developing Complex Sensory Profiles with Silicones, www.dowcorning.com/content/publishedlit/27-1072.pdf
3. Yoshiko Nakao; Relentless Quest for Purchase Intent with Kansei Engineering, Journal of Japan Society for Fuzzy Theory and Intelligent Informatics, 29(6), pp.214-216, 2017.
4. Kazunari Suzuki; Cosmetic Emulsions, Journal of the Japan Society of Colour Material, 54(10), pp.623-636, 1981.
5. T. Mezger; The Rheology Handbook, 3rd revised ed., Hanover, Vincentz Newyork, 2011.

6. Masato Suzuki; Development of Functional Cosmetics (3), CMC Press, 2007.
7. Sueo Kawabata, Masako Niwa and Yoshihiro Yamashita; Recent Developments in the Evaluation Technology of Fiber and Textiles: Toward the Engineered Design of Textile Performance, Journal of Applied Polymer Science, 83(3), pp.687-702, 2002.
8. Takashi Maeno; Analysis and Design of a Tactile Sensor Detecting Strain Distribution inside an Elastic Finger, Proc. IEEE/RSJ Int. Conf. on Intelligent Robotics Systems, pp.1658-1663, 1998.
9. Makoto Shimojo, Takashi Maeno, Hiroyuki Shinoda and Akihito Sano; Mechanism of Tactile Recognition and Application Technology – Tactile and Tactile Display -, S&T Press, 2014.
10. Yasutoshi Takekawa, Tatsuya Hasegawa, Yoshihiro Tanaka and Akihito Sano; Tactile Display Based on Skin-Propagated Vibration, in Haptic Interaction: Perception, Devices and Applications, Eds. H. Kajimoto, H. Ando, K-UK Kyung, pp.121-123. 2015.
11. Kouta Minamizawa, Masashi Nakatani, Soichiro Mihara and Susumu Tachi; TECHTILE toolkit: a prototype tool for design and education of haptic media, Proceedings of the 2012 Virtual Reality International Conference, p.26, 2012.
12. TOYOBO; Development of Method to Evaluate Application Feel of Cosmetics, The Syukan Syogyo, Jan. 25 p. 10, 2016.
13. Atsushi Sakuma and Yuma Sango; Viscoelasticity Measurement of Softness by Indentation Devices for Evaluation of Human Skin, Proceeding of ASME 2014 International Mechanical Congress and Exposition, 3, pp.1-4, 2014.
14. Yoshiyuki Nabata; Rheology of Cosmetics, Yoneda Press, 2015.
15. B. G. Rosen; On in-vivo Skin Topography Metrology and Replication Techniques, Journal of Physics, Conf. Ser., 13, pp.325-329, 2005.
16. Kyunghee Park and Teruko Tamura; Quantitative Analysis of Skin Surface Contour by Using Confocal Scanning Laser Microscope, Journal of the Japan Research Association for Textile End-Users, 51(4), pp.338-345, 2010.
17. Junko Morikawa; Optical and Thermal Imaging of Polymer Spherulites, OplusE, 381, 2011.
18. T. Dokland; Techniques in Microscopy for Biomedical Applications, World Scientific Publishing Co Pte Ltd, p.115, 2006.
19. Toshikatsu Nishioka and Norio Teramae; Microscopy-IR, IBC Press, 2003.
20. E. Lee; Infrared and Raman Spectroscopic Imaging, Eds. R. Salzer and H.W. Siesler, p.377, Wiley-VCH Verlag GmH, Germany, 2009.
21. Satoshi Yamaki; Micro-structure of Emulsion in Coated Form by Small Angle X-Ray Scattering, Spring-8/SACLA, SecB, 2(1), pp.35-36, 2014.
22. N. J. Harrick; Internal Reflection Spectroscopy, John Wiley & Sons Inc., 1967.
23. J. A. Fruetel, R.F. Renzi et.al.; Hand-held microanalytical instrument for chip-based electrophoretic separations of proteins, Analytical Chemistry, 77(2), pp.435-441, 2005.
24. Yoshiko Nakao and Haruka Yamada; Enhanced Infrared ATR Spectra of Surface Layers using Metal Films, Surface Science, 176(3), pp.578-592, 1986.
25. Hiroyuki Yamaba; Analysis of Transcutaneous Penetration Pathway Using TOF-SIMS, Journal of Japanese Cosmetic Science Society, 38(4), pp.237-243, 2014.
26. Hiroki Kitano; Study of Fine-structures and Mechanical Properties of Human Hair by Using Atomic Force Microscopy, Journal of the Surface Science Society of Japan, 29(7), pp.427-431, 2008.
27. Tetsuji Hirao, Mariko Egawa and Toyonobu Yamashita; Recent Advances in Technologies fir Measurement of the Skin, Journal of the Surface Science Society of Japan, 35(1), pp.17-22, 2014.
28. C. Marcott, M. Lo et.al.; Nanoscale infrared (IR) Spectroscopy and Imaging of Structural Lipids in Human Stratum Corneum Using an Atomic Force Microscope to Directly Detect Absorbed Light from a Tunable IR Laser Source, Experimental Dermatology, 22(6), pp.419-421, 2013.
29. A. G. Lafley, R. Charan; "The Game-Changer: How You Can Drive Revenue and Profit Growth with Innovation". Crown Business. Retrieved 12 March2018 – via Amazon.
30. Chie Muraki Asano, Akira Asano, Mitsuji Muneyasu and Takako Fujimoto; Analysis and Evaluation of Visual Identification of Texture Using Image Processing Methods, SCIS & ISIS 2006(0), 1789-1793, 2006.
31. J.D. Watson and F.H. Crick: A Structure for Deoxyribose Nucleic Acids, Nature. 171 (4356), pp.737-738, 1953.

ISASE-MAICS 2018

Relationship between thickness feeling and physical thickness under different compressive load

KyoungOk Kim*, Qiangwei Zheng **, Masayuki Takatera*

* Shinshu University, Institute for Fiber Engineering (IFES), Interdisciplinary Cluster for Cutting Edge Research (ICCER), Tokida 3-15-1, Ueda, Nagano prefecture, 386-8567, Japan
** Shinshu University, Graduate school of Science and Technology, Division of Textile & Kansei Engineering, Tokida 3-15-1, Ueda, Nagano prefecture, 386-8567, Japan

Abstract: In this study, we investigated the relationship between thickness feeling for various fabric types and physical thickness under different compressive loads to clarify the effective range for human about fabric thickness. We selected eight fabric types and prepared 8 or 9 fabrics with different thickness in one fabric type. We measured thickness of samples using compression tester KES-FB3 under compressive load 0.5 gf/cm^2, 10 gf/cm^2, 20 gf/cm^2, 30 gf/cm^2, 40 gf/cm^2, 50 gf/cm^2, respectively. Sensory evaluation for the thickness of each fabric was carried out using SD method (semantic differential scale method) for 60 subjects. The nine fabric types were divided into two kinds which fabric types having a significant correlation between physical thickness and sensory evaluation score under any pressures, and fabric types having significant correlations in thickness under the compressive load of 0.5 and 50 gf/cm^2.
Keywords: *thickness feeling, physical thickness, fabric type*

1. INTRODUCTION

Selection of fabric for clothing is carried out among samples taken from exhibitions or ones from trading companies and manufacturers [1]. Thickness, smoothness, softness, dry-moisture feeling (luster) are taken into account for fabric selection [2]. Among these, the thickness is the most fundamental characteristic for determining the use of a fabric.

According to ISO5084, compressive load in measuring the thickness of textile products is 1 kPa or less (0.1 kPa for piles and some kinds of knitted fabric). In Japanese Industrial Standards (JIS L 1018), the pressure is 0.7 kPa (7 gf/cm^2) for common knitted fabrics and 0.3 kPa (3 gf/cm^2) for hairy knitted fabric [3].

In hand prediction, the thickness feeling is considered to corresponding to the physical thickness. In the Kawabata Evaluation System, the thickness of the men's clothing is measured under compressive load at 50 Pa (0.5 gf / cm^2) [4]. However, an accuracy of human's discrimination on fabric thickness is still unclear. The feeling with respect to the thickness of the fabric may be related to many factors such as the type of yarns, hairiness of yarn, and the density of the fabric [5].

In this study, we investigated the relationship between thickness feeling for various fabric types and physical thickness under different compressive loads to clarify the effective range for human about fabric thickness.

2. EXPERIMENTAL

2.1 Measurement of physical thickness

We selected eight fabric types and prepared 8 or 9 fabrics with different thickness in one fabric type. The total numbers of fabrics were 67. The fabric type was in accordance with the category defined by a trading company.

We measured the thickness of samples using compression tester KES-FB3. The area of the compression plate was 2 cm^2. The maximum compressive load was set as 50 gf/cm^2. Then, the thicknesses were measured at 0.5 gf/cm^2, 10 gf/cm^2, 20 gf/cm^2, 30 gf/cm^2, 40 gf/cm^2, 50 gf/cm^2. For each sample, measurements of five times were carried out and the average was used. The experimental environment was 20 ± 1℃ temperature, 65 ± 4 % relative humidity. Before testing, the samples were preconditioned during 24 h under the experimental environment.

A fabric having an intermediate thickness among the respective fabric type is set as a standard sample for sensory evaluation. Table 1 shows the thickness of the standard sample for each fabric type and the maximum and minimum fabric thickness in each fabric type.

2.2 Sensory evaluation

Sensory evaluation for thickness of each fabric was carried out using SD method (semantic differential scale method). Subjects compared a sample to the standard

Keywords: thickness feeling, physical thickness, fabric type

Table 1: Thickness at 0.5gf/cm^2 of the standard sample for each fabric type (mm)

Fabric type	Minimum thickness in the fabric type	Thickness of the standard sample	Maximum thickness in the fabric type
Chiffon (nine kinds)	0.126	0.159	0.180
Taffeta (nine kinds)	0.137	0.183	0.289
Loan (eight kinds)	0.123	0.191	0.217
Denim (seven kinds)	0.256	0.282	0.424
Herringbone tweed (nine kinds)	0.195	0.313	0.428
Saxony (nine kinds)	0.282	0.347	0.485
Kersey (seven kinds)	0.246	0.369	1.28
Melton (eight kinds)	0.810	0.978	1.25

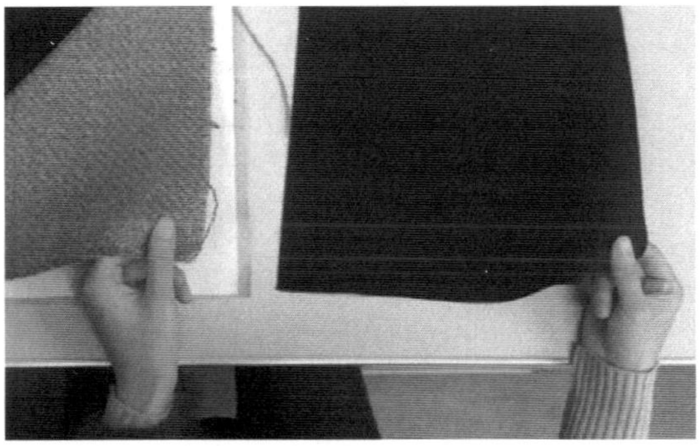

Figure 1: Evaluation method

sample for each fabric type. A subject touched the standard sample with 3 fingers of left hand and the other sample of the same fabric type with 3 fingers of right hand at the same time. Figure 1 shows the evaluation method. After comparing the thicknesses of the two samples, a subject fill in the evaluation sheet. Sensory evaluation value of the standard sample was set to 0, and the evaluation range was set to ± 3 scales. The thickest evaluation value was set to -3. The subjects were 60 university students in their 20's (30 women and 30 men).

3. RESULTS AND DISCUSSION

Figures 2-9 show the relationship between sensory evaluation score and measured thickness under different compressive load for each fabric type. The relationship between the thickness of the fabric under each compressive load and the sensory evaluation score was analyzed. We calculated the correlation coefficient and carried out tests for non-correlation. Table 2 shows the correlation coefficients and significant differences between the thickness under each load and the sensory evaluation scores. Chiffon, herringbone tweed, Saxony, and Kersey showed significant correlation at significant level 1% or 5% between the physical thickness and sensory evaluation scores, regardless of pressure. For fabric type of loan, a significant correlation was found between physical thickness and sensory evaluation scores value under the compressive loads of 0.5 gf/cm^2 and 50 gf/cm^2. For fabric type of Taffeta, the correlation coefficient between physical thickness and sensory evaluation scores under the compressive load of 0.5 gf/cm^2 was significant. For fabric type of Melton, a significant correlation was found between the physical thickness and the sensory evaluation value under the compressive load of 0.5 gf/cm^2, 10 gf/cm^2 and 50 gf/cm^2. However, fabric type of denim did not show a significant correlation between physical thickness and sensory evaluation score under any pressure.

For all seven types of fabrics except denim, all significant correlations were observed between physical thickness and sensory evaluation scores under the compressive load of 0.5 gf/cm^2. Moreover, six types of fabrics except for Denim and Taffeta showed significant correlations between physical thickness and sensory evaluation value under the compressive load of 50 gf/cm^2.

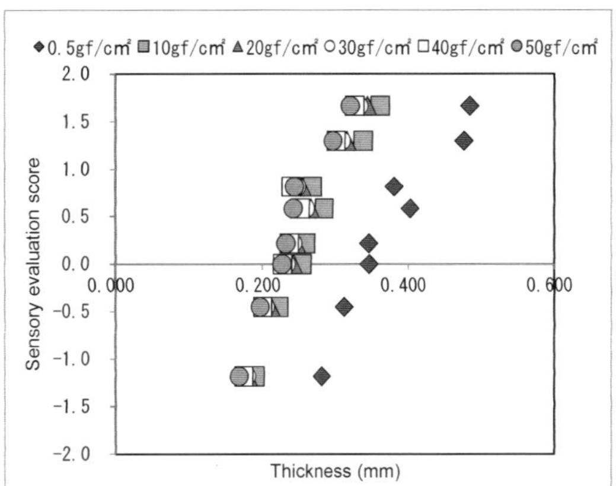

Figure 2: Relationship between sensory evaluation

score and measured thickness under different compressive load for fabric type of Saxony

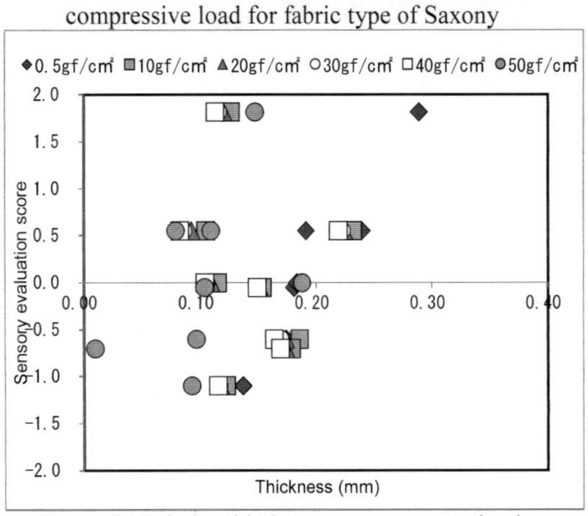

Figure 3: Relationship between sensory evaluation score and measured thickness under different compressive load for fabric type of Taffeta

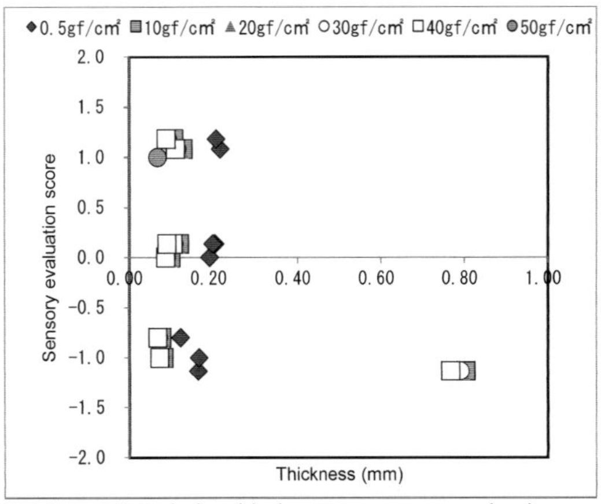

Figure 4: Relationship between sensory evaluation score and measured thickness under different compressive load for fabric type of Loan

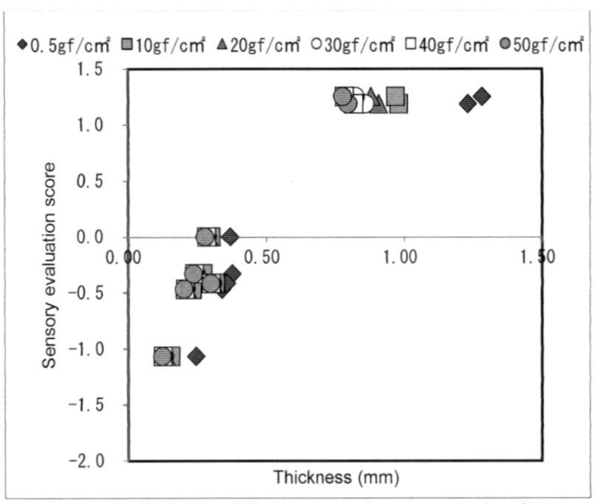

Figure 5: Relationship between sensory evaluation score and measured thickness under different compressive load for fabric type of Kersey

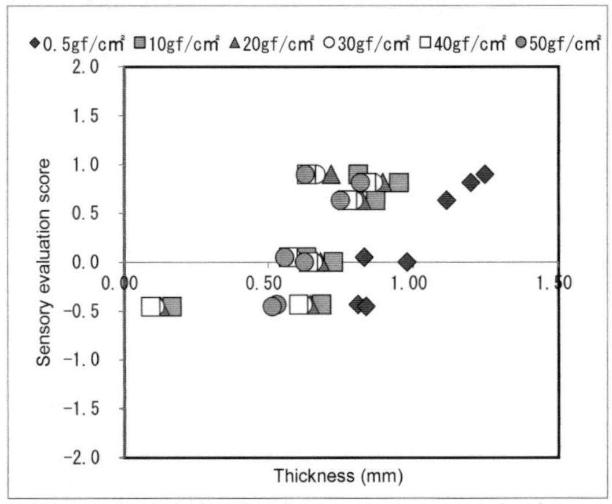

Figure 6: Relationship between sensory evaluation score and measured thickness under different compressive load for fabric type of Melton

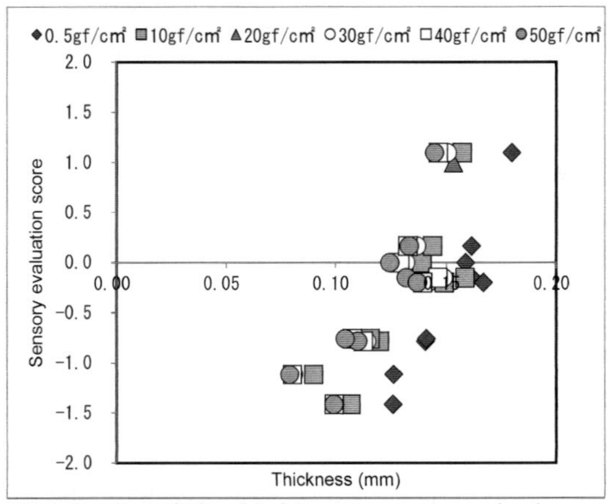

Figure 7: Relationship between sensory evaluation score and measured thickness under different compressive load for fabric type of Chiffon

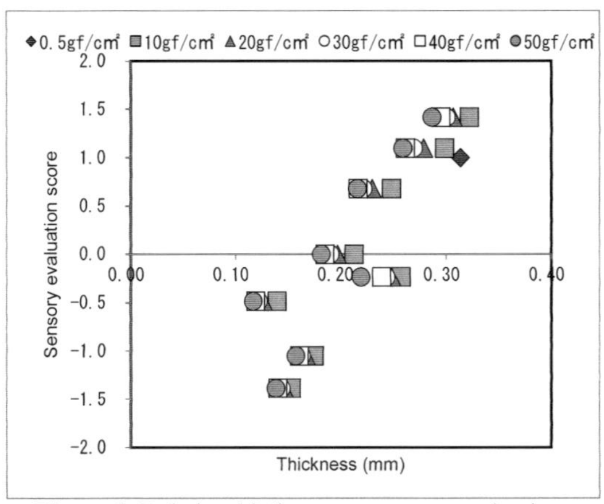

Figure 8: Relationship between sensory evaluation score and measured thickness under different

compressive load for fabric type of Herringbone tweed

Table 2: Correlation coefficient of sensory test results and physical thickness under each load.

Compressive load / Fabric type	0.5gf / cm²	10gf / cm²	20gf / cm²	30gf / cm²	40gf / cm²	50gf / cm²
Chiffon	-0.952 **	-0.846 **	-0.792 **	-0.922 **	-0.622 **	-0.870 **
Taffeta	-0.941 **	0.125	0.134	0.148	0.155	-0.453
Loan	-0.807 *	-0.858	-0.747	-0.667	-0.942	-0.839**
Denim	-0.671	-0.253	-0.178	-0.185	-0.215	-0.223
Herringbone	-0.987 **	-0.894 **	-0.868 **	-0.858 **	-0.855 **	-0.882 **
Saxony	-0.962 **	-0.970 **	-0.969 **	-0.968 **	-0.964 **	-0.975 **
Kersey	-0.960 **	-0.969 **	-0.971 **	-0.973 **	-0.974 **	-0.975 **
Melton	-0.951 **	-0.764 *	-0.728	-0.708	-0.694	-0.813*

**significant level 1%, * significant level 5%

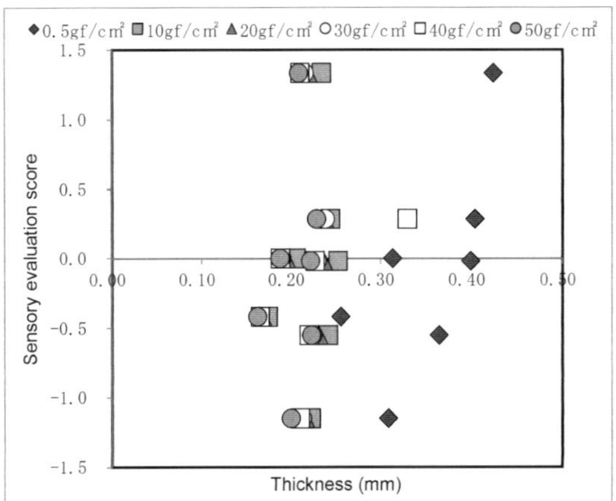

Figure 9: Relationship between sensory evaluation score and measured thickness under different compressive load for fabric type of Denim

4. CONCLUSION

We examined the relationship between the physical thickness of the fabric under different compressive load and the feeling of thickness. The eight fabric types were divided into two kinds which fabric having a significant correlation between physical thickness and sensory evaluation score under any pressures, and fabric having a significant correlation in thickness under compressive load 0.5 gf/cm²and 50 gf/cm². Except for fabric type of Melton, thick fabric types (Herringbone tweed, Saxony and Kersey) showed a high correlation between physical thickness and sensory evaluation score regardless of pressure. Chiffon which is the thinnest fabric type showed high correlation coefficient between the physical thickness and the sensory evaluation value. The subject was able to perceive the difference in the thin fabric. Denim showed low correlation coefficient under each pressure condition. It could be related to the structure and the surface roughness of the fabric because they have various materials which are different from the original definition of Denim even those named as Denim.

ACKNOWLEDGMENTS

This work was supported by JSPS (Japan Society for the Promotion of Science) KAKENHI under grant numbers JP24220012, 16K16255 and 17H01955.

REFFERENCES

1. Jones, S.J. (2005), Fashion Design, Laurence King Publishing.
2. Apparel Industry Promotion Center, "Organization for small & medium enterprises and regional innovation, Japan", Apareru Sozai Kikaku (Apparel Material Planning), 363–365, 1987 [in Japanese].
3. The Japanese Industrial Standards Committee, Japanese Industrial Standard, Japanese Standards Association, Tokyo, 2015.
4. Mitsuo Matsudaira, Sueo Kawabata and Masako Niwa, Measurements of Mechanical Properties of Thin Dress Fabrics for Hand Evaluation, Journal of the Textile Machinery Society of Japan, 37(4): T49-T57, 1984.
5. Aliouche, D., and Viallter, P. Mechanical and tactile compression of fabrics: Influence on handle.

Textile Research Journal, 70(11), 939-944, 2000

ISASE-MAICS 2018

Investigation on Psychological Structure of Wearing Comfort Sensation of Underwear Made of Yarn Blended with Polypropylene

Yuki KARASAWA*, Mayumi UEMAE*, Hiroaki YOSHIDA*, Masayoshi KAMIJO *

* *Faculty of Textile Science and Technology, Shinshu University, 3-15-1 Tokida, Ueda-shi, Nagano 386-0018, Japan*

Abstract: The purpose of this study is to clarify psychological structure of comfort sensation of underwear made of yarn blended with polypropylene (PP). As a result of wearing experiment, the fabric of one of the PP samples, which has low surface property, had a rough sensation even as a result of the sensory evaluation. The score of comfort sensation was also lowered and there was a bad sensation after exercise. In addition, as a result of multiple regression analysis to investigate the differences in impression evaluation of each sample, it was found that for the samples of PP blended yarn, the sensation caused by moisture-transport characteristics and air flow characteristics proved to affect the comfort sensation. In all of the samples, it was found that skin texture was important.

Keywords: *Polypropylene, Underwear, Comfort sensation, Psychological Structure,*

1. INTRODUCTION

In recent years, consumers have become increasingly interested in functional underwear with good moisture absorption, quick drying, and high thermal insulation. Polypropylene (PP) is the lightest among real fibers (specific gravity 0.91), has low thermal conductivity, and features hydrophobicity. Based on these characteristics, PP can be a material for high-performance underwear that is warm and extremely quick-drying. In fact, due to the high hydrophobicity and low thermal conductivity, PP can be used for knitted fabric using PP blended yarn. Our previous studies have shown the effect of changing heat and moisture-transfer characteristics [1]. In addition, as comfort factors for underwear made using yarns blended with PP, a hydrophobic material and moisture-absorbing quick-drying material, heat- and moisture-transfer characteristics and skin texture were selected [2]. Combining PP and a hydrophilic fiber or moisture- absorbing fiber to compensate for the moisture-transferring ability in this way makes it possible to design underwear that easily keeps moisture out of clothes during perspiration and does not chill the body [3].

Furthermore, since PP has a low Young's modulus [4], there is a possibility that cloths with soft texture can be made by using yarn blended with PP.

Therefore, in this study, we investigate the comfort sensation of underwear made from yarn mixed with PP and hydrophilic fiber from psychological point of view. And, we aim to clarify the difference of psychological impression given to cloth comfort by blending PP.

2. EXPERIMENT

2.1 Sample

In this study, three kinds of spun yarns were made and used for knitted fabric. Table 1 shows the total spun yarn used for each sample and the blend rate of all samples. The yarn of face fabric is unified to 100% cotton and the yarn of back fabric is different depending on the samples. PP is blended into the back yarns of PP/C/R and PP/C. The back yarns of C is 100% cotton and it was used to compare with the two kinds of samples mentioned above in which PP is blended. In all of samples, the knitting structure was unified to rib knitting and the gage number was 18.

The results of measuring the material property values of each sample, and machines / methods used for measurement are shown in Table 2. In all experimental environments, the temperature was 20°C. and the humidity was 65% RH. Compression characteristics, bending characteristics, surface characteristics, heat-transfer characteristics, and air flow characteristics

Table1. The ratio of blended yarn and total blend rate of samples

Symbol	Front Yarn	Back Yarn	Total Blend Rate
PP/C/R	Cotton100%	Rayon70%/Polypropylene30%	Cotton65%/Rayon25%/ Polypropylene10%
PP/C	Cotton100%	Cotton70%/Polypropylene30%	Cotton90%/Polypropylene10%
C	Cotton100%	Cotton100%	Cotton100%

were measured using KES-FB system (Kato Tech Co., Kyoto, Japan) [5-7]. KES-FB system is a texture measurement system that quantitatively evaluate the material properties of a fabric with various parameters. All experimental conditions were carried out by standard measurement. BOKEN method (BQE A 028) was used for water-transport property.

For PP/C/R, the value of B, 2 HB of the bending property is small, and it is soft and recoverable when bent. Moreover, it is a fabric having a relatively high heat-retention property because of the low value of q-max and thermal conductance. And it is a sample with excellent air permeability and fast drying property because it has low air flow resistance and good moisture-transport property.

For PP/C, although this has excellent breathability due to low air flow resistance, the sample has a relatively low heat-retention property, because the heat-retention rate is small. The values of MMD and SMD are large, so that the skin texture is poor.

Sample C is thick and soft and soft to the touch because C has large values of WC and TO of compression characteristics and the surface characteristics MMD and SMD are small.

2.2 Experimental Method

Initially, the participant entered a room with constant temperature and humidity levels at 24°C, 50% RH and rested for 15 minutes to let the body temperature adapt. Then, the participant wore a sample, and the experiment was begun. The experiment took 60 minutes (Figure1). First, the participant rested for 20 minutes, and after that exercised on a treadmill (AFR2115 manufactured by ALINCO) for 10 minutes at an intensity of 55% to 65% of the maximum heart rate (220 - age). After exercising, the participant rested again for 30 minutes.

During this time, we measured the psychological response at the time of wearing in order to evaluate the clothing comfort of the above three sample undershirts and to investigate the psychological sensation while wearing. To monitor psychological response, we used the semantic differential method (SD method) and measured

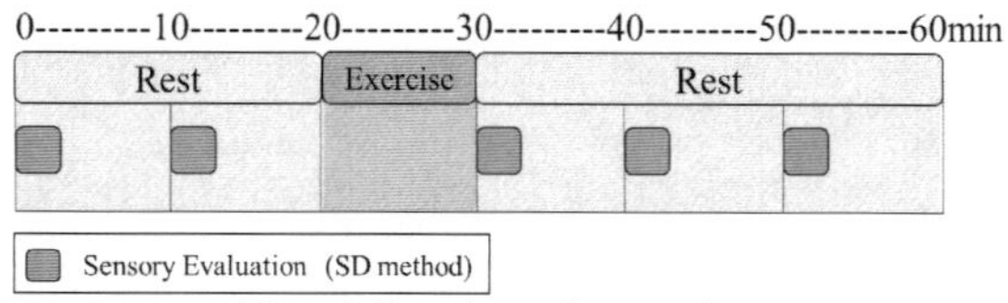

Figure1. Experimental protocol

Table 2. Material properties of samples

Blocked Property	Property		PP/C/R Mean / CV%	PP/C Mean / CV%	C Mean / CV%	Reference
Compression	LC ; Linearity (Compression rigidity) [-]		0.31 / 4.6	0.33 / 1.4	0.32 / 1.0	KES-FB3
	WC ; Compression energy [gf・cm/cm^2]		0.43 / 6.2	0.45 / 5.1	0.50 / 2.1	
	RC ; Regilience [%]		43.6 / 3.2	41.6 / 2.9	34.7 / 1.6	
	TO ; Thickness [mm]		1.22 / 3.2	1.26 / 2.4	1.31 / 1.4	
Bending	B ; Bending rigidity [gf・cm^2/cm]	wale	0.023 / 3.1	0.027 / 3.6	0.038 / 4.5	KES-FB2
		course	0.005 / 27	0.008 / 9.8	0.01 / 15	
	2HB ; Histerisis [gf・cm/cm]	wale	0.030 / 2.6	0.037 / 3.6	0.049 / 4.2	
		course	0.005 / 13	0.008 / 6.0	0.011 / 5.2	
Surface	MIU ; Mean value of the cofficient of friction [-]	wale	0.16 / 1.8	0.15 / 1.3	0.18 / 1.2	KES-FB4
		course	0.195 / 1.2	0.201 / 1.1	0.197 / 2.4	
	MMD ; Mean deviation of the cofficient of friction [-]	wale	0.007 / 21	0.012 / 25	0.007 / 6.6	
		course	0.013 / 16	0.015 / 19	0.011 / 21	
	SMD ; Mean deviation of surface roughness [micron]	wale	11.5 / 2.5	13.5 / 6.2	3.6 / 7.1	
		course	11.87 / 8.6	12.55 / 5.5	7.71 / 4.3	
Heat transport property	q-max [W/cm^2]		0.101 / 0.83	0.103 / 0.81	0.103 / 1.4	KES-F7
	Thermal conductance [W/(m^2・K)]		61.1 / 1.3	62.3 / 1.1	63.4 / 1.5	
	Insulation rate [%]		24.6 / 3.4	23.9 / 3.0	24.7 / 1.5	
Water transport property	Wicking & Quick drying [%]		15.0 / 15	14.4 / 11	14.0 / 12	BOKEN BQE A028
Air permeability	Air flow resistance [kPa・s/m]		0.044 / 2.6	0.041 / 3.7	0.084 / 3.3	KES-F8

Table 3. Evaluation terms of pair (SD method)

Terms of Pair	Property
Hot ⇔ Refreshing	Thermal
Cold ⇔ Warm	
Damp ⇔ Dry	Moisture
Poorly-ventilated ⇔ Well-ventilated	Air flow
Poor texture ⇔ Good texture	Mechanical
Rough ⇔ Smooth	
Hard ⇔ Soft	
Restrictive ⇔ Non-restrictive	
Thick ⇔ Thin	
Uncomfortable ⇔ Comfortable	Comprehensive

every 10 minutes except while exercising for 5 times in total (Table 3). The evaluation term pairs include "Hot ⇔ Refreshing", "Cold ⇔ Warm", "Damp ⇔ Dry", "Poorly-ventilated ⇔ Well- ventilated", "Poor texture ⇔ Good texture", "Rough ⇔ Smooth", "Hard ⇔ Soft", "Restrictive ⇔ Non-restrictive", "Thick ⇔ Thin", "Uncomfortable ⇔ Comfortable", with 7 grades (-3: Extremely, -2: Very, -1: Slightly, 0: neither, +1: Slightly, +2: Very, +3: Extremely).

In this experiment, participants were 10 male college students, each participant conducted the above experiment with one sample per day, which took three days in total.

3. RESULTS and DISCUSSION

3.1 Change in impression evaluation between samples and between processes

Figure 2 shows the scores of "Uncomfortable ⇔ Comfortable" in the sensory test. The value of PP/C decreased at 30 minutes and 40 minutes after the start of the experiment (after exercise), and statistically significant differences were found between PP/C/R and PP/C in these time zones. From this, PP/C has an evaluation of uncomfortable after exercise.

Figure 3 shows the scores of "Rough ⇔ Smooth". As in the case of "Uncomfortable ⇔ Comfortable" in this evaluation term, the value of PP/C is small at 30 minutes and after 40 minutes (after exercise), and there were statistically significant differences between PP/C/R and PP/C. The smoothness (touch sensation) of the fabric was low after the exercise, and then, the score of "Uncomfortable ⇔ Comfortable" of PP/C decreased.

Figure 4 shows the result of "Poorly-ventilated ⇔ Well- ventilated". For PP/C/R and PP/C, the score increased after exercise and the steamy sensation was relieved ten minutes after exercise, but the sensation for C was not relieved. For the score of C and PP/C/R, a significant difference of 1% significance was confirmed at that time. These results show the same tendency as the air permeability characteristic and moisture-transport characteristic of each sample, and the samples blended with PP had good breathability and were quick drying, so that there is little stuffiness in clothes due to perspiration after exercise. The steamy sensation that the person feels was reduced.

Two-way ANOVA was performed on two factors, samples and processes, for each evaluation term pair of 10 participants in the SD method. The level of the sample is 3 (PP/C/R, PP/C, C), and the level of process is 5 (every 10 minutes except for exercise). As a result, no interaction was observed in all evaluation term pairs. After that, multiple comparison (Tukey method) was performed to investigate whether statistically significant

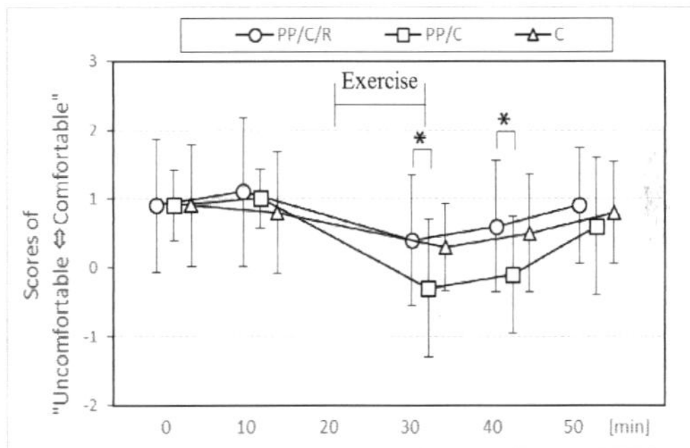

Figure 2. The scores of "Uncomfortable ⇔ Comfortable"

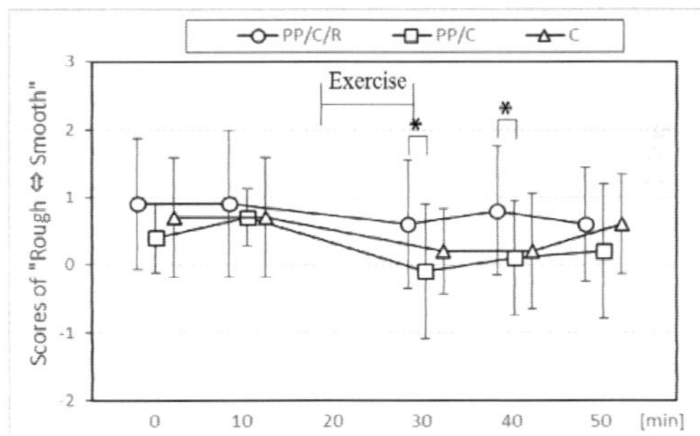

Figure 3. The scores of "Rough ⇔ Smooth"

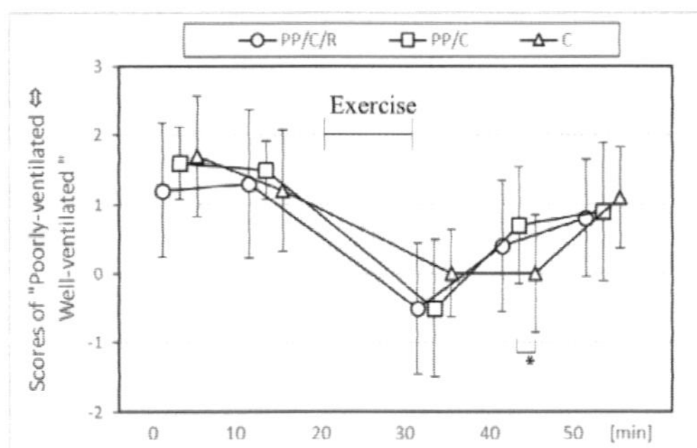

Figure 4. The scores of "Poorly-ventilated ⇔ Well-ventilated"

Table 4. Impression that affects "comfort sensation" for each sample

Sample	Explanatory variable (1st)		Explanatory variable (2nd)		Explanatory variable (3rd)		Constant term	Adjusted R^2
	Standardized partial regression coefficient	Terms of pair	Standardized partial regression coefficient	Terms of pair	Standardized partial regression coefficient	Terms of pair		
PP/C/R	0.393 **	"Poorly-ventilated ⇔ Well-ventilated"	0.323 *	"Poor texture ⇔ Good texture"	0.197	"Hard ⇔ Soft"	0.00804	0.669
PP/C	0.658 **	"Poor texture ⇔ Good texture"	0.436 **	"Damp ⇔ Dry"	0.202	"Cold ⇔ Warm"	-0.232	0.777
C	0.543 **	"Poor texture ⇔ Good texture"	0.351 **	"Hard ⇔ Soft"	0.114	"Poorly-ventilated ⇔ Well-ventilated"	-0.0263	0.816

** : p<0.01 * : p<0.05

differences exist between samples and between processes. Two-way ANOVA was performed on two factors, samples and processes, for each evaluation term pair of 10 participants in the SD method. The level of the sample is 3 (PP/C/R, PP/C, C), the level of process is 5 (every 10 minutes except for exercise). As a result, no interaction was observed in all evaluation term pairs. After that, multiple comparison (Tukey method) was performed to investigate whether statistically significant differences exist between samples and between processes.

3.2 Impressions that affects "comfort sensation" for each sample

Multiple regression analysis was performed for each sample in order to investigate what comfort sensation of 3 samples made from different blended yarns are produced. For this, in order to comprehensively evaluate each as a sample, the objective variable was set to scores of "Uncomfortable ⇔ Comfortable" for the whole time of each sample, and the explanatory variable were set as other evaluation term pairs. The Excel statistics tool ver.2017 (Social Information Service Co., Ltd.) was used for analysis, and forward selection method was used at this time.

Table 4 shows the results obtained from multiple regression analysis performed on each sample. For all samples, "Poor texture ⇔ Good texture" was used as an explanatory variable with a significance probability of 1%, and since the standard regression coefficient is high, it has been suggested that skin texture sensation has greatly influenced the comfort sensation while wearing the samples.

Considering each sample, "Poorly-ventilated ⇔ Well-ventilated" was selected for PP/C/R, and "Damp ⇔ Dry" was selected for PP/C as statistically significant. It seems that moisture sensation and air breathability greatly affect comfort sensation in samples using PP blended yarn. This also corresponds to the values of the material properties, and the PP blended yarn samples have remarkably small air permeability as compared with C and has good air permeability. In addition, the transpiration of moisture is also PP/C/R > PP/C > C. For this reason, the excellent breathability and the moisture-transport characteristics possessed by the PP blended yarn samples, show that the steamy sensation and the dry sensation greatly affect the comfort sensation.

For the sample C, "Hard ⇔ Soft" was an explanatory variable seen to have significant probability in addition to "Poor texture ⇔ Good texture". Therefore, for Sample C (with 100% cotton), the impression due to excellent mechanical properties (compression, friction) such as thickness, compression softness, and good skin touch feeling obtained from the material property measurement results had a big influence on the comfort sensation.

In this way, the comfort sensation at the time of wearing clothes is basically affected by the skin texture sensation, so the texture is important for making comfortable clothes. In addition, the impression with a high degree of influence changes depending on the differences in characteristics of each sample.

4. CONCLUSION

In this study, underwear was made with PP blended yarn, and the various material properties of fabric samples were measured. Using these samples, clothing experiments were conducted and psychological measurements were performed.

In the wearing experiments, as a result of seeing the evaluation terms of each sample over the passage of time, the fabric of the PP/C sample, which has a bad surface property because of higher values of SMD and MMD, felt rough even as a result of the sensory evaluation. That's why the scores of comfort sensation were also lowered and they felt bad after exercise. In addition, as a result of "Poorly-ventilated ⇔ Well-ventilated", although the scores of the PP blended samples recovered after exercise, the sample C took more time to recover.

This result corresponded to the moisture-transport characteristic and the air permeability of each sample. The PP blended samples have lower air flow resistance and higher transpiration rate than C. So we found that humans can perceive minute differences of material properties when wearing clothes.

As a result of multiple regression analysis to investigate the differences in impression evaluation from the evaluation results of the overall sensory evaluation for each sample, in the samples of PP blended yarn, the sensation caused by moisture-transfer characteristics and breathability characteristics affected the comfort sensation. Also, the softness of the cloth had a big influence on the sample of 100% cotton. In all the samples, skin texture was important. The results of this multiple regression analysis corresponded to the features of the material properties of each sample. PP blended samples, which have excellent moisture-transport properties and air permeability properties, also increased their impression of comfort sensation of these material properties. Likewise, for sample C which is a thick fabric and has a soft feature at the time of compression, the impression that is closely related to the comfort sensation was the softness sensation of the fabric. Therefore, we found that the evaluation factors of comfort sensation varies depending on the material characteristics of each sample.

Based on the results of this research, we obtained the possibility of developing comfortable underwear when making underwear using PP blended yarn by utilizing the hydrophobicity of PP, to improve moisture transfer characteristics, and to maintain good sensation by reducing wetness.

Acknowledgments

This study was supported by Grant-in-Aid for Scientific Research (B) (16H02888) by the Ministry of Education, Culture, Sports, Science, and Technology of Japan. The authors sincerely thank Mr. Masahiko Kubo, Mr. Toyokazu Nishiyama and Dr. Hideaki Mizuhashi from Daiwabo-Neu Co., Ltd for supporting about PP samples.

REFFERENCES

1. Hideaki Mizuhashi, Masayoshi Kamijo, Hiroaki Yoshida and Masahiko Kubo, J. Fiber Sci. Technol., 72(5), pp.104-111, 2016.
2. Hideaki Mizuhashi, Masayoshi Kamijo, Hiroaki Yoshida and Masahiko Kubo, J. Fiber Sci. Technol., 72(10), 220-226, 2016.
3. Masako Niwa, Uchino Masako and Humiko Morishita, Kansei Engineering International, 3(5), pp.49-55, 2000.
4. Japan Chemical Fibers Association,"KASEN HAND BOOK"
5. S. Kawabata, "The Standardizaition and analysis of Hand Evaluation" (2nd Ed.), HESC, The Textile Machinely Society Japan, 1980.
6. S. Kawabata, "Development of Autonomic Air-permiability Tester", J. Text. Mech. Soc. Japan, 40(6), T59-T67, 1987.
7. S. Kawabata, "Development of Device for Measuring Heat-Moisture-transfer Properties of Apparel Fabrics", J. Text. Mech. Soc. Japan, 37(8), T130-T141, 1984.

ISASE-MAICS 2018

Changes of tactile feeling for cotton knitted fabric by laundering – Differences between fabrics with Siro-spun and Ring-spun yarns –

KyoungOk Kim*, Nagisa Hirata**, Kyosuke Kanda***, Masatoshi Kawakami***, Masayuki Takatera*

* Shinshu University, Institute for Fiber Engineering (IFES), Interdisciplinary Cluster for Cutting Edge Research (ICCER), Tokida 3-15-1, Ueda, Nagano prefecture, 386-8567, Japan
** Shinshu University, Graduate school of Science and Technology, Division of Textile & Kansei Engineering, Tokida 3-15-1, Ueda, Nagano prefecture, 386-8567, Japan
*** Kondo Cotton Spinning Co, Marunouchi 2-18-25 Naka-ku Nagoya, Japan

Abstract: This study investigated the effect of spinning method of cotton yarn on the tactile feeling (hand) of the knitted fabrics by laundering. Two cotton knitted fabrics of rib stitch were made with two yarns of the same yarn count made by Siro- and Ring-spinning methods. Hand of samples for laundering 0 and 20 times were compared using Scheffe's paired comparison. Bending and surface properties of the samples were measured using Kawabata Evaluation System. It was found that the hand of the knitted fabric by Ring spun yarn was greatly changed by washing as compared with one of Siro-spun yarn. In particular, there was a significant difference by the spinning method in "smoothness". It was also found that B and 2HB of both C and E changed by laundering. However, MIU and SMD of C wan not changed by laundering although ones of E changed by laundering. However, those were not directly correlated with the hand changes. Therefore, other mechanical properties should be necessary to predict smooth feeling.
Keywords: *Tactile feeling, Hand, Knitted fabric, Siro-spun yarn, Ring-spun yarn*

1. INTRODUCTION

With the spread of the washing and drying machine, washing and drying by the machine have become common in the home. Although there have been problems of shrinkage and hand changes on cotton knitted fabric by laundering, the reason is still unclear. To make a fabric material that can maintain the hand and dimension changes after repeated laundering, it is necessary to investigate the effect of yarn on them.

The effect of laundering on various fabrics has been investigated by many researchers. Fletcher and Roberts [1] investigated the effect of laundering on the shrinkage of plain and rib knit cotton fabrics taking into account fabric structure. In their results, the effect of structural changes on fabric shrinkage was larger than the yarn shrinkage. Onal and Candan [2] investigated shrinkage of single jersey knits made with varying fabric tightness, yarn type, and fiber blend. They mentioned that yarn type and fiber blend have a relatively more significant contribution to fabric shrinkage lengthwise than widthwise. Quaynor et al. [3] investigated the effects of laundering and laundering temperatures on surface properties and dimensional stability for plain flat knit silk, cotton, and polyester fabrics with varying cover factors.

Fiber spinning method also affects the hand and mechanical properties of a fabric. Recently, Ring-spinning and Open-end spinning are commonly used to make cotton yarn. Siro-spinning is a method for making a pseudo-two-fold yarn in which the two components are untwisted stands rather than twisted single yarns. Siro-spun cotton yarn was less hairy and more extensible than conventional two-plied yarn [7]. Sun and Cheng [4] investigated the effect of cotton Siro-spun yarns on plain weft knitted fabrics and mentioned that the weft knitted fabrics made of cotton Siro-spun yarns are more durable and suitable for summer wear, and showed better hand. ÇELİK et al. [6] investigated physical properties of fabrics knitted with Siro-spun and Ring-spun yarns produced by short and long staple fibers. Mckinney and Broome [5] investigated the effects of laundering on the performance of Open-end and Ring-spun yarns in jersey knit fabrics. They demonstrated that the Open-end-spun cotton and cotton-polyester yarns in particular sizes displayed superior resistance to pilling, slow wickability, and good dimensional stability. However, the effect of Siro-spun yarns on tactile feeling (hand) of a knitted fabric by laundering is still unclear.

The purpose of this study is to investigate the effect of spinning method of cotton yarn on the hand of the knitted fabrics by laundering. We investigated the relationship between spinning method and hand changes.

2. EXPERIMENTAL

To investigate the effect of spinning method of yarn on hand and mechanical properties of a fabric, two cotton knitted fabrics of rib stitch were made with two yarns of the same yarn count made by Siro- and Ring-spinning methods as shown in Table 1. Laundering was carried out for the samples of 30cm×30cm according to the method of Japanese Industrial Standards [1]. Twenty times of laundering times were carried out and the laundering time denoted by the sample name.

Table 1: Specification yarn sample

Sample		C	E
Fiber	Fiber length (mm)	30.48	
	Fiber fineness (μg/cm)	1.76	
Yarn	Spinning method	Siro-spinning	Ring-spinning
	Yarn count Ne (tex)	16.3	
	Twist count (Turns/m)	697	900
	Apparent yarn thickness (μm)	251	216
	Apparent yarn thickness after 20 laundering (μm)	238	267
Fabric	Wale stitch density (/cm)	26.4	26.3
	Course stitch density (/cm)	19.7	23.3
	Mass per unit area (g/m^2)	168.7	175.7

Table 2: Measurements of the mechanical properties

Block	Symbols	Characteristic value
Bending	B (gf·cm^2/cm)	Bending rigidity
	2HB (gf·cm/cm)	Hysteresis
Compression	LC	Linearity
	WC (gf·cm/cm^2)	Compressional energy
	RC (%)	Resilience
	T0 (mm)	Thickness
Surface	MIU	Coefficient of friction
	MMD	Mean deviation of MIU
	SMD	Geometrical roughness

Hand of samples for laundering 0 and 20 times were compared using Scheffe's paired comparison using samples of 20 cm×20 cm under temperature 20±2℃ and relative humidity 65 ± 4%. Evaluation items were smoothness, softness, *shittori* (the Japanese word for smoothness accompanied with either a warm, moisture or soft feeling), estimated comfort in the summer, estimated comfort in winter and preference. We tested the significant difference of the average preference at significance level 5%. Subjects were Japanese University 10 female student in their 20's. Bending and surface properties of the samples in course direction were measured using Kawabata Evaluation System (KES) as shown in Table 2 [8]. The environmental condition was same as the hand evaluation. For the obtained values, T-test was carried out between C0 and E0, and C20 and E20 respectively.

3. RESULTS AND DISCUSSION

3.1 Hand changes

Figure 1 shows average preference of each fabric by the sensory test. Comparing to C0 and E0 samples, E0 was evaluated as smoother than C0 with a significant difference at significant level 5%. For other evaluation items, there were no significant differences. However, E0 was showed a tendency of softer, more comfortable in winter and preferred.

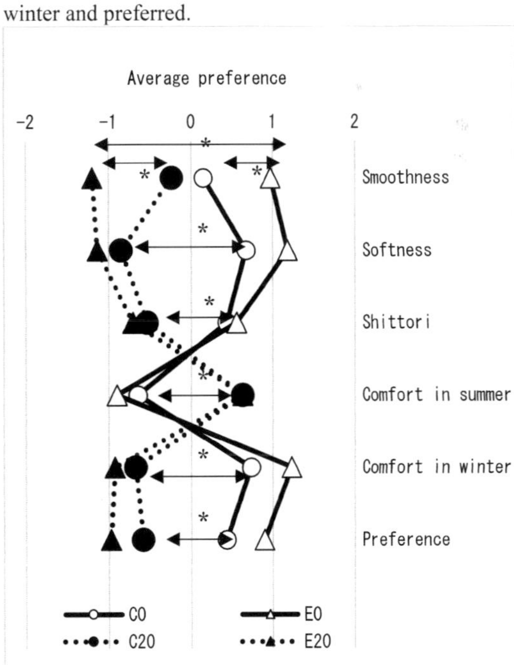

Figure 1: Average preference of each sample for fabric hand

Comparing C20 and E20 samples, C20 was evaluated smoother compared to E20 with a significant difference at significant level 5%, which was opposite with C0 and E0.

After laundering, both samples became stiffer, rougher, not *shittori*, uncomfortable in summer, comfortable in winter and not preferred with a significant difference at significant level 5%. Moreover, hand changes of E (Siro-spun yarn) were larger than C (Ring-spun yarn).

3.2 Changes of mechanical properties

Figure 2 shows changes of bending rigidity B for samples by laundering. Figure 3 shows changes of bending hysteresis 2HB for samples by laundering. About B and 2HB, E0 showed higher values than C0 which means hard to bend and difficult to recover from bending with a significant difference at significant level 5%. However, 2HB of E20 were lower than C20 which was opposite with the C0 and E0. However, those results were different from the result of hand changes.

Figure 4 shows changes of the coefficient of friction (MIU) for samples by laundering. MIU value of E20 was smaller than E0 although ones of C20 and C0 were similar. It means that unevenness of C was not changed by laundering. Figure 5 shows changes of mean deviation of MIU (MMD) for samples by laundering. MMD of C and E increased after laundering. Thus, it means that both samples became rougher by laundering which was same results with hand evaluation test. Figure 6 shows changes of geometrical roughness (SMD) for samples by laundering. About SMD, differences between C0 and E0 were observed. However, C0 and C20 showed similar values although E20 was smaller than E0.

Therefore, it was found that B and 2HB of both C and E changed by laundering. MIU and SMD of C wan not changed by laundering although ones of E changed by laundering. However, those were not directly correlated with the hand changes.

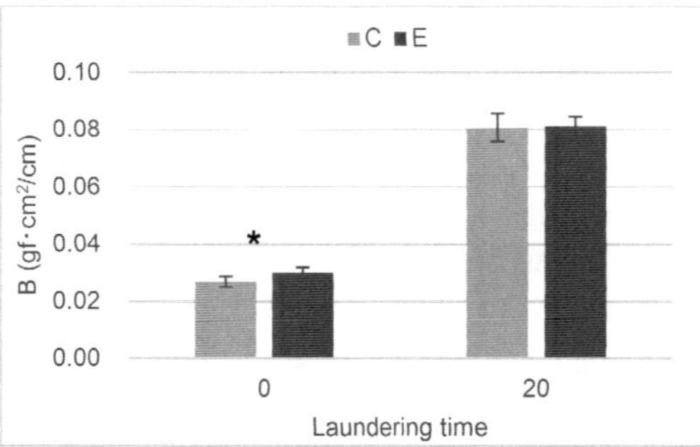

Figure 2: Changes of bending rigidity (B) for samples by laundering

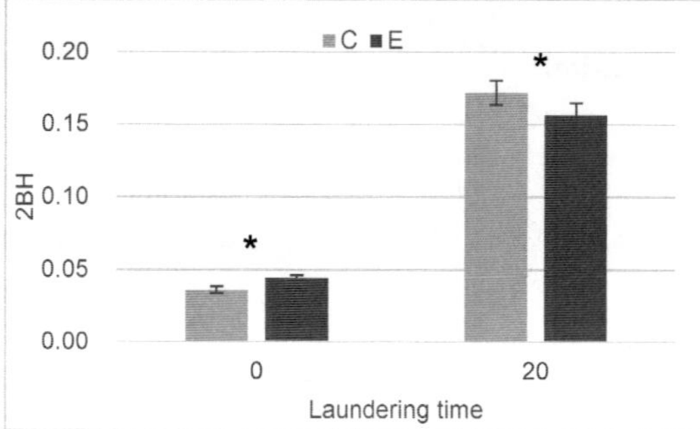

Figure 3: Changes of bending hysteresis (2HB) for samples by laundering

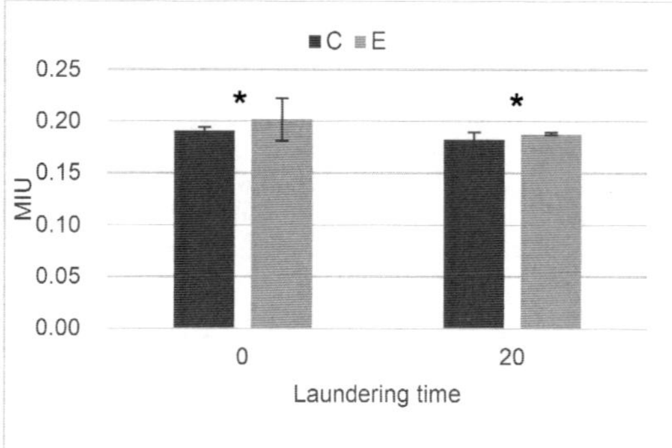

Figure 4: Changes of coefficient of friction (MIU) for samples by laundering

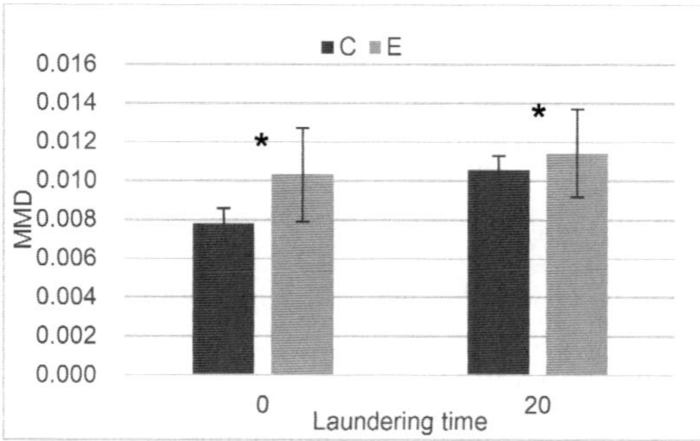

Figure 5: Changes of mean deviation of MIU (MMD) for samples by laundering

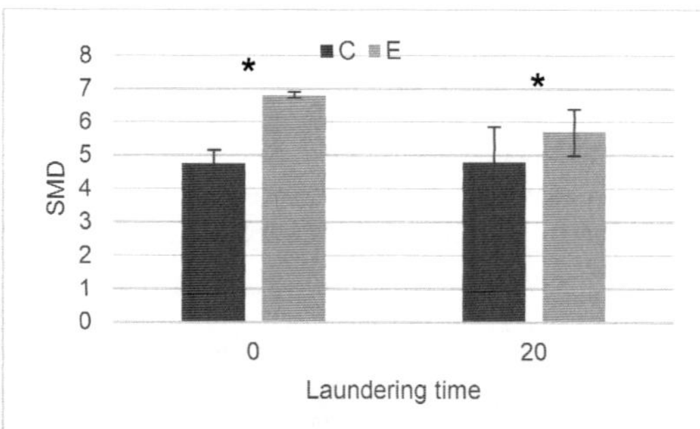

Figure 6: Changes of geometrical roughness (SMD) for samples by laundering

4. CONCLUSION

It was confirmed that the changes in the hand accompanying with the repeated laundering according to the yarn spinning method. The hand of the knitted fabric by Ring-spun yarn was greatly changed by laundering as compared with one of Siro-spun yarn. In particular, there was a significant difference by the spinning method in "smoothness".

About surface friction and surface roughness, there were differences by spinning methods. MIU and SMD of fabric with Siro-spun yarn wan not changed by laundering although ones of fabric with Ring-spun yarn changed by laundering. However, those were not directly correlated with the hand changes. Therefore, other mechanical properties should be necessary to predict smooth feeling.

ACKNOWLEDGMENTS

This work was supported by JSPS (Japan Society for the Promotion of Science) KAKENHI under grant numbers JP24220012 and 16K16255.

REFFERENCES

1. Fletcher, Hazel M., and S. Helen Roberts, The geometry of plain and rib knit cotton fabrics and its relation to shrinkage in laundering, Textile Research Journal, 22(2), 84-88, 1952
2. Onal, Levent, and Cevza Candan. Contribution of fabric characteristics and laundering to shrinkage of weft knitted fabrics. Textile Research Journal, 73(3) 187-191, 2003
3. Quaynor, Leticia, Masaoki Takahashi, and Masaru Nakajima. "Effects of laundering on the surface properties and dimensional stability of plain knitted fabrics." Textile Research Journal, 70(1), 28-35, 2000
4. M.N. Sun and K.P.S. Cheng, The quality of fabric knitted from cotton Sirospunl yarn, International Journal of Clothing Science and Technology, 12(5), 351-360, 2000
5. ÇELİK, Pınar, Tuba BEDEZ ÜTE, and Hüseyin KADOĞLU. Comparative analysis of the physical properties of the fabrics knitted with sirospun and ring spun yarns produced by short and long staple fibers, Journal of Textile & Apparel/Tekstil ve Konfeksiyon 22(4),324-331, 2012
6. Mckinney, Mary, and Esther R. Broome. The Effects of Laundering on the Performance of Open-End and Ring-Spun Yarns in Jersey Knit Fabrics, Textile Research Journal, 47(3), 155-162, 1977
7. C A Lawrence, Advances in Yarn Spinning Technology, Woodhead Publishing, 2010
8. Kawabata S. The standardization and analysis of hand evaluation, 2nd ed. Osaka: Textile Machinery Society of Japan, 1980.

ISASE2018

An Analysis on Color Characteristics of Website Images of Restaurants According to Price Range

Naoki TAKAHASHI *, Hiroko SHOJI **, Takashi SAKAMOTO* and Toshikazu Kato **

** National Institute of Advanced Science and Technology, 1-1-1 Higashi, Tsukuba-shi, Ibaraki 305-8566, Japan*
naoki.takahashi@aist.go.jp, takashi-sakamoto@aist.go.jp
*** Chuo University, 1-13-27 Kasuga, Bunkyo-ku, Tokyo 112-8551, Japan*
hiroko@kc.chuo-u.ac.jp, t-kato@kc.chuo-u.ac.jp

Abstract: In this study, we propose a method of Kansei analysis of aspects such as preference or impression using a large amount of automatically processed data. We focused on representative colors which are low colors representing many colors in an image because colors affect to people's feeling and impression and are easily quantify and express features. Our method consisted of automatic data acquisition by web crawling and automatic feature extraction through an algorithm of image processing. Data collected from restaurant websites were analyzed in order to verify the following hypothesis: expensive restaurants have more achromatic photographs on their websites. As a result, the hypothesis has been proven in several restaurant genres.

Keywords: Color, Data-analysis, Marketing

1. INTRODUCTION

Understanding how people feel about products is necessary to analyze consumer preference and apply that analysis to marketing research and product design. However, it is difficult to acquire large amounts of data for Kansei analysis, such as consumer preferences, because it requires some expert knowledge and manual labeling. An analysis using a large amount of data is very important considering the unsettled aspect of Kansei. An analysis that uses a large amount of data requires a system that can collect data and extract features that people selectively recognize.

In this paper, the representative colors of photographs automatically extracted from websites were analyzed so that relations between representative colors and photograph impressions could be found. The researchers collected advertising photographs of restaurant websites and extracted representative colors from them to be analyzed through an algorithm [1]. This study focused on colors because they are known to affect preferences and impression [2-4] and easily quantify and express features of large amounts of data.

2. Methods

The photographs analyzed in this study were downloaded from many restaurant websites. They included photographs not only of the food but also of the exterior and interior of the restaurants, as the photos of the websites were used not only to advertise the food but also atmosphere of the restaurant. They were also helpful to analyze Kansei characteristics, such as how high-class the restaurant is. Such photographs that deliver Kansei value are defined as "image photographs." The upper row of **Figure 1** shows examples of pictures analyzed in this study.

The websites' URLs were collected from Gurunavi, which is a Japanese foodspotting site. The analyzed websites were not created by Gurunavi, but by the restaurants themselves. The following restaurant genres were chosen: Izakaya (Japanese style bar), dining bar, Japanese, Western, Italian & French, Chinese, Korean, ramen, and café. All restaurants are located in Tokyo.

The analysis process consisted of three steps. In the first step, restaurant URLs, price averages, and images were collected from the Gurunavi API. A price average is defined as a nine-point scale on the Gurunavi page (see **Table 1**). Moreover, images whose height or width was less than 32 pixels were removed in order to exclude images that do not directly affect the impression on a restaurant, such as backgrounds, button interfaces, and white pixels for layout adjustment.

In the second step, representative colors from collected images were automatically extracted. Representative colors are defined as low colors that people perceive as representing many colors in an image. The algorithm determined the number of representative colors of each image while other means, such as k-means color reduction, extracted a predetermined fixed number of colors from all images. This algorithm consists of segmentation and clustering and requires segment-segment and cluster-cluster distance thresholds as parameters if clusters or segments are merged. The lower row of **Figure 1** shows examples of representative colors extracted from the source images.

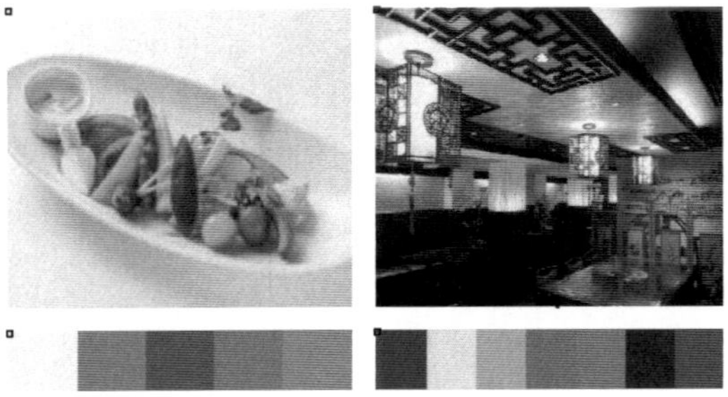

Figure 1: Examples of representative colors

In the third step, the distribution trends of the representative colors extracted from restaurant photos and the relations between the representative colors and the average prices of these restaurants were analyzed. We formed the hypothesis that high-class restaurants use more achromatic colors because of our previous study. Therefore, the relation between the average prices and the chroma of the representative colors extracted from the images of restaurants was analyzed.

3. Results

Through a web crawler, 13,424 pictures from 401 websites were collected. The average number of representative colors extracted per image was 5.55. **Table 1** shows the number of images by price range and genre of their restaurants. Most of the images were in price range of ¥1501 to 7,000, and the price range depended on genres.

3.1. Statistics on extracted representative colors

The tendency of the representative colors extracted to grasp features of colors used in restaurant photographs was examined. **Figure 2** shows histograms of saturation (the upper row) and hue (the lower row). A saturation s and a hue h are calculated by formula (1); a and b are CIELab values of the color. The bin widths of saturation and hue histograms are 5 and 10 respectively. The colors of the bins of the hue histogram indicate the correspondent hue values. The hue frequency was calculated excluding representative colors whose saturation was less than 20.

$$s = \sqrt{a^2 + b^2},\ h = \begin{cases} \frac{360}{2\pi}\tan^{-1}\frac{a}{b} & a \geq 0 \\ \frac{360}{2\pi}\left(\tan^{-1}\frac{a}{b} + \pi\right) & a < 0 \end{cases} \quad (1)$$

The saturation had a frequency peak in 0≤s<5 and tends to be generally low. Colors that satisfy 0≤s<5, which are almost achromatic, were extracted from the white backgrounds of retouched pictures rather than from photographs taken with natural backgrounds. The reason why the saturation of many colors used in photographs was low may be that low saturation colors are useful to maintain the balance of color theme for composition of pictures.

The hue had a frequency peak in around h=60° (from orange to green). These colors were extracted from food or interiors of restaurants. The colors of food are red and green; particularly, red has the effect of promoting appetite and green has the effect of making food more vivid in contrast to red. Moreover, the colors of the interiors were chosen considering their effect of promoting appetite, their harmony with food colors and their harmony with the design of the webpages.

Table 1: Quantity of images by price range and genre of restaurants

Price range	Izakaya	Dining bar	Japanese	Western	Italian & French	Chinese	Korean	Ramen	Café
¥501～1,000	0	0	0	0	0	0	0	23	0
¥1,001～1,500	0	0	0	0	0	0	0	11	0
¥1,501～2,000	37	58	27	167	59	50	20	415	494
¥2,001～3,000	689	554	338	266	331	245	221	40	252
¥3,001～4,000	512	629	471	403	660	454	354	0	151
¥4,001～5,000	8	15	42	76	20	31	60	0	0
¥5,001～7,000	22	0	30	78	0	10	43	0	0
¥7,001～10,000	0	0	0	14	0	0	10	0	0
¥10,001～15,000	0	0	0	16	0	0	0	0	0

Keywords: Color, Data-analysis, Marketing

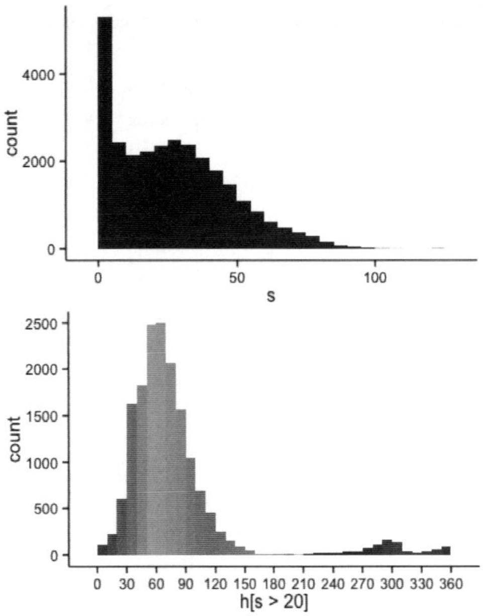

Figure 2: Histograms of saturation (upper row) and hue (lower row)

3.2. Correlation between saturation and average prices

Average saturation per average prices were calculated in order to verify the hypothesis that achromatic color tends to be used in high-class restaurants photographs rather than chromatic colors. Since price ranges depend on genre, saturations were compared in each genre.

As an example, **Figure 3** shows the saturation averages of representative colors from photographs of dining bars for each average price. As seen in the figure, the lower the saturation, the higher the price. Therefore, Kendall's tau correlation between prices and saturation of colors was calculated. In **Table 2**, "N" indicates the number of representative colors and "τ" indicates the Kendall rank correlation coefficient. A negative correlation was significant in the dining bar, Italian & French, Korean, Ramen, and café genres.

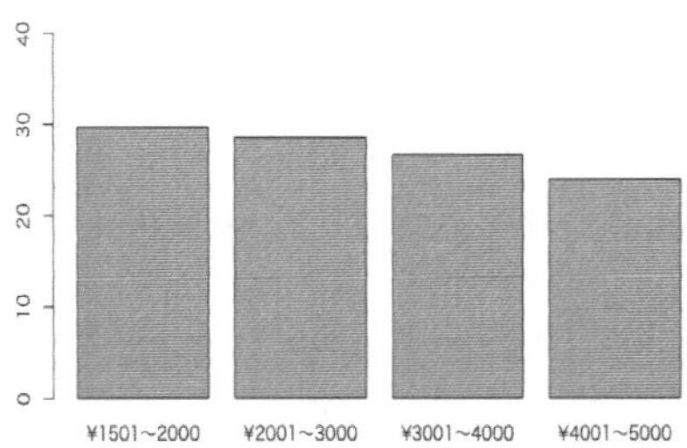

Figure 3: Average prices and saturation of dining bars

Table 2: Kendall rank correlation coefficients

Genre	*N*	*τ*	*p*-value
Izakaya	6751	-0.014	0.14
Dining bar	6960	-0.045	<0.01
Japanese	4847	0.014	0.21
Western	5183	-0.031	<0.01
Italian & French	5855	-0.043	<0.01
Chinese	4530	-0.013	0.25
Korean	3927	-0.076	<0.01
Ramen	2548	-0.005	0.75
Café	4861	-0.085	<0.01

4. Discussion

4.1. Analysis of statistics on the extracted representative colors

Most of the representative colors extracted showed low saturation or ranged from red to green. The role of low saturation color is to be the base-color of color coordination; colors ranging from red to yellow serve to promote appetite, while green emphasizes the liveliness of red.

In our previous research, a similar analysis was made with a home interior brand instead of restaurants. There were similar tendencies, such as a frequency peak at low saturation and orange. White and brown (dark orange) were extracted as base-colors mostly because they come from construction materials, such as wood. Orange is a natural color and makes people feel warm. Such effect can be expected regardless of the domain, be it a restaurant or a home.

4.2. Analysis of saturation and average prices

As a result of Kendall's test of correlation, significant negative correlations were obtained in 5 genres. High-class restaurants can be considered to use achromatic colors to create a sophisticated and extraordinary mood, while popular restaurants use warm colors to express relaxation and familiarity.

In 4 genres, no significant correlation was found between saturation and prices. This fact implies that the use of colors to direct high-class atmospheres is different among the genres of restaurants. For example, ramen restaurants tend to use food photographs, not interior photographs. In other cases, the difference may be a matter of national culture. For example, Chinese high-class restaurants prefer red while Western, Italian, French, and Korean high-class restaurants tend to use achromatic colors.

In this study, we focused on restaurant price ranges. However, an expensive restaurant does not always make people feel high class. Although the subjective feeling of whether subjects feel expensive or cheap is considered to be related to the price range of the restaurant, it is necessary to assess the subjective feeling of when photographs are given. If a significant correlation is obtained, the results can be applied to marketing research and product design.

4.3. Efficiency of the proposed analysis method

The analysis method can deal with a large amount of data easily, since it can collect data and extract quantitative features automatically. Moreover, it can be used for Kansei temporal analysis of preference and impression, which vary by season or fashion.

In this study, the numbers of samples are quite variable among the price ranges. The numbers were not standardized because the variability seems to reflect the characters of the parental population. In addition, automatic collection reduces data quality. Data was removed by simple filtering using the size of an image but some noise data has not yet been filtered. The detection of objects on the picture or on a white background will be required to obtain high quality data.

The proposed method focuses on the color of images. Although preference and impression can be undoubtedly affected by colors, they can also be affected by factors external to colors. However, the analysis was not extended to other factors because complicated features make it difficult to understand and to apply this method to another domain. We believe that developing an analysis method for understanding Kansei using only color features is challenging but useful for many analysts.

5. Conclusion

In this study, the tendency of color distribution in the restaurant domain and the relations between price ranges and features of representative colors were analyzed. Our future works will compare subjective feelings, price ranges, and features of representative colors. Moreover, this method needs a system to remove noise data automatically because the pictures used in this study included those that do not relate to Kansei.

This analysis can be applied to marketing research and product design. Moreover, it can apply to other domains without any changing a method and is used for modeling Kansei across some domains and analysis of temporal changing of features.

REFERENCES

[1] N. Takahashi, T. Sakamoto and T. Kato; Extraction of Perceptual Representative Colors for Kansei Data Analysis. Color Science Association Japan. 2016.

[2] S. Singh: Impact of Color on Marketing. Management Decision. 44(6), pp.783–789, 2006.

[3] Advanced Forward True Colors (Shikisai Kentei Kyokai): Official Textbook Supported by the Ministry of Education (Monbukagaku-sho Kouen Sikisai Kentei Koushiki Tekisuto). AFT, 2008.

[4] L. Ou, M. Lu, A. Woodcock, A. Wright; A study of colour emotion and colour preference. Part I: Colour preference modeling. Color Research and Application. 29(3), pp.232–240, 2004.

[5] N. Takahashi, T. Sakamoto, T. Kato: Color-analysis of Image Photography of Interior Brand based on Extraction of Representative Colors and Clustered Color-features. Journal of Japan Society of Kansei Engineering. Transactions of Japan Society of Kansei Engineering. 15(1), pp.203–212, 2016.

[6] Gurunavi Web Service. http://api.gnavi.co.jp/api/, (2018/01/28 accessed).

ISASE-MAICS 2018

Development of a Web Based Image Annotation Tool for Lung Immunofluorescent Confocal Images

Shu ISAKA *, Hiroharu KAWANAKA *, V. B. Surya PRASATH **, Bruce J. ARONOW ** and Shinji TSURUOKA *

* *Division of Electrical and Electronic Engineering, Graduate School of Engineering, Mie University, Mie, Japan*
** *Division of Biomedical Informatics, Cincinnati Children's Hospital Medical Center, Cincinnati OH 45299 USA*
** *Department of Biomedical Informatics, University of Cincinnati, Cincinnati OH USA*

Abstract: A molecular atlas of the human lung is important to inform basic mechanisms and treatments for lung diseases, and imaging data provide us the foundation upon which to build the lung atlas. For analyzing immunofluorescent confocal images, annotations describing precise anatomical structures are necessary. However, it is hard to annotate increasing images manually. Thus, this study aims to develop an automatic annotation system as a combination of automatic region detection and automatic structure classification modules. As an important and first step to achieving the aim, we developed an efficient annotation data collection tool that will be used collected data to develop the automatic annotation system for the lung atlas. We describe the details of our web based annotation tool that is web based and includes user control.
Keywords: *Image Annotation, Biomedical Informatics, Lung Image*

1. INTRODUCTION

A molecular atlas of the human lung is a critical platform for the future research to inform basic mechanisms and treatments for lung diseases. The LungMAP consortium aims to build a mouse/human lung atlas and an integrated database [1]. Currently, many research projects on RNA sequences, proteomics, and imaging [1]–[4] have been reported. In particular, imaging data provides us the foundation to build the lung atlas. Therefore, it is required to understand these visual data and identify a specific region in the images by annotation [1], [5].

The team of LungMAP has already developed the interactive web application, which identified the structures of the given area automatically [1]. This system, however, required the manual input for identification. Moreover, plenty of lung imaging data archived in the database will be extended for the 3D images in the future. It will be so hard for annotators to annotate all of them manually, and the demand for automatic annotation system has been growing.

The authors aim to develop an automatic annotation system for lung images using machine learning techniques. The annotation system will be developed by the combination of (i) Automatic Detection of Region of Interest and (ii) Structure Classification. As the first step of this study, we developed a web-based tool to collect annotated lung immunofluorescent images to realize this system. By using the developed system, each region of interest in the collected image will be linked to anatomical structure information, and biomedical informaticians would be able to use them for analyses, identification of tissues and so on. It is one of the benefits of our system.

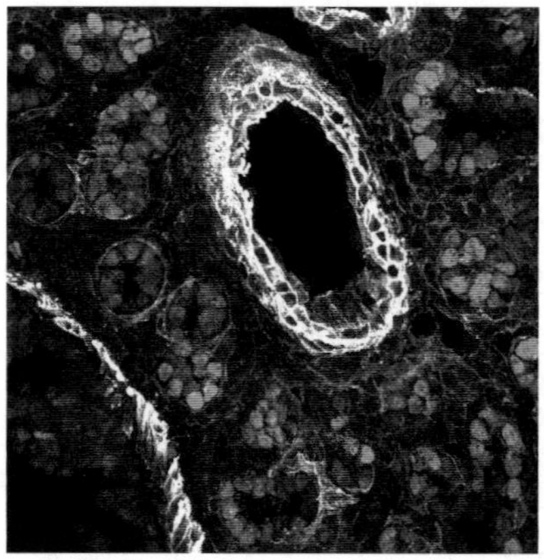

Figure 1: Example of a Lung Immunofluorescent (IF) Confocal Image. Three types of proteins were stained as red, green, and white. In this example, red pixels correspond to protein Sftpc. green, and white pixels mean protein Sox9 and Acta2, respectively.

2. MATERIALS

In this study, we focus on immunofluorescent (IF) confocal images of mouse and human lung. The images

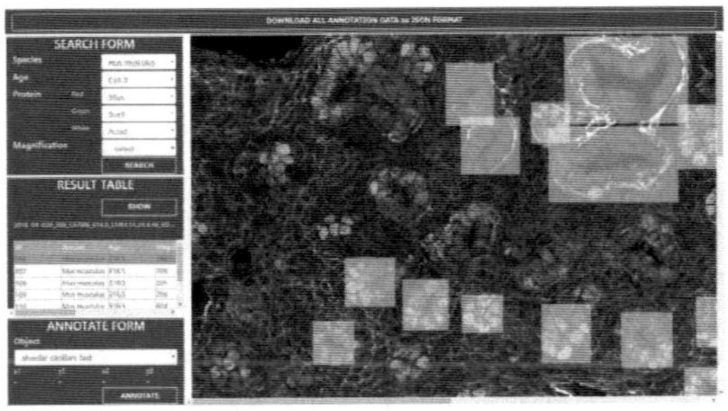

Figure 2: Screenshot of the developed web based annotation tool. System users can annotate with mouse control and all of the annotated data will be stored to the database. White rectangle means ROIs for annotation.

were collected from LungMAP website [6]. In the case of mouse, the IF images were collected from Mus musculus, whose age was from embryo 16.5 days to postnatal 28 days. Human means Homo sapiens and these ages were from 9 months old to 4 years old. All of the images were stained as red, green and white like Figure 1. The meaning of stained colors, i.e. set of stained proteins, depends on each image.

3. DEVELOPMENT OF DATA COLLECTION TOOL

A data collection tool is necessary to develop the automatic annotation system with machine learning techniques because machine learning methods require plenty of data to learn the features for classification. Therefore, the authors have developed a data collection and manual annotation tool on the web.

3.1 System Requirements

The developed data collection tool should be designed and developed considering the following three points.

1) Architecture for Ubiquitous System

The given lung images are usually provided by pathologists, and they will also annotate the given data. The annotated images are archived in the database for subsequent analyses. Also, most pathologists in the hospital are busy with daily works. Thus, the developed system should be ubiquitous; this means the developed system should not be subjected to any constraints on time and place. For these requirements, a web-based tool is one of the practical approaches because the web-based tool will be easy to ask specialists and able to connect the database with the tool.

2) Filtering of IF Images Based on its Information

The archived IF images have various information such as imaging condition, developmental stage (i.e. age) of the subjects, and the combination of antibodies for staining the lung tissue. This information is usually used to search the desired IF images for annotation. Thus, the developed system should have a function to search the images with specific conditions. This function will make the annotators possible to access their desired image(s) easily.

3) Data Structure for Analyses

In addition to the above information, each archived IF image has an experimental condition. Furthermore, the annotated image has many ROIs. In other words, the relationship between the annotated images and annotations is "many to many relationships." In this system, JSON was used to express the collected annotation data.

4) Tissue Extraction from ROI for Annotation

In the developed system, the desired tissue should be extracted with polygons because we cannot express the shape of ROI with a rectangle only. For instance, the shapes of some target tissues are like a circle, and then the ROI may or may not have surplus (or not enough) regions. Thus, automatic segmentation method of desired tissues is required for the developed system.

Table 1: Server Environment

Machine	Dell PowerEdge T320
OS	Ubuntu 16.0.4 (64bit)
CPU	Intel(R) Xeon(R) CPU E5-1410 0 @ 2.80GHz
Core	8
RAM	24 GB
Web Server	Apache 2.4.18 + Tomcat 8.0.32
Database	MySQL 5.7.19-Oubuntu0.16.04.1

3.2 Outline of Developed System

The authors have developed a web-based tool for annotation of IF images. To develop the system, we used Java with a web framework "Spring Boot", Apache 2.4.18 on Ubuntu 16.04 Server and Tomcat8.0.32. Table 1 shows specification of our server.

Figure 2 shows the screenshot of the developed tool. In the system, the screen consists of four parts; Search Form, Result Table, Annotate Form and Picturebox Area. After system users input (or select) conditions on the search form, and then this web tool connects to the database and shows search results in the result table. After this, we can select the desired IF image by clicking each row.

Further, system users can download all of the annotation data on the web tool, the format of the annotation data is a JSON file. If users develop a parser of the JSON File, they can import the annotated data to their computer and can do advanced analyses. Figure 3 shows

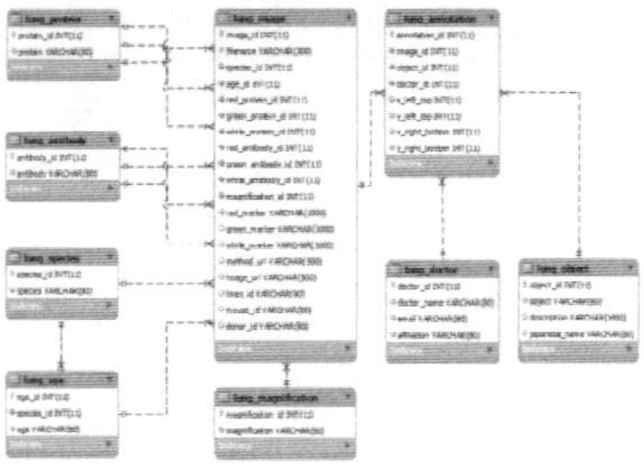

Figure 3: Entity Relationship Diagram. Each image file is related to its experimental condition (such as imaging condition, the set of antibodies, stained proteins, developmental stage of the subject), and multiple annotations will be linked to each image.

the entity-relationship diagram of the database.

3.2 Actual Use of Developed System and Data Stream

Figure 4 is the data stream among the user, client, server, and database.

1) Architecture for Ubiquitous System

The desired IF image can be extracted from the database by using specific search conditions. The flow of this process is the following steps (Steps from #1 to #9 in Figure 4).

1. (User) Input Filtering Condition
2. (Client) Send Filtering Condition to Server
3. (Server) Search Images from Database
4. (Client) Obtain Filtered Image List
5. (Client) Show Filtered Image List
6. (User) Select Image from the List
7. (Client) Send Image Information
8. (Client) Obtain Image
9. (Client) Show Selected Image

2) Annotating Images

After this, specialists can annotate the images by using a mouse, and all of the annotated data will be stored in the database. The flow of this process is the following steps (Steps from #10 to #12 in Figure 4).

10. (User) Annotate Image
11. (Client) Send the Annotation Data to Server
12. (Server) Store Annotation Data to Database

The annotation data can be the both of rectangles and polygons. Figure 5 shows an example of selected ROI with polygons and rectangles.

3) Downloading Annotation data

Users can download (and get) all of the annotation data on the tool, the format of the annotation data is downloaded as a JSON file. If users develop a parser of the JSON File, they can import the annotated data to their computer and can do advanced analyses.

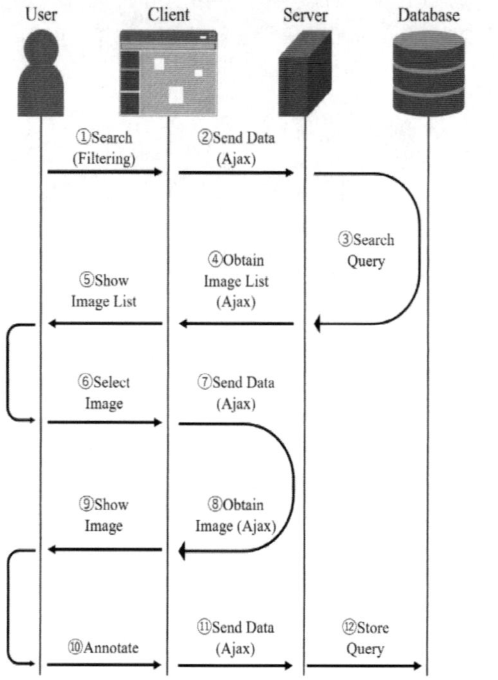

Figure 4: Data flow of developed tool among the users, client, server, and database. (1) Users can filter the images with drop-down lists of search criteria, and select one image from the given list (from #1 to #9). (2) Users can Annotate with simple mouse control (from #10 to #12).

4. TOWARD THE FUTURE

At the moment, the developed system is just a tool for data collection, that means it has no intelligent mechanism for automatic annotation and classification. For instance, system users have to put ROI(s) manually so far. Also, the tissue area should be extracted, recognized appropriately by image recognition techniques. To reach the final goal of this research project, we have to discuss the following methods as future works.

4.1 ROI Detection and Segmentation

The IF image has many target tissues for annotation and drawing ROIs on the image is a lot of burden to end users. Also, we have to extract appropriate tissue area from the ROI for accurate annotation. To realize this, we need a technique to detect ROI and get the desired tissue from ROI automatically and accurately. The ROI detection system scans the given image based on the concept of multi-resolution analysis, and then candidates of ROI are determined by using color, shape information. We are now discussing a method for this problem.

Another task is to extract the desired tissue from the

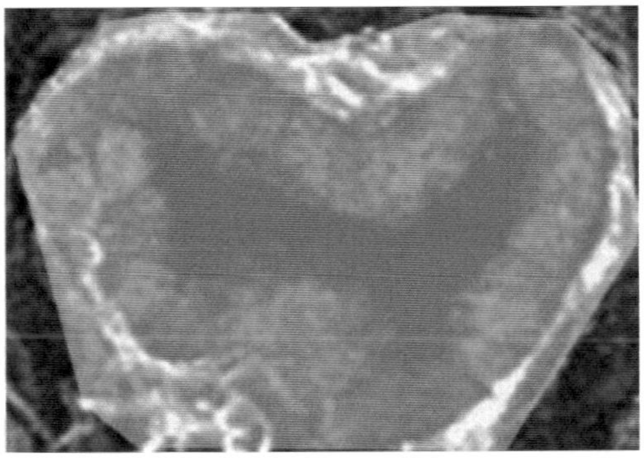

Figure 5: Polygon Annotation. Users can edit this polygon with simple mouse control.

ROI. As mentioned before, there are surplus regions for automatic annotation. We have to remove such area from the ROI for classification. Previously, many segmentation methods are proposed and discussed for practical use. However, the characteristics of medical images are different from others, and this makes the segmentation problem difficult. Figure 6 is an example of segmentation for distal acinar tubule bud of embryo 16.5 days mouse lung. To get this figure, we utilized the GrabCut algorithm [7], GrabCut algorithm is one of the segmentation methods, and its performance is high for general images. In the case of this particular example, the segmentation result looks good, but the obtained result has still surplus regions. It is difficult to apply such segmentation techniques to the given image directly, and some additional concept/techniques will be required [8].

4.2 Structure Recognition

The next task will be to develop a method to identify types of the extracted tissues automatically. We will use some methods for image recognition. As the first step, we will discuss features of the extracted tissues and a method to extract them from the tissue images to construct a classifier model [9,10]. Further, we will not only use statistical approaches but also state of the art machine learning techniques like Convolutional Neural Networks (CNNs) for highly accurate structure recognition [11,12,13]. These are important future work of this study.

5. CONCLUSION

A molecular atlas of the human lung is important to know the lung development mechanism, and it is useful for the future medicine and future research. The LungMAP consortium that works for integrated research of gene, protein, anatomy and imaging data to make molecular atlas.

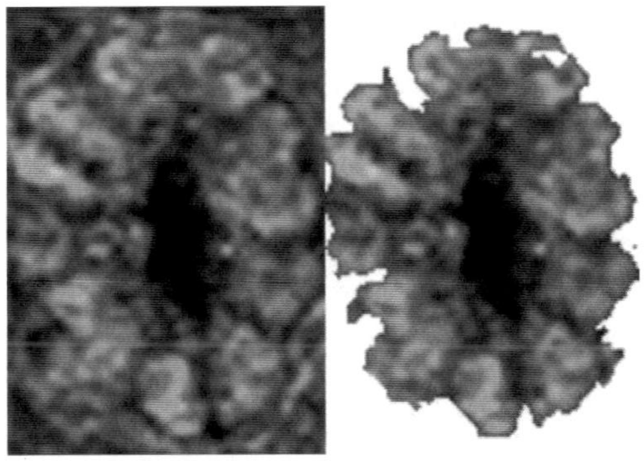

Figure 6: Segmentation Result Example. Distal Acinar Tubule Bud of Embryo 16.5 Days Mouse Lung. Left image is original and right image is the segmentation result.

This study aims to annotate the lung immunofluorescent confocal images automatically. As the first step of this study, the authors developed the manual annotation tool on the web to collect the manual annotation data. In this system, users can filter images, annotate images with both of rectangle and polygon regions easily. This paper also mentioned the current progress and remained problems in this study.

In the future, we will develop an automatic ROI detection and tissue extraction method, and also develop a tissue recognition system. And finally, these systems will be combined for effective automatic annotation for IF images.

REFFERENCES

1. M. E. Ardini-Poleske et al.; LungMAP: The molecular atlas of lung development program, Am J Physiol Lung Cell Mol Physiol, 313, L733L740, 2017.
2. M. Guo et al.; SINCERA: A Pipeline for single-cell RNASeq profiling analysis, PLoS Comput Biol, 11(11), e1004575, doi:10.1371/journal.pcbi.1004575, 2015.
3. Y. Xu et al.; Single-cell RNA sequencing identifies diverse roles of epithelial cells in idiopathic pulmonary fibrosis, JCI Insight, 1(20), e90558, doi:10.1172/jci.insight.90558, 2016.
4. G. Clair et al.; Spatially-resolved proteomics: Rapid quantitative analysis of laser capture microdissected alveolar tissue samples, Sci. Rep. 6, 39223, doi: 10.1038/srep39223 , 2016.
5. L. Barbe et al.; Toward a confocal subcellular atlas of the human proteome, Molecular & Cellular Proteomics, 7(3), 499-508, 2007.
6. LungMAP official web site, https://lungmap.net, [Accessed 24 April 2018].

7. C. Rother et al.; GrabCut - Interactive Foreground Extraction using Iterated Graph Cuts, ACM Transactions on Graphics (TOG), 23(4), 309-314, 2004.
8. V. B. S. Prasath et al.; Cell nuclei segmentation in glioma histopathology images with color decomposition based active contours, IEEE International Conference on Bioinformatics and Biomedicine (BIBM), 1734-1736, 2015.
9. Fukuma et al.; Feature extraction and disease stage classification for glioma histopathology images, IEEE International Conference on E-health Networking, Application & Services (HealthCom), 2015.
10. Fukuma et al.; A study on feature extraction and disease stage classification for Glioma pathology images, IEEE International Conference on Fuzzy Systems (FUZZ-IEEE), 2150-2156, 2016.
11. A. Yonekura et al.; Improving the generalization of disease stage classification with deep CNN for glioma histopathological images, IEEE International Conference on Bioinformatics and Biomedicine (BIBM), 1222-1226, 2017.
12. A. Yonekura et al.; Glioblastoma multiforme tissue histopathology images based disease stage classification with deep CNN, International Conference on Informatics, Electronics & Vision (ICIEV), 2017.
13. A. Yonekura et al.; Automatic disease stage classification of glioblastoma multiforme histopathological images using deep convolutional neural network. Biomedical Engineering Letters, 2018.

ISASE-MAICS 2018

A Tentative Theory of Primitive *Kansei*: Social Skills in Ancient Human Society

Takashi SAKAMOTO

National Institute of Advanced Industrial Science and Technology (AIST), AIST Tsukuba Central 2, Umezono 1-1-1, Tsukuba, Ibaraki 305-8568, Japan
takashi-sakamoto@aist.go.jp

Abstract: In this paper, a tentative theory that explains how human beings have acquired primitive *Kansei* as an essential intellectual ability to survive in severe conditions so that having social ability becomes evolutionary selective pressure is proposed. In the remote past, perhaps the Paleolithic age or later, *Kansei* ability was part of social ability that was indispensable for surviving in human society. *Kansei* ability enabled human beings to perceive, understand, estimate, and manipulate the influence of tangible and intangible entities; this is beneficial for the mental state of human beings. In this paper, this social ability is referred to as primitive *Kansei*. It was very important in ancient human society so as to secure a socially advantageous position, acquire more spouses, and leave descendants. The role of *Kansei* seems to have changed significantly since ancient times.

Keywords: *Selection pressure, Evolution, Theory of mind, Primitive Kansei, Social ability*

1. INTRODUCTION

Why do human beings have *Kansei*? In this paper, a possible answer to this question is proposed. It is a very important question and a research theme worthy of discussion. This may be regarded as the ultimate research topic in *Kansei* studies. However, to date, there is no widely recognized interpretation or theory on this question.

All the abilities with which human beings have been equipped are necessary for living. For example, human beings have the ability of language usage so as to convey information and their intentions to other people accurately. It is believed that Neanderthals who failed to acquire language usage abilities were culled in the process of evolution in contrast to Homo sapiens who succeeded in acquiring language usage abilities and have accordingly, survived the process of evolution [1–3]. In other words, having the ability to employ language was part of the selection pressure that encouraged human evolution. It is believed that all the intellectual abilities of human beings were acquired because they were indispensable for surviving such evolutionary selection pressures.

Was *Kansei* ability part of the selection pressure that influenced the chances of survival in the long history of human evolution? The author is of the opinion that the response to this question is yes and moreover, wishes to propose a tentative theory that *Kansei* ability was crucial for survival in ancient human society. This theory may appear to be very strange when one considers the role of *Kansei* in modern human society. It is a well-known fact the *Kansei* ability makes daily life richer and more varied, both internally and materially. For example, by acquiring *Kansei* ability, one can feel beautiful when looking at flowers, impressed when listening to music, and able to buy cute looking clothes for children. It may be hard to believe the proposed theory that postulates having *Kansei* ability influenced selective pressure and promoted the evolution of human beings.

The tentative theory proposed in this paper is outlined as follows: In the remote past, perhaps the Paleolithic age or later, *Kansei* ability was part of social ability that was indispensable for survival in human society. Such social ability involved perceiving understanding, estimating and manipulating the influence of tangible and intangible entities that are beneficial for the mental state of humans. Social ability was very important in society in order to secure a socially advantageous position, acquire more spouses, and leave descendants. In modern society, the social aspect of *Kansei* has been forgotten and only the psychological aspects related to impressions have been highlighted. Thus, the role of *Kansei* from ancient times to modern times seems to have changed significantly.

The social aspect of *Kansei* is referred to as primitive *Kansei* in this paper. Furthermore, primitive *Kansei* is discussed in contrast to modern *Kansei*. In accordance with the proposed method, the role and importance of primitive *Kansei* and the reason primitive *Kansei* has been deeply related to the selection pressure in human evolution is also discussed.

This paper is based on a Japanese article published in the *Journal of Japanese Society of Kansei Engineering* [4] that was written by the author.

2. SENSING OF HUMAN EMOTION

Changizi et al. (2006) [5] proposed an interesting theory that human color vision evolved from dichromatic color vision to trichromatic color vision because of acquiring the ability to sense a slight change in somebody's face color.

Compared with dichromatic color vision, trichromatic color vision has outstanding ecological merit. It is thought that trichromatic color vision functioned as selective pressure in the process of evolution and subsequently, human color vision evolved from dichromatic color vision to trichromatic color vision. In fact, many mammals have dichromatic color vision. However, primates including humans and old world monkeys (catarrhines) have been known to have acquired trichromatic color vision during the course of evolution approximately 30 million years ago [6]. Changizi et al. (2006) argued that the outstanding merit of trichromatic color vision was the ability to sense a slight change of complexion caused by emotional expression. In addition, Fernandez and Morris (2007) [7] also pointed out that trichromatic color vision played an important role in social communication such as individual identification, observation of health condition, recognition of facial expression, and reproductive behavior. These theories have argued that whether emotional sensing ability was acquired or not was functioned as selection pressure, and human color vision evolved. These arguments are consistent with theories that postulate that human brains developed in their quest to survive and leave offspring among complex social groups.

It is impossible to comprehend how one survived among complex social groups by only sensing other people's emotions. Changizi et al. (2006) revealed the importance of complexion sensing; however, the clues employed in sensing other people's emotions are not limited to complexion. For example, facial expressions, gestures, eyes, voices, behaviors, and attitudes toward others may be regarded as effective clues used to sense other people's emotions. After sensing, planning one's behavior and conducting the subsequent action must be necessary to acquire a social advantage. Unfortunately, Changizi et al. (2006) only revealed part of the ability to become socially advantageous and did not suggest the ability needed after emotional sensing.

3. THEORY OF MIND

Since ancient times, human beings have survived by belonging to social groups. Furthermore, it was believed that if social ability was high individuals would have an advantage in social groups. Emotional sensing ability, which was outlined in the previous section, is merely an aspect of social ability.

According to deductive reasoning, the ability to estimate and understand information acquired through emotional sensing is crucial after sensing. The ability to estimate and understand another person's state of mind is referred to as *theory of mind* [8]. Theory of mind is specifically studied in the field of developmental psychology. Generally, four- and five-year old children are able to answer the *false-belief task* correctly, and the task is employed to investigate whether children have theory of mind [9]. No study has shown that primates other than humans have succeeded in the false-belief task. In addition, there has been little evidence that non-human primates have theory of mind. This fact suggests that theory of mind is a highly intellectual ability that has only been acquired very recently in the course of human evolution.

Having theory of mind means that one acquires important mental functions of understanding others. Accordingly, one can consider other people's feelings based on one's own emotional experience and imagination; in other words, one is able to engage in intellectual activities that are equivalent to mental simulation such as empathy. These abilities are thought to afford human beings the opportunity to be superior to other individuals in a social group and to increase opportunities for survival and procreation.

4. PRIMITIVE KANSEI

By using theory of mind, one can estimate and understand the mental states of other people; however, by itself, one cannot obtain an advantage in social groups. It is necessary to make some action or feedback to others, depending on their mental states (Figure. 1).

For example, the action or feedback may be snatching food by intimidating others, or on the contrary, it may be sharing food. Furthermore, other social actions such as including others in a group, excluding others from a group,

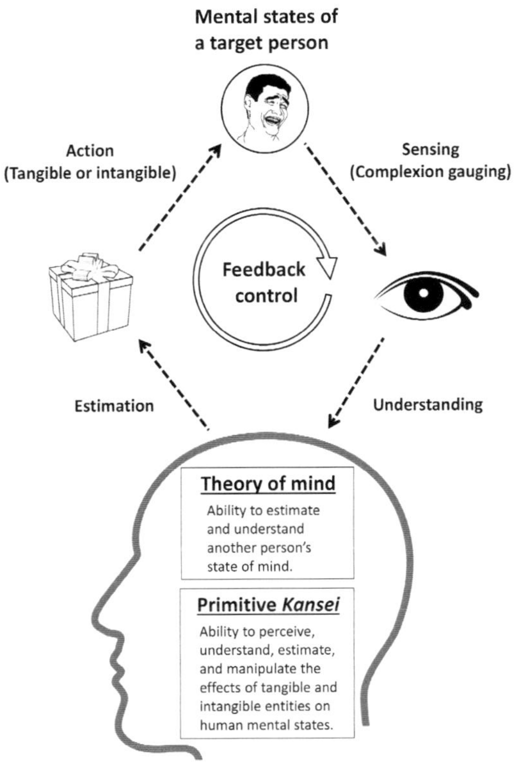

Figure 1: Feedback control is realized by emotional sensing, theory of mind, primitive *Kansei*, and action to improve the social relationship between oneself and a target person. (Adapted from [4]).

cooperating with others, fighting with others, grooming, and mating, are thought to be based on emotional sensing and the theory of mind. Thereafter, one needs intellectual abilities that can realize feedback control in order to plan strategies to change the mental states of others, act on the strategies, sense the result again, and modify actions to improve social relationships between oneself and others (Figure. 1).

In order to plan out a strategy to change the mental state of others to that which is desired, the intellectual abilities of perceiving and understanding the influence of tangible and intangible entities that are beneficial for the mental state of others are required. For example, tangible entities include natural or artificial objects such as craft objects, foods, animals, plants, the sun and the moon, and mountains. On the contrary, intangible entities denote human behavior and activities, various events, natural phenomena, imaginary concepts, and so forth. Furthermore, intellectual abilities are necessary to imagine influences from tangible and intangible entities and also estimate, simulate, and manipulate the effects of tangible and intangible entities on human mental states.

It should be noted that these intellectual abilities differ from the theory of mind. However, a literature search has not revealed an appropriate term, explanation or definition that illustrates such intellectual abilities. Therefore, in relation to the intellectual abilities of perceiving understanding, estimating, and manipulating the effects of tangible and intangible entities on human mental states, it is referred to as primitive *Kansei* in this paper.

By primitive *Kansei,* for example, one can plan out a strategy that a delicious food makes another person happy, and giving such a delicious food to another person makes a better social relationship, and accordingly, it increases opportunities for survival and procreation in the social group. Not only tangible objects such as a delicious food, but intangible actions such as grooming, dancing, playing music, and holding ceremonies were also carried out strategically in the social group in accordance with the primitive *Kansei.*

Sontaku, that is a recent vogue word in Japan and involves reading what someone is implying, are just carried out based on primitive *Kansei* in a complex social group. This example suggests that primitive *Kansei* also be found in the minds of modern people.

5. DISCUSSION: VERIFICATION METHODS

In this section, how to verify the proposed tentative theory is illustrated. It is necessary to verify whether the proposed theory is valid or not by employing scientific and reproducible methods. However, it would be difficult to reproduce the evolution of intelligence by using psychological experiments or observations of behavior. In addition, interdisciplinary studies that are not limited to science and engineering such as anthropology sociology, archeology, and philosophy are necessary to discuss the complex theme.

A few verification methods that can be employed are outlined: Firstly, brain activity measurement based on experiments using Magnetic Resonance Imaging (MRI) may be effective to verify this theory. This research method may reveal that the part of the human brain that executes *Kansei* evaluation has a relationship with the part of the brain that recognizes the effect of tangible and intangible entities for human mental states. Secondly, simulation is another effective method that could be used to verify the proposed theory. This could be performed on a computer as an evolutionary game that simulates social communication between individuals with or without a sensing ability of human mental states. These research methods may verify the proposed tentative theory.

6. CONCLUSIONS

The author proposed a tentative theory that human beings acquired primitive *Kansei* as an essential intellectual ability so as to survive severe situations and in which having social ability becomes an evolutionary selective pressure. Even if there was a development of superior human intelligence in the process of evolution, primitive *Kansei* as the intellectual ability would not have developed if human beings were not social beings. Primitive *Kansei* has evolved further with the times, and has been acquired as a human intellectual ability that has adapted to modern society and subsequently, developed into *Kansei* as it is known currently.

Primitive *Kansei* is only an aspect of the concept generally known as *Kansei*. Currently, *Kansei* seems to have lost its meaning as a social ability that has played an important role in the course of human evolution. On the contrary, social abilities such as reading the atmosphere of situations, and doing *sontaku* are generally not referred to as *Kansei*. These facts suggest that primitive *Kansei* has changed its role and meaning during a very long period of human evolution. Presently, *Kansei* makes our daily lives rich and colorful but originally it was indispensable for surviving as a social being in the course of human evolution. Consequently, human beings acquired it. Hence, the question posed at the beginning of the paper has been answered.

ACKNOWLEDGMENTS

This work was partially supported by JSPS KAKENHI Grant Number 18H03565, and AIST Research Division Grant.

REFERENCES

[1] P. Lieberman; The origins of some aspects of human language and cognition. In; P. Mellars, C. B. Stringer (Eds.) The human revolution, Edinburgh Univ. Press, Edinburgh, 1989.

[2] P. Lieberman; The Evolution of Human Speech: Its Anatomical and Neural Bases, Current Anthropology, 48(1), pp.39–66, 2007.

[3] P. Lieberman; The evolution of language and thought, Journal of Anthropological Sciences, 94, pp.127–146, 2016.

[4] T. Sakamoto; Evolutionary Perspective on Primitive Kansei as Social Skills, Journal of Japan Society of Kansei Engineering, 15(1), pp.16–19, 2017.

[5] M. A. Changizi, Q. Zhang, S. Shimojo; Bare skin, blood and the evolution of primate colour vision, Biology letters, 2(2), pp.217–221, 2006.

[6] C. Hiramatsu, Adaptive significance of primate color vision, Primate Res., 26, pp.85–98, 2010.

[7] A. A. Fernandez, M. R. Morris; Sexual selection and trichromatic color vision in primates: statistical support for the preexisting-bias hypothesis, The American Naturalist, 170(1), pp.10–20, 2007.

[8] D. G. Premack, G. Woodruff; Does the chimpanzee have a theory of mind?, Behavioral and Brain Sciences, 1(4), pp.515–526, 1978.

[9] S. Baron-Cohen, A. M. Leslie, U. Frith; Does the autistic child have a "theory of mind"?, Cognition, 21, pp.37–46, 1985.

ISASE-MAICS 2018

Influence of different characteristics of air flow on a person's sense evaluation

Tomoharu ISHIKAWA*, Kento MIURA*, Takaho ITOIGAWA*, Minoru MITSUI ** and Akio NOZAWA ***

* *Utsunomiya University, 7-1-2 Yoto, Utsunomiya, Tochigi 321-8585, Japan*
ishikawa@is.utsunomiya-u.ac.jp, itoigawa@cc.utsunomiya-u.ac.jp, miyoshi@is.utsunomiya-u.ac.jp
** *Institute of Technologists, 333 Maeya, Gyoda, Saitama 361-0038, Japan*
mitsui@iot.ac.jp
*** *Aoyama Gakuin University, 5-10-1 Fuchinobe, Sagamihara, Kanagawa 229-8558, Japan*
akio@ee.aoyama.ac.jp

Abstract: The purpose of this study is to clarify the effects of people's psychological evaluation based on different characteristics of air flow. In this study, we gave male subjects various air-flow stimuli made by an Air Flow Generating Device (AFGD), which had been developed in a prior study, along with a Dyson Air Multiplier AM01, to the back of their hand, palm, cheek, and back of the neck in a hothouse, with a temperature set to 20 degrees and a humidity of 45%. Results showed that higher wind speed air flow brought about cool and negative sensations and air flow created by AM01 made participants colder and more comfortable than air flow made by AFGD.
Keywords: *Air flow, Air sensation, Air Flow Generating Device*

1. INTRODUCTION

In addition to recognizing objects through sensory organ faculties such as vision and sound, humans also recognize their surrounding atmosphere. It is thought that when a human recognizes the atmosphere of a place, the air around the human body acts on the skin sensations and influences the person's sensation. Most research on skin sensations has been done using devices focused on touch. These studies include research on a multi-finger haptic presentation device [1], a device that presents a haptic sensation through the tension of a thread attached to an object [2], and a device that reproduces the feel of an object [3]. However, these devices present vibrations directly to the human body and do not use air as a medium. However, studies have been done on music therapy that focused on sensory acoustic vibrations in the air, and certain successful results have been reported [4,5]. However, in these studies, the interrelationships among physics, psychology, and physiology are unclear. To effectively use air vibrations, it is necessary to clarify the interrelationships among physical properties, sense evaluations, and physiological responses to fully illustrate the characteristics of the air.

Therefore, we developed an Air-Flow Generating Device (AFGD), which is a device that can generate various levels of air flow and thus, change the characteristics of the air [6]. These various "air flows" refer to air flows generated by giving a sine wave signal or an impulse signal to the input. That is, the wind speed is controlled by the amplitude of the sine wave signal, and the release cycle of the air flow is controlled by the frequency of the sine wave signal (FSS). A prior study (I) presented an air-flow stimulus that input sine waves and impulse signals using the AFGD and clarified the absolute threshold of wind speed and sensitivity characteristics [7]. Another prior study (II) was an experimental evaluation of cold sensations and preferences regarding several sine-wave air flows generated by an AFGD, simultaneously measuring decreases in skin temperature. It clarified the interrelationships among psychology, physiology, and physics based on differences in body parts and gender [8]. However, although these studies successfully clarified these interrelationships regarding air flow using an AFGD, the differences between this type of air flow and a general air-flow presentation device are unclear. Therefore, in this paper, we aim to clarify how characteristics of air flow influence sense evaluation using a fan as a general air-flow presentation device and an AFGD.

2. EXPERIMENT

2.1 Experimental devices

The AFGD is a device that has five dynamic speakers (AURASOUND NS3-193-8A) and one nozzle (air output portal diameter 30 mm) in a body with holes on each side (height 113 mm × width 113 mm × depth 113 mm, volume

1.16 L) (Figure 1 (a)(b)). By synchronizing and moving the five speakers instantaneously, the AFGD is a mechanism that increases the driving volume of the air and radiates external air flow. Note that in a preliminary experiment, the nozzle was formed into a shape that can efficiently release air.

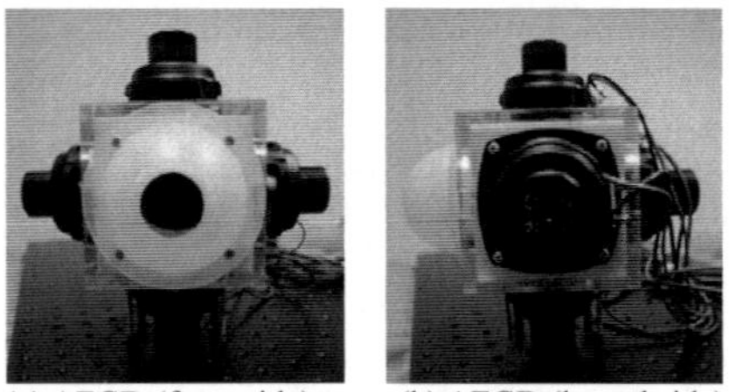

(a) AFGD (front side) (b) AFGD (lateral side)

Figure 1: Air Flow Generating Device (AFGD)

Through the system composition shown in Figure 2, the experimenters controlled the voltage and frequency of input signals to the speaker units and were able to generate air flows with different wind speeds and release cycles [6]. The Dyson Air Multiplier AM01 (AM01) was used as the fan to serve as a control compared to the AFGD (Figure 3). Note that the AM01 is equipped with a nozzle (air output portal diameter of 30 mm) that can present air flow locally, just as the AFGD can. By controlling the input voltage, it is possible to generate air flows with controlled wind speed.

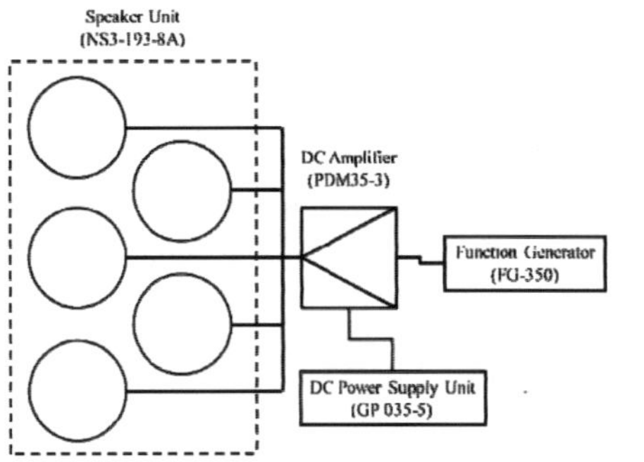

Figure 2: Design of Airflow Stimulus Generation System

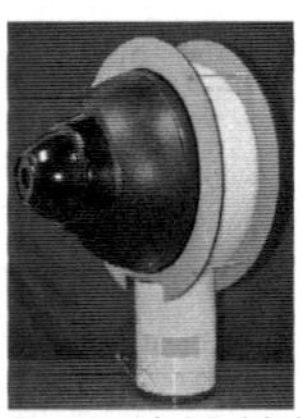

Figure 3: Dyson Air Multiplier AM01

2.2 Experimental stimuli, criteria, and scales used in the psychological evaluation

To compare the influence of the air flow from the AFGD with the air flow from the AM01, the experimental stimulation presented subjects with an air flow with controlled wind speed, and sense evaluation experiments were conducted on the participants' sense of coldness and their preferences. Note that with the AM01, there are three types of presented stimuli possible through input-voltage adjustments, and with the AFGD, there are nine types of presented stimuli possible through adjustments to input-signal amplitude and FSS. In this study, we considered the air-vibration detection threshold to be around 40 Hz [9], the resonance frequency of the muscular tissue of the human body (0–100 Hz) and the frequency for feeling tactile sensation (below 80Hz) [10]. There were three types of FSS: 40 Hz, 60 Hz, and 80 Hz. There were also three types of wind speed, 2 m/s, 5 m/s, and 8 m/s (7 m/s), which were decided based on a previous study in which the stimulus threshold of the sine-wave air flow was around 2 m/s [6]. For the AM01, we set the maximum wind speed to 7 m/s since that is the device's maximum wind speed. The participant group was made up of 10 men, and coldness and preference evaluations were conducted using the evaluation index shown in Table 1 as stimuli were presented to four body parts (back of the hand, palm, cheek, and back of the neck). The Visual Analog Scale (VAS) shown in Figures 4 and 5 was used as the evaluation scale. In the coldness evaluation scale (Figure 4), the evaluation values are digitized from 0% to 100%. We made the preference evaluation scale (Figure 5) compliant with the VA; evaluation values between 0% and 50% are positive evaluations, and values between -50% and 0% are negative evaluations.

Table 1: Psychological evaluation criteria

Coldness	Cold, Cool, Chilly
Preference	Comfortable/Uncomfortable, Agreeable/Disagreeable, Pleasant/Unpleasant

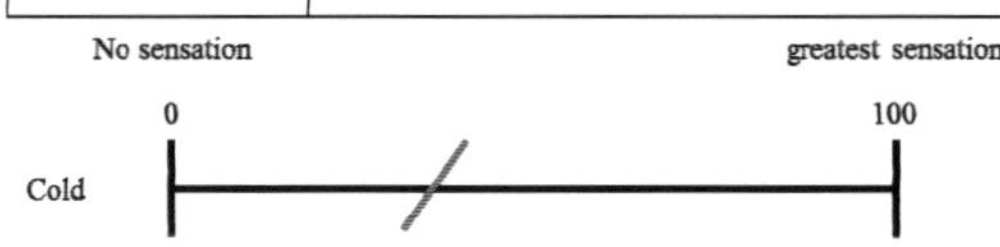

Figure 4: Psychological evaluation scale (example from the coldness evaluation)

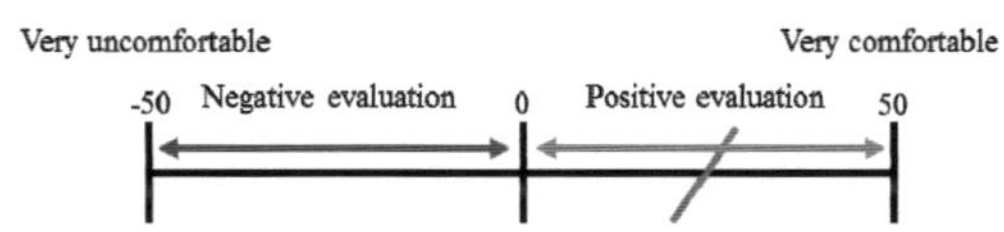

Figure 5: Psychological evaluation scale (example from preference evaluation)

2.3 Experiment environment and procedure

We conducted the experiment in a 2 × 5 m room (ceiling height = 2.4 m) in which we could maintain constant temperature and humidity levels. The temperature was 20 ± 1° C [11], and the humidity level was approximately 65%. For all body parts, we set the AFGD-generated stimulus 300 mm away from the target. To muffle the vibration noise of the AFGD during the experiment, we asked participants to wear a pair of headphones that emitted white noise (66 dB). Figure 6 illustrates the experiment procedure. The participants spent 20 min adjusting to the environment of the room and then 3 min adjusting to the white noise from the headphones. The participants rested for 45 s before each stimulus presentation to erase the psychological and physiological effects created by the immediately preceding stimulus. The participants undertook a series of iterations consisting of a 45-s pre-stimulus rest (Rest 1), a 15-s stimulus presentation and a 45-s post-stimulus rest (Rest 2), each iteration lasting for a total time of 1 min and 45 s. At the end of each iteration, the participants evaluated the relevant stimulus. Over the course of each iteration, we measured the participants' physiological responses. Each participant underwent a total of 36 iterations (3 FSS × 3 amplitudes × 4 body parts). To control for ordinal effects, we randomized the order of body parts and stimulus strength.

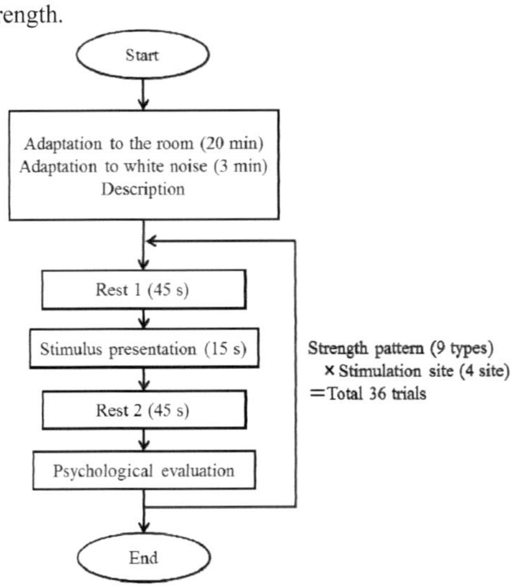

Figure 6: Experiment procedure

3. RESULTS

Coldness and preference evaluation values were calculated whenever air-flow wind speed, release cycles, and stimulus presentation devices were changed. Results are shown in Figure 7 (a)-(d) and Figure 8 (a)-(d). Note that mean coldness evaluation values were calculated for three items on the coldness evaluation index (cold, cool, chilly) and the means for those three times were calculated for each body part along with the stimulus, wind speed, FSS, and stimulus-presentation device. Similarly, for preference evaluation values, means were calculated for three items (pleasant/unpleasant, agreeable/disagreeable, and comfortable/uncomfortable) and the means for those three items were calculated for the body part along with the stimulus, wind speed, FSS, and stimulus-presentation device. Figure 7 shows the coldness evaluation values for wind speed in FSS and the stimulus-presentation device for each body part, and Figure 8 shows the preference evaluation values for wind speed in FSS and stimulus-presentation device for each body part. The diamond symbol (◇) represents the back of the hand, the square (□) represents the palm, the triangle (Δ) represents the cheek, and the circle (○) represents the back of the neck. A blue symbol represents AFGD 40 Hz, red shows 60 Hz, green indicates 80 Hz evaluation values and purple corresponds to AM01 evaluation values. For each symbol, a higher color density represents a higher wind speed (low density: 2m/s, medium density: 5 m/s, and high density: 8 m/s (7 m/s)). Additionally, for both coldness evaluations and preference evaluations, a multi-way ANOVA was conducted when the objective variable was "evaluation value" and when the fixed factors were "site," "stimulus-presentation device FSS," and "wind speed." The relationship between coldness evaluation values and preference evaluation values is shown in Figure 9. AFGD evaluation values in Figure 9 are mean values for the three FSSs (40 Hz, 60 Hz, 80 Hz) at each wind speed and site. As in Figures 7 and 8, the differences are shown in the shape of the symbols. Blue symbols show AFGD, red symbols show AM01 evaluation values, and higher color density shows higher wind speeds.

First, in Figure 7, both AFGD and AM01 coldness evaluation values showed a tendency to generally increase as wind speed in FSS increased for each body part. AM01 coldness evaluation values tended to be closer to and/or higher than AFGD values, and there was only a significant difference ($p<0.01$) between AM01 and AFGD when AFGD was 40 Hz. In contrast, coldness evaluations when AFGD was 80 Hz were close to the results from the AM01. Looking at each body part, there were significant differences between devices for the back of the neck with AFGD and AM01 at 40 Hz ($p<0.01$); however, for most body parts, no difference was observed.

Next, in Figure 8, preference evaluation values for

AFGD and AM01 showed a tendency to decrease slightly as wind speeds increased for each body part. AM01 preference evaluation values tended to be close than AFGD values. In particular, when AFGD was 60 Hz, preference evaluation values were closest to the results from the AM01. These tendencies can also be observed in the relationship between coldness evaluation values and preference evaluation values in each stimulus-presentation device, as shown in Figure 9. That is, preference evaluation values decreased as coldness evaluations increased, and the AM01 symbols showed high values for both coldness evaluations and preference evaluations. In particular, this tendency conspicuously shows the cheek and back of the neck. Although differences in body part site did not appear to influence evaluations for AM01, with the AFGD, coldness evaluations for cheek and back of the neck tended to be lower than for back of the hand and palm. Further, each symbol is a mean of the value in each FSS. Therefore, these results were not dependent on the frequency.

These results showed that air flow from AM01 had higher coldness and preference evaluation values as compared to AFGD for cheek and back of the neck. The AFGD FSS that had the closest coldness evaluations to AM01 was 80 Hz, and the closest preference evaluations was 60 Hz. Thus, it became clear that when the release cycle was higher through AFGD, sense evaluations were closer to AM01 air flow. Although AM01 air flow slightly influenced evaluations based on body part, with AFGD air flow, there tended to be different evaluations by body part, and there were lower coldness evaluations for cheek and back of the neck. The difference in this coldness evaluation was related to the difference in the cold spot density [12].

4. SUMMARY

In this paper, to clarify the influence of different characteristics of air flow on sense evaluations, we used an AFGD that had been developed in a prior study, as well as a general fan, and conducted an evaluation experiment with 10 male subjects on coldness and preference when stimuli were delivered to four body parts. Results showed that for both stimulus-presentation devices, as wind speed increased, coldness evaluations tended to increase and preference evaluations tended to decrease slightly. For any stimulation pattern and at any stimulus-presentation site, coldness and preference evaluations for cheek and back of the neck with AM01 were higher than with AFGD. That is, AM01 showed the potential to generate "chilly and comfortable" air flow while AFGD showed the potential to generate air flow where it is "difficult to sense the chill and is uncomfortable" for cheek and back of the neck. It also became clear that air flow with high release cycles released from the AFGD received (coldness and preference) evaluations that were close to those for AM01. Although air flow from AM01 slightly influenced evaluations by body part, air flow from the AFGD tended to produce different evaluations by body part, with lower coldness evaluations for cheek and back of the neck.

For future tasks, we would like to conduct the same experiment with female subjects and consider differences by gender, and in data organization; we would also like to measure the downward trend of skin temperatures of the stimulus-presentation sites and clarify the interrelationships among psychology, physiology, and physics from the viewpoint of device differences.

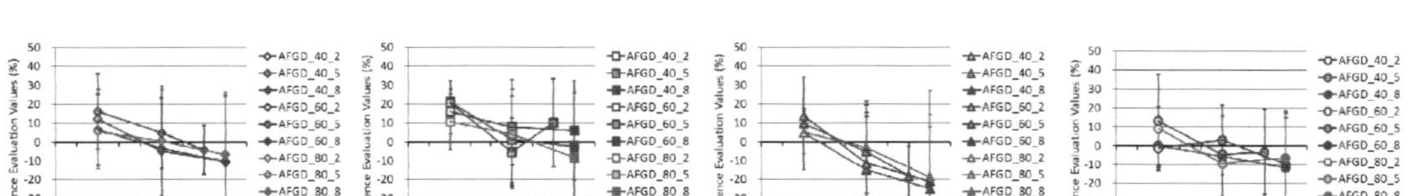

(a) Back of hand (BH) (b) Palm (PA) (c) Cheek (CH) (d) Back of neck (NE)

Figure 7: Coldness evaluations for airflow speeds according to body part and FSS

(a) Back of hand (BH) (b) Palm (PA) (c) Cheek (CH) (d) Back of neck (NE)

Figure 8: Preference evaluations for airflow speeds according to body part and FSS

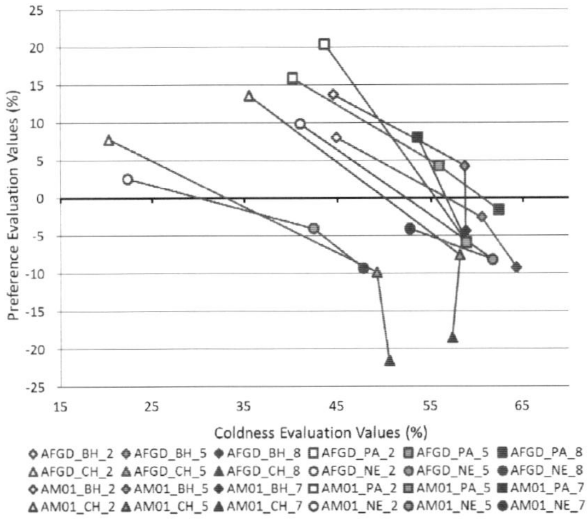

Figure 9: Relationship Between Coldness Evaluations and Preference Evaluations in Each Stimulus-Presentation Device

ACKNOWLEDGMENTS

This research was supported by the JSPS KAKENHI Grant Number 17K00387 and 18H03317.

REFFERENCES

1. Y. Adachi; Touch and Trace on the Free-Form Surface of Virtual Object, Proceedings of IEEE VRAIS93, IEEE, Seattle, pp.162-168, 1993.
2. H. Hashimoto, Y. Kunii, M. Buss and F. Harashima; Dynamic Force Simulator for Force Feedback Human-Machine Interaction, Proceedings of IEEE VRAIS93, IEEE, Seattle, pp.209-215, 1993.
3. S. C. Kim, A. Israr and I. Poupyrev; Tactile Rendering of 3D Features on Touch Surfaces, ACM Symposium on UIST2013, Scotland, 2013.
4. K. S. Chesky and D. E. Michel; The Music Vibration Table (MVTtm): Developing a Technology and Conceptual Model for Pain Relief, Music Therapy Perspectives; 9, pp.32-38, 1991.
5. O. Skille; Vibroacoustic Therapy, Music Therapy; 8, pp.61-77, 1989.
6. K. Hashimoto, M. Mitsui, A. Nozawa and T. Ishikawa; Development and Evaluation of a Device Stimulating Air Sensations for Air Media Technology, Proceedings of 16th, Tokyo, P-10, 2014. (in Japanese)
7. H. Takahashi, S. Bando, K. Oiwa, A. Nozawa, T. Ishikawa and M. Mitsui; Measurement of Psychophysical Quantities of Air-flow Stimulus; Institute of Electronical Engineers of Japan Transactions on Electronics, Information and Systems, 136(1), pp.1-3, 2016.
8. K. Miura, T. Ishikawa, T. Itoigawa, M. Mitsui and A. Nozawa; Psychological and Physiological Effects of Various Air-flow Stimuli Using Air Flow Generating Device -Difference in Subject's Gender and Body sites-, Proceedings of 12th JSKE spring, Osaka, 1B-01, 2017. (in Japanese)
9. T. Ooyama, S. Imai and T. Wake; New Edition Sensibility and Perceptual Psychology Handbook; Seishin shobo, Tokyo, Japan, 1994. (in Japanese)
10. M. Karkkainen and J. Mitsui; The Effects of Sound-based Vibration Treatment on the Human Mind and Body "The Physioacoustic Method"; Journal of International Society of Life Information Science; 24(1), pp.155-164, 2006.
11. Japanese Industrial Standards Committee; Standard Atmospheric Conditions for Testing; JISZ8703, 2014.
12. H. Strughold and R. Porz; Die Dichte der Kaltpunkte auf der Haut des menschlichen Körpers, Zeitschrift für Biologe; 91, pp.563–571, 1931.

ISASE-MAICS 2018

Characteristics of Modeling of Value Creative Consensus Building Process in Case of Multiple-Choice

Yuri HAMADA*, Tatsuya MARUYAMA ** and Hiroko SHOJI ***

* *Chuo University, 1-13-27 Kasuga, Bunkyo-ku, Tokyo 112-8551, Japan*
yhamada@kc.chuo-u.ac.jp
** *Graduate School of Chuo University, 1-13-27 Kasuga, Bunkyo-ku, Tokyo 112-8551, Japan*
*** *Chuo University, 1-13-27 Kasuga, Bunkyo-ku, Tokyo 112-8551, Japan*

Abstract: The authors have been conducting research on value-creating communication. It is a process where people embody and clarify their own values and form new values through communication. The authors have observed and modeled consensus building process that has few choice as an example of value-creating communication. Therefore, in this study, we observed and modeled the consensus building process in case of multiple-choices and compared the process based on quantity of choices. In multiple-choices, there was a group that they created the conception through communication and a group that they reach the consensus in terms of a viewpoint. It is considered that the conception is important if the appearance of viewpoints through communication is few or the degree of importance between viewpoints is not clear. However, as a result of comparison the process, it was suggested that the consensus building process can be caught the same structure regardless of the number of choices.
Keywords: *Consensus Building, Communication, Bayesian Network*

1. INTRODUCTION

The authors have been conducting research on value-creating communication. we refer to the case where people embody and clarify their own values and form new values through communication as "value-creating communication". Value created by value-creating communication refers to the internal value formed within the mind of each individual, not specific objects or services. The importance of value-creating communication has been stated. Fujii pointed out the limit of determining a solution rationally using an optimization method in consensus building because each individual's preference is not consistent enough [1]. Kuwako argued the importance of Kansei communication in consensus building through observation of field communication [2]. Kuwako stated not only the opinions of participants but also the history of reasons for opinions are important.

As described above, participants do not make solutions rationally in consensus building, but they share each opinions and history of it and make a solution that each person can convince each other through value-creating communication. However, there was no study that analyze value creative consensus building process in detail and evaluate it quantitatively.

Now, we will briefly introduce the observation and analysis of the consensus building process we have conducted. For more details, please refer to [3][4]. The theme of discussion is "going on a trip with lab members and teachers in spring for two days and one night" and gave six choices. Subjects were five college students belonging to the same laboratory and made discussions in four laboratories. We observed cases where decision by majority vote was different from that by discussion. Besides, a member who had negative impression on the chosen candidate were given a new viewpoint by remarks of other members and convinced by the "Reason" of choosing the candidates. Furthermore, there was a phenomenon where sharing the conception of "good for everyone" leads them to change their opinion. Therefore, we modeled consensus building process using Bayesian Network to show the structure of the process before and after creating the conception.

In this study, we observe the consensus building process that has thirty-five choices. In case of multiple-choice, it is not likely to determine a solution by majority vote. Iyengar also observed a decision making process and stated that decision making is difficult in case of multi-ple-choices [5]. Therefore, the purpose of this study was to model the consensus building process in case of multiple-choice and explain that structure. Further, we compared the process and the model depends on quantity of choices.

2. OBSERVATION

2.1 Observation Method

In this study, the theme of discussion is "going to a training camp to get a driving license in summer" and determine a site of training camp where all the member stay. The Subjects were five college students belonging to the same laboratory and made discussion in six laboratories. There are thirty-five choices, and a table that is created by referring to brochures. A table has such as location information, features or selling points of the site of training camp. We surveyed personal preferences by preliminary questionnaire. The scene of the discussion was recorded with a video camera, and the analysis target is the text data that the voice data was converted into.

2.2 Case Study

In this paper, we briefly introduce the flow of the consensus building for two groups.

In group A, members gave a candidate which each of them thought best, and shared it with reasons. In the process of comparing of choices, they narrowed choices according to viewpoints of "wireless LAN" and "to limit the expense to 230,000 yen". Further, they created the conception of "to have quality free time" and decided the school that has places to play and convenience stores, hot springs nearby according to the conception.

In group B, members gave a candidate which each of them thought the best, and stated features of candidate. In the process of discussion, all the members reached consensus to put emphasis on viewpoint of "low cost" and three candidates was narrowed. They eventually decided the school that matched viewpoints of "wireless LAN" and "a lot of surrounding facilities".

3. ANALYSIS BY BAYESIAN NETWORK

3.1 Bayesian network

The Bayesian network features the ability to predict the likelihood and possibility of the occurrence of an uncertain event by representing the causal structure as a network and then performing probabilistic reasoning [5]. The Bayesian network is a network-like probabilistic model defined by three variables: random variable, conditional dependency between random variables, and conditional probability. According to Motomura [5], the Bayesian network uses random variables as nodes and represents dependency relationships between variables as effective links. For example, the conditional dependency between random variables X_i, X_j is denoted by $X_i \rightarrow X_j$, and the node in front of the arrow (X_j in this case) is called a child node, and the node after the arrow (X_i in this case) is called the parent node. When there are multiple parent nodes, let $P_a(X_i)$ be a set of parent nodes of child node X_j. The dependence between X_j and $P_a(X_i)$ is quantitatively represented by the following conditional probability.

$$P(X_j|P_a(X_j))$$

Furthermore, considering each of the individual random variables as child nodes in the same way, the joint probability distribution of all the random variables is represented by the following equation.

$$P(X_1,\cdots,X_n) = P(X_1|P_a(X_1)) \cdot P(X_2|P_a(X_2)) \cdots \cdot P(X_n|P_a(X_n))$$

A probabilistic dependency between these variables can be modeled by a Bayesian network constructed by linking each child node and its parent node. The probability distribution of all variables is obtained by calculating the previous joint probability distribution.

In this study, we use BayoLink [6] to construct a Bayesian network. BayoLink is a Bayesian network construction support system implemented by Java developed by Motomura et al. [7-9]. In this study, "Reason" for "Choice" is a factor, while "Evaluation" is the result. We make a Bayesian network analysis by representing the remarks in the consensus building process as a causal structure.

3.2 Classification method of remarks

In order to classify the "Reason" into several nodes, we use the KJ method. As a result, it could be classified into nine categories: "Conception", "Cost", "Place", "Meal", "Life", "Entertainment", "Sports", "Tourism/Nature" and "Others." Table 1 shows the classification method. Therefore, a network was constructed using "Conception", "Cost", "Place", "Meal", "Life", "Entertainment", "Sports", "Tourism/Nature", "Others", "Choice", "Evaluation" as nodes (Figure1). The state of "Reason" is "A" if it is described for each item, and "None" if not described. The state of "Choice" is the school's number that has a range from 1 to 35. "Evaluation" status is "Positive" or "Negative". One sentence is one remark and the item of "Reason" necessarily selects "A" or "None". However, since BayoLink has a function to complement missing values using a neural network [7], "Choice" and "Evaluation" do not necessarily need to select a state and there may be a blank. A part of the data used for the analysis is shown in Table 2. The first line represents nodes of model. For example, the number 1 in Table 2 is a classification of the remarks that "⑫ is expensive.", "Choice" is "⑫", "Evaluation" is "Negative", "Cost" is "A", and the other nodes are "None".

Keywords: Consensus Building, Communication, Bayesian Net...

Table 1: Classification method of remarks

Conception	Remarks including intention, grounds
Cost	Remarks on expenses of a driving school, usage fee of surrounding facilities
Place	Remarks on place of a driving school
Meal	Remarks on meal of a driving school
Life	Remarks on life such as hot spring, wireless LAN etc.
Entertainment	Remarks on entertainment such as movie theater, Karaoke etc.
Sports	Remarks on sports such as tennis, football, bouldering etc.
Tourism / Nature	Remarks on tourism or nature such as castle, botanical garden, sea etc.
Others	Remarks on others such as a pickup bus, hospital etc.

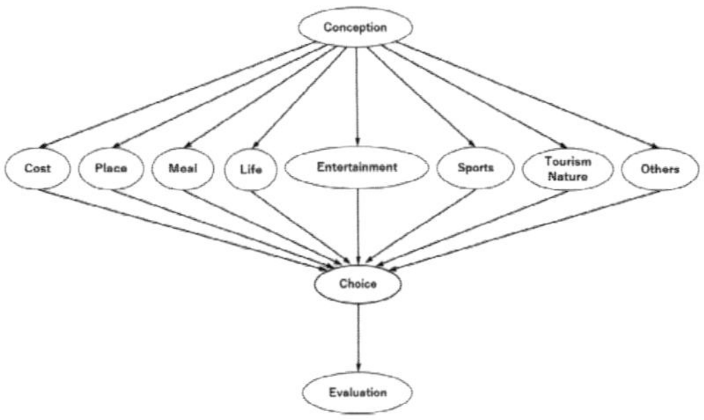

Fig 1: Bayesian network model 1

Table 2: Data 1 used for analysis (partial excerpt)

No.	Choice	Evaluation	Conception	Cost	Place	Meal	Life	Entertainment	Sports	Tourism Nature	Others
1	12	Negative	None	A	None	None	None	None	None	None	None
2			None	A	None	None	None	None	None	None	None
3			None	A	None	None	None	None	None	None	None
4	5	Positive	None	A	None	None	None	None	None	None	None
5	5		None	None	None	None	A	None	None	None	None
6	5		None	None	None	None	A	None	None	None	None

3.3 Sensitivity analysis

Sensitivity analysis was performed using the constructed Bayesian network model. Sensitivity analysis is a method of quantitatively calculating the influence of each factor in a model where an event is generated from a plurality of factors. BayoLink has a sensitivity analysis tool, which can infer with the specified explanatory variable and search for explanatory variable with a large influence on the objective variable. Therefore, we clarify by sensitivity analysis the "Reason" that greatly influences when "Evaluation" of "Choice". We made an analysis with "Evaluation" as an objective variable and "Conception", "Cost", "Place", "Meal", "Life", "Entertainment", "Sports", "Tourism/Nature" and "Others" as explanatory variables. In the sensitivity analysis, we made several pairs of values from explanatory variables and input them into the model to infer.

Here, it is possible to specify the upper limit of the number of input values to the model, but in this study the maximum number of combinations is set to 2. This is because "Conception" does not appear alone but often appears together with other items.

In chapter 2, it stated that group A created the conception by other member's remark that "we want to have quality free time." It also stated that group B reach consensus in terms of the view point that "low cost" by other member's remark that "the school where the cost is cheap is good." Therefore, we analyze separately for the first half and the second half of these remarks.

The results of the sensitivity analysis in group A are shown in Tables 3 and 4. "Probability value" in Table 3-6 denotes the probability value (posterior probability) of the objective variable under the condition that the value of the explanatory variable is input. This indicates the probability of "Evaluation" becoming "Positive" when a value of a specific explanatory variable is input. "Difference in probability" denotes the difference between the prior and posterior probabilities for the objective variable. "Lift value" represents the ratio of the probability (certain posterior probability) of occurrence of a certain state when observation is input and the probability (prior probability) of occurrence of that condition irrespective of the condition. That is, the higher the lift value, the greater the influence of the selected "Reason" set on "Evaluation". Tables 3 shows that they emphasize "Cost" in the first half. However, table 4 shows they emphasize "Entertainment" and there is also the combination of "Conception" and "Entertainment." This result indicates that the conception has created through communication, and what to put emphasis on has changed according to the conception in group A. Next, the results of the sensitivity analysis in group B are shown in Tables 5 and 6. Table 5 shows that they emphasize "Place" and "Cost" in the first half. However, table 6 shows they emphasize "Life" in the second half. This result shows that what to put emphasis on has changed without the conception. Thus, we visualized the process structure using Bayesian network model.

4. DISCUSSION

In this paper, we introduced two cases of consensus building process. Group A created the conception through communication. However, group B didn't create the conception and reached the consensus in terms of a viewpoint. In cases like group B, members reach consensus on which viewpoints to put on emphasis from the viewpoints appeared in discussion, and they make a decision meeting the conditions. In this case, even if the conception is not created it will reach an consensus. So we consider that the conception is important if the appearance of viewpoints through communication is few or the degree of importance between viewpoints is not clear.

Table 3: Sensitivity analysis result (Group A/First/Negative)

No.	Conception	Cost	Place	Meal	Life	Entertainment	Sports	Tourism Nature	Others	Probability value	Difference in probability	Lift value
1		A			None					0.302	0.033	1.121
2		A	None							0.300	0.030	1.111
3		A				None				0.298	0.028	1.105
4		A					None			0.295	0.026	1.095
5		A						None		0.295	0.025	1.094
6		A		None						0.294	0.025	1.091
7		A							None	0.294	0.024	1.090
8	None	A								0.293	0.023	1.086
9		A								0.293	0.023	1.085
10			None			None				0.282	0.012	1.045
11			None		None					0.280	0.010	1.037
12			None					None		0.278	0.008	1.030

Table 4: Sensitivity analysis result (Group A/Second/Negative)

No.	Conception	Cost	Place	Meal	Life	Entertainment	Sports	Tourism Nature	Others	Probability value	Difference in probability	Lift value
1						A		None		0.574	0.058	1.113
2					None	A				0.569	0.053	1.103
3				None		A				0.566	0.050	1.098
4		None				A				0.565	0.049	1.095
5						A	None			0.565	0.049	1.095
6						A			None	0.564	0.049	1.094
7			None			A				0.564	0.048	1.094
8	None					A				0.564	0.048	1.094
9						A				0.563	0.048	1.092
10		A				A				0.557	0.041	1.079
11	A					A				0.556	0.041	1.079
12						A	A			0.556	0.041	1.079

Table 5: Sensitivity analysis result (Group B/First/Positive)

No.	Conception	Cost	Place	Meal	Life	Entertainment	Sports	Tourism Nature	Others	Probability value	Difference in probability	Lift value
1			A							0.676	0.015	1.022
2			A		None					0.675	0.014	1.021
3	None		A							0.675	0.014	1.020
4		None	A							0.675	0.014	1.020
5			A				None			0.675	0.014	1.020
6			A					None		0.674	0.013	1.020
7			A			None				0.674	0.013	1.020
8			A						None	0.674	0.013	1.020
9			A	None						0.673	0.012	1.018
10			A							0.673	0.012	1.018
11		A								0.670	0.009	1.014
12		A			None					0.670	0.009	1.013

Table 6: Sensitivity analysis result (Group B/Second/Negative)

No.	Conception	Cost	Place	Meal	Life	Entertainment	Sports	Tourism Nature	Others	Probability value	Difference in probability	Lift value
1	None				A					0.398	0.113	1.399
2		A			A					0.398	0.113	1.399
3					A					0.398	0.113	1.399
4					A	A				0.398	0.113	1.399
5					A					0.398	0.113	1.399
6			A		A					0.398	0.113	1.399
7					A					0.398	0.113	1.399
8					A					0.398	0.113	1.399
9					A					0.398	0.113	1.399
10					A					0.398	0.113	1.399
11				A	A					0.398	0.113	1.399
12					A					0.398	0.113	1.399

Next, we compare the model based on quantity of choices. The model has the same structure regardless the number of choices, the top is the conception, underneath viewpoints, further choice, evaluation is at the bottom. However, nodes are different depend on the theme of consensus building, it is necessary to classify of remarks according to the theme. Further, the contents and number of conception is different depends on the theme or the group.

5. CONCLUSION

We modeled consensus building process in case of multiple-choice using Bayesian network. We showed the structure and characteristics of consensus building process in case of multiple-choice by quantitative analysis using the model.

In addition, we compared the process based on quantity of choices. As a result, we suggested that the consensus building process can be caught the same structure regardless of the number of choices, and it is possible to discuss various consensus building processes by quantitative analysis.

From now on, I would like to analyze the consensus building process when the subject is given a role or the subject's attributes are different.

REFFERENCES

[1] Satoshi Fujii; Examination On The Problem Of Con sensus Building, Operations research as a management science research 48(11), pp.795-801, 2003.

[2] Toshio Kuwako; Consensus Building and Kansei in Communications, The Journal of the Institute of Electronics, Information, and Communication Engineers 92(11), pp.967-969, 2009.

[3] Yuri Hamada, Hiroko Shoji; A Study on the Feature Analysis of the Success Pattern of Consensus Building Processes, Transactions of Japan Society of Kansei Engineering, Vol.16, No.1, pp.43-50, 2017.

[4] Yuri Hamada, Hiroko Shoji: How to Model Value-Creating Communication: Consensus Building Process as an Example, Proceedings of 3rd International Symposium on Affective Science and Engineering, Japan Society of Kansei Engineering, 2017.

[5] Sheena Iyengar: THE ART OF CHOOSING, Grand Central Publishing, 2011.

[6] Yoichi Motomura, Hirotoshi Iwasaki: Bayesian network technology-user and customer modeling and inference of uncertainty-, Tokyo Denki University Press, 2006.

[7] NTT DATA Mathematical Systems HP: http://www.msi.co.jp/bayonet/

[8] Yoichi Motomura, "BAYONET: Bayesian Network on Neural Network", Foundation of Real-World Intelligence, pp.28-37, CSLI calfornia, 2002.

[9] Yoichi Motomura; Bayesian network software, journal of the Japanese Society for Artificial Intelligence, vol.17, no.5, pp.559- 565, 2002.

[10] Yoichi Motomura; Bayesian network software Bayo Net, journal of the Society of Instrument and Control Engineers, vol.42, no.8, pp.693- 694, 2003.

ISASE-MAICS 2018

What type of hints can vitalize the brainstorming session?

Hidetsugu SUTO

Muroran Institute of Technology, 27-1 Mizumoto, Muroran-shi, Hokkaido 050-8585, Japan
suto@sdlabo.net

Abstract: A lot of supporting tools for vitalizing brainstorming sessions have been proposed. Some of them show the participants hints for discussions, e.g. keywords and images, to the members. The author's research group also has proposed a supporting system for vitalizing brainstorming sessions, in which related images of ideas thrown in the session are shown for the participants as hits. However, the effects of this type of hint had not been investigated yet. Thus, experiments were conducted to show the effects. In the experiments, effects of three types of hints, (1) relevant words of the words used in ideas presented in the discussion, (2) images retrieved by using words used in ideas presented in the discussion as keywords, and (3) images retrieved by using relevant words of the words used in ideas presented in the discussion as keywords, were compared. As a result, it became clear that the third type of hints can increase number of utterances and diversity of the subjects in discussions.
Keywords: *KJ-method, Idea creation, Group discussion*

1. INTRODUCTION

Brainstorming method is widely used in group meetings in companies, educational institutions, communities, etc. because of the facile introduction [1]. KJ-method is one of the most popular methods used in brainstorming sessions [2]. In KJ-method sessions, each idea thrown out by the participants is written on a small card. By organizing and grouping the posted cards, participants can find relationships between submitted ideas during the discussion, and it helps them to submit more ideas and conclude the discussion.

Although KJ-method is a powerful tool, several weak points also have been pointed out. For instance, participants have to throw out their ideas as much as they can, but generating many ideas is not so easy for ordinal participants. Moreover, in brainstorming sessions, creating unique and novel ideas is requested for the participants, but it is also hard for ordinal participants.

To solve such problems, many supporting systems have been proposed. Some of them show the participants some hints for discussions, e.g. keywords and images. The author's research group also has proposed a supporting system for vitalizing brainstorming sessions that shows relevant images about ideas presented in the discussion as hits [3]. However, the effects of these hints had not been investigated.

Thus, in order to compare the effects of the following three types of hints, experiments were conducted.

(1) Relevant keywords: related words of the words used in ideas presented in the discussion

(2) Relevant images: images retrieved by using words used in ideas presented in the discussion as keywords

(3) Semi relevant images: images retrieved by using related words of the words used in ideas presented in the discussion

Figure 1 illustrates each hint.

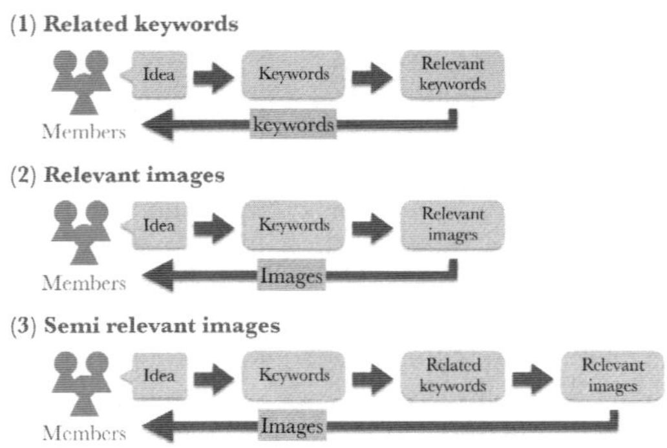

Figure 1: **Results of multidimensional scaling method**

In this paper, the results are shown and discussed.

2. BACKGROUND

Several systems for supporting idea creation have been proposed.

Watanabe et. al. proposed a tool to help the users meet new information which relates their interests [4]. The users make notes on cards on their PC screen same way as writing notes on sticky notes. When a user makes a note on a card, the card appears on the screen and move slowly for a direction. As two cards touch together on the screen, a new card appears on the screen. In the new card, information that is retrieved by using the two keywords on the original cards is described. This system shows the users relevant information about the users' idea for activating the users' imaginations.

Kang et. al. have developed a mobile application, called Category Camera, for supporting to create new idea in group meetings after fieldworks [5][6]. The users can put labels on photographs easily after taking them by using this mobile application. The labels help users to classify the photographs in the discussion phases. In this system, keywords associated with images are used as hints for creating new idea.

It is known that visual stimulate is one of the important types of hint for idea creating [7]. The author's group also has proposed a supporting system for vitalizing brainstorming sessions by using relevant images of thrown ideas in the session [3]. This system is designed as to activate discussions with KJ-method. Members of a discussion describe their ideas on cards on the screen. Then, images retrieved by using relevant words of important words used in the ideas described on the cards, we call them **semi relevant images**, appear on the screen. Here, it must be emphasized that not the words used in the ideas but relevant words of them are used as keywords for retrieving images. As a result, diverse kinds of images are obtained and they can extend users' imaginations.

All of these three systems use relevant keywords for providing hints for the users. The first two systems use keywords whereas the last system uses relevant images as hints for discussions. Thus, we discuss types of hints for discussions from two standpoints; keyword or image, and keywords used in ideas or relevant keywords of words used in ideas.

3. EXPERIMENTS

Experiments have been conducted in order to investigate the effects of hints displayed during group discussions.

The following three types of hints were given for the participants:

- **Type 1**: Relevant keywords; relevant words of the words used in ideas presented in the discussion
- **Type 2**: Relevant images; images retrieved by using words used in ideas presented in the discussion as keywords
- **Type 3**: Semi related images; images retrieved by using relevant words of the words used in ideas presented in the discussion

Numbers of utterances and presented ideas in the discussions were counted to evaluate the activation levels.

The participants are 16 students from an engineering course of a Japanese national university. 12 of them are the 1st grade of graduate school students and the others are 4th grade of under graduate school students (average 22.18 years old, SD 0.79). The participants were divided into 4 groups, Group A, B, C and D. Each group was asked to conduct discussions under two conditions as described in the section 3.1.

In the experiments, kizAPI [8] was used for generating relevant words, and Bing search [9] was used for obtaining relevant images.

3.1 Procedure of the experiments

The procedure of the experiments is shown below:

1. Instructions of brainstorming method and the experiments for the participants
2. Exercise of brainstorming method (5min)
3. Break (3 minutes)
4. Group discussion 1 (10 minutes)
5. Break (3 minutes)
6. Group discussion 2 (10 minutes)

The following two topics were discussed in the experiments:

- **Topic 1**: How to let children who do not like vegetables eat them.
- **Topic 2**: If your group has extra income of 5,000JPY, how to use it?

Table 1: Combinations of topics and hits for each discussion

	Group	A	B	C	D
Discussion 1	Topic	1	1	1	2
	Hint type	3	1	2	2
Discussion 2	Topic	2	2	2	1
	Hint type	1	3	3	3

Table 1 shows the combinations of topics and types of hints shown in the discussions. In order to reduce the effects of order, the orders were changed for each group.

3.2 Results

Table 2 and Table 3 show the number of idea thrown out and the number of utterances told in the discussions.

Table 2: The numbers of ideas and utterances in the discussion (Topic 1)

Hint type	Group	Ideas	Utterances
1	B	9	200
2	C	14	178
3	A, D	15, 15	225, 107

Table 3: The numbers of ideas and utterances in the discussion (Topic 2)

Hint type	Group	Ideas	Utterances
1	A	17	260
2	D	9	136
3	B, C	10, 7	266, 207

4. DISCUSSION

4.1 Number of utterances

It is difficult to find some trend from Table 2 and 3. Therefore, in order to investigate the effects of each type of hints, the number of utterances after displaying hints is counted for each condition, and they were compared.

First, each discussion was divided into 60 periods as each period has 10 seconds. Then the utterances in 5 periods from the next period in which a hint was displayed were counted, and the average was calculated for each condition. Table 4 shows the results.

Table 4: The average number of utterances after displaying a hint

Hint type	1	2	3
Topic 1	4.50	2.83	3.94
Topic 2	4.20	2.50	4.50

As a result of Kruskal-Wallis test, Marginally significant differences were found among the average numbers of Topic 1 ($p<0.10$). For the Topic 2, despite significant difference could not be found, the p-value is close to the threshold value ($p=0.137$).

From the results, it is expected that hints obtained form relevant keywords of submitted ideas is better than hints obtained from words used in presented ideas for vitalizing discussions.

4.2 Variety of topics in a discussion

In order to investigate diversity of the discussions, the utterances data were analyzed by using multidimensional scaling method. The process is shown below:

1. Obtain sets of words construct each sentence by using Japanese morphological analysis tool, ChaSen [10].
2. Eliminate words, which do not express the contents of discussions, i.e., Articles, numeral and preposition [11].
3. Make N-dimension vectors, N stands for the numbers of words used in all of the utterances. If the word is used in a sentence, then the element corresponding the word is 1, otherwise 0.
4. Project all sentences into a 2-dimensional space by using multidimensional scaling method.

The results are shown in Figure 2. The red circles in the figures indicate clusters of utterances. Utterances in a same cluster include many same words. Thus, we can think that if there are more clusters more wide varieties of topics have been discussed in the discussion. The table 5 shows the number of clusters under each condition.

Table 5: Number of clusters in the multidimensional scaling spaces

Hint type	1	2	3
Topic 1	6	5	8
Topic 2	5	3	6

We can see from Figure 2 and Table 5 that there are most clusters in the results of discussions with the hints of type 3, meanwhile there are least clusters in the results of discussions with hints of type 2. From the results, it is expected that relevant image is the most useful type of hint for make discussion topics widely.

4. CONCLUSION

In this paper, the effects of hints displayed in brainstorming sessions have been discussed based on the results of experiments.

Three types of hints, (1) relevant words of the words used in ideas presented in the discussion, (2) images retrieved by using words used in ideas presented in the discussion as keywords, and (3) images retrieved by using relevant words of the words used in ideas presented in the discussion as keyword, were compared. As a result, it is revealed that the third type of hints can increase number of utterances and variety of topics in

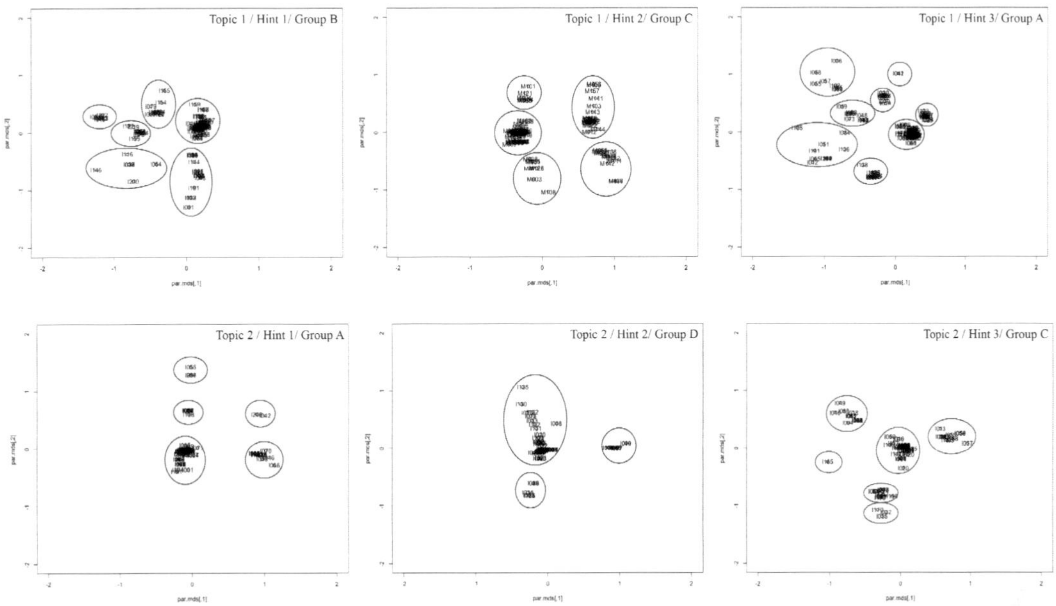

Figure 2: **Results of multidimensional scaling method**

discussions.

In this paper, only the types of hints shown in brainstorming sessions were discussed. However, it is predicted that the timing of giving such hints is also significant for idea creating, so it should be investigated in the future.

In the experiments, relevant words and images were obtained by using open APIs. It is also predicted that the effects of hints depends on the retrieving algorisms. The relationship between mechanisms of retrieving them and the activation level of brainstorming sessions also must be investigated in the future.

ACKNOWLEDGMENTS

This work was supported by JSPS KAKENHI Grant Number 15K00486 and 16K02807.

REFFERENCES

[1] Susumu Kunifuji; A Survey on Creative Thinking Support Systems and the Issues for Developing Them. J. Japanese Soc. AI., 8(5), pp.552-559, 1993. (Japanese)

[2] Jiro Kawakita; The original KJ Method (Revised Edition), Kawakita Research Institute, 1991.

[3] Hidetsugu Suto, Shuichi Miyo; A Support System for Vitalizing Brainstorming with Related Images, LNCS, 10274, Springer, Cham, pp.528-538, 2017.

[4] Keita Watanabe, Michiaki Yasumura; A Proposal of Persistent Interface and Its Implementation for Ubiquitous Environment, Trans. Information Processing Society, Vol.49, No.6, pp.1984-1992, 2008. (Japanese)

[5] Namgyu Kang, Hidetsugu Suto, Patchanee Pattitad; Role of Design Process Based on Expended ADT Model and TTS Model, Journal of Integrated Design Research, 13(1), pp.107-116, 2014.

[6] Hidetsugu Suto, Patchanee Patitad, Namgyu Kang: A Collaboration Support Tool for Multi-cultural Design Team Based on Extended ADT Model, LNCS8521, pp.548-557, 2014.

[7] Jonathan Littman; The Art of Innovation – Lessons in Creativity from IDEO, America's Leading Design Firm, Crown Business, 2001.

[8] kizasi.jp, http://kizasi.jp/about/ (accessed at February, 2018) (Japanese)

[9] Microsoft Azure, https://azure.microsoft.com/en-us/services/cognitive-services/bing-web-search-api/ (accessed at February, 2018)

[10] ChaSen, http://chasen-legacy.osdn.jp/ (accessed at February, 2018)

[11] Tetsuro Ito; Joho-Kensaku (Information Retrieval), SHOKODO Co.,Ltd., 1986. (Japanese)

ISASE-MAICS 2018

Classifying Personalities of Comic Characters Based on Egograms

Byeongseon PARK**, Kanae IBAYASHI * and Mitsunori MATSUSHITA *

* *Faculty of Informatics, Kansai University, 2-1-1, Reizanji-cho, Takatsuki-shi,Osaka 569-1052, Japan*
mat@res.kutc.kansai-u.ac.jp
** *Graduate School of Informatics, Kansai University, 2-1-1, Reizanji-cho, Takatsuki-shi,Osaka 569-1052, Japan*
K281401@kansai-u.ac.jp

Abstract: The aim of this research is to develop a search system for comics based on the personalities of appearing characters. For this purpose, this paper describes the classification of characters using egograms, which are used to classify personalities. In the proposed method, texts that express a comic book character's personality are acquired from web resources, and semantic vectors are allocated based on these texts using egograms. The resulting egogram pattern is used to estimate typical properties. Our experiment reveals that the performance accuracy of this classification method is 55.0%.
Keywords: *Personality Classification, TEGII, Web Resource, Comic Computing*

1. INTRODUCTION

In Japan, the number of newly published comic book titles is increasing every year, with more than 12,000 titles published in 2017. It is difficult to find comics with content that conforms to the interests of users from this huge number. In order to solve this problem, it is necessary to create an information access support system that can grasp the contents of each comic, and select and present them according to a user's interests[10].

In this research, we aim to achieve such a solution by creating a retrieval system that considers the personality types of appearing characters. Users tend sympathize deeply with characters who embody many of their favorite elements or emotions they identify with. Therefore, comics in which characters with such traits appear are highly likely to match a user's preferences. In addition, characters play an important role in composing the story of a comic. For example, even for comics following the same concept, the story development can differ considerably if the characters' personalities are different. For this reason, in this research we aim to realize a comic search that focuses on the similarity between the character's personality and the user's preferences, with the belief that the attributes of an appearing character form a criterion for selecting comics.

2. DIAGNOSIS OF PERSONALITY BY EGOGRAM

An egogram [1] is a personality diagnosis method based on the theory of exchange analysis, and it identifies character types using the question paper method. This method is said to have high objectivity, reliability, and validity, and is utilized in various situations such as educational and medical approach [4-9].

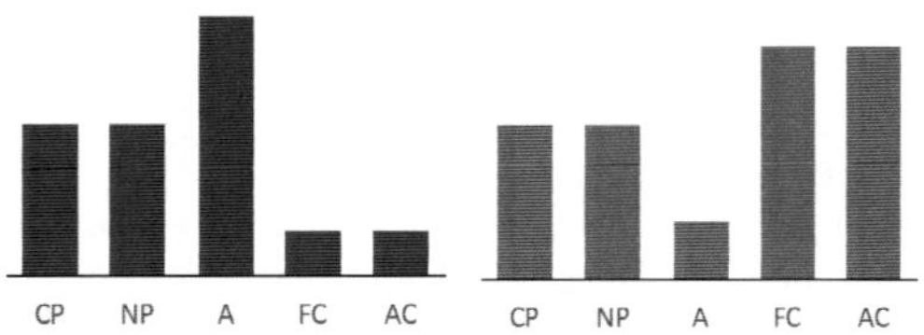

(a) C dominant type **(b) A dominant type**

Figure 1: Example of Egogram pattern in TEGII

Currently, the egogram that is most widely employed in Japan is the second version of the Tokyo University Egogram (hereafter referred to as TEGII) [3]. In TEGII, we measure the character of a person divided into the following five ego-state areas.

- Critical Parent (CP): Mind-concerning aspects such as obligation, sense of responsibility, belief, and pursuit of ideals.
- Nurturing Parent (NP): Mind-concerning aspects such as acceptance, compassion, development of self, and other mind and body aspects.
- Adult (A): Mind-concerning aspects such as logicality, rationality, objectivity, and plannability.
- Free Child (FC): Mind-concerning aspects such as autonomy, activity, aggressiveness, and creativity.

Table 1: Example of words acquired from the web

Gong Freaks (ゴン フリークス)	Uzumaki Naruto (うずまきナルト)	Son Goku (孫悟空)
bright(明るい)	never give up (諦めない)	bright (明るい)
full of curiosity (好奇心旺盛)	Justice (正義感)	Fool (お人好し)
honest (裏表がない)	self-indulgence (我が儘)	honest (裏表がない)
honest(素直)	reckless (無鉄砲)	overconfidence (自信過剰)
calm(冷静)	straight (まっすぐ)	honest(素直)
sore loser (負けず嫌い)	sore loser (負けず嫌い)	friendly (優しい)
friendly (優しい)	friendly (優しい)	calm(冷静)

- Adapted Child (AC): Mind-concerning aspects such as cooperativeness, social nature, compromise, and dependence.

TEGII classifies the personality into 29 types according to the degrees of correspondence to these five areas. For example, in the left diagram of Fig. 1, focusing on the fact that FC and AC are of similar height, the personality is classified as "C dominant type." This shows that even if the subject is an adult, they exhibit a childlike selfish state, and behave according. Furthermore, the right diagram of Fig. 1, focuses on the point that only A protrudes, and is classified as "A dominant type." This indicates that the subject exhibits many logical, intellectual, and planned actions.

In this research, we propose a method to classify personalities of comic book characters according to TEGII.

3. PERSONALITY CLASSIFICATION OF A COMIC BOOK CHARACTER

3.1 Proposed Method

In the proposed method, we first extract sentences that express briefly a character's personality from document data that can be collected from the web, and create a personality word dictionary for the personality classification. In our research, personality words refer to words (e.g., bright, calm, friendly) and short sentences (e.g., caring person, deep affection) that briefly express personality.

In order to judge the personality type of a character, we create a vector (hereafter referred to as a personality vector) by referring to the personality words obtained

Table 2: Examples of personality features

Egotic condition	value is high	value is low
CP	mandatory	easygoing
	responsibility	friendly
	stubborn	loose
NP	caring person	nervous
	kind	own pace
	meddle	frank
A	rational	naive
	calm	fool
	cold	not realistic
FC	curiosity	quiet
	free-roaring	meek
	bright	moderate
AC	cooperativeness	lively
	honest	positive
	obedience	own pace

from the resources on the web and the created dictionary. The degree of similarity between this personality vector and the preregistered basic egogram pattern is calculated, and those closest in shape are taken as the personality type of the character.

3.2 Personality Word Dictionary Creation

First, we collected descriptions expressing character 's personalities from Wikipedia[1], Niconico Pedia[2](ニコニコ大百科), pixiv encyclopedia[3](pixiv 百科事典), and Aniota wiki[4](アニヲタ wiki), and created a dictionary, which represents the cornerstone of each character' s personality classification.

The basic vocabulary for creating a dictionary targets those words used in relation to each of the main 100 characters appearing in the top 19 comic books (ranked in June 2017) published in the manga chronological issue number stated on the Mangazenkan.com[5](漫画全巻ドットコム). From the document collected from the above website, the words and short sentences that briefly express personalities are manually handled as personality words for the corresponding character. Table 1 shows examples of extracted personality words.

We created a personality word dictionary based on the personality words that were collected and extracted as a result of the above process. Each of the five regions of the egogram described in TEGII represents a different personality, and various personality features can be read

1 https://ja.wikipedia.org/wiki/
2 http://dic.nicovideo.jp/
3 https://dic.pixiv.net/
4 https://www49.atwiki.jp/aniwotawiki/
5 https://www.mangazenkan.com/

Table 3: Example Personality Word dictionary

Word	Area of Egogram				
	CP	NP	A	FC	AC
calm	0	0	1	0	0
mandatory	1	0	0	0	0
easygoing	-1	0	0	0	0
kind	0	1	0	0	0
fool	0	1	-1	0	0
own pace	0	-1	0	0	-1
free-roaring	0	0	0	1	0
honest	0	0	0	0	1

from the high and low values. For example, a high value of CP indicates personality features such as "mandatory (義理堅い)" or "stubborn (頑固)," and a low value of CP indicates character characteristics such as "easygoing (おっとり)" or "loose (ルーズ)." Table 2 shows examples of personality features. In this paper, the vector created in this manner is called the personality vector.

With respect to these 664 personality words, an evaluation is performed with reference to the vocabulary described in TEGII as to whether there is a match with personality traits of each region of TEGII, and a vector based on the five regions (CP, NP, A, FC, and AC) of TEG II is created. At this time, values of "1" and "-1" are assigned when the values of a region are high and low, respectively, with "0" corresponding to not matching at all. For example, because the personality word "stubborn (頑固)" is a feature that appears when the CP value is high, the personality vector corresponding to "stubborn (頑固)" is (1, 0, 0, 0, 0), where CP is 1. Because there are not many personality features described in TEGII, we have expanded it to include words within two hops of similar words recorded in weblio zisyo[6]. Through this processing method, 534 words out of the 664 used to create the dictionary could be given vectors. A part of the result is shown in Table 3.

3.3 Method of Estimating Personality Types of Comic Characters

We propose a method of judging the personality of each character with reference to the personality word dictionary created in 3.2. In the proposed method, we characterize a comic character's personality type by examining the personality words from the personality word dictionary contained in web descriptions related the character.

Next, a personality vector is generated by referring to the personality word dictionary. The personality vector is obtained as a linear sum of the personality vectors of each personality word. Because the number of personality words obtained for each comic character is different, an adjustment is made such that the total numbers are the same among characters.

Based on the value of the personality vector obtained for each comic character and the value of the basic type of the egogram, the similarity f was calculated according to Equation (1) to estimate the personality of the a character.

Equation (1) measures the distance between the personality vector $(x_1, x_2, x_3, x_4, x_5)$ of each comic character and the basic type $(y_1, y_2, y_3, y_4, y_5)$ of the egogram. The closer the calculated value is to 0, the higher the similarity.

$$f = \sum_{i=1}^{5}(x_i - y_i)^2 \qquad (1)$$

Table 4: Personality words of "Monkey D Luffy"

Responsibility (責任感)	King (王様)	Leadership (リーダーシップ)
Charisma (カリスマ)	Daring (豪胆)	Tolerance (包容力)
big heart (器が大きい)	Humanity (人情)	Friendly (優しい)
Flexible (柔軟)	Argumentative (理屈)	free-roaring (自由奔放)
Spontaneously (行動力)	self-oriented (自分本位)	Renewal (根明)
Fierce (凶暴)	Reckless (無鉄砲)	Rough (荒い)
Reckless (無謀)	Carefree (能天気)	Optimism (楽観主義)
Simple (単純)	Innocence (無邪気)	Serious (真面目)
Pure (純粋)	Strict (厳しい)	Dignity (威厳)
Straight (ストレート)	Capricious (気まぐれ)	Messenger (お調子者)
never give up (諦めない)	Insensitivity (鈍感)	easy to be fooled (騙されやすい)
Bright (明るい)	Magnificent (豪快)	

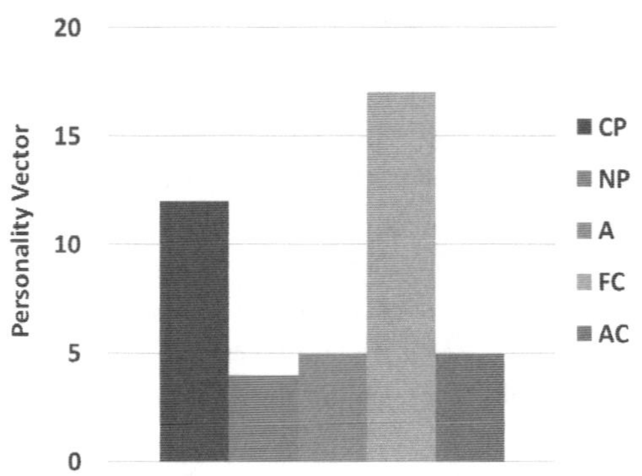

Figure 2: Egogram of "Monkey D Luffy"

6 https://www.weblio.jp/

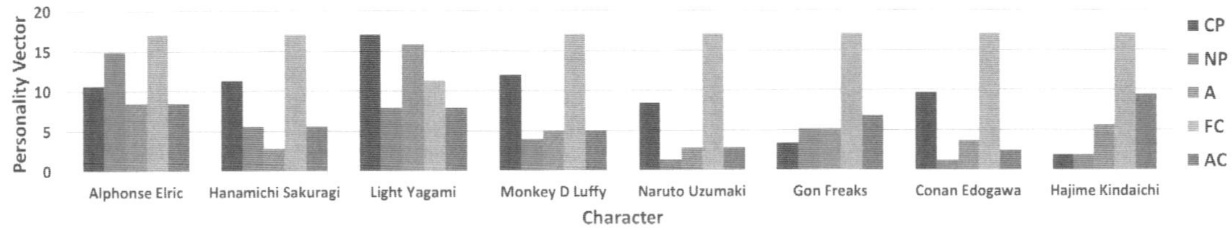

Figure 3: Personality Vector obtained by proposed system

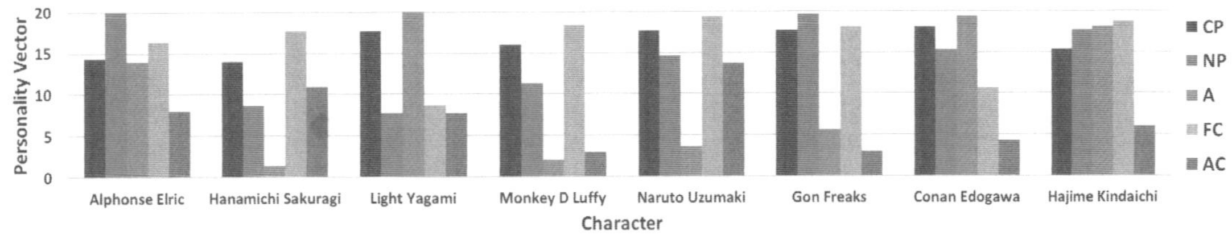

Figure 4: Personality Vector obtained by experiment

For example, for "Monkey · D · Luffy", the hero of "One Piece" (written by Eiichiro Oda, Shueisha), the personality words shown in Table 4 were extracted.

In this case, the personality vector is calculated based on these words (12, 4, 5, 17, 5) (see Figure 2). When this personality vector is applied to Equation 1, it becomes "inverse N type 3," "reverse N type 2," "FC dominant" in descending order of the degree of agreement with the basic types of the egogram, so that the personality type of the character is determined to be "reverse N type 3." "Reverse N-type 3" has the characteristics of self-centered, selfish, intimidated, emotional, and so on, and can be said to be valid for the personality of this character.

4. EXPERIMENT

4.1 Experimental Procedure

We conducted a user experiment to verify whether the personalities of comic characters extracted using the proposed method match the personalities recognized by users.

First, we asked the users to create an egogram of characters using the question paper method. The subject data of the experiment consisted of 20 characters from 17 comics, and data was collected from three experimental collaborators per character.

Fifteen people (nine men and men women) aged from their 20s to 40s participated as experiment collaborators in this experiment. Because one cannot provide answers without being familiar with a character, it was necessary to (1) read the comic in which the character to be evaluated appears, and (2) recognize the character to be evaluated. As a condition, we decided which characters would be assigned each experimental collaborator. Under this condition, between one and 18 characters were assigned to each collaborator. The reason for the different number of assignments is that the number of comics that had been read varied greatly for each collaborator.

In the experiment, we asked how the assigned comic characters corresponded to the questions (e.g., "is it easy to be influenced by what others say?" or "has a sense of humor?") of all 50 egograms described in TEGII. In this case, we calculated the total value following TEGII, with a scale of two points if applicable to the question, zero points if not applicable, one point if not sure.

We compared the judgment results for the top three using the proposed method, with the type indicated by the judgment result of three experimental collaborators and verified by the coincidence ratio. At this time, if the types indicated by the judgment results of three experimental collaborators included in the top three personality types extracted using the proposed method, this was regarded as being consistent.

4.2 Experimental Result

The results for the proposed system and the top three types resulting from the questionnaire assigned 55.0% of the comic characters with the same types (11 out of 20 characters). Figure 3 shows the personality vectors for each character calculated using the proposed method, and Figure 4 shows the judgment results from the experiment partners. Table 5 shows a part of the results of comparing

Table 5: Experiment results (matched personality types are bold)

Character name	Similarity	Result of system 1st	Result of system 2nd	Result of system 3rd	Result of experiment collaborators
Alphonse Elric	0.057	**Flat type 1**	Trapezoid type 1	P dominant type	**Flat type 1**
Hanamichi Sakuragi	0.081	**Reverse N type 3**	Reverse N type 2	U type 2	**Reverse N type 3**
Light Yagami	0.086	**Reverse N type 1**	Flat type 1	P dominant type	**Reverse N type 1**
Monkey D Luffy	0.140	**Reverse N type 3**	Reverse N type 2	FC dominant type	**Reverse N type 3**
Tatsuya Uesugi	0.145	**N type 1**	C dominant type	Flat type 1	**N type 1**
Kankichi Ryotsu	0.171	**Reverse N type 3**	FC dominant type	Reverse N type 2	**Reverse N type 3**
Gintoki Sakata	0.263	M type	FC dominant type	**Reverse N type 3**	**Reverse N type 3**
Kurosaki Ichigo	0.286	NP dominant type	**P dominant type**	Flat type 2	**P dominant type**
Zaodyeek Killua	0.323	Flat type 3	FC dominant type	C dominant type	W type
Souma Yukihira	0.366	FC dominant type	Reverse N type 2	**Reverse N type 3**	**Reverse N type 3**
Edward Elric	0.373	FC dominant type	Flat type 3	Flat type 1	Reverse N type 3
Roronoa Zoro	0.494	Reverse N type 1	Flat type 3	A dominant type	AC recessive type
Syouyou Hinata	0.526	U type 2	Reverse N type 2	**Reverse N type 3**	**Reverse N type 3**
Ellen Yeager	0.561	Reverse N type 2	Reverse N type 3	FC dominant type	Reverse N type 1
Son Goku	0.647	FC dominant type	Flat type 3	C dominant type	Reverse N type 3
Kenshin Himura	0.664	M type	NP dominant type	Flat type 1	P dominant type
Naruto Uzumaki	0.837	Reverse N type 2	**Reverse N type 3**	FC dominant type	**Reverse N type 3**
Gon Freaks	1.006	FC dominant type	C dominant type	Flat type 3	Reverse N type 3
Conan Edogawa	1.380	Reverse N type 2	Reverse N type 3	FC dominant type	P dominant type
Hajime Kindaichi	1.416	AC dominant type	C dominant type	FC dominant type	Flat type 1

the types of egogram.

In the experimental results, the highest degree of coincidence between the system and usesr was "Alphonse Elric" (0.057), who is a character from "Full Metal Alchemist (鋼の練金術師)" (written by Hirohiro Arakawa, Square Enix). The lowest was "Hajime Kindaichi" (1.416), who is a character from "Kindaichi Boy's Case Files (金田一少年の事件簿)" (written by Sato Fumiya, Kodansha).

4. DISCUSSION

The accuracy of the proposed method was shown by the experiment to be 55.0%. Because the ratio corresponding to three of the 29 personality types would be 10.3% under random conditions, the estimation of the personality type using the proposed method seems to have demonstrated an effect. From this, it is suggested that the egogram method used in this paper can be applied not only to the personalities of humans, but also of comic characters.

On the other hand, the reasons why the classification accuracy remained at 55.0% are as follows. The first factor is the extraction of unnecessary words as personality words of comic characters. In this approach, a method of extracting personality words matching with words registered in a personality word dictionary was adopted. Here, it is not possible to consider the meanings of words by context. For example, it is desirable that only the words "bright" and "energetic" are extracted from the sentence "rather than calm, bright, and energetic," but "calm" is also extracted using the current method. In addition, although the sentence "severe person" represents a "severe personality," "severe reality" does not indicate that the personality is severe. By wrongly extracting these words, the classification accuracy is deteriorated.

The second factor is that personality words cannot be extracted according to style. For example, from sentences such as "I care about my friends more than anyone, I care very much" and "I have a strong commitment to protect important people," traits such as "gentle," "friendly," and "passionate" can be estimated. However, because the proposed method extracts words and short sentences through superficial matching, personality words cannot be extracted from these sentences, and the intended personality cannot be estimated.

The third factor is that as a story evolves, the personality can change. This is a tendency found in many long-term serial works, and sometimes there are differences in personality depending on the selected time period. In comics, characters are often subject to extreme characterization, and there are cases where characters with a gentle personality change to having a cruel personality because of certain events. An egogram cannot capture such personality changes due to narrative features.

In the future, we will consider these influences and improve the accuracy of the method.

5. CONCLUSION

In this paper, in order to construct a comic book search support system, a focus was given to the personalities of characters, which considerably affects the story. A method was proposed to classify the personalities of characters based on egograms. Experimental results confirmed that the classification of personalities using egograms is possible. Thus, because the similarities between the personalities of characters and a search request is to be calculated, results such as "a comic book character with a personality that is similar to this character appears" are expected. In the future, we will extend this research by expanding the personality word dictionary and improving the accuracy of the personality type estimation.

ACKNOWLEDGMENTS

This work was supported by JSPS KAKENHI Grant Number 15K12103.

REFFERENCES

[1] John M. Dusay, M.D.; Egograms and the constancy hypothesis, Transactional Analysis Journal, Vol.2 No.3, pp.37-41, 1972.

[2] Shunji Hirose, Manabu Tatebayashi, Kumi Saito, and Satoru Yoshikawa; A study of psychological factors of bruxism: Analysis of risk factors, Japanese Society of Psychosomatic Medicine, Vol.55, No.7, pp.864-872, 2015. (In Japanese)

[3] Michiko Wada, Asami Watanabe, Miho Ichimura and Yutaka Matsui; New egogram developed by web survey, Tsukuba Psychological Research, Vol.53, pp.63-71, 2017. (In Japanese)

[4] Liang Cai, Sakae Kaneko and Eishin Morita; Changes in salivary chromogranin A levels in adults with atopic dermatitis are correlated with changes in their condition, The Journal of Dermatology, 2018.

[5] Min Jung; Influence of ego states, self-esteem, and empathies on interpersonal relationship of nursing students, Journal of the Korea Academia-Industrial cooperation Society, Vol.16, No.7, pp.4614-4620, 2015.

[6] Gao Xu, and Minoru Uehara; Design of a sports mental cloud, Advanced Information Networking and Applications Workshops, 31st International Conference on. IEEE, pp.443-448, 2017.

[7] Ng Annalyn, Maarten W. Bos, Leonid Sigal, and Boyang Li; Predicting personality from book preferences with user-generated content labels, IEEE Transactions on Affective Computing, 2018.

[8] Teruyuki Iijima and Shin Tezuka and Ryuya Uda; Method for Extraction of characteristics of personal characters from life log, Proceedings of the 8th International Conference on Ubiquitous Information Management and Communication, pp.110:1-110:8, 2014.

[9] Margaret L. Kern, Johannes C. Eichstaedt, H. Andrew Schwartz, Lukasz Dziurzynski, Lyle H. Ungar, David J. Stillwell, Michal Kosinski, Stephanie M. Ramones, and Martin E. P. Seligman; The online social self: An open vocabulary approach to personality, Assessment, Vol.21-2, pp.158-169, 2014.

[10] Byeongseon Park, Kahori Okamoto, Ryo Yamashita, and Mitsunori Matsushita; Designing a comic exploration system using a hierarchical topic classification of reviews, Information Engineering Express International Institute of Applied Informatics, Vol.3, No.2, pp.45-57, 2017.

ISASE-MAICS 2018

A Consideration to Estimate Spoiling Pages in Comics

Yoshiki MAKI, Yuji SHIRATORI, Kenta SATO, and Satoshi NAKAMURA

Graduate School of Advanced Mathematical Sciences, Meiji University, Tokyo 164-8525, Japan
tekkanomaki01@gmail.com

Abstract: Previous studies suggested that spoilers might increase the enjoyment of novels. However, the problem of spoilers has not been sufficiently clarified. The objective of our work is to clarify the effect of comic spoilers and to apply clarified knowledge for applications. In our past work, we constructed a spoiler dataset and investigated the spoilers' effect by changing the spoiler timing for readers. However, in the past work, we could not clarify the characteristics of spoilers. In this work, we clarified that spoilers reduced the interest in continuing reading the comics and analyzed the characteristics of spoilers by using the dataset. Then, we considered how to construct a comic spoiler dataset and investigated how to determine the spoiling pages automatically using image processing, and character detection and so on.
Keywords: *Comics, Spoiler, Automatic Detection, Characteristics*

1. INTRODUCTION

People enjoy reading with the variety of literary forms such as novels, comics, and so on. Comics, as one of those forms, excite readers and evoke laughter, surprise, and other emotions through pictures and stories. The popularity of comics in Japan is very high; the size of the Japanese comic market reached nearly 3.77 billion U.S. dollars in 2013. Japanese comics became popular around the world, partly due to the promotion by the Japanese government. Comics are also of interest to the field of information engineering, in which various studies on comics are being conducted. Among them, spoilers stand out as one of the significant problems that attract the interest of the researchers.

Spoilers ruin contents by revealing the endings, e.g., the winning or losing of matches, or the life or death of characters. Readers often want to avoid encountering spoilers before enjoying the content. Nakamura et al. [4, 5] proposed several methods for reducing the risk of encountering spoilers.

There are several studies on the characteristics of story spoilers. Leavitt et al. [1] studied the effect of novels' spoilers, and Levine et al. [2] studied the effects of novels' spoilers based on their timing. However, they did not look into comics' spoilers and considered spoilers as plots in and of these stories. Hassoun et al. [3] studied the effect of comics' spoilers depending on the comic panel layout. However, they only focused on spoilers on one page and did not focus on the entire of comics.

In our previous study [6], we investigated the degree of effect of the spoiler depending on the reading progress. We revealed that there were two types of comics: one is the spoiler-acceptable type that did not reduce the reader's enjoyment after providing spoiler information, and the other is the spoiler-unacceptable type that reduced the reader's enjoyment after providing spoiler information. However, our previous study could not show the essential spoiler effect because we only compared the emotions at the end of the reading. In addition, it is necessary to clarify what kind of page people felt spoilers because in estimating spoiler pages, there is no study to define what kind of elements we should use.

In this paper, we firstly analyze the comic spoiler's effect more deeply such as the degree of reducing enjoyment after encountering a spoiler depending on the spoiler timing and any other characteristics in chapter 2. In addition, in chapter 3, we analyze the aspects of spoilers which were constructed in the previous work. Then, in chapter 4, we discuss the guideline to construct the useful spoiler dataset and a method to identify which pages recognize as spoilers.

2. ANALYSIS OF SPOILER EFFECT

2.1 Experiment on spoiler effect

In our previous study [6], we prepared eight comics and constructed the dataset of spoiler information which made by four participants who were hired to label spoiling pages and conducted an experimental test about the spoiler effect depending on the spoiling timing. To do that, we divided each comic into three parts according to the number of volumes. In addition, we prepared four patterns of providing spoiler information and asking to answer questionnaires (see Figure 1). Note that subjects who were assigned to Pattern 0 did not encounter spoiler information while reading the target comic.

42 undergraduate students at Meiji University participated in the experimental study. We assigned five subjects to each spoiling pattern in each comic randomly. Each subject had never read their target comic. As a result, 20 subjects enjoyed and tried the experimental test in each comic.

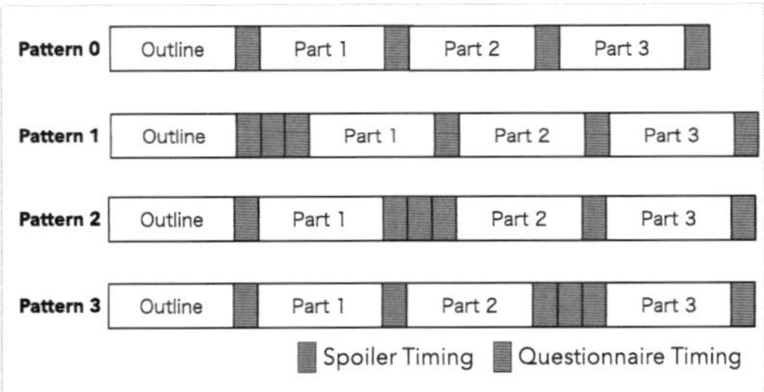

Figure 1: The timing of asking to answer questionnaires and providing a spoiler page in each pattern.

2.2 Results

Figure 2 shows the average of enjoyment value at the end of reading the comics in each pattern. The difference between Pattern 0 and others was not significant. In fact, there was no difference in the final enjoyment between subjects who were exposed to the spoilers and subjects who were not. In this experimental test, we forced subjects to read the comics to the last. In addition, the comics that we prepared were very popular and successful in their sales. In other words, this result only clarified that people could enjoy popular comics, regardless of whether or not to encounter spoiler information, when they read such comics to the last.

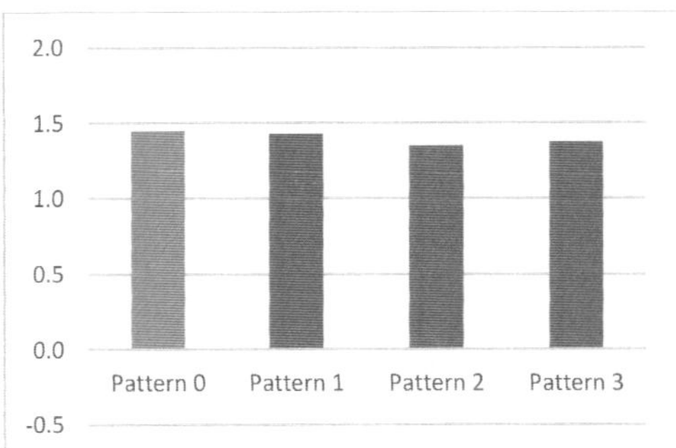

Figure 2: The average last enjoyment value in each pattern.

Here, in this paper, we analyzed the spoiler effect by comparing the level of enjoyment between before and after encountering the spoiler to reveal the impact of the spoiler.

There were two independent variables in this experiment: the difference in just before and after the spoiler (spoiler factor) and the difference in the spoiler timing (spoiler timing factor). There were also dependent variables, i.e., two questions in the questionnaire about the subjects' subjective impressions.

The dependent variables in the questionnaire on enjoyment value and interest in continuation value were analyzed by two (spoiler factor) x two (spoiler timing factor) mixed-design analysis ANOVA (see Figures 3 and 4).

In the questionnaire on enjoyment value (see Figure 3), we observed the significant differences between Pattern 1 and 2 ($p < 0.05$), and between Pattern 1 and 3 ($p < 0.05$). However, there was no interaction effect.

In the questionnaire on interest in continuation (see Figure 4), we observed that there were significant differences between Pattern 1 and 2 ($p < 0.05$), and between Pattern 1 and 3 ($p < 0.05$). There was an interaction effect between the spoiler factor and the spoiler timing factor ($F2, 117 = 8.04$, $p < 0.01$). In addition, there were significant differences in Pattern 1 and 2 ($p < 0.05$) in the spoiler factor.

Figure 5 and 6 show a transition graph evaluating enjoyment and interest in continuation about reading progress and spoiler timing. In Figure 5, enjoyment tends to increase from the start to the end. Also, in Figure 5 and 6, in the pattern in which the subjects encountered spoilers, enjoyment and interest in continuation decreased after viewing the spoiler. But, in the pattern 1, interest in continuation increases after viewing the spoiler.

Figure 3: The difference of enjoyment before and after spoiler in each pattern.

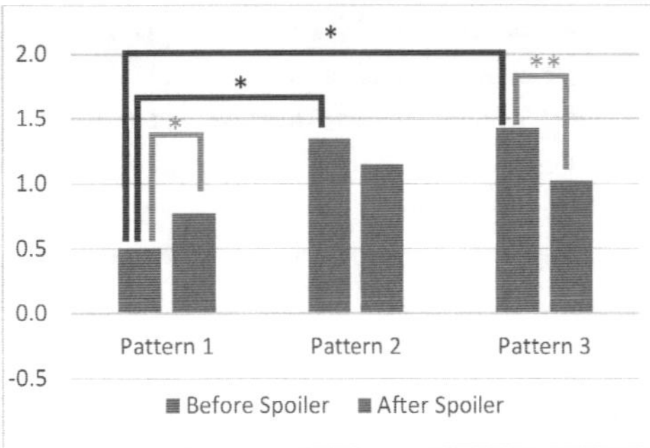

Figure 4: The difference in interest to continue before and after spoiler in each pattern.

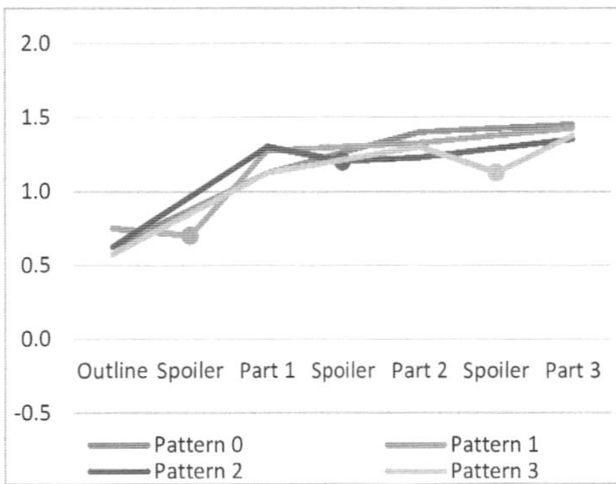

Figure 5: Transition of enjoyment value in relation to reading progress in each pattern.

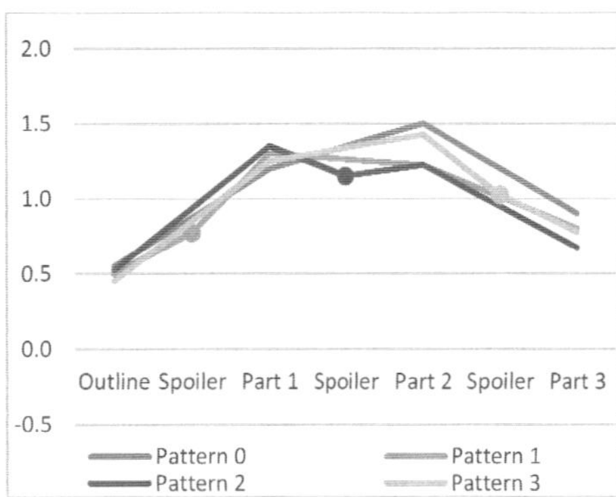

Figure 6: Transition of interest value to continue in relation to reading progress in each pattern.

Table 1 shows the data on the interest in continuation depending on the conditions ("With spoiler" condition vs. "Without spoiler" condition). In this table, Pattern 0 is classified to "Without spoiler," and Pattern 1, 2 and 3 are classified to "With spoiler." This result clarified that 10% of the subjects who did not encounter a spoiler lost interest in continuation, and 37% of the subjects who saw a spoiler lost interest in continuation. In other words, spoilers reduce the readers' interest in continuation.

Table 1: The ratio of lost interest with a spoiler or without a spoiler.

	Number of subjects	Lost interest	Ratio
Without spoiler	40	4	10%
With spoiler	120	44	37%

2.3 Discussion

As shown in Figure 2, there was no significant difference in the degree of enjoyment value in each pattern. So, we could say that spoilers do not affect enjoyment if readers complete reading whole of the major comics. It means that even with a spoiler, readers can still enjoy other excellent parts and read to the last. In addition, Figure 3 shows that there was no significant difference in the degree of enjoyment between before and after encountering spoiler information.

Here, we could classify these eight comics into two groups. One is a spoiler-acceptable comic, and the other is a spoiler-unacceptable comic from the previous study [6]. Furthermore, we found a difference in ideas about spoiler information among the experimental subjects. For that reason, we should redesign a method to construct spoiler dataset in comic. We discuss the method to construct spoiler dataset in section 3. Then, we should increase the number of each group's comic for experimental test and analyze them depending on the group in the future work.

In Figure 4, we could see the interaction effect between the spoiler factor and the spoiler timing factor. At first, the result of Pattern 1 showed that spoilers increased the interest in the continuation if the readers who only read the outline encountered the spoiler information. On the other hand, the result of Pattern 2 showed that the interest in continuation value dropped if the readers encountered the spoiler information before reading the final part of the comic. In addition, Table 1 shows that the readers might give up reading the comics if they encountered the spoiler information.

These results showed that it might be possible to motivate people who have never read the target comic to buy it by providing its outline and spoiler information. On the other hand, we also might be able to demotivate people who have already read the target comic except the final part to buy a next volume of the target comic by providing its spoiler information.

3. PRE-ANALYSIS OF SPOILERS IN DATASET

In the future work, we will realize a system which estimates the degree of spoiling of each facing pages in a comic based on the spoiler dataset which we will construct as soon as possible.

In this paper, we preliminarily find out the characteristics of spoiler pages by analyzing the current spoiler dataset which is constructed in the previous work [6]. In the dataset, four the participants selected three spoiler pages and ranked them in eight comics in four genres.

3.1 Characteristics of spoiling pages in a comic

Figure 7 shows the degree of spoiling in each page in each comic. The horizontal axis shows the page number of the final volume in each comic, and the vertical axis indicates the total score of spoiling evaluated by four the experimental participants. First-ranked spoiling page got five points, second-ranked spoiling page got three points, and third-ranked spoiling page got one point. *YuYu Hakusho*(by Yoshihiro Togashi) and *All You Need Is Kill*(by Takeshi Obata and Hiroshi Sakurazaka)are classified into the battle genre, *Ping Pong*(by Taiyo Matsumoto) and *GIANT KILLING*(by Tsujimoto) are classified into sports genre, *Prophecy*(by Tetsuya Tsutsui) and *The Shadow Spirit*(by Natsuhiko Kyogoku and Aki Shimizu) are classified into the mystery genre, and *ReRe Hello*(by Toko Minami) and *Snow White With The Red Hair*(by Sorata Akizuki) are classified into the romance genre.

In the battle, sports and romance genres, the experimental participants selected one or two scenes as a spoiler. On the other hand, in the mystery genre, the participants selected some pages as a spoiler. The reason for this result on the mystery genre would be that there are many highlighting scenes such as scenes about a mystery, mysterious killer, trick, solution of a mystery and so on. Thus, in the mystery genre, each comic has many mysteries and these mysteries drawn more than three pages. Then, the participants could not select all the spoiler pages.

As seen in Figure 7, the participants frequently chose the continuous pages, so it seems that several pages illustrated one spoiler content. Therefore, it is necessary to reconsider how to instruct the participants to select a spoiler in comics.

We found from Figure 7 that the comics can be classified into two types. One type tends to increase the score of spoiling (*YuYu Hakusho*, *All You Need Is Kill*, and *GIANT KILLING, Ping Pong*) and the other type tends to decrease the score of spoiling (*ReRe Hello*, and *Snow White With The Red Hair*). In our previous study, we also classified these comics into two types. One type is comics in which spoiler is acceptable (spoiler-acceptable comics), and the other type is comics in which spoiler is unacceptable (spoiler-unacceptable comics). Note that the spoiler-acceptable comics and the comics that tend to increase the score of spoiling are similar. In addition, the spoiler-unacceptable comics and the comics that tend to decrease the score of spoiling are similar. It seems that there is a relationship between the classification of comics into spoiler acceptable and spoiler unacceptable and the way of gingering up the comic stories.

3.2 Characteristics of content on a spoiler page

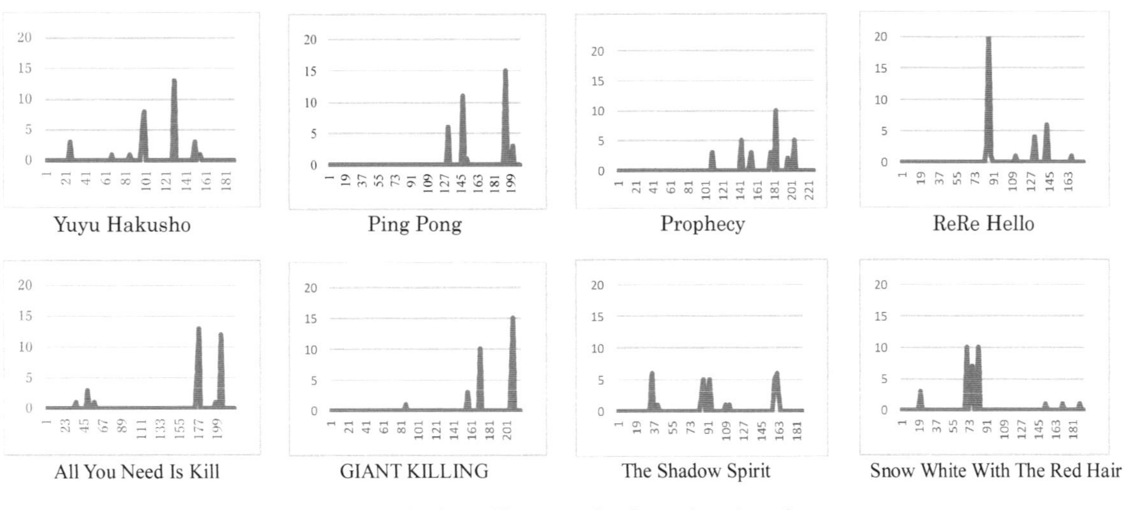

Figure 7: The spoiling score of each page in each comic.

In the battle genre, there were specific terms on the pages chosen as a spoiler that are related to the result of the battle, such as "*I won*" or "*Finished.*" In addition, on the pages close to a spoiler page, bigger frames were used than on other pages.

In the sports genre, in the selected pages, there was character information which clarifies Win-Lose. The difference between the sports genre and the battle genre can be seen in the types of characters selected. In the sports genre, the numeric character is selected as the spoiler. For example, in the *GIANT KILLING* and *Ping-Pong*, there are little numeric characters in near the spoiler page. In addition, there are big frames near the spoiler page.

On the other hand, in the comics of the mystery genre, there are no specific terms selected as a spoiler. However, there are many big frames near the spoiler page. In particular, in *The Shadow Spirit*, the size of terms is small on the first, fourth and fifth-ranked spoiler page. In the *Prophecy*, there are small terms in the second, third, and fourth-ranked spoiler page.

In the romance genre, there are terms "I love you" and "I know" near the spoiler page with a big frame. All of the above suggests that there are specific terms, a specific frame size, and a big frame near a spoiler page.

4. HOW TO CONSTRUCT SPOILER DATASET

From the experimental results and pre-analysis of spoilers, we conclude that the spoiler effect depends on how much the book is read. For example, when he/she is reading volume 1 of a long story, he/she cannot identify spoiler information in volume 20 and may ignore the spoiler. Therefore, to construct spoiler dataset, we must take hold readers' condition to select a spoiler page.

In our previous spoiler dataset, we asked the participants to select three spoiling pages and to rank these pages subjectively. Since there was a possibility that the participants' criteria for judgment were different, we could not choose the real spoiler page in each comic. In addition, it might be very difficult for the participants to reduce the number of the spoiler pages up to three (see Figure 7). In the first place, they could not find any spoiler pages in a comic. In addition, the participants had a conflict to judge what page should be a spoiler.

In order to solve these problems, we must set a rule whether the page is the spoiler page or not and take hold a condition to think about a spoiler.

At first, we define facing pages as a spoiler in a comic. In addition, we will enable the participants (readers) to set three levels of spoiler in each facing pages in a comic. Next, to take hold readers' condition, if facing pages in the next story of a comic reduces the enjoyment of readers who already read up to the most current story in the comic, we define that the facing pages is the spoiler. For example, if a reader already read until the story number N in a comic, the reader evaluates whether each page is a spoiler or not in the story number $N+1$ in the comic.

Here, it is difficult for the participants to judge whether the page is the spoiler or not by thinking about the degree of reducing their enjoyment. Then, we will change the direction as follows; "*Please evaluate the degree of spoiling in each page based on the following basis. Imagine the situation that you show facing pages in the story number N+1 to your friends who have read the comic until the story number N and have not read the story number N+1. If you assume that your friends will have an awful time by reading the page, the page is a spoiler. If you assume that your friends will have no thought by reading the page, the page is not a spoiler.*" By changing the direction like this, we expect that the evaluation becomes easier for the participants than the previous one because it requires thinking about the relationship with others.

Furthermore, in the previous dataset, we asked the participants who have read the whole of the comic to decide spoiling pages. Here, it was difficult for these participants to judge spoiler pages because they knew everything about the story, such as who will die, what will happen, how things go and so on. In the future, we will recruit new participants who have never read the target comic.

5. HOW TO ESTIMATE SPOILER PAGES

The pre-analysis of spoilers in the previous dataset showed several characteristics. However, it is not clear what kind of dimensions there are on the spoiler page.

It is considered that there are many features of spoiler pages, one of them being the frame size. There are small frames in the general scenes and big frames in the exciting scenes. Exciting scenes include scenes crucial to the story, such as battle results or truth about the incident, so these scenes look like spoilers. In other words, it might be possible to identify spoiler pages by their frame size. In the estimate frame method, Tanaka [7] proposed a frame estimating technique utilizing the direction of the concentration gradient. We are considering using this method to estimate the frame size.

Another feature is the terms in the speech bubbles or

cutline. Comics show the results using not only the picture but also the cutline and the characters' remarks. In the previous study [6], the spoiler page feature was the frame with the terms expressing the results of games or battles. So, we will extract the terms from each page and use these terms to estimate spoiler pages. As for the character recognition method, we are considering using Google's Vision API [8]. In addition, we are going not only to use the frame size and the terms but also to extract and use face information and bubble speech.

6. SUMMARY

In this paper, we attempted to clarify the effects of spoilers depending on the reading progress. We revealed that the degree of enjoyment was not changed even if the reader encountered a spoiler. Based on the results of the test on the interest in continuation, the number of the subjects who lost interest after seeing a spoiler was about four times higher than in the case where no spoilers were encountered. So, we conclude that the willingness to buy comics decreases if the reader sees spoilers.

We found many problems in the spoiler dataset. In this paper, we explained about how to construct the spoiler dataset. In the future work, we will construct the new spoiler dataset based on the method. In addition, from the analysis of spoiler pages, we discovered that the features of the spoiling pages were different depending on the genres. However, there are some common features around the spoiling pages, e.g., the size of the frame and the number of terms, and so on. In the future work, we plan to estimate the spoiler pages by using machine learning techniques.

ACKNOWLEDGMENTS

This work was supported in part by JST ACCEL Grant Number JPMJAC1602, Japan.

REFERENCES

[1] J. D. Leavitt and N. J. S Christenfeld; Story Spoilers Don't Spoil Stories. Psychological Science; 22 (9), pp.1152–1154, 2011.

[2] W. H. Levine, M. Betzner and K. S. Autry; The Effect of Spoilers on the Enjoyment of Short Stories. Journal of Discourse Processes; 53 (7), pp.513–531, 2016.

[3] D. Hassoun; Sequential outliers. The role of spoilers? Need for cognition, need for affect, and narrative selection and enjoyment. Psychology of Popular Media Culture; 4 (2), pp.346–358, 2013.

[4] S. Nakamura and K. Tanaka; Temporal Filtering System for Reducing the Risk of Spoiling a User's Enjoyment. 2007 International Conference on Intelligent User Interfaces; (IUI2007), pp.345–348, 2007.

[5] S. Nakamura and T. Komatsu; Study of Information Clouding Methods to Prevent Spoilers of Sports Match. Advanced Visual Interfaces; (AVI 2012), pp.661–664, 2012.

[6] Y. Maki and N. Satoshi; Do Manga Spoilers Spoil Manga? The Sixth Asian Conference on Information Systems; (ACIS 2017), 2017.

[7] T. Tanaka, K. Shoji, F. Toyama, and J. Miyamichi; Layout Analysis of Tree-Structured Scene Frames in Comic Images, Proc. 20th International Joint Conference on Artificial Intelligence; pp.2885–2890, 2007.

[8] Google Cloud Platform; Cloud Vision API; 2018.

ISASE-MAICS 2018

Effects Comparison between English and Chinese Speakers in Learning Japanese Role Words with Comic Scenes

Yoko NISHIHARA*, Kohei MATSUOKA ** and Ryosuke YAMANISHI*

* *College of Information Science and Engineering, Ritsumeikan University, 1-1-1 Nojihigashi, Kusatsu-shi, Shiga 525-8577, Japan*
nisihara@fc.ritsumei.ac.jp, ryama@media.ritsumei.ac.jp
** *Graduate School of Information Science and Engineering, Ritsumeikan University, 1-1-1 Nojihigashi, Kusatsu-shi, Shiga 525-8577, Japan*

Abstract: The role word is one of the expressions for letting people imagine one's character. It is difficult for people to learn the role words from conversation examples written in textbooks of foreign language because few examples are shown to learn the role words on the textbooks. Comic scenes have the examples of conversation in their line texts of character's speech. We have proposed a support system for learning Japanese role words with comic scenes. The system classifies comic scenes according to a role word included in the scenes. System users can learn how to use role words by watching comic scenes and lines. We have verified the efficiency of the system for Chinese speakers whose language culture is similar with Japanese language culture; both of them use Kanji in writing. The good results might be caused by the similarity of language culture. In this paper, we report results of an experiment with English speakers. The results of English speakers were compared with those of Chinese speakers. We verified that the system can support English speakers to learn Japanese role words. We also discuss improvements of our system by referring comments from English speakers. They said that the system should enables the users to learn the role words in enjoying comic stories.
Keywords: *language learning support, comic engineering, role word*

1. INTRODUCTION

With the rapid progress of globalization, many people are learning foreign languages that are different from their native languages. Japanese language was learned by 2,979,820 learners as one of the examples of foreign language in 2006 [1]. The number in 2015 was 3,655,024 [2] that is 1.2 times bigger than that in 2006. Other languages like Chinese and English also have been learned by many foreign learners. Though the machine translation technique is generally used in daily lives, the needs of learning foreign languages are increasing in the world.

The learners are practicing their skills of foreign language. Their skill levels can be evaluated by examinations like TOEIC and TOEFL for English learners. The examinations evaluate their language levels from the four points: reading, writing, listening, and speaking. The learners practice their skills by exercises. For reading skills, they may read many sentences. As writing many sentences, they may improve their own writing skills. Their listening skills would be improved by listening to varied and many speeches. And, they may talk about something with others for their speaking skills. The three kinds of the skill (reading, writing, and listening) of those can be practiced by many learning materials. There are many documents such as news, books, and weblogs that can be used for practicing reading and writing skills. And, a lot of music, news programs, and TV dramas are very useful for practicing listening skill. A plenty of contents in the real world and the Web are available for learners of foreign language.

In contrast, there are few learning materials for practicing speaking skill; the practicing of the speaking skill has been less supported. Speaking skill can not be improved by just speaking sentences one-sided, and that should be improved by talking with other people. That should be the reason why the number of learning materials for the speaking skill is less. Moreover, speaking manner is different from writing manner. If words generally used in speaking are used in writing, the written sentence gives a strange impression to the readers. If words generally used in writing are used in speaking, the speech also might give too formal impression. People need to use proper words according to the situation and their characters: a role word is one of the typical examples of such words.

1.1 Role words for speaking in foreign language

The role word is one of the expressions for letting

people imagine one's character [3]. The characters are one's age, gender, occupation, class, era, looks, appearance, personality, and so on. When a young girl talks with others, she uses proper words for her character. In Japanese language, the young girl may use "ATASHI" (that equals to "I" in English) as a word concerning herself. Japanese people can imagine the character of the speaker from the phrase and the voice of "ATASHI." In another case, a little boy uses usual words that may be different from his mother, and a little girl uses also different words in her talking. Though the number of role words is different among foreign languages, people tend to use proper words and expressions according to their characters. People unconsciously have obtained the knowledge of the relationships between role words and characters in their native languages from their daily talking. However, it is hard to obtain the knowledge in foreign languages because the knowledge has not been clearly described in language textbooks and learning materials.

We insist that learning materials for practicing the speaking skill must include the knowledge of the relationships between role words and characters. The learning materials should give learners the pairs of characters and sentences with role words. Through the survey on comic data, we found that lines of the comic scene are good examples of the pairs. In a comic, many characters appear and act their roles. A story of comic basically flows by conversations of the characters. The comic characters use their proper words for speech in the conversations. Especially, comic contains living words and phrases in the current real world. The existing study has confirmed that the lines and images of anime are useful learning materials for living words and phrases [4]. There are several characters in general comics. Each character uses proper role words to let readers know one's feature. That means characters merely use the same role words. Readers of comic often use lines and character's faces to identify each character. If the readers have trouble in the identification, they may not enjoy reading the comic because the story becomes unclear. Learners might obtain the knowledge of a role word from a few comic characters in a comic. In learning role words, the learners should check many examples of such scene and must find common features of characters using the corresponding role word. Then, it is necessary to use several comics for learning to find common features. Moreover, in order to learn a role word from several comic scenes, the scenes with lines have to be classified into several groups according to the role words. The learners should do these tasks by themselves; it costs a lot of time.

1.2 Learning support system of role words

We have already proposed a support system for learning the role words [5]. The outline is explained in this section though the details of the system are described in Section 2. The system extracts role words in lines of comics, and classifies the scenes into some groups according to the role words. As far as we know, there are few systems to support learning the role words for practicing speaking skills. The system provides the learners with a set of classified comic scenes corresponding to the role word; the learners can learn how to use the role words. This idea can be categorized into the application of comics in comic computing [6].

We did an experiment of the system with Chinese participants. They learned how to use the role words by using the system and took quizzes to answer proper role words. Their scores of quiz were compared with scores by other participants who learned how to use the role words by reading a textbook of role word. The scores by the participants using the system were higher. We verified the efficiency of the system from the results.

Chinese language culture is similar with Japanese language culture; both of them use Kanji in writing sentences. The good results might be caused by the cultural similarity. We need to conduct an experiment of the system with other participants of different language culture.

1.2 Objective of this paper

In this paper, we conducted an experiment of the system with English speakers and report experimental results. The results are compared with the results obtained from Chinese speakers in the previous experiment [5].

2. LEARNING SUPPORT SYSTEM OF ROLE WORDS

Figure 1 shows the outline of the system. The system consists of two parts: a data processing module and an interface.

In the data processing module, the system takes comic data as the input. The comic data is processed through optical character recognition machine to obtain text data of lines of comics. The system extracts role words from the obtained lines. The system classifies scenes into groups according to the extracted role word. The classified scenes are sent to the interface.

On the interface of the system, a list of the role words and classified comic scenes are visualized. The overview

Keywords: language learning support, comic engineering, r...

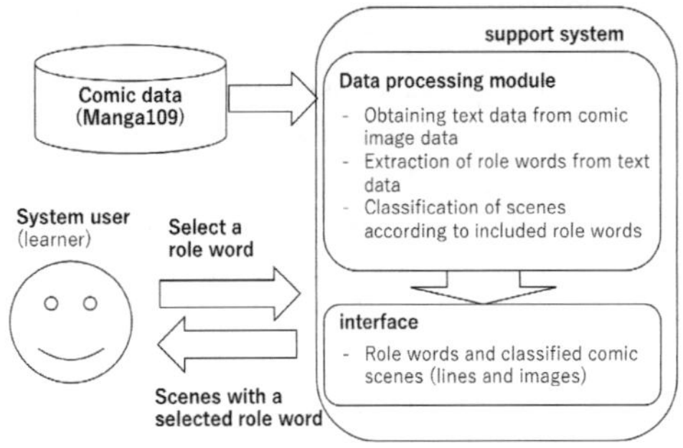

Figure 1: Outline of the learning support system of role words

Figure 2: Example of output from an interface of the system. The right frame shows the scenes including a role word selected by the system user. Each scene is from Manga109.

of the interface is shown in Figure 2. The interface works on a Web browser. The interface has two part: a list of the role words on the left side, and comic scenes including a role word selected by the system user on the right side. As the system user selects a role word, the system shows comic scenes including a selected role word on the interface. The system user checks the images and reads the lines in the scenes to learn how to use the role word. The following sections will explain the procedures of the system from input to output.

2.1 List of Japanese role words

The system uses a list of role words defined in a previous study. Many academic papers and books related to the role words have been published [3,7]. In Japanese language, most of the expressions for role words are personal pronouns and sentence-end expressions.

2.2 Texts of line of comic scene

The system obtains texts of line from comic image data. As the experimental dataset of comics, this study uses a dataset of comics named Manga109 [8]. Manga109 dataset has been compiled by Aizawa and Yamasaki Laboratory of the University of Tokyo. In Manga109, 109 comics made by professional manga artists between 1970s and 2010s are collected.

The system obtains text lines of comic from Manga109 through an optical character recognition machine (OCR machine). The system uses Google Cloud Vision API (https://cloud.google.com/vision/?hl=ja) as the OCR machine which has a function to extract texts in an image. Many languages can be detected by the Vision API, and the language type is also detected automatically. As an image is sent to the API, a recognition result is back to the console as a json format. The proposed system extracts role words from the json files.

2.3 Japanese role word detection and scene classification

Some of the obtained lines include role words. The system extracts the role words from the lines by using a parser (morphological analyzer). In the system, MeCab (http://taku910.github.io/mecab/) and Neologd (https://github.com/neologd/mecab-ipadic-neologd) are used as the parser and the dictionary for parsing, respectively. The parser returns the parsed words and their parts of speech.

After parsing, the system detects role words by collating the list of role words. If a role word is detected in a line text, the system gives the role word as a label for classification to the scene including the line text. Some of the scenes includes several role words. Then, multiple labels are given to such scenes.

The labeled scenes are classified according to the labels of role word. If a scene has multiple labels of role word, the scene is classified into multiple classes.

3. EXPERIMENT

We conducted an experiment for English speakers as participants with our support system. The results were compared with the results of Chinese participants obtained in the previous experiment. We obtained comments from the English participants after the experiment. The comments were considered to improve the system.

The experimental procedures were the same as those in the previous experiment. We set evaluation items in Section 3.3 to evaluate the effect concretely. An experimenter (the second author) coordinated the experiment in the following procedures.

1) The experimenter gathered participants (called English participants).

2) The participants learned how to use the role words by using the system.

3) After learning, the participants took quizzes to

answer proper role words.

4) The experimenter compared quiz scores between English participants and Chinese participants.

The participants were English people who were learning Japanese language. They lived in Vancouver, Canada. The number of the participants was 12. Most of them have obtained scores of JLPT like TOEIC and TOEFL for English. Five of them have obtained N1 that was highest, three of them have obtained N2, and two of them have obtained N3.

3.1 Used role words in the experiment

The used role words were the same as those in the previous experiment. There are 53 labels of role word to learn in the system. The experimenter selected some role words for the experiment because it might be impossible to learn all of the role words in the experiment period. The experimenter counted up the number of scenes for each role word, then sorted the role words according to the number of scenes. Top, middle, and bottom 10 role words were respectively selected for the experiment.

3.2 Quizzes for evaluating participant's level

We evaluated levels of participant with quiz scores. The quiz sheet was almost the same as that in the previous experiment. A role word was removed from the sheet. The quiz sheet had two kinds of quiz. One type of quiz (Quiz 1) was to answer appropriate/inappropriate to each role word in a line text spoken by a comic character. An example of the quiz is shown in Figure 3. The another type (Quiz 2) was to choose the most appropriate role word for the shown scene from a list of three role words. An example of the quiz is shown in Figure 4. For the Quiz 1, we selected two or three role words from each top, middle and bottom category, respectively. Eight role words in all were selected. As same as this, we also selected each two or three role words respectively for Quiz 2. There was no common role words between the two sets of role word. Table 1 shows the role words used for the quizzes.

3.3 Evaluated items

We evaluated the following six items. The items were also the same as those in the previous experiment.

- Average score
- Average score for Quiz 1
- Average score for Quiz 2
- Average scores for top 10 role words
- Average score for middle 10 role words
- Average score for bottom 10 role words

四角の中の役割語が最も適切な役割語かどうか○×で回答してください.

○ ○

○ ×

Figure 3: Example of Quiz 1. ("Platinum Jungle," © Masami Shinohara, Manga109.

空欄に当てはまる最も適切な役割語を選択肢から選んでください.

○ よ

○ じゃ

○ ですわ

Figure 4: Example of Quiz 2. ("Heisei G-men," © Koichi Yamada, Manga109)

Table 2: Role words used in the quizzes

	Quiz 1	Quiz 2
Top 10	さ、ぜ	ね、じゃ
Middle 10	あら、かしら、ぼく	あたし、あんた、わし
Bottom 10	たまえ、拙者、申す	えらい、貴様、わたくし

3.4 Experimental results

Table 2 shows the experimental results. The average total score was 13.9. The average score for Quiz 1 was 7.1. The average score for Quiz 2 was 6.8. The average score for top 10 was 3.5. The average score for middle was 5.2. The average score for bottom was 5.3.

They learned the role words about 40 minutes for the three days, respectively. The average of the 1st day was 42.9 minutes, that of the 2nd day was 43.7 minutes, and that of the 3rd day was 40.3 minutes.

Table 2: Average quiz scores obtained in the experiment

	Average score (Average rate)
Total	13.9 (87%)
Quiz 1	7.1 (86%)
Quiz 2	6.8 (85%)
Top	3.5 (88%)
Middle	5.2 (86%)
Bottom	5.3 (88%)

4. DISCUSSION

This section discusses the results by comparing the results obtained from Chinese participants in the previous experiment. We will discuss the comments from the English participants.

Table 2 shows that the average correct rate was 87%. The rate of Chinese participants was 80%. As both of the rates was almost the same, we verified that our system can support English people in learning how to use Japanese role words.

We considered three role words of low correct rate. Table 3 shows the three role words on the left column. The right column shows three role words of low correct rate by Chinese participants. English participants marked low correct rates for answering "あら, " "さ," and "えらい." The correct rates were 53%, 67%, and 67%, respectively. Chinese participants marked low correct rates for answering "さ," "ぜ," and "申す." The correct rates were 38%, 63%, and 63%, respectively.

Both of the participants marked lower correct rates in answering a quiz of "さ." The word is used to express for multiple roles (countryside people, Okinawa people, Man, and Boy). Therefore, it may be difficult to find the relationships between the word and specific roles. We need to improve the system to learn such role words more efficiently.

Table 3 shows that five of six quizzes were to answer appropriate/inappropriate for a buried role word (Quiz 1). The option quiz shows the list of role words. The participants can answer proper role words by referring the other role words. The Quiz 1 does not show any candidates of role word. The low correct rate for Quiz 1 might be caused by the reason.

Parts of speech in Table 3 were different between English participants and Chinese participants. English participants marked lower correct rates in answering quizzes of adverb role words. "あら" and "えらい" are adverbs mainly used in a sentence though "さ" is a particle mainly used in the end of sentence. In contrast, Chinese participants marked lower correct rates in answering role words mainly used in the end of sentence. "さ" and "ぜ" are particles, and "申す" is a verb. All of them are used mainly in the end of sentence. We need to consider the reason as the future work.

Table 3: Role words of low correct rate

English group	Chinese group
あら (53%: Quiz 1)	さ (38%: Quiz 1)
さ (67%: Quiz 1)	ぜ (63%: Quiz 1)
えらい (67%: Quiz 2)	申す (63%: Quiz 1)

We obtained comments from English participants after the experiment. Most of them commented the improvements of visualization of the system interface. They advised us that the system should enable the users to learn the role words in enjoying reading comic stories. The system uses comic scenes. However, the system does not use comic stories. We would like to improve the point. The improvements will also give benefits in enjoying comic nuances.

5. CONCLUSION

This paper reports experimental results of English speakers with our support system for learning Japanese role words. The system extracts line texts of comic scene and detects role words included in the lines. Then, the system classifies comic scenes into classes according to the included role words. Each of the classes is given a role word as a label of class. We had already done an evaluation experiment of the system with Chinese speakers. The experimental results were good that might be caused by the similarity of language culture with Japanese. In this paper, we did another experiment of the system with English speakers as the participants and compared the results with those in the previous experiment.

In the experiment, we asked English participants to learn how to use role words with the system. They took quizzes to answer proper role words after learning. We compared the quiz scores of English participants with the scores of Chinese participants. They were almost the same. We verified that the system can support English people to learn how to use role words.

English participants marked lower correct rates in answering quizzes of adverb role words. In contrast, Chinese participants marked lower correct rates in answering particles and a verb mainly used in the end of sentence. We need to consider the reason as the future work.

We obtained comments from English participants after the experiment. They said that the system should enable the users to learn the role words in enjoying comic stories. We would like to improve the point and the usability of system interface. We also try to evaluate the difficulty of line texts of comic scene by using our evaluation method [9].

ACKNOWLEDGMENTS

The experiments in this paper were conducted with the great support of Yokoso Japan Association.

REFFERENCES

[1] Japan Foundation, Survey Report on Japanese-Language Education Abroad 2006, 2006.
[2] Japan Foundation, Survey Report on Japanese-Language Education Abroad 2015, 2015.
[3] Satoshi Kinsui, Yakuwarigo to Nihongo Kyoiku (in japanese), Japanese Education, vol. 150, pp. 34–41, 2011.
[4] Junjie Shan, Yoko Nishihara, Ryosuke Yamanishi, and Junichi Fukumoto, Analysis of Dialogues Difficulty in Anime Comparing with JLPT Listening Tests, in 21st International Conference on Knowledge-Based and Intelligent Information and Engineering Systems, vol. 112, pp. 345–352, 2017.
[5] Yoko Nishihara, Kohei Matsuoka, and Ryosuke Yamanishi, Learning Support System of Role Words by Using Classified Lines of Comic Scene, in the 2018 IAENG International Conference on Data Mining and Applications, 2018.
[6] Ryosuke Yamanishi and Mitsunori Matsushita, Comic Computing: a Conceptual Framework for Decomposition and Utilization of Comic Contents, in The 6th Asian Conference on Information Systems, 2017.
[7] Satoshi Kinsui, Virtual Nihongo Yakuwarigo no Nazo (in Japanese). Iwanami Syoten, 2003.
[8] Azuma Fujimoto, Toru Ogawa, Kazuyoshi Yamamoto, Yusuke Matsui, Toshihiko Yamasaki, and Kiyoharu Aizawa, Manga109 Dataset and Creation of Metadata, in International Conference on Pattern Recognition workshop MANPU (The First International Workshop on coMics ANalysis, Processing and Understanding), 2016.
[9] Junjie Shan, Yoko Nishihara, Ryosuke Yamanishi, and Junichi Fukumoto, Analysis of Japanese Animation Dialogue Level using Japanese Expressions, in the fifth Asian Conference on Information Systems, 2016, pp. 322–325.

ISASE-MAICS 2018

Supporting Gift Selection to Encourage Consideration of Gift-Receivers from Various Perspectives

Saki NISHINO*, Takafumi OHSUGI ** and Mitsunori MATSUSHITA *

** Faculty of Informatics, Kansai University, 2-1-1 Ryozenji, Takatsuki, Ohsaka 569-1095, Japan*
{k241072,t080164}@kansai-u.ac.jp
*** Graduate School of Informatics, Kansai University, 2-1-1 Ryozenji, Takatsuki, Ohsaka 569-1095, Japan*
k715328@kansai-u.ac.jp

Abstract: The purpose of this research is to encourage consideration of gift-receivers in the gift selection process from various perspectives. People often purchase gifts for their loved ones, such as partners and friends. There are various e-commerce websites that recommend gifts for loved ones; however, selecting an appropriate gift is difficult because these recommendations do not consider gift-receivers' hobbies and preferences. Entering all their hobbies and preferences into the system in advance will solve this problem, but it takes time and effort. To solve this problem, we proposed a system that encourages consideration of gift-receivers by themselves. To achieve this, the proposed system provides questions about the gift-receiver and facilitates deeper consideration in gift selection. Using this proposed system, we conducted an experiment to observe the participants' gift selection process. As a result, we confirmed that the system increases people's consideration of gift-receivers.
Keywords: *Gift selection process, Various perspective, Consideration of gift-receiver, Questions about the gift-receiver*

1. INTRODUCTION

With the spread of the Internet in recent years, many shopping websites, such as Amazon and Rakuten Market, have arisen online. Users can select and buy various products on such websites, and the number of users is increasing every year. The range of product selection has also expanded. However, it is not easy for the website to choose the desired product from the wide variety of available products. The technique of recommending products that match a user's preferences is one way of solving this problem. For example, a collaborative filtering method has been proposed [1] that guesses each user's preferences from past purchase data and recommends products that match the user's preferences. As another example, when a user chooses a desired item on Amazon, he/she receives product recommendations such as "people who bought this product also bought the following products" [2]. Such recommendations support an individual's purchasing behavior.

Such purchase behavior happens not only when users buy products for themselves, but also when they select gifts for others. Various websites offer products suitable as gifts, including COCOMO (https://cocomo.to/) and GIFT DINOS (https://www.dinos.co.jp/gift/). On these websites, when searching for gifts, users can select the age and event (e.g., birthday) of the person they are buying a gift for, and products that correspond to each selection are recommended. Many websites also provide information on selecting gifts based on questionnaires. For example, "Recommended gifts for 20 to 30-year-old people" and "Birthday gifts list." Since the Internet is easy to use, many users use such websites for selecting gifts. Many websites provide such gift recommendations. However, the recommendations made by these gift websites do not consider gift-receivers' hobbies and preferences. For this reason, the recommended products are not necessarily suitable. It is not always possible for a person giving a gift (hereinafter referred to as "gift-sender") to find a satisfying gift item on such websites. Therefore, in this research, we focus on a system that can help increase consideration of gift-receivers during the gift selection process. Unlike the conventional gift recommendation system, in the proposed system in this study, users think about gift-receivers from various perspectives when choosing gifts. Through this system, we will help gift-senders find a satisfying gift.

2. RELATED STUDIES

The factors related to a user's purchasing decision when buying products as gifts for other people are different than those when buying products for himself/herself [3,4]. Clarke et al. have shown that people who buy gifts consider more products and visit more stores compared to those who buy products for themselves [3].

Kudo et al. proposed a simple product recommendation system [5]. This system uses a rough set theory. In this system, rules for a recommendation method are first created from users' queries. Next, based on that, the system estimates the implicit condition of the products that users want to search and then recommends the products.

Sarwar et al. explored item-based collaborative filtering techniques [6]. In particular, they analyzed an item-based recommendation generation algorithm. They examined various ways to measure the similarity between different items, for example, correlation between items and cosine similarity between the vectors of items. Further, they examined ways to recommend products from item similarity, for example, a weighted sum or regression model.

In this research, we do not purchase products themselves but support the purchase of products as gifts for others. We focus on the gift selection process.

By urging gift-senders to consider gift-receivers (e.g., preferences, favorites, belongings), we aim to help gift-senders select a convincing gift item. Our purpose is to develop a system that encourages gift-senders to increase their consideration of gift-receivers, not a system that recommends traditional products.

3. PROPOSED METHOD

3.1 Methods to increase consideration of gift-receivers

It is difficult for a gift-sender to consider gift-receivers from various perspectives without the opportunity to consider the opponent. In this paper, to encourage gift-senders to increase their consideration of gift-receivers, the proposed system uses a method of asking questions about gift-receivers. We aim to make gift-senders select gifts considering the gift-receiver based on responses triggered by the questions. We conducted a preliminary experiment aimed at setting questions to make the user think about the gift-receiver. Two university students were selected as experiment participants. They decided to whom to send gifts and selected gifts. The selection process was observed using a think-aloud protocol. This is a way for participants to utter what they think or think during the experiment as much as possible. For example, they said the following when choosing: "What kind of wallet did she use?" and "If the wallet was not damaged, she used the same thing all the time." In addition, their thoughts concerned what the gift-receiver wears frequently or which of the gift-receivers belongings were damaged. In this, it seems that they thought about the gift-receiver.

Based on such utterances, we selected 18 questions about gift-receivers. For example, "gift-receiver's environment," "gift-receiver's hobby," "gift-receiver's favorite color," and "consideration of gift-receiver (metal allergy, dislike of smells, etc.)."

3.2 Overview of the proposed system

In the proposed system, the gift-sender generates keywords associated with the gift-receiver by answering questions presented by the system, which then conducts a product search based on keywords. An example of the assumed interaction is shown below, which shows how college students conducted a product search to find gifts for friends.

One participant thought about gifting her friend cosmetics, considering the friend's likes. She searched for cosmetics and set it as an option. Looking at the question column, she considered the question "what has the gift-receiver bought recently?" As a result, she recalled that the friend recently purchased new cosmetics, and hence removed cosmetics from the options. She considered which product might be ideal. Her gaze stopped at the question "what item is damaged among the gift-receiver's belongings, and what item should be replaced?" She reconsidered the gift. She remembered that the gift-receiver's pass holder was damaged. When searching for a pass holder, she found one illustrated with the friend's favorite character. Through the above actions, she decided to choose the pass holder.

As mentioned above, asking such questions promotes the consideration of gift-receivers, thereby widening the range of gift items. Based on this, we proposed a system using the questions shown in section 3.1.

The proposed system can be used on a webpage, and is implemented with HTML and JavaScript. In this paper, we used the Rakuten product search API (version: 2017-07-06) of the Rakuten web service developed by Rakuten Co., Ltd. The interface of the proposed system is shown in Figure 1. Answers are entered using a filling formula, and the questions are always presented from the time of system startup (see Fig. 1-A). Questions are fixed, not changing for each user. This is to allow gift-sender to consider gift-receiver from various perspectives. A question can be answered arbitrarily while a user is selecting a gift. By inputting a search keyword with a question as a trigger (see Fig. 1-B), a product corresponding to that keyword is displayed (see Fig. 1-C).

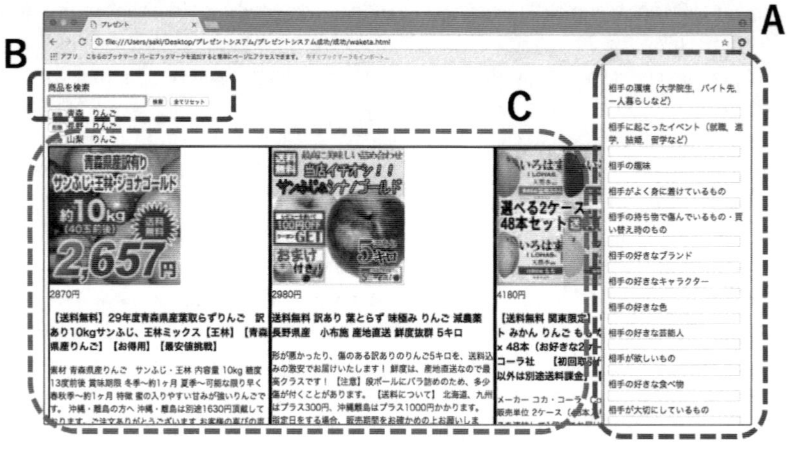

Figure 1: Proposed system

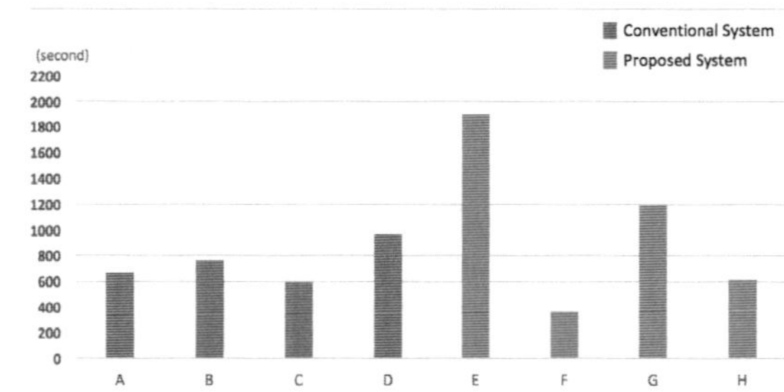

Figure 2: Search time

The questions are presented in the question column.

4. EXPERIMENT

4.1 Outline of experiment

In this experiment, we focused on the gift selection process. This experiment aimed to verify whether the gift-sender will be encouraged to consider the gift-receiver using the proposed system. A system with only a product search function, excluding the question column from the proposed system, was used to represent a conventional system and compared with the proposed system. Four experiment participants were selected for each the conventional system and the proposed system. For the conventional system, four college students (one male, three females) from the information systems department were selected. For the proposed system, four college students (two males, two females) from the same department, but who did not participate in the experiment using the conventional system, were selected. Experiment participants made their gift choices using the system assigned to each group. The following three experimental conditions were explained to the experiment participants: (1) The experiment participant decides a gift-receiver, but as an exception, he/she must avoid choosing a person who he/she has already decided what to give or for whom he/she has already decided on a category; (2) When choosing a gift, the experiment participant must utter what he/she thinks as much as possible; and (3) When a gift is determined, the experiment is terminated. We first communicated the experiment contents to the participants and explained how to use the system. Next, to help them get used to the system, experiment participants were directed to enter specified search keywords and conduct a product search. When explaining the proposed system, we only told them that they can fill in the question column of the system. We did not encourage use of the question column. After that, the first participant decided on a gift-receiver and started the experiment. The experimenter waited next to the participants in order to respond immediately to any remarks. During the experiment, we asked the question "Why did you search by that word?" This was to clarify their reason for searching when participants selected a gift. After obtaining the participants' consent, we recorded the search screen and their utterances during the experiment.

4.2 Search time and questionnaire result

The average time for gift selection using the conventional system was 12 minutes 29 seconds. On the other hand, the average time for gift selection using the proposed system was 17 minutes 00 seconds. Figure 2 shows the time taken by experimental participants A to D using the conventional system, and by participants E to H

Table 1: Table caption

Conventional system		Proposed system	
Participant	Number	Participant	Number
A	6	E	36
B	8	F	1
C	6	G	39
D	5	H	18
Average	6.3	Average	23.5

using the proposed system. The questionnaire results of participants A, B, C, and D, who used the conventional system, are as follows. Participant A made the final decision by considering the gift-receiver's looks and price of the gift. Participant B selected items based on price, functionality, novelty, and looks. Participant C made a decision based on price, the gift-receiver's preferences, and looks. Participant D selected products based on whether the gift will be easy to use for the gift-receiver. The questionnaire results for participants E, F, G, and H, who used the proposed system, are as follows: Participant E made product decisions based on whether the product is a consumable item, the thoughts of the gift-receiver (filial piety), and the gift-receiver's preferences. Participant F selected the product considering the season, the their own preferences, and price. Participant G made the final decision based on the feelings of the gift-receiver and what he/she wears. Participant H made product decisions considering practicality and the gift-receiver's feelings.

5. DISCUSSION

5.1 Search time

The average time taken by the experiment participants' using the proposed system was longer than that taken by those using the conventional system. However, there was no significant difference between the two groups, as there were differences in the time to choose for each gift-sender. After the experiment, we formed a question "Do you usually take time when you choose a gift?" Regarding the participants who replied that the time spent choosing a gift is short, it was observed that they promptly determined the gift item in the experiment.

Moreover, looking at time taken to choose a gift by participants E and F, who used the proposed system, it can be seen that there is difference of 25 minutes between the two. From their utterances, we observed that participant E looked at all the questions in the proposed system and answered all of them. On the other hand, participant F did not use the question column to make the product decision. This shows that using the question column affects the time taken to choose a gift.

5.2 Analysis of search process

First, in order to analyze the search process, we generated text from speech data obtained from the experiment process. Next, we divided the recorded utterances by sentence, giving them a label and briefly describing the contents, and then grouping them into categories based on similar labels. In the conventional system and the proposed system, we categorized utterances into "categories including consideration of gift-receivers," such as gift-receiver's hobby and gift-receiver's favorite celebrities, etc. We also categorized utterances into "categories not including consideration of gift-receivers," such as product discovery and evaluation of products. This was to make it easier to examine whether the search process promoted consideration of gift-receivers. In the conventional system, 12 categories including consideration of the gift-receiver were generated.

On the other hand, 17 categories were generated in the proposed system. Both systems had nine common categories. They are "Gift-receiver's situation," "Gift-receiver's event (e.g., birthday, marriage)," "Gift-receiver's hobby," "Gift-receiver's clothes," "Gift-receiver's episode (e.g., filial piety)," "Gift-receiver's favorite color," "Gift-receiver's favorite entertainer," "Gift-receiver's taste," and "Recollection of what you bought before." This shows that both systems encouraged consideration of the gift-receiver. However, the remaining categories were obtained only when those obtained using the proposed system were the same as those obtained from the questions. Based on their utterances, three out of four people who used the proposed system confirmed only that they read all the questions aloud and confirmed that the product was searched for using that question as a trigger. Therefore, these categories are considered to have been obtained by presenting questions. In addition, by presenting questions based on the number of categories, it can be suggested that the proposed system, using questions, increases consideration of gift-receivers from various perspectives compared to the conventional system.

5.3 Number of considering points for gift-receivers

We measured the number of participants' utterances in which the gift-receiver was considered for each divided sentence at the time of category generation. This was done to measure the number of utterances that considered gift-receivers by each participant for both systems. The results are shown in Table 1. The average number of such utterances by the participants using the conventional system was 6.3, and the average number of such utterances by participants using the proposed system was 23.5. Two of the experiment participants using the proposed system made more than 30 utterances that considered the gift-receiver.

5.4 Questionnaire results

Three out of four experiment participants in the conventional system and all four in the proposed system made utterances (e.g., preference of the gift-receiver and ease of use) that considered the gift-receiver. However, utterances (e.g., prices and appearances of products) that did not consider the gift-receiver were obtained from three out of four participants in the conventional system and two out of four in the proposed system. This indicates that in both systems, gifts were selected by considering gift-receivers. Furthermore, participants did not select other possible items because they considered gift-receivers using both systems. This is the same as the decisive factor for the final gift. When selecting a gift, it is necessary for the gift-sender to consider the gift-receiver (e.g., preferences, favorites, belongings).

5.5 Overall discussing

In this paper, we conducted experiments aimed at promoting consideration of gift-receivers when selecting gifts by presenting questions about gift-receivers. The questionnaire results showed that experiment participants considered the gift-receiver using both systems. By observing the amount of consideration given to the gift-receiver in the search process, many categories, including consideration of the gift-receiver, were obtained using the proposed system. In addition, more utterances were observed in the proposed system than in the conventional system. From these results, it seems that presenting questions about gift-receivers could encourage consideration of gift-receivers from various perspectives. Further research should examine the question items.

6. CONCLUSION

In this paper, we aimed to have gift-senders select a satisfying gift by encouraging their consideration of gift-receivers in the gift selection process. We conducted an experiment aimed at promoting consideration of gift-receivers using the proposed system that presented questions about gift-receivers. After that, we analyzed the utterances of participants. It was found that the proposed system helped them consider the gift-receiver (e.g., preferences, favorites, belongings) from various perspectives. The study results also confirmed that the proposed system led to more utterances that considered gift-receivers. In future studies, we will consider adding more questions and improving the present question items to encourage gift-senders to consider the preferences of gift-receivers from various perspectives.

ACKNOWLEDGMENTS

A part of this work was supported by JSPS KAKENHI Grant Number 15H02780.

REFFERENCES

[1] Breese, J. S., Heckerman, D., and Kadie, C. Empirical Analysis of Predictive Algorithms for Collaborative Filtering, Proceedings of the 14th Annual Conference on Uncertainty in Artificial Intelligence, pp. 43–52 (1998).

[2] Linden, G., Smith, B., and York, J. Amazon.com Recommendations: item-to-item Collaborative Filtering, IEEE Internet computing, Vol. 7, No. 1, pp. 76–80 (2003).

[3] Clarke, K. and Belk, R.W. The Effects of Product Involvement and Task Definition on Anticipated Consumer Effort, Advances in Consumer Research, Vol. 6, pp. 313-318 (1979).

[4] Scammon, D. E., Shaw, R. T., and Bamossy, G. Is a Gift Always a Gift? An Investigation of Flower Purchasing Behavior across Situations, Association for Consumer Research, Vol. 9, pp. 531-536 (1982).

[5] Y. Kudo, S. Amano, T. Seino, and T. Murai. A Simple Recommendation System Based on Rough Set Theory, Kansei Engineering International, Vol. 6, No. 3, pp. 19-24 (2006).

[6] B, Sarwar., G, Karypis., J, Konstan., and J, Riedl. Item-Based Collaborative Filtering Recommendation Algorithms, Proceedings of the 10th International Conference on World Wide Web, pp. 285-295 (2001).

ISASE-MAICS 2018

A Fundamental Study Evaluating Child Resistant Containers for Pharmaceutical Products

– Report on Container-Opening and Impression-Evaluation Experiments Using the New Easy Seal Open Pack (ESOP) Type of Pill Container –

Naoshige AKITA*, Yoshitsugu MORITA* and Hisao SHIIZUKA**

*Kyushu University, 4-9-1 Shiobaru Minami-ku Fukuoka 815-8540, Japan
**Fuzzy Logic Systems Institute, 680-41, Kawatsu Iizuka-shi Fukuoka 820-0067, Japan
**Shiizuka Kansei Engineering Laboratory, Co., Ltd., 4-10-5 Sendagaya Shibuya-ku Tokyo 151-0051, Japan

Abstract: Cases of accidental ingestion of pharmaceutical products by children are increasing and have become a serious social concern. In this study, we investigated a new type of soft plastic, child resistant pill container, called ESOP (easy seal open package). We first conducted a container-opening experiment on children aged 12 to 36 months, and were able to identify a relative strength of the container and a point for improvement. Next, using the improved ESOP and an existing PTP (press through package), we performed an impression-evaluation experiment regarding the safety of the respective drug container, in the opinion of guardians with 24- to 36-month-old children. By investigating the guardians' satisfaction level and degree of ascribed importance, we determined their impression of the safety of the two containers, and conclude that it is necessary to improve the items of which the degree of ascribed importance was high and the satisfaction level low.
Keywords: *Design Evaluation, Child Resistant Pill Containers, User Satisfaction*

1. INTRODUCTION

In recent years, cases of accidental ingestion of pharmaceutical products by children are increasing and have become a serious social concern. From January to December, 2012, the Japan Poison Information Center collected data regarding the accidental ingestion of pharmaceutical products by children under 5 years of age. Over this period, the Consumer Safety Investigation Commission analyzed 764 cases of children accidentally swallowing pharmaceutical products, and found that 549, or 71.9% of the total, involved children of 1 to 2 years of age. Of the products ingested, 871 were individual pills and 442 were tablets, which accounted for 50.7% of the total cases. With regard to the individual pill containers, the structure of the containers of 558 pills was confirmed, and 133 (15.3%) of the 871 total pills ingested were stored in PTPs (press through packages), the most common type [1].

In such circumstances, the development and standardization of child resistant (CR) pill containers, which are difficult for children but easy for others to open, are required in order to prevent children from accidentally swallowing pharmaceutical products [2]. Currently, new types of CR pill containers are under development by several pharmaceutical companies. Among them, a 'hard-push' type PTP uses a stronger sealing material, requiring greater force to open; a 'peel-off' type requires peeling off an aluminum seal; a 'peel & push' type requires both peeling off a seal and pushing out the pill, an unusually intricate combination for children; and a 'slide-pack' type requires that the holes of the PTP must be slid into alignment with those of a cardboard or plastic case. In addition to these, a soft plastic container called 'ESOP (Easy Seal Open Pack)' (Figure 1) has been designed to be very difficult for children to open. To remove a tablet from the ESOP, a flap must first be lifted, and the tablet squeezed upwards (as one would squeeze a pea from a pod), until it breaks a weak plastic seal, allowing the tablet to be removed [3].

As noted, a variety of CR pill containers have been developed in Japan; however, no appropriate method or standards have been established to evaluate their child resistant features, making it difficult to determine the quality of these products.

Some studies have conducted pill container-opening experiments with children, based on the respective standards of the United States and Europe. However, the U.S. standards (16CFR1700) and European standards (EN14375) differ for non-resealable containers. For example, in such experiments, children are permitted

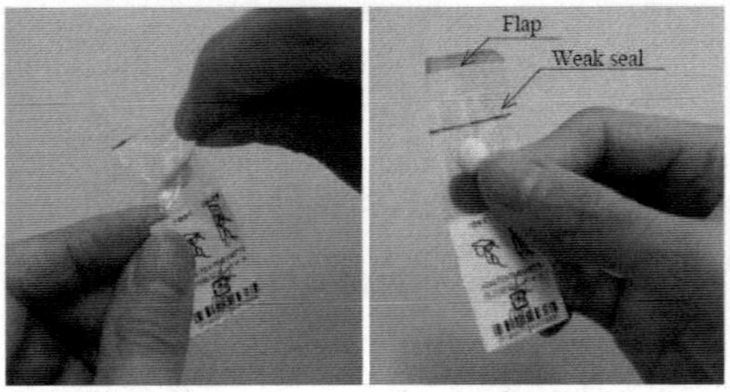

(1) Lifting the flap

(2) Squeezing the tablet past the weak seal

(3) Removing the tablet from the container

Figure 1: How to open an ESOP

to use their teeth whenever they desire, but some children do not recognize this. In such cases, after five minutes, according to the U.S. (but not European) standards, observers may suggest that such children try using their teeth. Thus, we must determine which elements of these respective standards should apply in Japan.

With respect to container opening with the teeth, the Safety Committee of the Federation of Pharmaceutical Manufacturers' Associations of Japan submitted a written opinion regarding the prevention of accidental ingestion of pharmaceutical products by children to the Ministry of Health, Labour and Welfare of Japan, in May 2015. The document notes many cases of children accidental ingesting pharmaceutical products by biting the container, and argues that merely changing the PTP sealing material would not prevent such incidents, and thus would be an inadequate safety measure. Thus, we must continue to experimentally investigate container opening with the teeth [4].

Further, we must consider the time restrictions in such experiments. Accidental pharmaceutical ingestion by children may well take more than merely 5 or 10 minutes.

In light of the foregoing, in this study, we conducted a container-opening experiment with children, observing their behavior over time, using an ESOP under development by Morimoto Pharma Co., Ltd. The aim was to develop guidelines for the improvement of ESOP quality by examining the relationship between the experimental results and the actual actions taken by children. In addition, using a conventional PTP and an improved ESOP, we conducted an impression-evaluation experiment involving the children's guardians, regarding the safety of the respective pill containers, and investigated the evaluation method.

2. CONTAINER-OPENING EXPERIMENT

2.1 Purpose and method

The purpose of the experiment was to evaluate children's difficulty in opening an ESOP containing a placebo tablet with no medical ingredients. The experiment was conducted from November 22 to December 15, 2016, and involved 15 12- to 36-month-old children. Reproducing the ambience of a typical living room, we observed the children's behavior when handling the pill container, and whether they were able to open the container.

The container used in the experiment has been under development by Morimoto Pharma Co., Ltd., a collaborator with our laboratory in exploring child resistant pharmaceutical technology. As aforementioned, the ESOP container requires a sequence of two different actions in order to open and remove the tablet.

The experimental procedure was as follows.

(1) Explain to the guardian the purpose and procedure of the experiment, countermeasures against risk and misfortune, and measures in case of an emergency; and obtain his/her consent regarding the details.

(2) Hand an ESOP containing a tablet to the child, and invite him/her to try to open the container to remove the tablet. Do not explain how to open the ESOP at this time. Staff members observe his/her behavior while recording, with two video cameras, how he/she handles the container. The experiment should be continued until the child opens the container or gives up.

(3) The staff and guardian show the child how to open the ESOP. Open the container slowly in front of the child, and then encourage the child to open it themselves, while continuing to observe and record his/her behavior.

(4) Review the child's behavior in the recorded video, including whether he/she was able to open the container. Specifically, first determine the overall pattern of their actions. Next, determine which action the child took over each time period. Finally, determine the respective actions taken by the child in each of the three stages ('lifting the flap', 'breaking the weak seal', and 'removing the tablet'), and whether he/she was finally able to open the container.

2.2 Experimental results

Table 1 summarizes the different actions taken by subjects, and Table 2 the respective actions for the three stages of tablet removal. The symbol "×" in Table 2 indicates that the subject was not able to perform the task, and "○" indicates that the subject was able to perform the task by taking the action written in the column.

Subjects 3 (13 months old) and 5 (16 months old) pulled at the container with their teeth, but were unable to open it (Figure 2).

Table 1: Actions taken by children (subjects)

Subject	Age in months	Gender	Holding	Feeling with fingers	Biting	Grasping	Twisting	Bending	Putting fingers in the package	Trying to break the package	Pulling the mouth of the package	Pulling the entire package	Pulling the weak seal part with the hand	Pulling the upper part	Pushing	Pressing the tablet on the desk	Shaking	Hitting	Throwing	Fingering the tablet
1	12	M	•																	
2	12	M																		
3	13	F	•		•							•								
4	15	F	•																	
5	16	M	•	•	•		•				•	•								
6	17	F	•								•	•			•					
7	17	M	•	•							•									
8	19	M	•	•																
9	20	M	•	•					•		•									
10	23	F	•	•								•			•					
11	24	F	•	•					•		•		•							
12	26	F	•									•			•					•
13	27	F	•	•					•		•	•	•							
14	32	F	•	•			•			•	•		•	•	•	•	•			•
15	35	F	•	•						•	•		•		•					•

•: Indicates that the subject took the action.
M: male child, F: female child

In addition, it was found that even those who were able to unfold the flap were unable to squeeze the tablet through the weak seal. Thus, it appeared that it was generally difficult for children to open the container in the way determined by the manufacturer.

Figure 2: Children attempting (and failing) to open the ESOP by pulling on it with their teeth

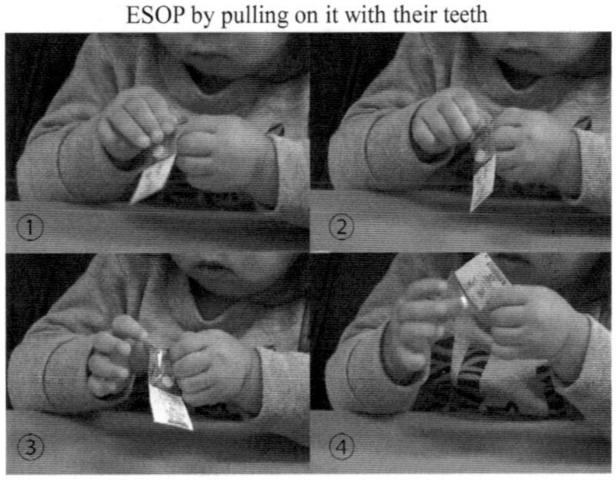

Figure 3: A child opening the ESOP (before elimination of the 3-mm extension)

Table 2: Results of actions taken by children (subjects) in the three container-opening stages

Subject	Age in months	Gender	(1) Lifting the flap	(2) Breaking the weak seal	(3) Removing the tablet
1	12	M	×	-	-
2	12	M	×	-	-
3	13	F	× Lifting the flap by hand while	-	-
4	15	F	×	-	-
5	16	M	○ Lifting the flap with hands × Lifting the flap by hand while	× Pulling at the tablet -	- -
6	17	F	○ Lifting the flap with hands	× Pulling at the weakly sealed part	-
7	17	M	× Holding the flap with hands	-	-
8	19	M	○ Lifting the flap with hands	-	-
9	20	M	×	-	-
10	23	F	× Pushing, pulling, etc., the flap	-	-
11	24	F	○ Lifting the flap with hands	○ Putting a finger in the weak seal	○ Putting a finger in the package
12	26	F	× Pushing, holding, etc., the flap	-	-
13	27	F	○ Lifting the flap with hands	○ Pinching and pulling the weak seal with hands	○ Putting a finger in the package
14	32	F	○ Lifting the flap with hands	×	×
15	35	F	○ Lifting the flap with hands ○ Lifting the flap with hands ○ Lifting the flap with hands	× Unable to push out the tablet ○ Pinching and pulling the weak seal part with hands ○ Pinching and pulling the weak sealed part with hands	- ○ Squeezing out the tablet with hands ○ Putting a finger in the package

M: male child, F: female child

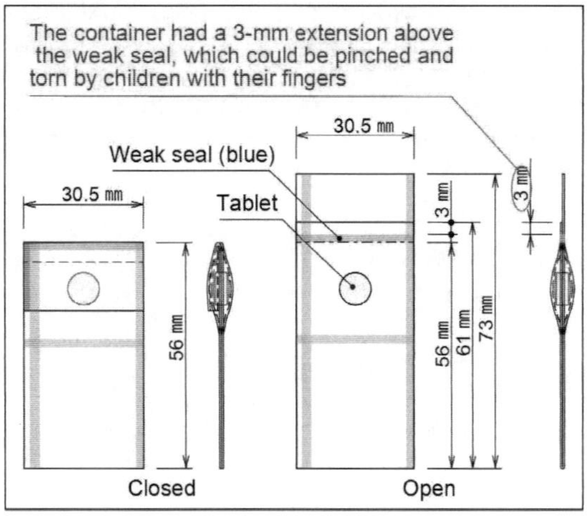

Figure 4: Schematic of the ESOP (before elimination of the 3-mm extension)

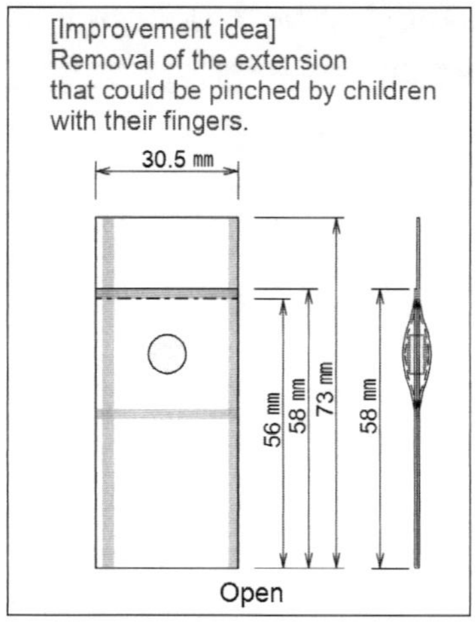

Figure 5: An example of the improved ESOP (without 3-mm extension)

However, Subjects 11, 13, and 15 picked, pulled, or poked with their fingers the roughly 3-mm soft plastic extension above the weak seal; and as a result, were able to break the seal and open the ESOP. Figure 3 shows Subject 11 opening the container in this manner.

2.3 Discussion and means of improvement

In the case of conventional PTP containers, some children have accidentally swallowed a tablet by biting the container. In this experiment, children could not open the ESOP in this manner, suggesting that ESOPs are difficult-to-open for those at the age when children tend to put things in their mouth. However, the subject number in the experiment was small, and thus further experimentation is necessary in order to verify this.

As noted, the samples in this experiment had a 3-mm extension above the weak seal, which could be pinched with the fingers; and in some cases, children of 24 months or older noticed this and opened the container by pulling at this extension (Figure 4). Thus, eliminating this extension should significantly reduce the risk of an ESOP being opened by children up to 3 years old (Figure 5).

3. IMPRESSION-EVALUATION EXPERIMENT USING AN IMPROVED ESOP

3.1 Purpose and method of the experiment

The purpose of this experiment was to evaluate guardian impressions regarding the safety of the improved ESOP (without extension) versus a conventional PTP(Figure 6). The subjects were 15 guardians of children aged 24 to 36 months, and the experiment was conducted after they had observed how their children handled an ESOP.

3.2 A method for applying customer satisfaction analysis in the evaluation of pill container safety

Customer satisfaction (CS) indicates, in general, the degree of satisfaction that people feel when they are purchasing a product. Based on the assumption that people purchase a product when they feel satisfied with the product, companies sometimes define evaluation items and evaluate customers' satisfaction level, using the results as material for determining product development policy.

The degree of importance ascribed to these evaluation items by customers can be determined based on the simple correlation coefficient between the value for each evaluation item and the overall evaluation. This degree of importance, then, reflects the relation between customers' satisfaction with individual items and their overall evaluation [5] [6] [7].

In this study, we investigated guardian impressions of the safety of the respective pill containers, by evaluating their satisfaction level and degree of ascribed importance in each case.

3.3 Selection of evaluation items

We conducted an interview survey of three pharmacists, and one writer for the medical publication, NPO Kodomo-to-kusuri, and based on the results, determined the following seven evaluation items, which were considered to be important for children's safety: 1) Difficulty in removing the tablet from its container, 2) Difficulty in understanding how to remove the tablet from its container, 3) Difficulty in removing the tablet by biting the container, 4) Difficulty in distinguishing the pill container from a candy container, 5) Risk of being injured

Table 3: Results of actions taken by children (subjects) in the three container-opening stages (PTP)

	Evaluation items	Subject														
		1	2	3	4	5	6	7	8	9	10	11	12	13	14	15
a	Difficulty in removing the tablet from the container	2	5	7	3	5	5	2	2	7	7	2	2	7	2	2
b	Difficulty in understanding how to remove the tablet from the container	2	5	7	2	3	4	2	5	6	7	2	2	4	1	1
c	Difficulty in removing the tablet by biting the container	1	4	6	3	2	2	4	2	4	6	1	1	7	4	4
d	Difficulty in distinguishing the pill container from a candy container	2	4	6	1	1	2	1	1	2	3	1	3	7	6	6
e	Risk of being injured when handling the container	2	5	6	2	2	2	1	1	2	2	1	1	2	2	2
f	Size of the container (for preventing a child from putting it in the mouth)	1	4	7	6	2	2	3	7	3	4	4	5	7	6	6
g	Hardness of the container material (in case it is put in the child's mouth)	1	3	6	2	1	2	1	1	1	1	1	1	7	1	1
	Overall evaluation	1	4	7	3	4	2	1	1	4	5	1	2	6	3	3

Table 4: Results of actions taken by children (subjects) in the three container-opening stages (ESOP)

	Evaluation items	Subject														
		1	2	3	4	5	6	7	8	9	10	11	12	13	14	15
a'	Difficulty in removing the tablet from the container	6	7	7	6	3	6	6	7	7	7	6	6	6	5	6
b'	Difficulty in understanding how to remove the tablet from the container	6	7	7	6	2	6	7	7	7	7	6	7	7	6	7
c'	Difficulty in removing the tablet by biting the container	5	6	7	6	2	6	6	7	4	7	5	7	7	5	2
d'	Difficulty in distinguishing the pill container from a candy container	6	7	7	6	6	4	4	6	2	3	4	3	7	6	6
e'	Risk of being injured when handling the container	5	7	7	6	6	5	7	7	6	7	3	4	7	7	7
f'	Size of the container (for preventing a child from putting it in the mouth)	4	7	7	2	6	3	4	6	3	4	4	5	5	7	7
g'	Hardness of the container material (in case it is put in the child's mouth)	4	7	7	7	5	5	7	6	2	6	2	4	7	7	7
	Overall evaluation	6	7	7	6	4	5	6	6	4	6	5	6	6	5	6

Table 5: Results of analysis

	Evaluation items	PTP		ESOP (after improvement)	
		Degree of ascribed importance	Satisfaction level	Degree of ascribed importance	Satisfaction level
a	Difficulty in removing the tablet from the container	0.84	0.27	0.56	0.87
b	Difficulty in understanding how to remove the tablet from the container	0.60	0.20	0.59	0.93
c	Difficulty in removing the tablet by biting the container	0.81	0.20	0.58	0.60
d	Difficulty in distinguishing the pill container from a candy container	0.64	0.27	0.47	0.60
e	Risk of being injured when handling the container	0.68	0.07	0.33	0.73
f	Size of the container (for preventing a child from putting it in the mouth)	0.38	0.40	0.32	0.40
g	Hardness of the container material (in case it is put in the child's mouth)	0.73	0.13	0.60	0.60

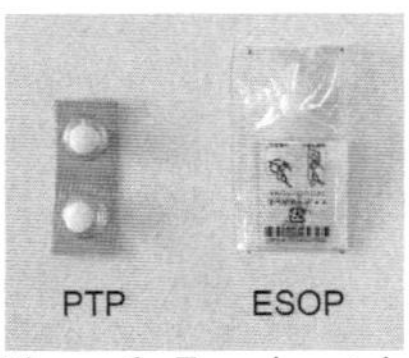

Figure 6: Experimental sample

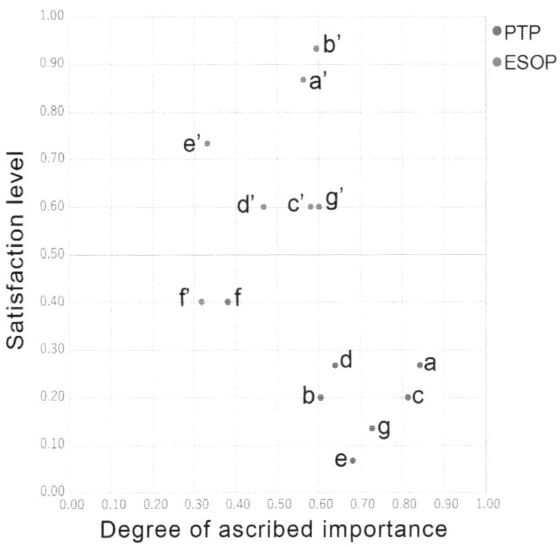

Figure 7: CS charts for PTP and ESOP

when handling the container, 6) Size of the container (for preventing a child from putting it in the mouth), and 7) Hardness of the container material (in case it is put in the child's mouth).

3.4 Evaluation of individual items and the overall evaluation

Setting seven levels (scores) for the evaluation: 1, Very dissatisfied; 2, Dissatisfied; 3, Somewhat dissatisfied; 4, I don't know; 5, Somewhat satisfied; 6, Satisfied; 7, Very satisfied; we asked the subjects (guardians) about their impression for each evaluation item.

Next, we asked for their overall evaluation of the safety of the drug containers, based on the same seven levels. Table 3 and table 4 show the results.

3.5 Calculation of the satisfaction level and degree of ascribed importance

We gave scores (1 to 7) to the evaluation answers for each item, and divided these into three groups: 'Good (6, 7)', 'Normal (3, 4, 5)', and 'Bad (1, 2)'. Among these, the percentage of 'Good' answers, out of the total answers, was considered to represent guardian satisfaction.

Next, we determined the degree of ascribed importance by calculating the simple correlation coefficient between the value for each evaluation item and the overall evaluation. Table 5 shows the results.

Finally, we created a customer satisfaction chart (CS chart), with the degree of ascribed importance on the horizontal axis and the satisfaction level (the percentage of 'Good' answers) on the vertical axis (Figure 7).

3.6 Calculation of the satisfaction level and degree of ascribed importance

(1) In the evaluation of the PTP sample, though the subjects' degree of ascribed importance was generally high, their satisfaction level was low, meaning that the guardians considered that the PTP had serious need of improvement with regard to safety.

(2) For most items, the guardians' ESOP satisfaction level was higher than for the PTP, suggesting that they felt the ESOP was safer than the PTP.

(3) For the "difficulty in understanding how to remove the tablet from the container", the satisfaction level for the PTP was 0.20, and for the ESOP 0.97, indicating that the guardians considered it more difficult for children to understand how to open the ESOP.

(4) For the "difficulty in removing the tablet from the container", the satisfaction level for the PTP was 0.27, and for the ESOP 0.87, indicating that the guardians thought the ESOP was more difficult for children to open.

(5) For the "size of the container (for preventing a child from accidentally putting it in the mouth)", the degree of ascribed importance was low for both the PTP and ESOP, indicating that the guardians considered other items more important.

(6) Given that, for the degree of ascribed importance in particular, the results may vary with the number of subjects, further experimentation, with increased numbers, is required in this respect.

4. SUMMARY

In this study, we investigated a new type of soft plastic, child resistant pill container, called ESOP. We first conducted a container-opening experiment on children aged 12 to 36 months, and were able to identify a relative strength of the container and a point for improvement. In the experiment, children were unable to open the ESOP container with their teeth. Thus, it would appear that the ESOP would be difficult to open for those at the age when children tend to put things in their mouth.

After the making the improvement that we identified, the ESOP used in the experiment was more effective in preventing children from opening it.

Next, using the improved ESOP and an existing PTP, we performed an impression-evaluation experiment regarding the safety of the respective drug container, in the opinion of guardians with 24- to 36-month-old children. By investigating the guardians' satisfaction level and degree of ascribed importance, we determined their impression of the safety of the two containers, and conclude that it is necessary to improve the items of which the degree of ascribed importance was high and the satisfaction level low.

In future, we will conduct further evaluation experiments, with increased subject numbers, and improve the evaluation method.

REFFERENCES

[1] Consumer Safety Investigation Commission; Investigation cause investigation report based on Article 23 paragraph 1 of consumer safety law -the accidental ingestion of pharmaceutical products-, December 2015.

[2] The Safety Committee of the Federation of Pharmaceutical Manufacturers' Associations of Japan; A written inquest report regarding the prevention of accidental ingestion of pharmaceutical products by children, October 2017.

[3] Shuji Morimoto; Development of "ESOP", CRSF Medicine Packaging, to Prevent Accidental Ingestion and Swallowing of PTP (Press Through Package), Packaging Technology , Vol.54, No.5, pp.357-363, May 2016.

[4] The Safety Committee of the Federation of Pharmaceutical Manufacturers' Associations of Japan; A written opinion regarding the prevention of accidental ingestion of pharmaceutical products by children, May 2015.

[5] Tamio Kan; Introduction to multivariate analysis learned in Excel, Ohmsha,Ltd., 2013.

[6] Masaaki Koyama, Yuki Takahashi, Hisao Shiizuka; Analysis and Evaluation of the Sign by Deviation Value, Journal of Japan Society of Kansei Engineering, Vol.12, No.1, pp.193-205, 2013.

[7] Naoshige Akita, Yoshitsugu Morita, Hisao Shiizuka; Evaluation of Product Design User Satisfaction based on the Systematic Analysis of Kansei, Journal of Japan Society of Kansei Engineering, Vol.15, No.2, pp.265-277, 2016.

ISASE-MAICS 2018

Affective Color Theme Generator for Visual-Textual Design: The Exploration of 3-Color for Banner Design

Qianru Qiu*, Xuan Luo*, Shu Watanabe* and Kengo Omura*

* *Fuji Xerox Co. Ltd, 6-1 Minatomirai, Nishi-ku, Yokohama-shi, Kanagawa-ken, 220-8668, Japan*

Abstract: Color design is a crucial component in creating an appealing media presentation. Designers always prepare many color themes in their design work, while it is not an easy work for non-designers to obtain suitable colors. In this paper, we propose an affective color theme generation approach for exploring of 3-color themes. Banner design acts as an initial application. First, we create a color form with overlapped blocks for the evaluation samples of color theme, and conduct the evaluation experiment to gain the affective data for color themes which are created by designers. Second, we analyze the relationships between color features and impressions, and create the estimation model. Then, we propose to generate new color themes corresponding to specified impressions based on the affective color model. A recommender system is developed to create banners with different colors corresponding to specified impressions. Moreover, we implement the mechanism of color unification with input image and text color legibility checker in the design system.
Keywords: *Color Theme; Affective Design; Hue & Tone; Visual-Textual Design; PCCS*

1. INTRODUCTION

People are very sensitive to color and effective use of color is extremely important in graphic design. Choosing suitable colors is a difficult task and it even confuses professional designers to use appropriate color in their design works. In practice, there are many online color design services, such as Adobe Kuler or known as Adobe Color, and COLOURLovers [1, 2], offering abundant user-provided color sets, called color themes, i.e., ordered combinations of 1-5 colors. These color themes have related ratings. The rating data only express the preference of users. A well-known research of colors and various human impressions, Kobayashi's art work, maps color themes to a color image-scale space [3]. Many researchers adopt this image-scale space in their works, such as the affective image colorization and adjustment [4, 5, 6], semantic image indexing [7]. These color themes are originally designed for image presentation, without considering textual description.

Nowadays, people are creating greater amounts of rich-media content on the Web than ever before. One of the fundamental challenges is how to create a visual design object consisting of multiple media elements, e.g., image and textural description [8]. The design object combining image and text contents, is called visual-textual presentation media, e.g., poster, magazine cover, banner, and any other rich media. The automatic colorization for visual-textual presentation media is becoming ubiquitous in both commercially printed publications and online digital advertisements. Generally, color themes are extracted from well-designed images and photographs, or created by designers, and applied for image colorization. To our knowledge, there are less researches and applications about the colorization for visual-textual design which is referring to image color, text color, and background color of text contents.

For color system, modern color theory began with Isaac Newton, who devised hue wheel by arranging seven spectral colors into an incomplete circle [9]. Subsequently, many psychologists and artists devoted to developing a color space. In the first decade of the 20th century, a true color system, Munsell Color System was developed in 3-dimensional space of hue, lightness, and chroma, known as saturation. With the development of color theory, many industrial color standards have been produced. Practical Color Co-ordinate System (PCCS), developed from 1964 by the Japan Color Research Institute, is a color-order system similar with Munsell's system. The color space in this system is indexed by hue and tone, and tone is the mixing of lightness and saturation. PCCS color chart is set with 288 colors for practical use and it is widely used for color investigation, color recording, and color education [10]. We use PCCS to help extract color features and generate color themes in this study.

In this paper, we explore the approach for affective color theme generation for visual-textual design. 3-color theme are set as the first trial and it is applied to web banner design which requires personalized design for millions of users and frequent updating for new contents. We first conduct an evaluation experiment to gain the affective data for color themes which are created by designers. Different from the general color themes with ordered color bar, the colors are shown as overlapped blocks with different color areas in our work. Then color features based on PCCS are extracted, and the estimation model of affective color features is learned by a multiple linear regression. Based on this model, we propose to generate new color themes corresponding to specified impressions, and develop a recommender system for automatic colorization for banner design.

2. AFFECTIVE EVALUATION OF COLORS

2.1 Color themes for evaluation

Considering that people prefer in themes which are neither too simple (i.e., monochromatic), nor too complex (more than 2-3 different hues) [1], the color theme in our study contains 3 colors and the 3 colors in a theme almost have different hues. Generally, color themes in online communities and related researches are shown in the form of ordered homogeneous bars. Considering of visual-textual presentation media that texts overlay on the background color or image, the samples of color themes in our study are designed with several overlapped blocks with different areas as shown in Figure 1. In our form, each 2 colors have adjacent edges for easier comparison and evaluation. The arrangement of overlapped color blocks brings more intuitive feelings to an actual visual-textual presentation. These 3 colors are called as base color, assort color, and accent color [10]. The base color is expected to be used as the background color with largest area in a design. The assort color, or called main color, is used to enrich the whole design with relative less area. The accent color aims to be used to capture people's attention with least area. For the areas of 3 colors, there are some popular design principles for color ratios, such as 70-25-5 rule [11], and 60-30-10 rule [12]. These rules are derived from the experience of designers and adjusted in practical application scenarios. After the discussion with color coordinators and seasoned designers, we set the final proportion nearly as 74-22-4 with best color balance for evaluation samples.

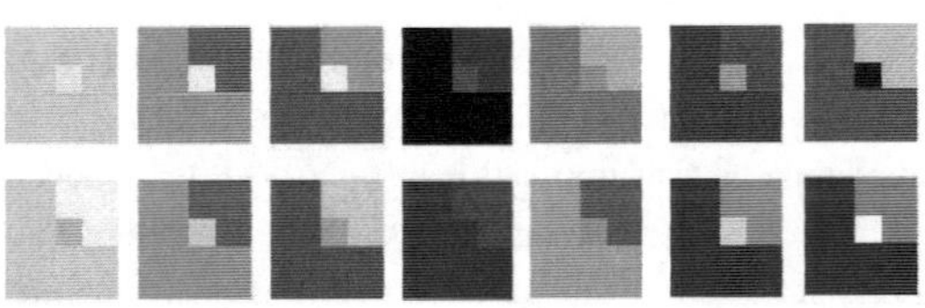

Figure 1: Parts of 3-color evaluation samples

We ask designers to create 232 color themes for several specified design images, as pretty, dynamic, etc., which are well-distributed in Kobayashi's Color Image Scale [3]. The colors in the evaluation samples contain different hues, and different segments of saturation and lightness.

2.2 Affective evaluation experiment

We extracted 30 kansei words including 26 affective words based on color image scale and 4 seasonal words. All these words can be found in Table 1 in section 3. The evaluation experiments for these 232 color themes were conducted for 109 designers. These color themes were divided into 8 groups and each group of them was evaluated by 12 to 15 participants with 30 kansei words. The evaluation experiment was executed through online questionnaire survey by 5-scale method and entrusted to a research company, Macromill. In this experiment, all participants are ensured without color deficiency and their monitors are larger than 20-inch. The age of these participants have a distribution in twenties, thirties, forties, fifties, and sixties.

3. PREDICTION MODEL OF 3-COLOR

This section describe method for learning the affective models by color features and evaluation data. As a widely used multiple linear regression model in Kansei Engineering (KE), Quantification Theory Type 1 (QT1), is used to analyze the quantitative relationships between kansei words and color features.

3.1 Feature vectors

For an input color theme λ, we define a vector x_l where $l \in [1, 2, 3]$ which are corresponding to base, assort and accent colors. A vector x_{li} expresses the presence or absence of hue and its categories. We extract 13 categories for each color hue, that is $i \in [1, 2, \ldots, 13]$. The categories for hue H include 12 interval hues from 24 hues and the neutral one in PCCS, that $H \in [2, 4, \ldots, 24, N]$. A vector x'_{lj} expresses the presence or absence of tone and its categories. 12 tones are extracted as categories for each tone, as vivid (v), bright (b), strong (s), deep (dp), light (lt), soft (sf), dull (d), dark (dk), pale (p), light grayish (ltg), grayish (g), dark grayish (dkg), that is $j \in [1, 2, \ldots, 12]$, and $T \in [v, b, s, dp, lt, sf, d, dk, p, ltg, g, dkg]$. The tone of neutral color is represented by its closest color tone for analysis. Besides hue and tone of each color, we add hue relations of 3 colors, and tone relations of 3 colors into learning model which are defined as $Q(x_{1i}, x_{2i}, x_{3i})$ and $Q'(x_{1j}, x_{2j}, x_{3j})$.

For hue relations, there are several common definitions for 2 hues, as identical, adjacent, similar, ambiguous, contrast, split complementary, and complementary types, shown in Figure 2. In this study, we clarify them into 4 groups, signed as, I: Identical hues; S: Similar hues, including adjacent and similar types; M: Ambiguous hues, or called Intermediate hues; C: Contrast hues, including contrast, complementary, split complementary types.

The relations of 3 hues φ are the unordered combination of the relations of base-assort colors, base-accent colors, and assort-accent color. Then, 14 categories are collected shown as Figure 3, that $\varphi(H_1, H_2, H_3) \in [CCC, CCM, CMM, CSM, CCS, MMS, MSS, CCI, MMI, ISS, CN, MC, SN, IN]$ and $h \in [1, 2, ..., 14]$. N means having a neutral color.

For tone relations, tone is consisted with two concepts of lightness and saturation. The lightness and saturation are both divided into 3 groups, signed as high, medium,

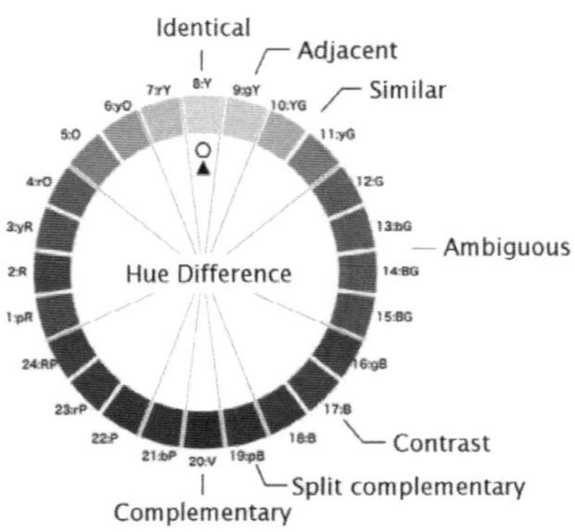

Figure 2: Hue difference in PCCS

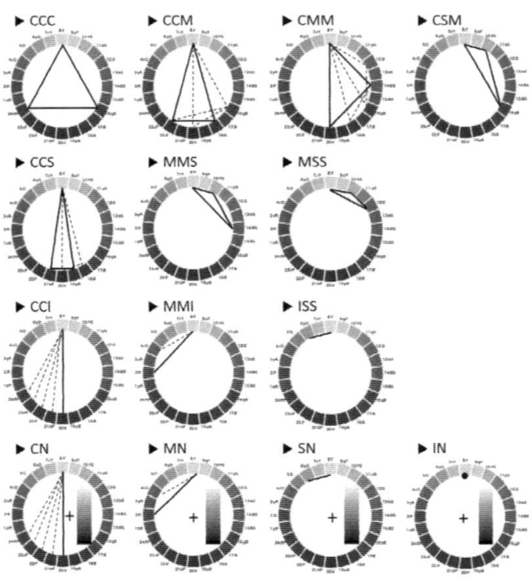

Figure 3: Hue relations of 3-color

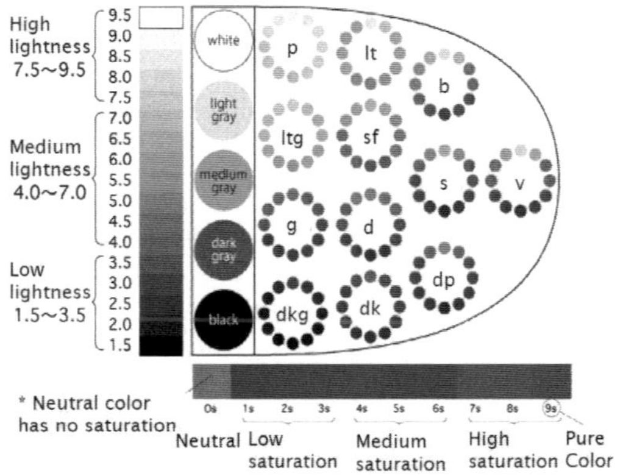

Figure 4: Tone classification in PCCS

and low. As Figure 4 shows, high lightness contains p, lt, and b. Medium lightness contains ltg, g, sf, d, s, and v. Low lightness contains dkg, dk, and dp.Meanwhile, b, s, dp, and v belong to high saturation. lt, sf, d, and dk belong to medium saturation. p, ltg, g, and dkg belong to low saturation. The relations between high and low groups are defined as contrast (C), and the relations between medium and high groups or medium and low groups are defined as similar (S). In this defination method, the relations of lightness for 3 tones are signed as, 1L: 3 tones correspond to 1 lightness group; 2L_S: 3 tones correspond to 2 similar lightness groups; 2L_C: 3 tones correspond to 2 contrast lightness groups; 3L: 3 tones correspond to 3 lightness groups. The relations of saturation for 3 tones are signed as, 1S: 3 tones correspond to 1 saturation group; 2S_S: 3 tones correspond to 2 similar saturation groups; 2S_C: 3 tones correspond to 2 contrast saturation groups; 3S: 3 tones correspond to 3 saturation groups.

The relations of 3 tones $\varphi'(T_1, T_2, T_3)$ are the combination of lightness and saturation, such as 1L&1S. For the evaluations in this study, there are 15 categories extracted for the relations of 3 tones, that $t \in [1, 2, ..., 15]$. Here, 2S_S and 2S_C are merged as 2S for 2L_C.

3.2 Regression model

Given an objective variable for an evaluation with a kansei word y_λ for each sample λ (λ = 1, …, m).

$$y_\lambda = \sum a_{li} x_{li\lambda} + \sum b_{lj} x'_{lj\lambda} + \sum c_h Q_h(x_{1i\lambda}, x_{2i\lambda}, x_{3i\lambda}) + \sum d_t Q'_t(x'_{1j\lambda}, x'_{2j\lambda}, x'_{3j\lambda}) + \varepsilon_\lambda \quad (1)$$

where,

$$x_{li} = \begin{cases} 0 \ (H_{li} \neq H_l) \\ 1 \ (H_{li} = H_l) \end{cases} \quad (2)$$

$$x'_{lj} = \begin{cases} 0 \ (T_{lj} \neq T_l) \\ 1 \ (T_{lj} = T_l) \end{cases} \quad (3)$$

$$Q_h(x_{1i}, x_{2i}, x_{3i}) = \begin{cases} 0, \ r_h \notin \varphi_h(H_1, H_2, H_3) \\ 1, \ r_h \in \varphi_h(H_1, H_2, H_3) \end{cases} \quad (4)$$

$$Q'_t(x'_{1j}, x'_{2j}, x'_{3j}) = \begin{cases} 0, \ r_t \notin \varphi'_t(T_1, T_2, T_3) \\ 1, \ r_t \in \varphi'_t(T_1, T_2, T_3) \end{cases} \quad (5)$$

Only a variable assigned as a category of an item is set to 1, otherwise be set to 0. a_{li} denotes for the coefficient of hue of color l with categories i. b_{lj} denotes for the coefficient of tone of color l with categories j. c_h denotes for the coefficient of hue relations of 3 colors with categories h. d_t denotes for the coefficient of tone relations of 3 colors with categories t. r_h denotes the relation of 3 color hues, and r_t denotes the relation of 3 color tones.

3.3 Estimation precision

The multiple correlation coefficient R determines how well the estimation model fits the observed data. In the long experience of KE, R^2 should be more than 0.6 [13]. As a preliminary attempt, we built models with CC-features [4] including 10 hues, 12 tones for 3 colors, and 6 color patterns with some decision rules. We found that the decision rules for color patterns is ambiguous to classify color themes. Then we built affective models with our features including 13 hues and 12 tones for each color, 14 hue relations of 3 colors, and 15 tone relations of 3 colors. The Table 1 shows the results of R^2 for the evaluation data of 3-color themes. It is found that the estimation models with CC-features are reliable for 23 kansei words, that is 7 kansei words have a result of R^2 which is less than 0.6, and the estimation models with our features are reliable for 27 kansei words. Our method is precise and scalable for classifying hue relations and tone relations, and the decision rules in our work have better performance than the rules of CC-features.

Table 1: Multiple correlation coefficients R-squared of estimation models for 3-color themes

Emotions	Multiple R-squared	
	CC-features	Our features
Pretty	0.827	0.834
Casual	0.770	0.806
Dynamic	0.759	0.793
Romantic	0.783	0.870
Mild	0.842	0.858
Feminine	0.837	0.818
Natural	0.783	0.838
Elegant	0.599	0.693
Gorgeous	0.548	0.641
Wild	0.696	0.745
Classic	0.757	0.780
Formal	0.733	0.780
Dandy	0.800	0.841
Chic	0.789	0.842
Fresh	0.745	0.791
Clear	0.722	0.773
Modern	0.436	0.515
Pop	0.754	0.789
Retro	0.648	0.757
Noble	0.567	0.631
Friendly	0.760	0.811
Contemporary	0.386	0.485
Expressive	0.460	0.561
Readable	0.503	0.627
Attractive	0.686	0.722
Spring-like	0.820	0.817
Summer-like	0.661	0.802
Autumn-like	0.679	0.758
Winter-like	0.671	0.733
Beautiful	0.676	0.702

4. COLOR THEME GENERATION IN PRACTICE

4.1 Color generation method

The coefficients in regression model, which are called category scores in QT1, denote the degree of relevance with kansei words. Generally, we can get a color theme with maximum of categories scores, that is, the best result is $\{a_{1max}, a_{2max}, a_{3max}, b_{1max}, b_{2max}, b_{3max}\}$. Then the hues and tones for 3 colors should be set as $\{H_{1max}, H_{2max}, H_{3max}, T_{1max}, T_{2max}, T_{3max}\}$. However, when c_{max} is larger than a_{lmax} and the relation of selected hues does not fit $\varphi_{max}(H_1, H_2, H_3)$, the result has conflict and the hues should be adjusted. Similarly, when d_{max} is larger than b_{lmax} and the relation of selected tones does not fit $\varphi'_{max}(T_1, T_2, T_3)$, the result has conflict and the tones should be adjusted. The process for adjustment is to keep the categories which have larger coefficients and change other categories which are fitting the relation of hues or tones.

Moreover, we create several color themes in order. The pseudo code is shown as follows:

Algorithm: Color theme generation in order

```
Require: Kansei k, ThemeNumber N
Define<Object> colorThemes
Define<Object> allScores = GetKanseiDB(k)
Define<Object> bestCat = GetBest(allScores)
Define<Object> restCat = GetRest(allScores)
sortDescending(restCat)
for n = 1 to N step 1 do
    if n == 1 then
        catSet = bestCat
    else
        catSet = bestCat.replace(restCat [n-2])
    end if
    if catSet has conflict then
        adjustCategories(catSet)
    end if
    if 3 colors are all not same then
        colorThemes.add(catSet)
    end if
end for
```

4.2 Color unification with input image

In our study, color themes are applied for design objects that have image contents and text contents. It is known that designers always extract colors in image and unify the text colors or background colors with the colors of image. Hence, in the design case that have image and text contents, we extract the main colors of the input image, and select unified color themes from generated color themes in order. The main colors of picture are mapping to PCCS colors. If the generated color theme has a color which has same or similar hue and same tone with main colors of picture, the color theme is selected. If there is no suitable color theme for the input picture, it denotes that the picture has a conflict with the specified impression, and it will be suggested to change the kansei word or input a new picture.

4.3 Text color legibility checker

In our design scenarios, the legibility of text color on background color should be ensured. We extract all 144 colors and 9 neutral colors in PCCS color chart, and settle them as text color and background color. There are 23409 pairs of combinations in total. We asked people without color deficiency to label the legibility of these color combinations with 6-scale method. The evaluation score being larger than 4 means the text color is readable on the background color. We create a color legibility checker based on these evaluation data. Universal color design has not been concerned in our current work.

Figure 5: System outputs for pretty, formal, clear, elegant, dynamic, natural, fresh, and dandy

4.4 Color recommender system

Based on the results of affective color models, we implemented a color generation engine in our automatic design system. The color generation engine could be used in many fields of graphic design, as card design, poster design, web design, etc. In this study, we explore the color recommendation for affective web banner design. Once the user chooses a kansei word, the colors for the design will be reset corresponding to the selected impression. Text colors are adjusted to be readable by color legibility checker. Hence, we just extracted 3 pairs of outputs shown in Figure 5 which are corresponding to pretty, formal, clear, and elegant which are created in 240×240 pixels.

5. CONCLUSION

In this paper, we describe the study for 3-color theme generator and a trail application in banner design. The key contribution of our work is to break the regular form of color bars and create a form with overlapped blocks to show the color theme for visual-textual design. Our proposed color form in blocks is considered with an appropriate area ratio for 3 colors which brings more intuitive feelings to an actual visual-textual presentation media. For analyzing the affective evaluation data of created color themes, we make the decision rules for classifying hue relations and tone relations to optimize the estimation model for the relationships between color features and impressions. Then we develop a recommender system for generating color themes and colorizing web banner automatically. Additionally, we implement color unification with input picture and text color legibility checker. Next we will conduct verification experiments to explore the effect of unification of text and text-background colors to picture's colors. We hope to have a further study about the unification rules of picture colors and other colors in design.

As we know, the legibility is important in text design, while the adjustment of text legibility may change the emotional expression of design. Our current adjustment method is to change the color to its closet legible color in PCCS chart. We will explore some other methods and verify their affective effect in our future work.

Our current study has some limitations that the evaluated samples are 3-color themes and the main application scenario is for a simple design work with a small number of colors and contents. Moreover, when input picture is disharmonious with color theme, how to adjust the colors of elements should have an in-depth consideration in our future work. Though our prototype is only initial explorations, we hope that further works will yield tools or systems for industrial cases and business scenes that help non-expert work easier.

ACKNOWLEDGMENTS

This work was supported by Research & Technology Group, Fuji Xerox Co., Ltd.

REFFERENCES

1. P. O'Donovan, A. Agarwala and A. Hertzmann; Color Compatibility from Large Datasets; ACM Transactions on Graphics (TOG), 30(4), No.63, 2011.
2. P. O'Donovan, A. Agarwala and A. Hertzmann; Collaborative Filtering of Color Aesthetics; Proceedings of the Workshop on Computational Aesthetics, pp.33-40, 2014.
3. S. Kobayashi; The aim and method of the color image scale; Color research & application, 6(2), pp.93-107, 1981.
4. X. Wang, J. Jia and L. Cai; Affective Image Adjustment with a Single Word; The Visual Computer, 29(11), pp.1121-1133, 2013.
5. X. Wang, J. Jia, H. Liao and L. Cai; Affective Image Colorization; Journal of Computer Science and Technology, 27(6), pp.1119-1128, 2012.
6. K. Peng, K. Karlsson, T. Chen, D. Zhang and H.Yu; A Framework of Changing Image Emotion Using Emotion Prediction; Image Processing (ICIP) 2014 IEEE International Conference on.
7. M. Solli and R. Lenz; Color Semantics for Image Indexing; Proceedings of 5th European Conference on Colour in Graphics, Imaging, and Vision, pp.353-358, 2010.
8. X. Yang, T. Mei, Y. Xu, Y. Rui and A. Li; Automatic Generation of Visual-Textual Presentation Layout; ACM Transactions on Multimedia Computing, Communications, and Applications, 12(2), No.33, 2016.
9. S. Westland, K. Laycock, V. Cheung, P. Henry and F. Mahyar; Colour Harmony; Journal of the International Colour Association, 1(1): 1, pp.1-15, 2007.
10. H. Kawasaki; Introduction to Color Arrangement for Color Coordinator; Japan Color Enterprise Press, 2002.
11. M. Kobayashi; Studies on the exterior color of shops: Effect on the motives for entering boutiques; Osaka Shoin Women's University Proceeding, No.46, pp.121-131, 2009.
12. K. Ferris, and S. Zhang; A Framework for Selecting and Optimizing Color Scheme in web design; 49th Hawaii International Conference on System Science, 2016.
13. M. Nagamachi and A.M. Lockman; Innovation of Kansei Engineering; CRC Press, 2010.

ISASE-MAICS 2018

Affective Data Visualization: A Preliminary Study

– Manipulating Emotions with Data Visualizations–

Peter MATSON*, Molly MUELLER ** and Elizabeth TIPTON ***

* *Eastern Washington University, 526 5th Street Cheney, Washington 99004, United States of America*
pmatson@eagles.ewu.edu
** *Eastern Washington University, 526 5th Street Cheney, Washington 99004, United States of America*
mmueller@eagles.ewu.edu
*** *Eastern Washington University, 526 5th Street Cheney, Washington 99004, United States of America*
etipton@ewu.edu

Abstract: This paper details the findings of a study that was conducted to explore how data visualizations could be used to get a targeted emotional response. In total, there were ten original graphs created that were then manipulated in some manner to attain another emotional response, giving the study twenty graphs. The study was conducted in an electronic survey format. Characteristics examined were color choices, font type, and scale. Faculty and students of Eastern Washington University were asked to partake in the survey. We found that it was possible to affect the emotional responses to a graph by changing the colors. Changing the font and scale of the graphs did not yield significant results.
Keywords: *Affective, Data, Visualization*

1. INTRODUCTION

Data visualizations have been used for many years to influence and inform people on a wide variety of topics. In the modern age of big data, it is becoming more important for us to be aware of the ways in which data visualizations can be used to influence our understanding the of the data and the world at large.

To this end we designed a short survey as part of a course to help demonstrate the ways in which modifying data visualization can influence the emotional responses of the viewer. To demonstrate this, we created 10 different data visualizations using both real and manufactured data. We then modified the graphs by changing the font, color, and/or scale. The survey also collected basic demographic information: gender, age, ethnicity, and level of education.

2. REVIEW OF LITERATURE

In the article "Speak to the Eyes: The History and Practice of Information Visualization" by Jefferson Bailey and Lily Pregill [2014], the authors give an overview of the data visualization. Bailey and Pregill give several examples of people who have shaped the field of data visualization. Bailey and Pregill first organize their paper by important people in establishing data visualization as a field and then move into different type of data visualization organized by data of inception. The authors conclude by summarizing the functions of data visualization in the modern context. Namely, that data visualizations "support new modes of understanding, serve an administrative function, and play a unique role in mediating how users explore and understand groups of material" (Bailey and Pregill, 2014, p. 191).

The article "A Picture Is Worth A Thousand Words: Visualization in Data Analysis" was published in 2017 by Tricia Leggett. In her article she discusses different types of data and data visualizations and how different visualizations are better suited for displaying different results. Leggett discusses pie, column, and scatter plot charts outlining the uses and misuses of each of the chart types. Leggett concludes that pie charts "best [communicate] data that can be shown … to represent parts of a whole" (Leggett, 2017, p.2). Column charts, on the other hand, are best for categorical data over time. Finally scatter plots are useful for shown relationships between two variables and outliers in the data.

The UM/3M paper by Vogel, Dickson, and Lehman in 1986 details a study that measured how computer visual supports affect the persuasiveness of a presentation. In this particular study used variables such as "color vs. black and white, plain text vs. text plus pictures and graphs, and 35mm slides vs. overhead transparencies." The study found that "audience attention, comprehension, yielding, and retention culminating in action" when visual aids were used increased compared to when they were not.

Specifically, the persuasiveness of the presentation increased by 43% when visual aids were used.

At the time of the study there only other study of its like was conducted in 1981 by the Wharton School of the University of Pennsylvania. The UM/3M study sought to expound upon the Wharton study since they claimed that while the UM/3M study was often cited, claims exceeded the study's explanatory capabilities.

The UM/3M study used two measures, time and money, to see whether or not visual aids were more persuasive. hey then narrowed it down to just time on the basis that college students had on average the same amount of time available. However, student's financial situations could be drastically different and therefore willingness to spend money to go to a seminar was not the best measure to use. It was concluded that groups getting visual supports planned to spend 16.4% more time and 26.4% more money on seminars.

The article "How the Brain Processes Images" written by Barron explains that no matter where someone comes from, people process images in the same manner. Everyone has visual centers that control specific neurons that fire when things like vertical or horizontal lines are detected. There are two different types of visual orientating, top-down and bottom-up. Top-down, or goal-directed, is when we choose to shift our attention to certain objects. Bottom-up, or stimulus, orientating is when our attention is almost forced to focus onto something. Busy things, such as a lot of crisscrossing lines, use our stimulus driven orientation to force our attention onto it. An artist, Sima, uses geometric shapes, "atypical" colors, and angles to force attention to his works. He uses offsetting colors to evoke feelings of "awe, turmoil, and passion" and color combinations with bold or faded lines to grab attention and affect the desired emotional response.

3. HYPOTHESIS

It is possible to manipulate data visualizations is small ways such as, color, font, scale or a combination of, to affect the triggered emotional response to the data. Table 1 indicates the aspects of each graph pair that was manipulated for the survey. Figure 1 is the graph for Name Things in Group 1. Figure 2 is the graph for Name Things in Group 2, where the color and font have been changed. Respondents were exposed to all ten graphs in group 1 in a random order before seeing all ten graphs in group 2 in random order. Figure 3 is all pairs of graphs in decreasing order of significant response difference with group 1 on the left and group 2 on the right.

Table 1: Graph Aspects Changed between Groups by Topic

Graph Topic → Changed ↓	Energy Prod.	Name Things	YMCA Lyrics	Magazine	Political	Pillow	Debt	Live Without	Salary	Orange
Color	x	x	x	x	x	x				x
Font		x		x				x	x	x
Scale							x			

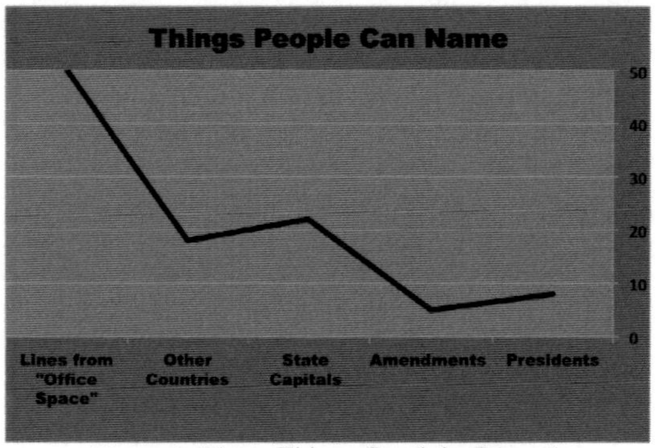

Figure 1: Name Things Graph in Group 1

Figure 2: **Name Things Graph in Group 2**

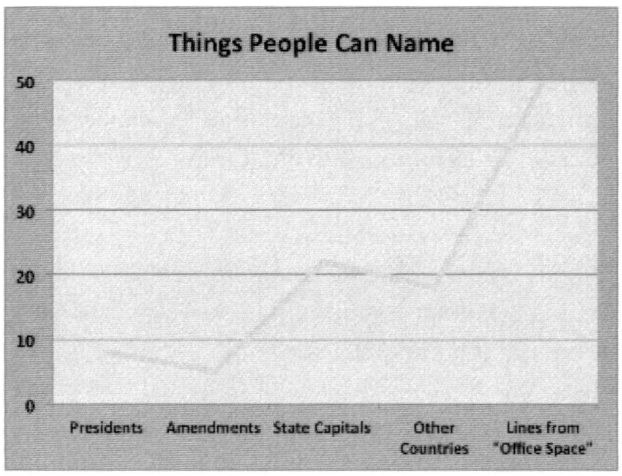

4. SAMPLE DESCRIPTION

The sample population for this study was comprised of students at Eastern Washington University. The survey was managed electronically through Qualtrics to ensure anonymity. The survey was only available for a two week period due to course limitations. Of the 40 responses kept after data cleaning, there were 25 respondents in the age group of 18-24, 6 in 25-34, 1 in 35-44, 5 in 45-54, and 3 left blank. There were 24 male respondents and 16 female respondents. The ethnic demographics were 32 White, 1 Black or African American, 3 Asian, 3 Hispanic or Latino/a, and 1 Middle Eastern.

Affective Data Visualization: A Preliminary Study
Keywords: Affective, Data, Visualization

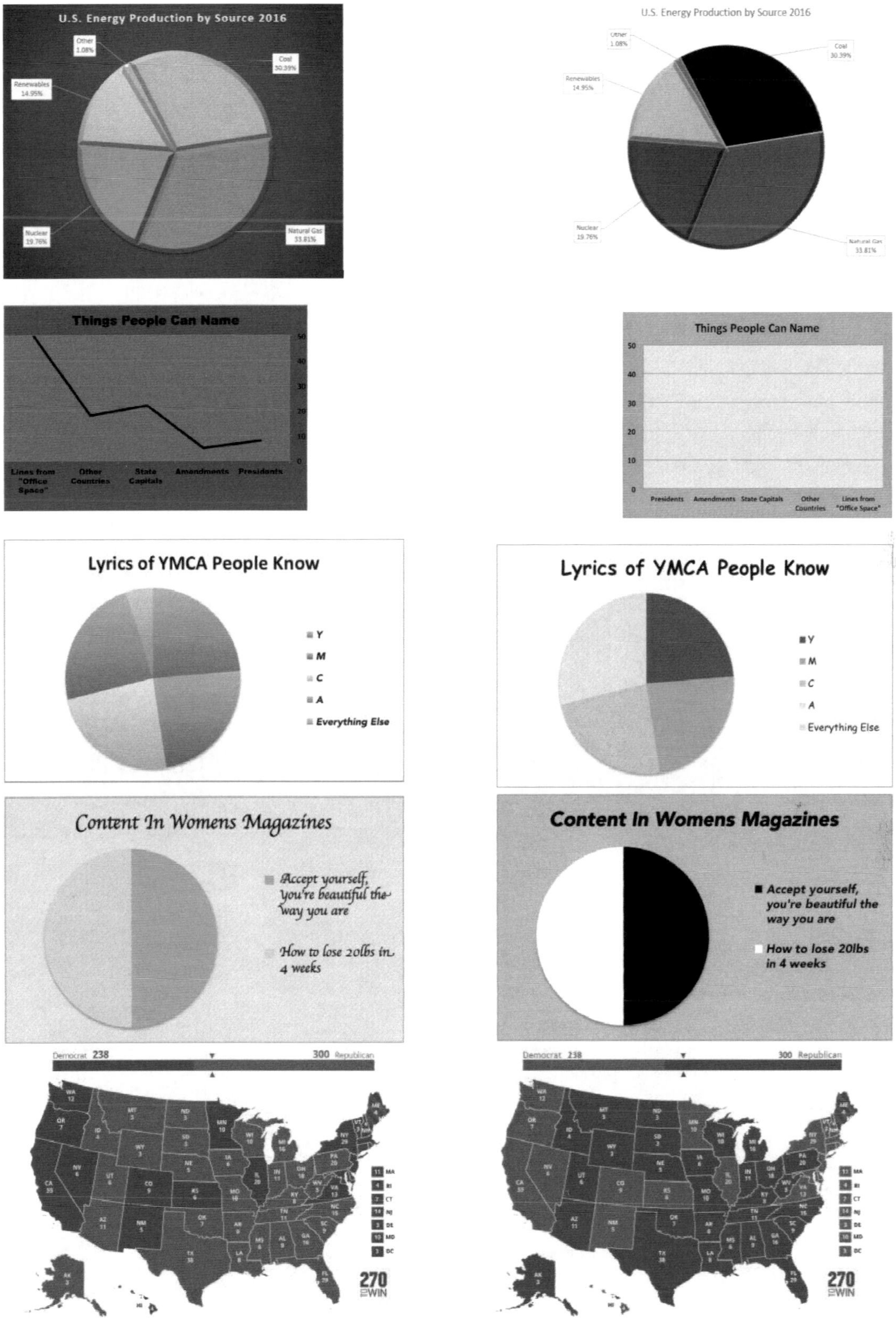

Figure 3a: Graph Pairs in order of decreasing significance – Group 1 on left, Group 2 on right

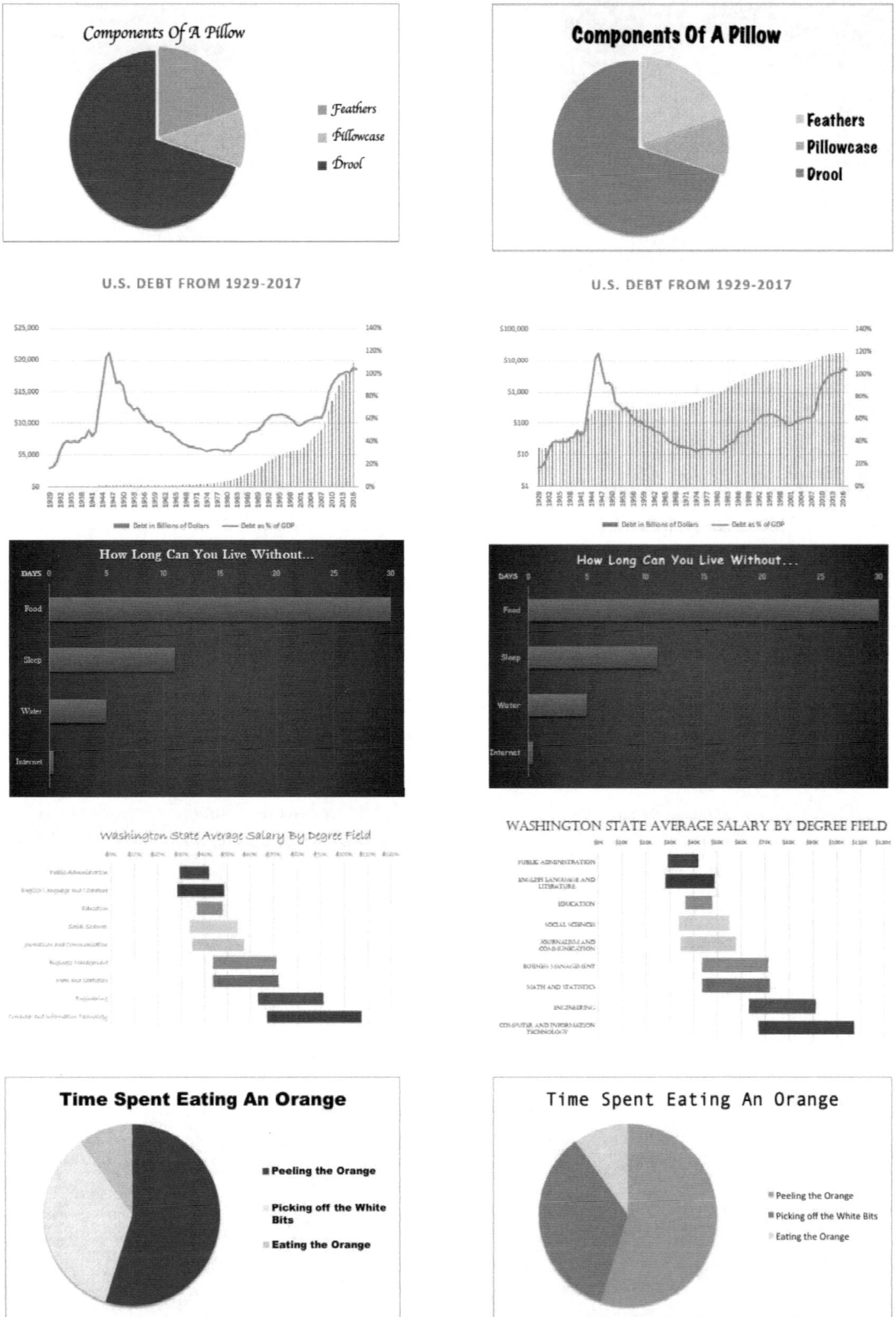

Figure 3b: Graph Pairs in order of decreasing significance – Group 1 on left, Group 2 on right

5. METHODS

After collecting the results of our survey, we had a total of 45 responses. Before analyzing the data, we removed any of the responses that did not start the second half of the survey since there was no data to compare across the responses. This left us with 40 responses fully completed.

We then categorized the emotional responses into three categories: Positive, Negative, and Neutral. The emotions captured in the positive category were happy, optimistic, and some responses from the other category such as amused and intrigued. The emotions captured in the negative category were angry, sad, pessimistic, disgust, and responses in the other category such as depressed and powerless. The emotions captured in the neutral category were indifferent, surprise, and responses in the other category such as confused and none.

Once the data was grouped into the three categories, we created tables for each of the matching pairs of graphs to perform a Chi-square test goodness-of-fit to compare the distribution of responses from the graphs in the first half of the survey to the corresponding graphs in the second half. After creating the tables, we checked to see if we needed to further group the data to have at least five for each category for the graphs in the first half of the survey. In such cases, we collapsed either the Positive or Negative grouping into the Neutral grouping to create only two groups Positive and Not-Positive or Negative and Not-Negative. We reduced the groups from three to two in three cases. For the YMCA Lyrics Graph, and Salary by Degree Field we collapsed the negative category and aggregated the responses into the neutral to form the Not-Positive Category. The Things People Can Name Graph had the Positive Category collapsed and added the responses into the neutral category to form the Not-Negative category.

We then performed three different tests. A Chi-Square test for Goodness-of-Fit between on each of the pairs of graphs was performed to determine which pairs yielded significant results in terms of different emotional response. We also aggregated the data and repeated the Chi-Square Tests for Goodness-of-Fit on each of the types of treatments to determine if changing the color, font, scale, or color and font of the graphs yielded significant differences overall. Finally, we considered whether our result could be the artifact of inadequate randomization. We tested each of the response pairs using an F Test to determine if we could assume equal variance and a Two Sample T-Test to determine if the number of graphs seen between pairs could have been a significant factor in determining if responses were the same or different.

Table 2: Chi-Square Goodness-of-Fit Tests for Individual Graph Topics

Graph topic → (* positive & neutral collapsed; ** negative & neutral collapsed)		Energy Prod.	Name Things*	YMCA Lyrics**	Magazine	Political	Pillow	Debt	Live Without	Salary**	Orange
Group 1	Negative	9	21	0	13	13	16	20	11	1	6
	Neutral	22	16	16	19	20	7	14	22	22	16
	Positive	9	3	24	8	7	17	6	7	17	18
Group 2	Negative	20	10	6	19	16	13	26	6	2	3
	Neutral	17	21	20	17	22	12	10	26	17	17
	Positive	3	9	14	3	2	15	4	8	20	20
Goodness of fit of Group 2 to Group 1	Chi-sq	18.581	12.13	10.417	6.2357	4.4637	4.3692	3.6095	3.1429	1.2308	1.7847
	df	2	1	1	2	2	2	2	2	1	2
	p	**<0.0005**	**<0.0005**	**0.001**	**0.044**	0.107	0.113	0.165	0.208	0.267	0.410

Table 3: Chi-Square Goodness-of-Fit Tests for Aggregated Graph Topics

Graph topic → (* positive & neutral collapsed; ** negative & neutral collapsed)		Color	Font	Scale	Color and Font
Group 1	Negative	78	52	41	40
	Neutral	116	95	30	51
	Positive	86	53	9	29
Group 2	Negative	87	40	36	32
	Neutral	126	98	31	55
	Positive	66	60	13	32
Goodness of fit of Group 2 to Group 1	Chi-sq	6.57159	3.80656	2.42087	2.23436
	df	2	2	2	2
	p	**0.037**	0.149	0.298	0.327

6. RESULTS

We determined that of our ten graphs, four were found to be statistically significant when the differences in emotional responses were analyzed (Table 2): Energy Produced, Name Things, YMCA Lyrics, and Magazine. Only color was significant when the attributes were aggregated (Table 3).

Two of the graph pairs had significant differences in viewing order when split by whether the responses were different or not. The two in which order may have played a significant role were Name Things (F = 0.9393, p = 0.4753, pooled-t = -2.3161, p(two-tailed) = 0.0259) and Salary (F = 0.5488, p = 0.1731, pooled-t = -2.1717, p(two-tailed) = 0.0360). It is important to note however that only Things People Can Name had statistically different responses while Salary by Degree Field did not. The other three graph pairs with statistically different responses were not statistically different in the viewing order test. Furthermore, the remaining five graph pairs were also not statistically different in the viewing order test. As no systemic pattern was apparent, inadequate randomization does not appear to be a factor driving the results of this study.

7. DISCUSSION AND FUTURE RESEACH

The conclusions from our study are limited and may not apply to most of the population as our sample was only from people currently in college and specifically only in a few departments at Eastern Washington University. Of our sample of 41 people, 31 were between the ages of 18 and 34 and 32 of 41 identified as White. The disproportionate numbers of young and white respondents coupled with the size of the sample cast doubt on the applicability of the results to the general population. It is necessary for further research to be done to generalize the results to a larger population. For further analysis, we would suggest using a sample that has a wider variety in ages, ethnicities, and other demographic variables.

It is also probable that cultural context may play a key role in how individuals responds to changes in color, font, and scale, though it may be most influential in color. Accounting for such difference in future studies will likely be necessary to improve the power of the study results.

Further analysis should also be done to refine and codify how visualization can affect emotions. Specifically, with a wider variety of graphs and a larger sample size, it may be possible to account for when changes in color are likely to influence a change in emotional response. Determining when magnitude of change in color or if specific colors are more effective at eliciting specific emotional responses is the next logical progression for follow up research.

The other two changes in graphs (font and scale) could similarly be expounded upon further to see if they could be codified in such a way as to predict when changes in emotional response will occur. This would require more extensive testing and a larger sample size. It is believed that further research may be able to determine what types of changes are most likely to influence changes in emotional response.

Further research would help areas such as marketing. Knowing what specifically would elicit the response that marketers would want would save time and resources. Broadening the research to include more cultural backgrounds would be necessary since color was statistically significant and research shows that certain colors mean different things in different places of the world.

REFERENCES

[1] Bailey, J. j., & Pregill, L. l. (2014). Speak to the Eyes: The History and Practice of Information Visualization. Art Documentation: Bulletin Of The Art Libraries Society Of North America, 33(2), 168-191.

[2] Leggett, T. (2017). A Picture Is Worth a Thousand Words: Visualization in Data Analysis. *Radiologic Technology*, 89(1), 79-82.

[3] D. R. Vogel, G. W. Dickson, and J. A. Lehman; June, 1986; Persuasion and the Role of Visual Presentation Support: The UM/3M Study; Management Information Systems Research Center School of Management, University of Minnesota, Minneapolis, Minnesota 55455.

[4] Barron, D. (2016, May 10). How the Brain Processes Images. Retrieved January 25, 2018

ISASE-MAICS 2018

Impression Evaluation between Color Vision Types

Yasuyo G. ICHIHARA*

* *Kogakuin University, 1-24-2 Nishi-Shinjuku, Shinjuku-ku, Tokyo 163-8677, Japan*
ichihara@cc.kogakuin.ac.jp

Abstract: Red is not a color that stands out brightly for dichromatic individuals who have a different sense of color from the majority. However, they know that the color of passion is red. They also know that the color of sadness is of bluish color.
But these understandings are learned a posteriori. If so, there must be a discrepancy in terms of the impression between the stimulation of letters by the color name and the stimulation by color itself. Impression is also expected to be different between the majority and the minority. This study conducted the impression survey by SD method using stimulations by letters and colors to understand instinctively the color world as seen by individuals with different sensation of color.
Keywords: *Color vision, Impression evaluation, dichromatism, Protan, Deutan*

1. INTRODUCTION

In a variety of situations in everyday life, many colors appear. Colors are used not only in designing product, and apparel for aesthetic purpose, but are also used in illustrations and signs that convey information.

However, human color vision is non-uniform and in most cases variation is genetically linked to L-cones and M-cones. Therefore, the way color appears is not the same for all color vision types. Some people experience a high saturation red as quite striking, but other people with a different type of color vision may feel that it is dark and is not a striking color.

In Japan, approximately 95% of men and 99.8% of women are trichromats (have normal, or common-type color vision). The other 5% of men, and 0.2% of women confuse red and green. This is known as defective red-green color vision. The percentage is different by country, for example approximately 8% of men have red-green confusion in Europe.

Individuals with red-green confusion fall into the category of either protanopia or deuteranopia, depending on their cone cells.

In this paper, we define color vision type of trichromats as C-type, that of protanopes as P-type, and that of deuteranopes as D-type color vision in conformance with the NPO Color Universal Design Organization.

Color combinations used for most products and signs are designed with reference to C-type color vision, even though colors are used to communicate information for everybody. Therefore, color combinations that C-type people can discriminate clearly may not be clear for individuals with red-green color confusion (i.e. P- or D-type people). Such color combinations may cause problems or even accidents.
Color Universal Design (CUD) is an easy-to-understand system that was created to convey color-coded information accurately to most people by taking color vision types into consideration.

Recently, various designs and products for which CUD is applied have started appearing, but their number is still limited. For effective application of CUD, more research is needed on the color cognition systems and the color perception characteristics of individuals with red-green color confusion.

In Our previous study, we analyzed color discrimination levels of C-types and P-types on the CIELAB uniform color space[1]. The study suggested that the theoretical confusion locus of P-types might not match with our results1. The confusion locus is define as a line, and colors represented along this line look identical if no luminance contrast is present.

In our previous research[2] about color classification using color-chips, we were able to determine common color categories between C-types and P-types.

In our another research[3], we analyzed the validity of the theoretical confusion locus of individuals with red-green color confusion using a custom-made color chart on the CIELAB uniform color space. In addition, we experimented with color classification using the 100 Hue Test to find color categories that do not depend on color names, because our previous results may have been affected by the recognition of color names.
Characteristics of color perception in P-types or D-types were investigated by these experiments.

This study conducted the impression survey by SD method using stimulations by letters and colors to understand instinctively the color world as seen by individuals with different sensation of color.

2. Experiment method

Test subjects

1st group: ten individuals that passed the Ishihara test plate (type C) in their 20s ~60s

2nd group: nine type 2 dichromatic individuals (type D intensity) in their 20s ~60s

3rd group: 13 type 2 dichromatic individuals (type P intensity) in their 20s ~60s

Stimulations: Color and letter stimulations for 11 basic colors

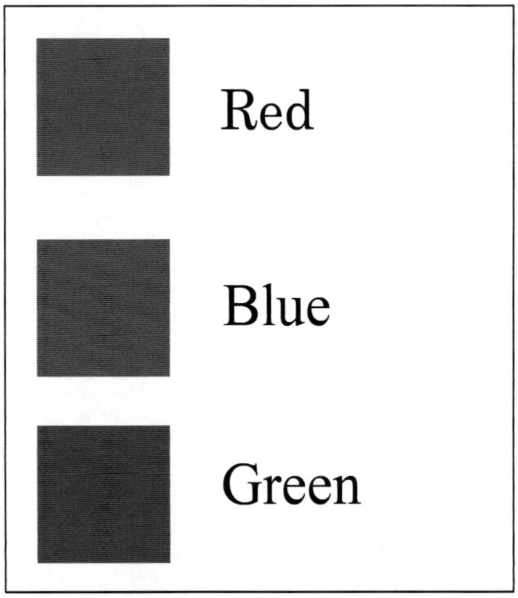

Figure 1. Stimulations
3x3cm size

Table 1. Names stimulations

Notation	Name
5B	Blue
N1.0	Black
5R	Red
N9.5	White
5YR3.5/4	Brown
5Y	Yellow
5P	Purple
5RP8/6	Pink
N5.0	Gray
5YR	Orange
5G	Green

An evaluation sheet with printed color names and color stimulations was prepared, and the test was conducted using the SD method. Data was collected from nine individuals in the first group and ten individuals in the second group, and factor analysis (principal factor analysis) was performed using the SPSS for each group.

Table 2. Opposite adjectives in SD method

bright-dark
warm-cold
wet-dry
hard-soft
heavy-light
lively-lonely
strong-weak
flamboyant-subdued
thick-thin

3. Results

Table 3. P-type factors

Opposite adjectives		factor 1	factor 2	factor 3
flamboyant	subdued	0.91	−0.04	−0.01
lively	lonely	0.90	−0.06	0.02
warm	cold	0.66	0.05	−0.15
bright	dark	0.63	−0.44	−0.25
heavy	light	−0.34	0.82	0.15
thick	thin	0.13	0.72	0.36
hard	soft	−0.34	0.65	−0.12
strong	weak	0.31	0.59	−0.06
wet	dry	−0.10	0.06	0.62
Sum of squared loading		2.80	2.18	0.63

Table 4. D-type factors

Opposite adjectives		factor 1	facror 2	factor 3
lively	lonely	0.92	0.09	−0.10
flamboyant	subdued	0.88	0.04	−0.10
warm	cold	0.81	−0.01	−0.25
bright	dark	0.74	−0.48	0.00
thick	thin	0.01	0.90	0.04
heavy	light	−0.49	0.70	0.21
strong	weak	0.32	0.66	0.34
hard	soft	−0.48	0.36	0.67
Sum of squared loading		3.40	2.09	0.69

Table 5. C-type factors

Opposite adjectives		factor 1	factor 2	factor 3
lively	lonely	0.95	0.13	−0.17
warm	cold	0.87	0.06	−0.29
flamboyant	subdued	0.82	0.31	0.23
bright	dark	0.79	−0.33	−0.07
thick	thin	0.01	0.77	0.28
strong	weak	0.39	0.68	0.08
heavy	light	−0.30	0.61	−0.23
wet	dry	−0.17	0.18	0.55
Sum of squared loading		3.42	2.07	1.02

Factor analysis results showed that values with the greatest factor loading were all positive. First factor had an impact on adjective groups "lively, flamboyant, warm, bright" for type P,D and type C.,
Second factor had an impact on "thick, heavy, strong", for type P,D and type C.
Third factor had an impact on "hard " for type D and "dry" for type P, C. First and second factors were of same components for both type D and type C.

From each adjective groups, the first factor and the second factor were labeled "sensation" and "physicality", respectively.

As expected, type C (majority) exhibited a similar value for each factor in letter stimulations and color stimulations.

Red is not appear a bright color for dichromatic people. But in this paper result, a similar trend was observed for color and letter stimulations for the color red in type P, D. Red color stimuli and letter stimuli both impression "lively", "warm", "flamboyant", and "bright".
This result supports the understandings are learned a posteriori against Red.

A similar trend was not observed for color and letter stimulations for the color blue in type P, D.

Type P has in the color stimulations, sensation factors such as the "lonely", "cold", "subdued", and "dark" exhibited large values for factor 1, but these factors did not appear in letter stimulations where physicality factors such as "lively", "warm", "flamboyant ", "bright" had greater values.

In type D in the color stimulations, sensation factors such as the "lonely", "cold", "subdued", and "dark" exhibited large values for factor 1, but these factors did not appear in letter stimulations where physicality factors such as thin, weak, and light had greater values.

Color and letter stimulations greatly varied also for the color pink.
Second physicality factor showed large values in color stimulations for pink. However, sensation factor was great in letter stimulations.

Green showed a tendency similar to brown color and was found to be in a position similar to purple.
With respect to the difference with type C, the difference was expected to be significant for red color stimulations before the experiment, but such a difference was observed for green instead. Sensation factors in letter stimulations were great for type C which perceived the color to be a lonely, cold, subdued, and dark color, while type D perceived the color in an opposite manner as lively, warm, flamboyant, and bright.

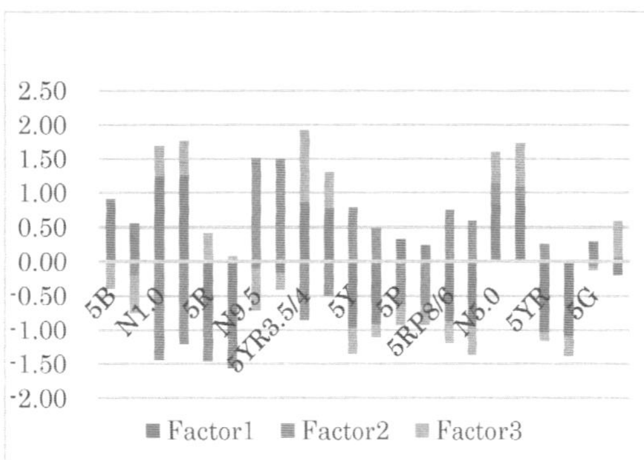

Figure 2. Differences between letter and color stimulations per factor for type C

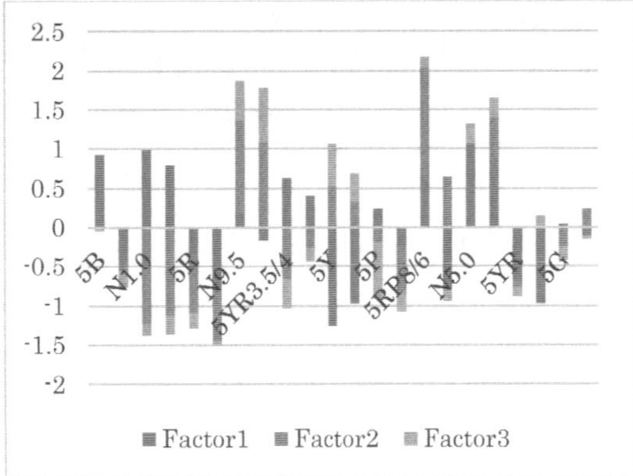

Fugure 3. Differences between letter and color stimulations per factor for type P

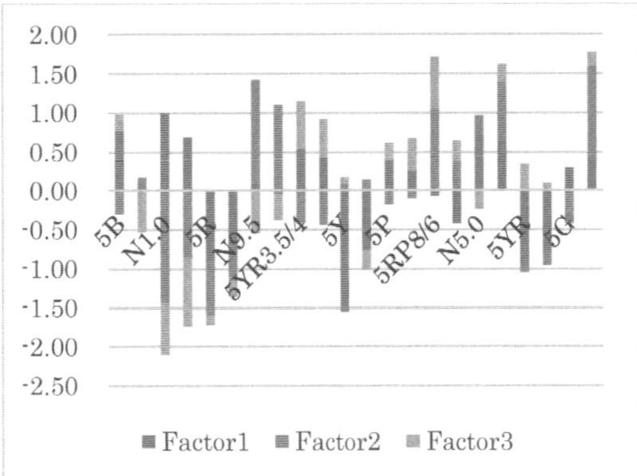

Figure 4. Differences between letter and color stimulations per factor for type D

CONCLUSION

Red is not a color that stands out brightly for dichromatic people.
But in this paper result, Red color stimuli and letter stimuli both impression "lively", "warm", "flamboyant", and "bright".

This result is the understandings are learned a posteriori against Red.
They know that the color of passion is red.
In this study, blue, pink and green has different impression between the majority and the minority.

There are a discrepancy in terms of the impression between the stimulation of letters by the color name and the stimulation by color itself.

ACKNOWLEDGMENTS

The authors would like to thank everyone at the Color Universal Design Organization (CUDO) for their cooperation in conducting the experiment.
This research is supported by Grants-in-Aid for Scientific Research (KAKENHI C No.25350027 (Multi-year Fund)).
The authors would also like to thank Mr. Ren Nakano, Mr. Daichi Kuromaru and Daiki Yamashita from our laboratory for their help in analyzing the results.

REFFERENCES

[1] Natsuki Kojima, Tomohiro Ikeda, Miyuki G.Kamachi, Yasuyo G. Ichihara, Kei Ito,Color Universal Design –Analysis of Color Dependency on Color Vision Type(3) - EI2012 Internet Imaging, Color Imaging XI:Processing, Hardcopy, and Application SPIE-IS&T/Vol.8092 pp .809206 -1-8, 2012

[2] Natsuki Kojima,Miyuki G.Kamachi, Yasuyo G. Ichihara, Kei Ito Color Universal Design – Analysis of Color Dependency on Color Vision Type(2) - EI2011 Internet Imaging, Color Imaging XI:Processing, Hardcopy, and Application SPIE-IS&T/Vol.7866 pp .78660J-1-8, 2011

[3] Tomohiro Ikeda, Yasuyo G. Ichihara, Natsuki Kojima, Hisaya Tanaka, Kei ITO, Color Universal Design –Analysis of Color Dependency on Color Vision Type(4) , EI2013 Color Imaging XVIII: Displaying, Processing, Hardcopy, and Application SPIE-IS&T/ Vol.8652 pp.86520G-1-8, 2013

[4] T. Oyama, S. Takimoto, and H. Iwasawa: A study on synesthesia using a semantic differential method - a comparison of factor structure and factor scores, Journal of Beaviormetrics, 20 (2) , 55-64, 1993.

[5] T. Fukuda and R. Fukuda, Human Engineering Guide

ISASE-MAICS 2018

The Impact of Imagery versus Graphical Information

– An Experimental Comparison –

Mason KUPP*, Tej SIDHU*, Matt CRANER*, and Elizabeth TIPTON *

* *Eastern Washington University, 526 5th Street Cheney, Washington 99004, United States of America*
mkupp@eagles.ewu.edu, teptejsidhu@eagles.ewu.edu, mcraner@eagles.ewu.edu, and etipton@ewu.edu

Abstract: : To measure the difference between the recognition of pictorial images and simple data displayed in a graph or chart, a survey with varying images was developed with the intent of eliciting some type of reaction. The images were either pictorial or graphical in nature and covered multiple themes. Topics ranged included both from politically charged issues as well as sedate ones such as puppies running in a park. For each subject, there was both a picture and a graph and any of the images had the potential to emote a response. Each image, along with a slider to measure strength of response and a hidden timer, was on a separate page and the order of the pages was completely randomized. The reaction strength and time of participants to the various image pairs was compared.
Keywords: *Data Visualization, Emotion, Image Perception*

1. INTRODUCTION

With the ever-increasing pace of data collection and analysis comes the growing need for understanding how to present the information gleaned to a non-technically focused audience. While the techniques of data visualization are intended to allow viewer to grasp complex patterns easily, the affective impact of data visualization is also critical. Beginning with the idea of how AI could be developed or programmed with the aid of visualizations, this study evolved into a survey evaluating how strongly, and how quickly, the human brain responds affectively to graphs or pictorial information on similar topics.

2. LITERATURE REVIEW

How are data visualizations processed? In other words, how does a person perceive, remember, and respond to an idea presented to them as visual information?

Images have a long history of having an effect on humans in an academic setting. It is known, from a 1986 study at the University of Minnesota, that instructors using pictures in their teaching were 43% more persuasive than NOT using some type of pictorial method [1]. A 2016 study done by Manolis Mavrikis at the UCL Knowledge Lab in London [2] demonstrated a connection between eye movement and student success in a coding project. A test at the University of Sussex [3] concluded that humans are drawn to areas in photos that are sharper and brighter. Furthermore, they found a preference for sharper darker areas over blurry areas.

While people are exposed to thousands of visual stimuli each day, only certain experiences stick with them. How and why some memories are retained better than others is also key in understanding the affective impact of data visualization. As explained by one study [4], "explicit memory refers to the memory that involves conscious recollection of information; on the other hand, implicit memory does not depend on conscious recollection." Furthermore, this study examined how two perception styles affected this: global and local. Someone with a global perception style would view an entire object, while someone else with a local perception style would focus on the individual parts of the whole. When shown a letter 'D' made up of smaller letter 'L's, one with a global perception style would recognize the D first, while one first noticing the L's would have a local perception style. Implicit memory is correlated ($r = 0.52$) with perception style, while explicit memory is not.

Image processing speed by the brain is also of note. Neuroscientists have found that the brain is able to identify images seen for as little as 13 milliseconds. This was a significant difference in the previously record of 100 milliseconds. The brain has rapid-fire processing abilities, which allow it to direct the eyes from one thing to the next, such as where to look next in a coding project. The eye moves, on average, about 3 to 4 times per second, and the brain processes not just the image, but also understands and directs what the eyes need to look at next

[5]. Neuroscientists at MIT did this research by showing new images to members of a test group for decreasing set amounts of time: 80 milliseconds, 53 milliseconds, 40 milliseconds, 27 milliseconds, and 13 milliseconds. The lower bound was determined by the capability of the computer monitor used [5]. Even though there was a decline in performance between 53 and 40 milliseconds, it was found that the brain was generally able to process information such as shape, color, and orientation. As the images were mixed up in six or twelve picture sequences, it appears that there a one-way flow of information to the brain allowing for continued processing of information even while the eyes were receiving a new image.

The use of data visualization for conveying complex concepts, the effects of images on students, the concepts of explicit and implicit memory, and the speed and accuracy of human processing and memory were all influential on the development of the research question: "How do responses differ, in affect strength and in speed, when exposed to either a graph or pictorial image on the same topic?"

3. EXPERIMENTAL COMPARISON

3.1 Survey Design

A set of potential graph/picture topics was prepared and then pretested on Dr. Tipton's DSCI 450: Data Visualization class. The topics chosen from this set for the actual survey were in three groups: Anxiety (Global Warming, Test), Political (President, Immigration, Gun), and Leisure (Movie, Super Bowl, Dog). Each image in a pair was given its own page on the survey. All images used in the survey may be found in Section 5, after the conclusion. Each page had the question "How strong is your reaction to this image?" below the image with a slide for responding. The response options available were "Skip", "1 = None", "2", "3". "4" and "5 = Strong". Intermediate responses were not possible and the slider initially presented in position "3". Time to first click, time to last click, time to page submit and click count was collected internally on the server side by the Qualtrics system used to electronically manage the survey. Respondents were told that this was happening and requested to "please answer all questions as quickly as possible as they are being timed." However, respondents did not have access to the timing information. The pages with the images were completely randomized by the Qualtrics system to limit the impact of an ordering effect.

After the block with the images, the survey ended with a section where demographics were requested: Age, Gender, and Race. Respondents had the option of providing write-in answers to the gender and race questions if they did not prefer to use the options provided. Not answering any of these questions was also allowed.

3.2 Procedure

Once IRB approval was obtained, the survey was sent to undergraduate students at Eastern Washington University (EWU) in the Information Systems and Business Analytics (ISBA) Department and the Accounting Department (ACCT) by their instructors midway through the Winter Quarter of 2018. It was also sent to graduate students at EWU in the MBA program by the graduate director. The survey was administered electronically and anonymity was guaranteed through the set-up of this system. The survey was available for two weeks. The survey was available via mobile devices or a computer. It was accessed either general link generated by Qualtrics or by a QR Code that redirected to that link.

Timing information (click count) and the standard deviation of the scores across all images for a respondent was used to assist in the cleaning process by helping identifying people who were just rapidly clicking "next" without actually choosing their reactions. Of the 47 responses recorded by Qualtrics, 6 were removed for this reason, resulting in a usable sample size of 41. The demographics of the resulting cleaned sample are in Figures 1-3.

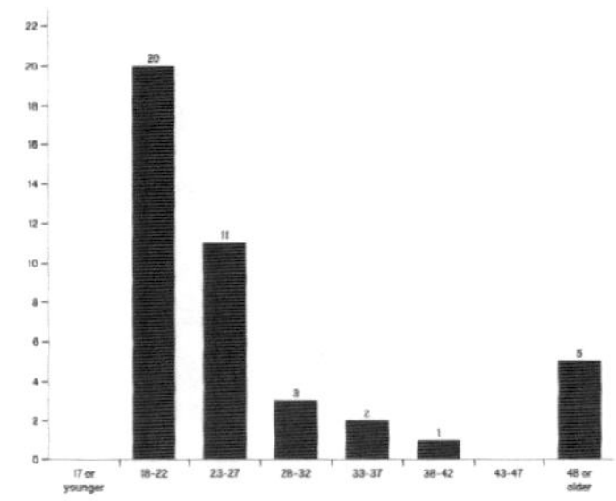

Figure 1: Age Distribution of the Sample

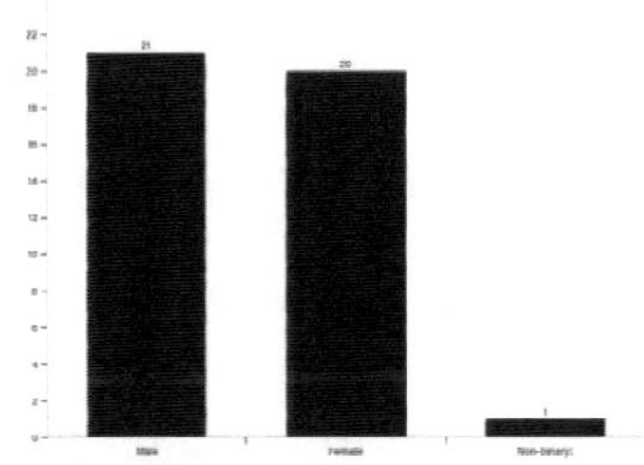

Figure 2: Gender Distribution of the Sample

Keywords: Data visualization, Emotion, Image Perception

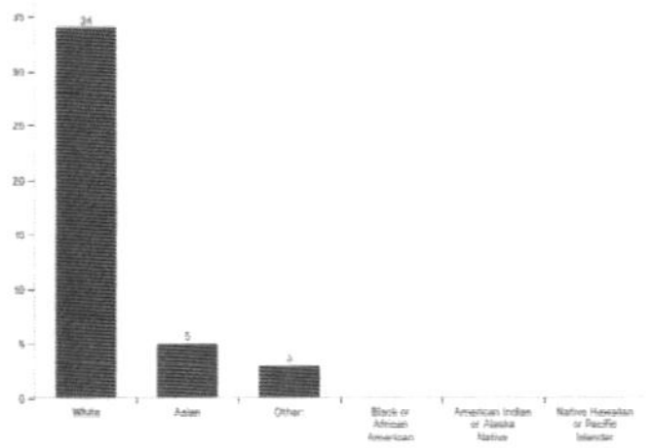

Figure 3: Race Distribution of the Sample

3.3 Analysis

Median differences in slide viewing time and median differences in the strength of reactions between pictures and graphics for a single topic were examined using matched-pairs Wilcoxon tests. For comparing median differences in slide viewing time segmented on the difference in reaction strength (graph-picture = negative, zero, positive), the Kruskal-Wallis test was used. Medians, rather than arithmetic means, were chosen to measure the centers of the distributions of the responses due their robustness in the presence of skew.

Figure 4 and Table 1 contain the results for the analysis of median difference in slide viewing time. It is worth noting that all pairs except Movie were statistically significantly greater than zero at the 10% level. All pairs except Movies and Global Warming were statistically significantly greater than zero at the 5% and 1% level.

Table 2 contain the results for the analysis of median difference in response strength. It is worth noting that only Dog is statistically significantly different at any typical level, while Gun and Global Warming join Dog at the 5% level and Movie joins these at the 10% level.

Table 3 contain the results for the analysis of median differences in slide viewing time segmented on the difference in reaction strength (graph-picture = negative, zero, positive), No topic pairs are statistically significant, suggesting that the relationship between time spent viewing an image and reaction strength may not be related. However, this may also be a result of the limited number of responses.

Table 1: Results for matched-pairs Wilcoxon test on Difference in Time Spent (Graph – Picture)

Testing for the median of (graph-picture) > 0 for time spent					
Topic pair	Median of Graph	Median of Picture	Median of (Graph-Picture)	W	p-value
Gun	7.53	4.83	3.33	812	<0.0005
President	8.30	4.57	4.70	796	<0.0005
Global Warming	5.20	4.66	0.56	549	0.063
Super Bowl	6.48	4.08	2.26	624	0.006
Movie	6.20	5.33	0.01	432	0.495
Dog	8.11	4.17	4.18	799	<0.0005
Immigration	7.62	4.67	3.73	680	0.001
Test	9.31	6.44	3.00	624	0.006

Table 2: Results for matched-pairs Wilcoxon test on Difference in Response Strength (Graph – Picture)

Testing for the median of (graph-picture) ≠ 0 for response strength					
Topic pair	Median of Graph	Median of Picture	Median of (Graph-Picture)	W	p-value
Gun	3.00	3.00	-0.50	67	0.018
President	3.00	3.50	-0.50	90	0.144
Global Warming	4.00	4.00	-0.50	102	0.013
Super Bowl	2.50	3.00	0.00	179	0.810
Movie	3.00	3.00	0.50	260	0.093
Dog	3.00	4.00	-1.00	35	<0.0005
Immigration	3.00	3.00	0.00	81	0.380
Test	3.00	2.00	0.50	269	0.270

Table 3: Results for Kruskal-Wallis test on Difference in Time Spent (Graph – Picture) vs Differences in Response Strength

Testing for at least one median different of (graph-picture) for time spent separating on recoded response strength					
Topic pair	Median of time spent for negative strength difference	Median of time spent for neutral strenght difference	Median of time spent for positive strength difference	H	p-value
Gun	2.52	3.70	2.08	0.95	0.622
President	3.40	5.13	3.64	1.00	0.606
Global Warming	0.15	0.98	0.04	2.66	0.264
Super Bowl	0.97	4.34	1.02	1.61	0.448
Movie	-0.38	0.10	-0.55	1.42	0.492
Dog	3.58	2.96	3.08	0.48	0.787
Immigration	3.05	2.21	3.51	1.53	0.466
Test	1.58	0.14	2.73	1.42	0.491

3.4 Interpretation

Unsurprisingly, people seemed to take longer to digest specific information and conclude when viewing graphics than when making a gut decisions based off viewing a picture. Trends regarding respondent reaction strength were not as clear. While people generally appeared to care about pictures more than graphs, this difference was only statistically significant at the 5% level for three topics, Guns, Global Warming and Dog.

3.5 Limitation

Due to the small sample size and limited population to draw from, results from this study should be considered suggestive only.

3.6 Future Research

Expansions of this research should include using the heat map function within Qualtrics to include respondent perception styles. Follow-up focus groups or one-on-one interviews may help shed light as to what specific aspects of particular images may have been driving certain responses. A link between global and local perception style preference and differences in response speed depending on graph vs. picture is a potential area of future investigation. Mixed-method research methodology is suggested as a future path for this work.

4. CONCLUSION

While this experiment did not break major new ground with respect to its result that "people generally appeared to care about pictures more than graphs," it did successfully serve as a pilot study into the viability of using Qualtrics as a platform for gathering data on affective data visualization design.

5. SURVEY IMAGES

The image pairs below and on the following pages were used for the experimental comparison survey. They are in the same order as in tables 1-3.

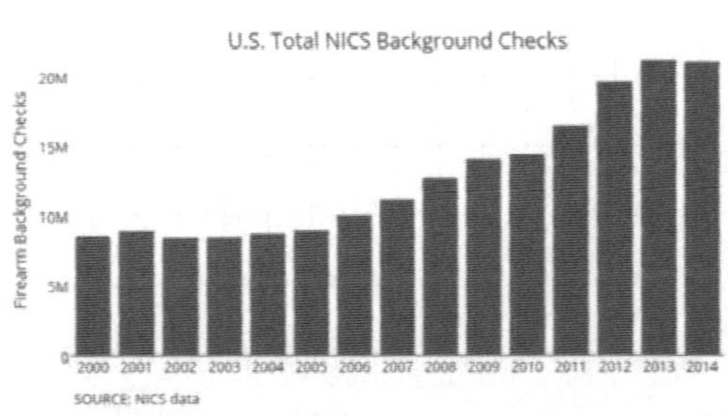

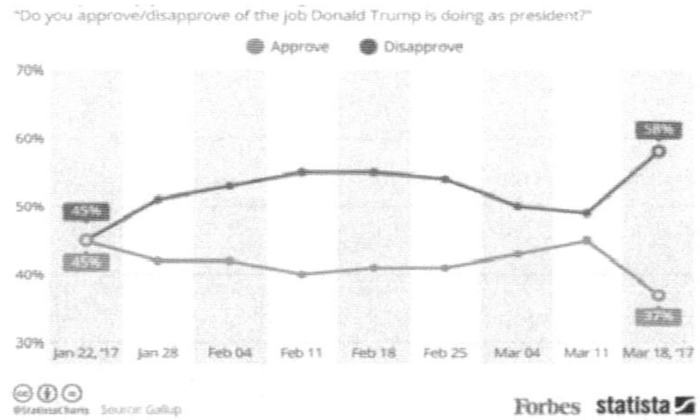
"Do you approve/disapprove of the job Donald Trump is doing as president?"
Approve
Disapprove
70%
60%
50%
40%
30%
45%
45%
58%
37%
Jan 22, '17
Jan 28
Feb 04
Feb 11
Feb 18
Feb 25
Mar 04
Mar 11
Mar 18, '17
Source: Gallup
Forbes
statista

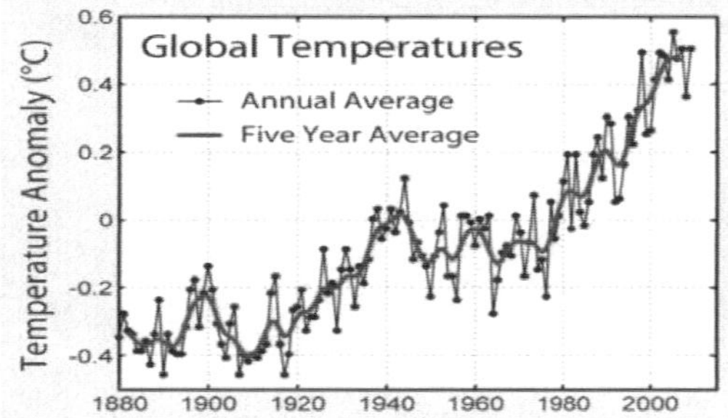
Global Temperatures
Annual Average
Five Year Average
Temperature Anomaly (°C)
0.6
0.4
0.2
0
-0.2
-0.4
1880
1900
1920
1940
1960
1980
2000

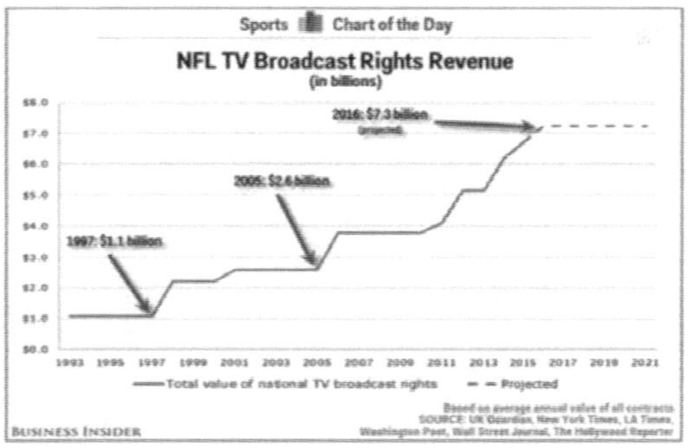
Sports
Chart of the Day
NFL TV Broadcast Rights Revenue
(in billions)
1997: $1.1 billion
2005: $2.6 billion
2016: $7.3 billion
Total value of national TV broadcast rights
Projected
BUSINESS INSIDER

MARVEL STUDIOS
BLACK PANTHER

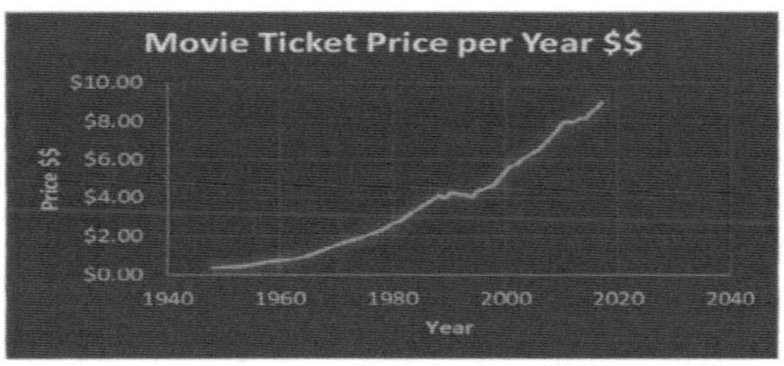
Movie Ticket Price per Year $$
$10.00
$8.00
$6.00
$4.00
$2.00
$0.00
Price $$
1940
1960
1980
2000
2020
2040
Year

THE 3RD MOST POPULAR DOGS BY STATE
BULLDOG
mental_floss

Keywords: Data visualization, Emotion, Image Perception

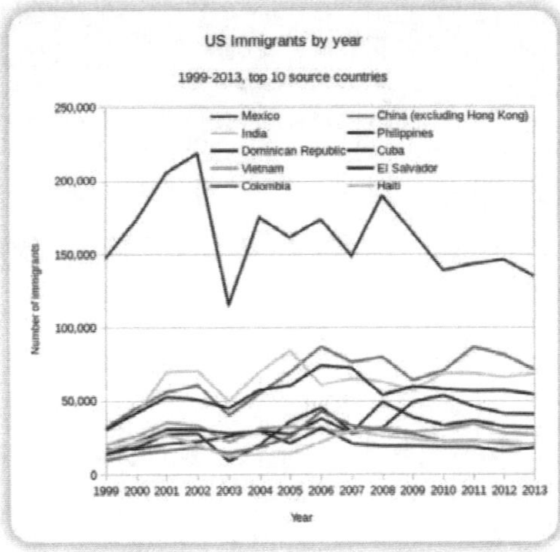

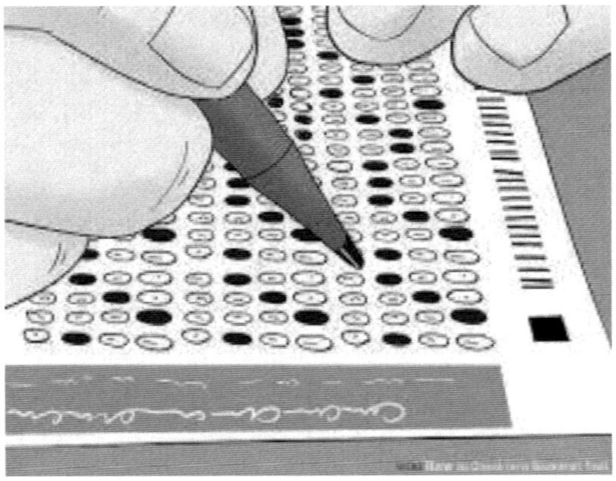

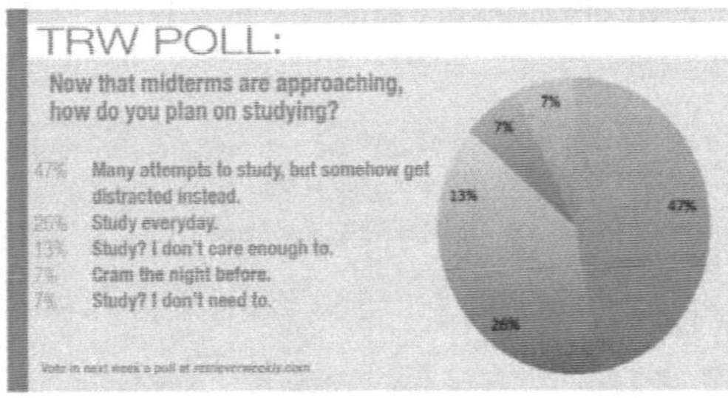

REFERENCES

[1]D. R. Vogel, G. W. Dickson, and J. A. Lehman; June, 1986; Persuasion and the Role of Visual Presentation Support: The UM/3M Study; Management Information Systems Research Center School of Management, University of Minnesota, Minneapolis, Minnesota 55455

[2] M. Manolis; A Study On Eye Fixation Patterns of Students in Higher Education Using an Online Learning System; April 2016; UCL Knowledge Lab, 23-29 Emerald Street, London, WC1N 3QS United Kingdom.

[3] B.W. Tatler, R.J. Baddeley, I.D. Gilchrist; Revised November 2003; Visual correlates of fixation selection: effects of scale and time; Sussex Centre for Neuroscience, School of Life Sciences, University of Sussex, Brighton BN1 9QG, United Kingdom and b Department of Experimental Psychology, University of Bristol, 8 Woodland Road, Bristol BS8 1TN, United Kingdom

[4] K. Hine, Y. Tsushima; Not explicit but implicit memory is influenced by individual perception style, Plos ONE; 13(1) pp. 1-10, 2018.

[5] A. Trafton; In the Blink of an Eye, MIT News, 16 Jan. 2014, news.mit.edu/2014/in-the-blink-of-an-eye-0116.

AUTHOR INDEX

AUTHOR INDEX

Japan Society of Kansei Engineering (JSKE)
Grand Heights 1003
2-55-5 Nihombashi Hamacho
Chuo-ku, Tokyo 103-0007
Japan

ISBN 978-1-5108-8376-5
9 781510 883765

CURRAN ASSOCIATES INC.
proceedings.com

28th Italian Symposium on Advanced Database Systems (SEBD 2020)

Online
21 – 24 June 2020